FINANCE, ACCUMULATION AND MONETARY POWER

This accessible yet rigorous book examines the development of 'financial socialism' in advanced capitalist economies in the decade since the global financial crisis of 2007–2009. This new term refers to an attempt to resolve the accumulation crisis of capital through coordinated central bank activism, where state circuits of monetary capital assume a critical role in the reproduction of capitalist social relations.

The book explains the dynamics of the crisis as it has developed and assesses the response of monetary elites to systemic financial risk in the global economy. Their failure to re-engineer growth following the technology boom of the late 1990s and the global financial crisis are driving fundamental changes in the form and function of capitalist money, which have yet to be theorized adequately.

Finance, Accumulation and Monetary Power presents a revealing and radical critique of the failure of the International Political Economy to apprehend changes taking place within capitalism, employing a critical-theoretical analysis of contradictions in the capitalist reproduction scheme. The book will be of key interest to scholars, students and readers of international political economy, critical political economy, heterodox economics, globalization, international relations, international political sociology, business studies and finance.

Daniel Woodley teaches politics at DLD College in London, UK, and is the author of numerous books and articles on political theory and international politics, including *Fascism and Political Theory* (2010) and *Globalization and Capitalist Geopolitics* (2015).

In *Finance, Accumulation and Monetary Power*, Daniel Woodley expertly depicts and uncovers the key structural problems that contemporary 'postliberal' capitalism faces. As the book shows, we are moving towards what Woodley terms 'financial socialism', in which nation-states and international organisations are required to stabilise an increasingly unstable global capitalism, using monetary policy to prop up the value of money and assets – and in doing so, to sow the seeds of the next crisis. The book is a must-read for anyone with an interest in the ongoing stagnation of the global economy, and the likely sources of the current crisis to come. At the end of a ten-year period of quantitative easing and ultra-loose monetary policy we still exist in a period of 'secular stagnation' – this book goes beyond the surface-level explanations of both mainstream and heterodox economics, to show why this is the case.

David J. Bailey, University of Birmingham, UK

FINANCE, ACCUMULATION AND MONETARY POWER

Understanding Financial Socialism in Advanced Capitalist Economies

Daniel Woodley

 Routledge
Taylor & Francis Group

LONDON AND NEW YORK

First published 2020
by Routledge
2 Park Square, Milton Park, Abingdon, Oxon OX14 4RN

and by Routledge
52 Vanderbilt Avenue, New York, NY 10017

Routledge is an imprint of the Taylor & Francis Group, an informa business

Library of Congress Cataloging-in-Publication Data
Names: Woodley, Daniel, author.
Title: Finance, accumulation, and monetary power : understanding
financial socialism in advanced capitalist economies / Daniel Woodley.
Description: New York : Routledge, 2019. | Includes bibliographical
references and index.
Identifiers: LCCN 2019028253 (print) | LCCN 2019028254 (ebook) |
ISBN 9780367338558 (hardback) | ISBN 9780367338527 (paperback) |
ISBN 9780429322419 (ebook)
Subjects: LCSH: Finance. | Finance--Social aspects. | Socialism.
Classification: LCC HG101 .W66 2019 (print) | LCC HG101 (ebook) |
DDC 332.01--dc23
LC record available at https://lccn.loc.gov/2019028253
LC ebook record available at https://lccn.loc.gov/2019028254

ISBN: 978-0-367-33855-8 (hbk)
ISBN: 978-0-367-33852-7 (pbk)
ISBN: 978-0-429-32241-9 (ebk)

Typeset in Bembo
by Lumina Datamatics Limited

MIX
Paper from
responsible sources
FSC
www.fsc.org   FSC™ C013985

Printed in the United Kingdom
by Henry Ling Limited

In memory of Rosaline Mary Bernadette Woodley 1942–2017

CONTENTS

LIST OF TABLES

PREFACE

The following study examines the trend towards 'financial socialism' in advanced economies, developing themes raised in two previous works, *Fascism and Political Theory* (2010) and *Globalization and Capitalist Geopolitics* (2015). The study draws on an extensive range of academic, official and journalistic sources to demonstrate how accumulation and monetary power are interlinked in the present economic crisis, and how political and monetary elites have utilized this crisis to extend their power of disposal over the surplus product of the global economy. Although the title suggests an analysis of 'collectivist' trends in postliberal capitalism, the corporate-synthetic character of financial socialism should be understood less as an antechamber on the road towards universal political emancipation than a compulsive, unstable and authoritarian form of capitalist monetary power that concentrates capital and magnifies inequality for the exclusive benefit of investor elites. The oligarchic structures of legal and political organization that sustain 'socialism for the investor class' constitute a form of socioeconomic change *within* capitalism, presaging a further aggregation of power within a multifaceted corporate governing class whose apparatus of direct and indirect social control lies beyond the 'grasp of the average citizen' (Suarez-Villa 2015: 296). This is consistent with the disintegration of universal ideologies of progress in advanced economies in which first state socialism then liberalism have been exposed as failed legitimation strategies to contain the working class and suppress the global South (Wallerstein 1992). On the one hand, financial socialism indicates a specific moment in capitalist development where state circuits of capital assume a critical role in the reproduction of oligarchy. On the other hand, financial socialism facilitates the deferral of a catastrophic unwinding of fictitious capital in the global financial system, enabling capital accumulation without a corresponding augmentation of value through the profitable valorization of socially necessary labour. This 'deferral' is manifest in the determination of global monetary and political elites to sustain the illusion of liquidity and rising asset prices and to institutionalize new macroprudential regulations to mitigate global systemic risk and delay an alteration of capitalist relations of power through the continual multiplication of debt as a condition for the accumulation of capital without value.

The accumulation crisis of capital, and the failure of elites to re-engineer growth following the technology boom of the 1990s and the global financial crisis of 2007–2009, are driving fundamental changes in the form and function of capitalist money which have yet to be theorized adequately. The text is intended not simply as another study of the global financial crisis, but as a critique of the failure of political economy to comprehend changes taking place in capitalism employing a critical-theoretical analysis of contradictions in the capitalist reproduction scheme. The aim is to explain the dynamics of the crisis as it has developed *within* capitalism, and to assess the response of elites to systemic financial risk in the global economy. A further aim is to render a complex topic – the evolution of monetary power in response to the accumulation crisis of capital – as accessible as possible for non-specialists while addressing academic debates in the fields of economics, political economy and global governance.

The book is divided into two sections. Part I begins with a critical assessment of neoclassical, Keynesian and Marxian economic theories and their relevance for understanding the accumulation crisis of capitalism. The analytical focus is the origins of the long deflationary recession in the advanced economies, and the attempt by governments to evade a catastrophic deleveraging of capital values through central bank activism, that is, through the use of monetary policy to compensate for the incapacity of market economies to return to some form of profitability. Attempts by mainstream economics to comprehend the dynamics of the crisis are shown to be ephemeral at best. Neoclassical theory retains a preeminent position in academia, yet remains dogmatically confined within the paradigm of marginal utility theory and behaviourism, reduced – like Marxism-Leninism in the former Soviet Union – to the level of a 'legitimation science' unable to apprehend the economic reality of postliberal capitalism. The paradigm survives not because it offers answers to structural contradictions in capitalism but because the prevailing discourse of neoliberalism is institutionally embedded, creating false confidence in the viability of 'free markets' which even the present financial crisis has failed to upend.

Heterodox approaches, on the other hand – albeit critical of neoclassical theory – misdiagnose the origins of the crisis. Chapters 2 and 3 show that financialization is not the reason for the collapse of capitalism but is rather symptomatic of it. The logic of financialization is linked to the functional requirements of capital accumulation, and the intensification of this process has increased instability in capitalist economies, triggering recurring market disturbances which amplify underlying structural deficiencies in the capitalist mode of production. In addition, the 'return to Keynes' since the global financial crisis is shown to be pragmatic and selective, devoid of serious commitment to strategic investment as governments return to pre-crisis policy perspectives to satisfy bond markets and rating agencies. The crisis did place in question neoliberal ideology, but 'embedded neoliberalism' continues to develop at an institutional and ideological level in both advanced and emerging economies.

Part II examines the development of financial socialism as a monetary response to the crisis of accumulation in the advanced economies. Financial socialism is defined as a postliberal-capitalist formation in which central banks assume a de facto monopoly of control over the monetary system, where currency loses its function as a store of value for most citizens, and where states attempt to coerce investors and depositors into bond markets to sustain credit flows and counter a trend towards corporate and sovereign insolvency. The aim of this extension of state power is to prevent a rerun of the banking crisis of 2008. Given the scale of additional debt created by Western governments since 2008, a repeat of the credit seizure which threatened the survival of the global banking system would result in a destruction of capital value on a scale adequate to bankrupt low-growth economies and limit the power of investors to appropriate the surplus product of the global economy.

To understand financial socialism, it is essential to consider the evolution of capitalist money and the development of 'modern money theory' in monetary political economy. While neoliberal economic theory is concerned with the ideological and institutional logic of market rationality, critical political economy pays attention to the nature of monetary power and the role of the state form of capital in sustaining unprofitable 'market' economies. Understanding the causes of the present crisis requires an adequate understanding of the forms and functions of money in capitalist economies and the changing nature of money in postliberal capitalism specifically. The aim in Chapter 4 is to shed light on the role played by the capitalist credit money system in the historical and contemporary development of market societies. Credit money has become a condition *sine qua non* for the evolution of advanced economies which require 'elastic' money to accommodate the inflation of capital values created by continual expansion of debt. In contrast to Austrian political economy, modern money theory holds that money must be infinitely elastic to maintain liquidity and facilitate growth in capitalism. Yet infinite elasticity is unfeasible in the long run, as it leads to the loss of money as a measure of wealth, creating incoherence. Just as there are limits to capital in its illusory or 'fictitious' form, so there are limits to the expansion of immaterial money.

Chapter 5 presents financial socialism as a postliberal-capitalist strategy to reduce systemic risk through controls on capital and controls on investment decisions by banks. While it is important to avoid determinism, there is evidence to suggest we may be approaching the limits of capitalist commodity production as a basis for the valorization of surplus value. Financial socialism seems to imply that system-immanent forces in the capitalist mode of production are creating economic and technological conditions for the future evolution of capitalist property relations *beyond* market individualism independently of human agency – yielding postcapitalist outcomes as an unintended consequence. Viewed from a historical perspective, however, financial socialism in fact manifests striking similarities to economic fascism: as the economic history of the twentieth century shows, fascism is based on a corporate model of postliberal-capitalist development which coincides with the transition to pure fiat money. It ensures the survival of capitalist class societies in a new and politically repressive form, based on a fusion of corporate and political power and the imposition of government controls over the economy to stabilize accumulation and suppress political challenges to capitalist hegemony. While espousing market rationality and wealth creation, financial socialism reveals the sclerotic expansion of debt-based accumulation generated through the capture of future value, and recalibrates governmental strategies for defending elite accumulation through capitalist central planning and the erosion of property rights among intermediate strata in favour of corporate interests tied to the state. While this does not rule out the possibility of political opposition or resistance to capital among downwardly mobile or highly marginalized social groups, it does suggest a further disorientation and disempowerment of progressive social forces confronted by the hegemonic rearticulation of capitalist hegemony through the growth of state-based authoritarian populism.

Finally, Chapter 6 examines elite responses to systemic risk in financialized capitalist economies, focusing specifically on macroprudential strategies to reduce systemic risk in the global banking system in periods of future financial instability. These strategies reflect not just systemic risk, however, but a more fundamental change in the phenomenal forms and legal basis of finance capital driving the institutional consolidation of co-governance mechanisms in elite global forums like the G20, the Financial Stability Board (FSB) and the Basel Committee on Banking Supervision (BCBS) whose function is to stabilize rather than transform a global finance-led accumulation regime. Preparations for the next financial crisis are in place, and the new regulatory framework will not only socialize private losses to public balance sheets but also place an additional penalty on ordinary depositors whose assets are liable to be appropriated by financial institutions to placate creditors and prevent bankruptcy. This transnational regulatory framework constitutes a new form of monetary internationalism. It is intended not only to mitigate risk in the global banking system but to address instabilities created by opposing pressures in capitalism between global economic integration and the fragmentation of the international economy into segmented networks of global capital flows and value chains, connecting financial centres in the advanced economies with manufacturing and commodity-rich zones in the periphery.

A core assumption of the text is that while labour struggles have historically played a key role in rebalancing capital-labour relations and transforming political outcomes, the structural contradictions of capital cannot be 'fixed' through specific political interventions. Capitalism is an enduring historical-social formation which expanded in the sixteenth century through European colonialism into a global accumulation regime, inflicting actual and symbolic violence on non-Western peoples in the core and periphery. Capitalism, argues Stiegler,

> is a process of transformation of which we are ignorant of the end. It had a beginning, and one day it will come to an end – but we have no way of knowing where or when this will occur. The only way of living this process is to make it possible for it to follow itself out, until that moment when, coming to completion, it could perhaps engender a new process, of which we remain utterly ignorant, because it is incalculable. Insofar as it is an *epoch* of psychic and collective individuation, capitalism has been preceded by a western, precapitalist past, and it will be followed by a future which is already no longer simply western, and which may not be capitalist. (Stiegler 2004: 40)

The postliberal phase of capitalist development is likely to continue this trend in approaching decades, with ever more intense exploitation of workers in advanced economies as global economic convergence forces G7 nations into a race for the bottom with non-Western nations to sustain profitability, limit capital flight and defend bond markets. The consequences of this will be increasing violence among, and repression of, disaffected subject populations in North America and Europe, as liberal political structures disintegrate and transnational economic blocs compete for geoeconomic pre-eminence in a multipolar global growth system.

Yet while G7 economies are running out of policy options to counter a long-term decline in the profit rate and debt deflation, accumulation *might* be stabilized in the short to medium term through financial repression and the imposition of new rules to reduce systemic risk in the global financial system. As we enter a period of renewed turbulence approaching 2020, the text assesses whether financial socialism can resolve the accumulation crisis of contemporary capitalism, or whether this decadent model of economic reproduction is fast approaching its vanishing point, revealing the illusory character of fictitious capital as a phantasmagorical form of wealth based on infinite multiplication of debt and accumulation without value.

ACKNOWLEDGEMENTS

I would like to thank Richard Milner for reading a draft of the manuscript and for his useful observations, as well as the editors at Routledge for their professional support and guidance in the production of the book. I am also grateful to Oxford University Press for allowing me to reprint data from one of its publications on financial regulation. Any errors or omissions in the text are of course my responsibility alone.

LIST OF ABBREVIATIONS

BIS	Bank for International Settlements
BRICS	Brazil, Russia, India, China, South Africa
BRRD	Bank Recovery and Resolution Directive
CDO	collateralized debt obligation
CLO	collateralized loan obligation
DLT	distributed ledger technology
ECB	European Central Bank
EESA	Emergency Economic Stabilization Act
ERU	equilibrium rate of unemployment
FDIC	Federal Deposit Insurance Corporation
FRB	Federal Reserve Bank
FSB	Financial Stability Board
FSF	Financial Stability Forum
GDP	gross domestic product
G7	Group of Seven industrialized economies
G20	Group of Twenty industrialized economies
G-SIFI	global systemically important financial institution
HQLA	high-quality liquid assets
ICT	information and communication technology
IMF	International Monetary Fund
LCR	Liquidity Coverage Ratio
LSAP	large-scale asset purchase
LTCM	Long-Term Capital Management
MI	methodological individualism
MPE	multiple point of entry resolution
MREL	Minimum Requirement for Eligible Liabilities
NCWOL	no creditor worse off than in liquidation

NFA	new financial architecture
OECD	Organization for Economic Cooperation and Development
QE	quantitative easing
SDR	special drawing right
SPE	single point of entry resolution
SPV	special purpose vehicle
SRR	special resolution regime
TARP	Troubled Asset Relief Program
WRC	world reserve currency

PART I
Theorizing the crisis

1

THE FAILURE OF NEOCLASSICAL ECONOMICS

Introduction

During the last decade there has been no shortage of studies on the global financial crisis and its political consequences, with a vast range of books examining
everything from the excesses of financialization and the failure of regulatory
regimes to the history of the eurozone crisis and the economic consequences of
mounting debt for advanced economies. Is there anything to add to this growing
list of titles? The answer, it seems, is yes. The dramatic events of the 2008 market
collapse are fascinating in themselves and provide excellent subject matter for
narrative histories. However, very little that is useful can be learnt from the crash
in isolation from a broader understanding of the material determination of value
in capitalist society and the evolving sociopolitical structure of contemporary
postliberal-capitalist accumulation regimes. This requires a critical-theoretical
approach to political economy, dispensing with simplistic notions of 'parasitic
finance' which condemn speculation on normative grounds or which miscon-
strue finance capital as an imaginary value detached from the 'real' economy.
Too many recent studies start from the hackneyed assumption that the global
financial crisis occurred due to the avarice of bankers (Augar 2018), the failure of regulation (Friedman & Kraus 2011) or the dishonesty of accountants
whose complicity in financial fraud illustrates the failure of traditional fiduciary
accountability in modern financial markets (Brooks 2018). Notwithstanding the
extensive evidence of financial cupidity and corruption revealed by the crash, and
the embezzlement and fraud which accompany financial liberalization (Bullough
2018; Shaxson 2018), a singular emphasis on criminality and greed distorts our
field of vision by shifting the focus towards cases of individual malfeasance while
ignoring the underlying structural development of commodity-determined society and its changing political form.

To address this deficiency, the following study develops a new approach to the crisis based on a critique of *financial socialism*, defined as a specific stage in the evolution of postliberal capitalism where state circuits of financial capital assume a critical role in the reproduction of capitalist social relations and the stabilization of corporate power. This suggests the development of capitalism beyond its so-called 'neoliberal' moment in an attempt to understand not simply the stagnation of advanced monetary economies, but the failure of economics itself as form of 'legitimation science' – that is to say, an ideologically distorted mode of social-scientific inquiry adequate to the defence of capitalist social relations. With the collective failure of the economics profession to predict or accurately diagnose the underlying causes of the crisis, it is evident that the ideological function of economics in contemporary capitalism is to reproduce *paradigm mentalities* in order to deflect counterhegemonic narratives, reconciling at a theoretical level the gulf between academic orthodoxy and economic reality. The claim of science to superior knowledge is based on the assumption that methodologically consistent work on the material world is likely to generate a more accurate picture of reality than can be obtained via intuition. Yet a scientific research programme characterized by paradigm mentalities inevitably aspires to the status of 'normal science', where the collective commitment of adherents obviates the need for evidence to defend theoretical claims (Kuhn 1970; cf. Walker 2010). Otherwise put: no matter how deep the irresolvable internal contradictions in a given paradigm, its recognized status as 'normal science' relieves adherents of the tiresome requirement to continuously justify a programme, reaffirming their claim to possession of scientific and methodological rationality.

The text is intended further as a contribution to value theory (*Wertkritik*), linking the accumulation crisis of capitalism with contemporary developments in global finance and monetary policy. Marxism has traditionally focused on capitalist crises from the standpoint of labour (Postone 1993), emphasizing class conflict and revolution as vehicles of social change; but with the collapse of state socialism and the retreat from historical teleology, Marxian critiques from the standpoint of labour have become less relevant. Class-theoretical approaches correctly locate social-structural change in the material development of commodity-determined societies yet fail to consider the categorial primacy and inner contradiction in the capitalist value form as a driving force of change *within* the capitalist mode of production. While the determinants of crisis are central to his investigation, the 'object of Marx's analysis is not crisis, but the capitalist process of reproduction in its totality. Given his method of investigation Marx examines the unending circuit of capital and its functions through all the phases of the process of reproduction' (Grossmann 1929: ch. 2: 17). In addition, there is a failure to comprehend the eclipse of liberalism as a political technology with its origins in eighteenth-century political economy. The atrophy of liberal capitalism is well advanced; yet despite concerns over the rise of anti-establishment populism in western democracies, this trend is obscured by the hegemonic force of 'neoliberalism' as a discursive strategy which misrepresents the complex link between corporatism and oligarchic power as a necessary feature of globalizing capital. This system depends not simply on access to new markets and new sources of accumulation but on the growth of financial market capital (interest-bearing capital) to extend, intensify and amplify the accumulation of future value in the present, extending the parameters of accumulation while delaying a deflationary crisis that overshadows debt-leveraged economies in the capitalist metropole.

The emphasis, therefore, is on the contradictory development of *value* in commodity-determined societies as a social relation between agents realized at a higher level of abstraction through the process of exchange. *Value* is a central analytical category in Marxian political economy yet is one which is obscured in mainstream economics (and traditional Marxism) as a result of the 'fetish' nature of exchange value. That is to say, Marx (1978, 1973) observed that economics fails to distinguish between the technical character of the commodity and its social form in capitalism where the exchange-value of a commodity is entirely distinct from its intrinsic worth or utility as an object. This is necessarily so because commodity-determined society *renders all values commensurable*: their value is not intrinsic or given but realized via exchange. Relations between actors are mediated by and assume the form of relations between things in the market – a process which Lukács (1975 [1923]) famously termed 'reification'. This economic mystification is not just ideological; it is a feature of social being in commodity capitalism which arises principally with respect to credit money as interest-bearing capital – the 'main lever of overproduction and overspeculation in commerce' (Marx 1959: 441). As Kurz argues:

> We must not forget that value, which must appear as exchange value, does not by its nature express an in some way mythical substance inherent to things as such, as the fetish structure of exchange value suggests, but rather a social relationship between partial or private producers who are isolated from one another, whose social division of labor can only be realized by means of the sphere of circulation that has been separated from it. (Kurz 1986: 26)

Although it should be stated that – in contradistinction to Rubin (1973) and Heinrich (1991) – the sphere of exchange is not the exclusive realm in which value is created (Kurz 2016), the exchange-value of commodities realized through the intermediation of financial markets is the context in which social relations of capitalist production achieve their highest level of abstraction: finance is a sphere of money-creation which is integral to the expanded reproduction of global capital.

Complex financial instruments (equities, securities, derivatives) traded in financial markets represent *fetishized forms of appearance of capitalist social relations* – 'new kinds of rationality for the promotion of exploitation strategies based on the circuits of capital, rather than [...] aberrations or dysfunctional developments of the "real" economy' (Sotiropoulos et al. 2013: 33; 2). Yet finance not only intermediates risk, it also generates an 'attitude of compliance with the laws of the capitalist system [and] these new rationalities systematically push for an underestimation of risks' (ibid.). Through the commodification of risk and anticipation of future value, financialization indicates not only the expanded role of finance in the reproduction of total social capital but the performative enactment and legitimation of commodity fetishism (the assumption that the value of a commodity is intrinsic, detached from the investment of human labour power in its production) among subjects always already *'captured within* and *dominated* by the "supersensible" but objective forms of appearance of the existing complex of capitalist power relations' (ibid.: 153).

While the origins of the present crisis lie less in the implosion of the US subprime mortgage market in 2007 than in the slump of the 1970s, the event that exposed most dramatically the *structural weakness* of the advanced capitalist economies was the collapse of the new technology boom in the US between 1999 and 2001. Following a series of escalating crises in emerging economies during the 1990s, the coincidence of financialization with the global digital communications revolution induced what some observers define as a 'metaphorical heart attack' in the accumulation structure of capitalism – an economic trauma derived from the inner contradiction in the value form (Lohoff & Trenkle 2013). That is, the unprecedented expansion of capital value generated by the combination of the 'dot.com bubble' and the acceleration of global digital communications technology accelerated a process of 'accumulation without value' in the advanced economies. As a consequence of the diminished contribution of labour power in the creation of surplus value, the capacity of firms to *valorize* capital (to yield a profit from capital invested) has diminished sharply. This, in turn, has exacerbated a deflationary recession that persists two decades on despite attempts by elites to disguise the crisis by inflating new asset bubbles to perpetuate the fiction of rising prices, liquidity, prosperity and growth that sustain the advanced economies. This leads one critic to conclude that while the 'visible hand of central banks has taken over administration of a burned out capitalist future, private business seeks out new speculative bubbles which have become indispensable for a continuation of the global accumulation process' (Lohoff 2016: 4). With the rise of 'financial market socialism on a global scale, an ironic outcome of the neoliberal revolution, politics has bought the decadent global capitalist system a reprieve' (ibid.).

The implosion of the US mortgage market in 2007 triggered a market collapse which is now routinely – yet mistakenly – blamed on financialization, as if financial market risk and greed in and of themselves could explain escalating internal contradictions within the capitalist mode of production as a historical mode of production (Kliman 2012). The phenomenal growth of finance is less a historical aberration, however, than a structural feature of globalizing capital, which provides a powerful engine to generate value through manifold forms of credit and debt-leveraging. But it is more than this. To employ a concept from Althusser, in the present global order interest-bearing capital functions as a 'structure in dominance' within the capitalist mode of production: a critical element of a complex whole which determines and organizes all other social and economic practices. For Althusser, the concept 'totality' indicates 'unity of complexity', in the sense that the 'mode of organization and articulation of complexity is precisely what constitutes its unity' (Althusser 2005: 201–202). Marx, of course, recognized the importance of interest-bearing credit money in the nineteenth century, observing how finance capital 'accelerates the material development of the productive forces and the establishment of the world market' (Marx 1959: 441). He also recognized the logical contradiction in the capitalist credit system, namely that interest-bearing capital simultaneously 'accelerates the violent eruptions of this contradiction – crises – and thereby the elements of disintegration of the old mode of production' (ibid.). In the present era, finance intensifies the process of *commodity abstraction*, where the global money-form of capital – the realization of human labour power in the abstract (La Berge 2014), creates complex financial entitlements which facilitate and intensify the reproduction of value in the sphere of circulation. This, in turn, augments and compensates for a declining profitability of labour power in commodity production itself – although these two modes of valorization are not necessarily antithetical.

Nevertheless, financialization *is* economically and politically unstable because the growth of credit money – falsely understood as a 'limitless' quantity – continually tests the limits of liquidity in the international monetary system. That is, the growth of financial market money tests the capacity of monetary authorities to defend liquidity which is not itself money but rather 'money that is virtual and latent in an asset' (Lozano 2014: 16). This is so because, in pursuit of rapid gains, modern financial instruments are fluid, fungible, over-extended and impermanent, dependent for their valorization on the continual multiplication of debt and the appropriation of future value to sustain an illusion of rising asset values and prosperity in the present. At the same time, the intermediating function of finance alters the social basis of property ownership in favour of investor elites. Despite the shrill propaganda of 'popular capitalism' and 'share-owning democracy' in the 1980s, and despite the relative diffusion of finance capital to post-communist and emerging economies in the present period of globalization, property ownership still remains highly concentrated among a transnational investor class whose deracinated location at once removed from the domestic political ties and regulatory constraints of sovereign territorial states affords it immense global financial power and operational autonomy. At the other extreme, new macroprudential regulations in the international financial system mean that assets held by *ordinary* depositors in banks and financial institutions are increasingly insecure: not only are depositors denied a real rate of return for lending to banks due to negative real interest rates (where the rate of inflation is higher than base rates) or negative nominal rates (where rates are below the zero lower bound), but a regulatory regime is being implemented which will limit the entitlement of depositors to assets in the event of future liquidity crises.

Central to the development of financial socialism is the changing form and function of money in advanced capitalism which must be understood in response to the accumulation crisis of capital, which is characterized by a tendential decline in the rate of profit, a search for new sources of value in the sphere of circulation and the field of information. At the heart of this problematic, however, is the unprecedented leveraging of debt in developed and emerging economies which renders the return to a 'normal' monetary policy cycle unthinkable without the risk of triggering sovereign and corporate default (Mai 2018). According to the International Financial Reporting Standards Foundation, the critical issue of debt has intensified since the global financial crisis:

> The combined debt of consumers, banks, corporates and governments amounted to no less than 269% of [global] GDP at the outbreak of the financial crisis. Never in history had global debt been so high as it was in 2008. […] Normally excessive leverage is reduced after a financial crisis. This time, however, total debt continued to grow to a staggering 318% of global GDP in 2018, almost 50 percentage points higher than the historical record of 2008. (Hoogerverst 2018: 1)

The ever-increasing magnitude of private, corporate and sovereign debt in a slowing global economy means not only that accumulation is maintained to a great extent by the growth of fictitious capital, but also that capitalism (barring the unlikely occurrence of a modern debt 'jubilee' – a universal cancellation of outstanding unpayable debt) is caught in an irreversible debt trap. A debt trap is triggered where escalating levels of debt keeping capitalism in motion increase because interest rates are low, but where interest rates cannot be raised because the edifice of leveraged debt is vulnerable to even small movements in the base rate by one or more of the world's major central banks. This extended interruption in the 'normal' cycle of monetary policy since 2008 – particularly in the advanced economies – reinforces the trend towards financial socialism as a specific stage in the evolution of postliberal capitalism where state circuits of finance capital assume a critical role in the reproduction of capitalist social relations and the stabilization of the financial system.

Stated otherwise: finance capital (credit money) is generated through new forms of debt, perpetuating at ever-higher levels of magnitude the moment of repayment which might announce the 'end' of capitalism as a mode of production in which a settling of accounts (debt repayment) might signify a limit to the potential valorization and self-expansion of capital. Streeck (2014) argues that measures introduced to stabilize the global economy since 2008 are a means of 'buying time' – a strategy to delay the sociopolitical crisis of state-democratic capitalism. He also argues convincingly that the financial crisis has been used by political and monetary elites – particularly within the eurozone – to realize the political-economic conditions for Hayek's (1980) vision of 'interstate federalism' and to further reduce the capacity of sovereign democracies to manage their economic and financial affairs independently. Yet while Streeck may be correct in his evaluation of the political exigencies of the global financial crisis – which have further reduced the scope of eurozone states to determine economic and monetary policy, it is also possible to understand the concept of 'buying time' in a historical-philosophical sense, namely as a *katechontic deferral*. Applying Benjamin's (2004) opaque yet prescient critique of capitalism as a cult that rules out salvation yet renders debt pervasive, the goal of an infinite expansion of debt as a precondition for continued accumulation can be seen as a contemporary instantiation of the classical figure of the *katechon* – that is, a deviation or detour to 'extend history into the dead eternity of surplus time' through the further capture of future value (Hamacher 2002: 89). If capitalism is a mode of production in which debts do not have to be repaid (merely extended and deferred), then this process must in theory be repeated *ad infinitum* to avoid a catastrophic collapse of commodity-determined society triggered by the uncontrolled draining of liquidity from the monetary system. Infinite accumulation of debt has, in effect, become a necessary (but perhaps insufficient) process to delay a change in capitalist social relations caused by a cataclysmic unwinding of global debt, thereby delaying a potential collapse of the global economy. For global monetary and political elites, the political implications of such a 'final' event are so nightmarish as to be literally unimaginable, and must therefore be repressed – whatever the cost. If financial socialism leads to economic fascism – where independent capital is extracted through a coercive accumulation of private assets and overaccumulation is resolved through wasteful and unproductive investment, this may be considered a price worth paying by elites to defend the global economic order of capital.

Whereas the figure of the *katechon* was conceived originally in theological terms as a force that defers the arrival of the end times (*eschaton*), in contemporary European philosophy the concept is secularized to denote a generalized deferral of change that delays the catastrophic implosion of a mode of production that is at once 'out of time' yet compulsively celebrates its own existence. This critical association of capitalism and religion is theoretically distinct from Weber's (2002 [1905]) economic sociology of Calvinism in the *Protestant Ethic*. Following Agamben (2007) and Debord (1994), Racy argues that Benjamin's formulation of capitalism as a 'cult without a theology' which withholds the possibility of atonement effectively 'terminates the distinction between sacred/profane, divine/ human. In so doing, not only is the split eradicated, but also profanation itself becomes an absolute consecration without content' (Racy 2016: 87). This division, he notes, reflects a parallel division in the commodity form itself – the contradiction between exchange-value and use-value which

> inflicts irreparable damage on social life, since the gap opened by it is filled by the spectacle itself which in the end reveals 'itself for what it *is*: an autonomously developing separate power, based on the increasing productivity resulting from an increasingly refined division of labour [...] working for an over-expanding market'. (Debord 2002, cited in Racy 2016: 90)

Benjamin's interpretation of the *katechon* as debt is complex and sophisticated, and considerations of space rule out a detailed exposition in the present study. However, its significance for the analysis should be clear: 'If the god whose cult is celebrated in capitalism is indebtedness itself [...] then this process can have no end' (Szendy 2012: 9). For capital to continue its relentless self-expansion into the 'dead eternity of surplus time', the moment of redemption *can have no end* and 'the cult to debt can only be celebrated by generating more debt to sustain debt, to avoid absolution from debt [...]' (ibid.; emphasis in original).

What this implies in more transparent language is that in its present secularized form the relentless yet non-expiatory power of the debt-relation functions as a historical device to enable a withholding of the moment of capital's supersession – normally defined in Marxism as 'sublation' (*Aufhebung*). This 'katechontic deferral' is evident in the determination of global monetary and political elites after the global crisis to sustain the illusion of global liquidity and institute new macroprudential mechanisms to reduce systemic risk and increase financial repression and thus delay a more significant alteration in capitalist relations through the continued multiplication of debt as *conditio sine qua non* for the uninterrupted self-expansion of the capitalist value form. Their aim is to prevent a repeat of the global financial crisis, for given the scale of new debt created since 2008, renewed instability could lead to a deleveraging of capital values sufficient to bankrupt unproductive economies, *limiting the power of investor elites to appropriate the surplus product of the global economy.*

Yet the dramatic expansion of credit money in the global financial system and the concomitant failure of elites to re-engineer growth since the termination of the long boom in the early 2000s are driving important changes in the form and function of capitalist money itself, leading to the potential elimination of the zero lower bound and a complete transition to electronic bank money as a unit of account. As we shall see in Chapters 4 and 5, these changes reflect not only the increasing abstraction of interest-bearing capital in the banking system and the disappearance of physical monetary assets (for all but wealthy investors), but the growth of financial market money sustained by a supply of state-issued sovereign currency to maintain liquidity (quantitative easing). In the emerging framework of financial socialism, central banks seek to maintain a de facto monopoly over money, as a result of which the traditional function of currency as a store of value is being eroded by negative (real) interest rates and as capital controls are (re)introduced under the rubric of a 'cashless society', ostensibly to deter the preservation of private wealth outside the banking system. These dynamics are driving investors into bond markets, which serve to sustain credit flows and counter a tendency towards corporate and sovereign insolvency.

To understand the present structural fragility of capital, therefore, it is necessary to examine contradictions in the capitalist form of value, and the changing forms and functions of commodity money, fiat money and credit money in advanced capitalism. To counter deflationary tendencies and compensate for declining profitability in advanced capitalism, central banks have deluged markets with liquidity, allowing financial institutions to 'capture' future value through the accumulation of *fictitious* capital – an *abstract manifestation of capital value* gener-ated through a multiplication of paper claims on value in excess of the aggregate surplus value generated through productive activity. In Marxian theory, capital is defined as 'fictitious' not because it is imaginary or immaterial but because it derives from investments based on an 'expectation of future returns. Since the expected returns might be produced in the future, they do not currently exist, and, so are fictitious' (Cooper 2014: 3). Yet capital gains of this type are made at the expense of future accumulation and must therefore be classified as a form of 'accumulation without value' (Lohoff & Trenkle 2013).

Four salient issues arise from the Marxian critique of value, discussed at length in the course of the present study. These can be summarized in the following form:

1. The exhaustion of commodity production as a basis for the generation of abstract surplus value through exploitation of labour power;
2. The character of fictitious capital (equities, securities, derivatives, etc.) as 'financial market' money;
3. Limitations on the preservation of fictitious capital through central bank activism and financial repression;
4. The impact of oligarchy and financial repression on the nature of property ownership in postliberal capitalism.

For Stiegler, fictitious capital constitutes a 'system of anticipations' – an organi-zation of risk-taking, one which 'gives the capitalist system its dynamic: capital-ism presupposes the existence of free capital open to speculation [...]' (2011: 84). Confronted by the ontological limits of its own self-expansion, however, capital may be testing the ontological limits of exchange society. Financial socialism is not simply a new form of regulation to manage contradictions in market societ-ies but a necessary evolution of capitalist commodity relations beyond the 'free' market to sustain oligopolistic banking capital confronted by a crisis of valo-rization specific to technologically advanced economies where human labour power plays a diminished role in the production of material commodities and services. Financial socialism reveals the ideological/institutional flexibility of postliberal capitalism as 'socialism for the investor class'. The neoliberal 'revolu-tion', argues Kurz, 'was not a subjective, political project. It was rather an escape strategy from the objective problems of a shortage of actual surplus produc-tion, based on the rapid acceleration of current processes without any change in direction' (Kurz 2010: 334). A similar logic informs the transition *within* capi-talism from competition to oligopoly. This articulation of postliberal capitalism is characterized in the sphere of circulation by an intensification of demand through the proletarianization of the consumer (Stiegler 2011), by the continual expansion of credit markets, and by a change in the form and function of capi-talist money itself.

We cannot approach this issue, however, until we have assessed the limi-tations of neoclassical economics as a method for explaining the crisis, before examining in Chapter 2 the failure of heterodox economics (neo-Marxism/left-Keynesianism) to provide adequate alternative explanations for the persistence of capitalist crisis. It is important to note that although it was a financial crisis originating in the US which *triggered* the present economic downturn, contrary to the claims of heterodox economics, the causes of the present recession are not 'irreducibly financial' (Kliman 2012). Instead, they lie in the exhaustion of the capitalist value form as the 'necessary dimension of labour and of the useful objects produced by it in the bourgeois mode of production. It is a *social* dimension and a social universal' (Reuten & Williams 1987: 60). In capitalist societies, the particular 'products of labour necessarily have to take on a social-universal form which is the value form, for without them being *validated* as such they are socially non-existent' (ibid.: 60–61). It is not financialization which explains the crisis but a crisis of valorization in the sequence of money, production and profit which underpins capitalist commodity production. Here lies an explanation for the failure of governments to engineer 'recovery' by deleveraging debt (austerity), by purchasing distressed financial assets and by allowing interest rates to fall below the zero lower bound to stimulate economic activity.

Methodological contradictions in neoclassical theory

Despite the political triumph of neoliberalism, neoclassical economics increasingly resembles the shambolic state of Marxism-Leninism in the former USSR, which descended into a sophisticated yet intellectually barren legitimation science for the maintenance of Communist Party rule. In the final years before the Soviet command economy collapsed, only party *apparatchiki* and intellectual sycophants continued to parrot the ossified narrative of scientific socialism as a superior organizational model of industrial society. In the present crisis, neoclassical economics retains a preeminent position in academia, yet the dissonance between this legitimation science and the reality of postliberal capitalism is increasingly clear. As a social-scientific orthodoxy, an institutionally legitimated mode of scientific production (Althusser 1969), neoclassical economics possesses a *material existence* by virtue of the fact that it is performed in educational and administrative apparatuses and reproduced discursively by excluding alternative discourses. Neoclassical theory has 'seen off many attacks not because it has been strong enough to withstand them, but because it has been strong enough to ignore them' (Keen 2011: 4). Yet the survival of the paradigm has created false confidence in the stability of capitalism which even the financial crisis has not destroyed, and the discipline is clearly overdue an 'intellectual revolution' (ibid.). Contradicting the intentions of its founders, neoclassical economic theory is the *real* source of the authoritarian logic of postliberal capitalism – a suboptimal market economy which depends on centralized administrative control over currency and the regimentation of consumer behaviour. Just as marginal utility theory praises stable and predictable consumer behaviour as a condition for equilibrium, financial socialism presupposes manipulation of consumer spending/

borrowing, continuous real-time market research, reward-based spending and so forth. This correlates with the securitization discourse of neoliberalism, pointing towards a modern monetary tyranny in which wealth is expropriated by negative interest rates and limitations on the movement of independent wealth in cashless economies.

In the present era we are living with *unresolved consequences of a deflationary disturbance that can only be understood as a crisis of capitalism itself.* The origins of this disturbance predate the global financial crisis and have their ultimate source in the crisis of Fordist accumulation regimes in the 1970s, which brought to an end an exceptional period in the history of western capitalism. While economists have produced sophisticated attempts to explain the global financial crisis (largely to justify specific policy responses), there has been a failure to examine the weakness of capitalist commodity production itself, which predates the present crisis and cannot be attributed to it. This is not because mainstream economists are fools, but because they prefer to ask very limited questions within the restrictive framework of 'general equilibrium theory'. Put simply, general equilibrium theory is a social-scientific dogma which holds that the default state of markets is stability: 'breakdowns of the market system, as opposed to imbalances in particular markets, are out of the question; what general difficulties do occur must be the effect of some non-economic factor, such as the weather, human psychology or mistaken government policies' (Mattick 2011: 18). Yet capitalism has always been prone to accumulation crises caused by factors beyond financial instability, greed or regulatory failure. The present downturn stems less from sectoral imbalances or irrational exuberance, but from a contradiction in the capitalist value form itself, which Marx observed in his mature critique of political economy. In the absence of a sustained critique of capitalist commodity production, attempts to explain the weakness of advanced economies in terms of 'irrational exuberance' or a lack of fit between the 'real' economy and finance yield only partial insights into the declining profitability of capitalism and the failure of attempts to revitalize a decadent mode of production. That falling profit rates are largely disguised by inflated asset prices not only conceals the underlying problem from general view; it also makes it less likely that monetary and political elites can recognize and address the problem at all.

From a philosophical perspective, neoclassical economic theory is based on a rigid commitment to methodological individualism (MI), an approach to economics and social science concerned exclusively with the determining effect of individual preferences – the intentional states which motivate individuals to engage in specific actions.[1] Neoclassical theory is also self-consciously reductionist in its choice of assumptions about human agency. To use a term favoured by leading exponents, neoclassicism is 'parsimonious' in its theoretical claims and choice of relevant criteria, in relation to individuals acting alone, and the social or affective relations which exist between agents. Neoclassical theory also excludes more from its models of economic behaviour than it includes, eschewing structural or diachronic analysis in favour of micro-level explanations (within imaginary delimited economic spaces), while avoiding theoretical generalization in the search for minimal lawlike ('positive') hypotheses concerning causation. Such hypotheses are devoid of any *normative* considerations which cannot be reconciled with the assumption of rational optimizing individuals engaged in self-interested action.

This is not simply an academic question: commitment to MI has direct implications for the theoretical failure and ideological distortions of neoclassical economic theory, whose postulates and assumptions are taken as axiomatic by academics, policymakers and corporate CEOs, and which are assumed to possess a 'scientific basis' by ordinary mortals mystified by finance and global political economy. Our specific concern with MI is not identical to that of critical authors such as Weeks (1989), Fine (2004) or Lawson (2009), representatives of 'critical realism in economics'. These writers advance important critical anti-positivist positions to support the assumption that causality is a question of the real powers that objects and structures possess (Groff 2004), in contradistinction to neoclassical orthodoxy which uses deductivism to falsely justify Menger's essentialist insistence on individual preferences as a basis for scientific explanation (Lawson 1999; cf. Boyle & McDonough 2010). Neither are we concerned with presenting historical materialism as alternative economic science in the manner of Analytical Marxism, a revisionist approach which explains the emergence of structural inequalities (and thus social classes) in terms of the 'rational choices of unequally endowed utility-maximizers, that is, uncoercively, and within the context of circulation' (Roberts 1997: 5; cf. Roemer 1982; Elster 1985; Cohen 2000). Rather, our specific aim is to show how MI undermines the capacity of neoclassical economics to explain market failure and recession, and why this leaves orthodoxy open to charges of ideologization. Orthodox economists are wedded to Hayekian individualism as a prior basis for analysing collective economic behaviour, yet as Denys (2014: 8) notes, Hayek himself did not consistently adhere to MI in his career and departed from 'mistaken precepts' of MI in later works. Hayek concluded that networks of relationships cannot be reduced to logically prior asocial individuals, and that marginal choices made by individuals depend to a very large extent on the collective outcome of preceding choices and decisions determining social structures that ultimately constrain and/or facilitate autonomous agency (ibid.: 15).

How therefore do neoclassical economists explain recession? Are their reductive models of equilibrium adequate for understanding more than simple microeconomic processes in which real-world events and dynamics are controlled for or excluded? In what follows, we outline some key assumptions in neoclassical theory and criticisms of its philosophical assumptions and methodological foundations. The intention is not to declare an 'end' to economics (cf. Perelman 1996) but to specify the limitations of the discipline in its capacity to address the causes of capitalist recession and market collapse. The weakness of neoclassical equilibrium models derives not simply from flawed assumptions concerning unsatisfied demand or unsold supply but from the subjectivism of marginal utility theory. Symbolized by the Chicago School tradition of Friedman and the MIT tradition of Samuelson, neoclassical theory is a successful rhetorical strategy which *reproduces itself through continual verification of its own standard models*. These models are based on questionable assumptions about the operation of free markets, including perfect competition, certainty, stable preferences and optimizing behaviour.

Neoclassical economics has its roots in the 'marginalist' revolution of the nineteenth century, which rejected the labour theory of value developed in classical political economy (that the value of a commodity is a function of the labour power employed in its production) in favour of marginal utility theory. The *New World Encyclopedia* defines neoclassical economics as a

> general approach in economics focusing on the determination of prices, outputs and income distributions in markets through supply and demand. These are mediated through a hypothesized maximization of income-constrained utility by individuals and of cost-constrained profits of firms employing available information and factors of production. Neoclassical economics [...] developed from the classical economics dominant in the eighteenth and nineteenth centuries. Its beginning can be traced to the Marginal revolution of the 1860s, which brought the concept of utility as the key factor in determining value in contrast to the classical view that the costs involved in production were value's determinant.[2]

This new approach to market behaviour is based on a subjective (psychological) rather than objective (material) conception of value which assumes (a) that economic behaviour is driven by the quest for utility (preference satisfaction), and (b) that rational actors seek to satisfy needs or preferences with a higher priority, such that no higher preferences are left avoidably unsatisfied in an attempt to satisfy secondary preferences. Leading representatives of the marginalist revolution such as Jevons, Walrus and Menger – and Böhm-Bawerk, Pareto and Marshal – rejected the labour theory of value as a 'metaphysical relic', abandoning historical materialism for logical positivism in the search for a universal model to explain the determination of prices in markets with an ideal equilibrium state. Whereas classical economists and Marxists had been concerned with the objective realization of surplus value in the production process, neoclassical theory was concerned with the subjective derivation of value in the sphere of exchange – with the emphasis on rational choice as a key determinant of supply and demand.

Although the notion of a marginalist revolution is mythic – economics has always evolved in parallel with the political-institutional development of capitalism (Henry 1990) – marginal utility theory achieved intellectual hegemony in academic and political circles until Keynes challenged neoclassicalism in the 1930s. After 1945, mainstream theory absorbed elements of Keynesianism to become the 'neoclassical synthesis', which remains the leading school of positive economic science in western universities today (Weeks 1989). Positivism is not exclusively concerned with the fact-value distinction (Katouzian 1980); yet as Clark (2016: 310–311) observes, it is based on the idea of a 'clear distinction between *de*scription and *pre*scription. Only positive statements dealing with the world as it is can potentially be proved wrong'. Neoclassical theory welcomes logical positivism because 'it treats normative claims about how society ought to be structured as "meaningless", and therefore unworthy of consideration by economists' (ibid.: 311). This normative/positive distinction in social science reflects the paradigm in which logical positivism developed and imposes a strict ontological divide between 'empirical facts about the world and our appraisal of such facts' (Keita 1997: 84).

Developing Bernal's (2010 [1939]) critical sociology of science, Henry observes that despite its pretension towards value-free science, neoclassical economics in fact 'reflects the dominant relationships within capitalist society and has been developed and modified to accommodate changes within this form of social organization [...] neoclassicism does not stand above or apart from society, but is, as with all social ideas, conditioned by that society' (Henry 1990: xvii). In fact, the development of neoclassical theory corresponds with the transition from competitive to uncompetitive capitalism in the nineteenth century, signalling a *retreat* from historical materialism into positivism and pseudo-science. This period witnessed an unprecedented flowering of irrational political and philosophical ideas, including logical positivism, vitalism, existentialism and revolutionary conservatism, which 'bear one essential characteristic in common: the denial of an objective, real world that exists independent of one's ideas and can become known through observation and experimentation. In other words, materialism had to be denied' (ibid.: 55). As Lukács (1962) observed, the rise of subjectivism and irrationalism signalled the end of progressive bourgeois political and economic thought and the marginalization of Marxian materialism within the labour movement. Capitalism had brought into being a numerically significant working class which was susceptible to materialist ideologies linking scientific progress and rational economic development, which threatened to undermine the legitimacy of capitalist institutions founded on liberal equality and private property. A striking example of the new subjectivism in social science was neoclassical theory, which employs ahistorical deductive-nomological methods to test hypotheses concerning the microeconomic behaviour of individuals and firms – hypotheses derived from intuition rather than experimentation. At the level of macroeconomics (analysis of aggregate market behaviour) neoclassicism is still more restrictive, and even the crowning achievement of neoclassicism (Walrasian equilibrium analysis) is in practice only applicable in short-run static models composed of a limited number of market actors with specific resource endowments – models which can be controlled for exogenous shocks and disequilibrium trades (Weeks 1989: 42–43).

Neoclassical economics is also based on a faulty and simplistic model of *marginal utility* which – despite denials from disciples like Samuelson – is psychologistic in orientation. Marginal utility is viewed as a function of stable preferences, ranked by consumers according to subjective estimates of hedonic value: if the supply of a given preference increases and its market value falls, then to compensate for *diminishing marginal utility*, rational consumers will seek to satisfy alternative preferences instead. According to marginalism, consumers manifest consistent market behaviour, which shifts only in response to price signals. Individuals are rational not on the basis of the quality or integrity of choices, but on the basis that their choices are stable and maximize marginal utility at all times. In addition, it is assumed all market societies are fundamentally alike, that is to say, all societies are understood as abstract ahistoric aggregations of optimizing individuals who respond appropriately to price fluctuations in perfectly competitive markets.

As Henry notes, 'adoption of the utility theory of value as the standard from which all subsequent theory would flow satisfied the general requirements that the dominant view of economics would have to fulfil' (ibid.: 227). Henceforth, value would be determined not by the surplus value generated in production but by the hedonistic calculus of individual consumers in the absence of antagonistic class relations and market distortion. Neoclassicism is thus very narrow in its theoretical premises and horizons: while in the real world individuals are inconsistent, emotional, irrational and often self-defeating, in the marginalist fantasy of a static universal social space, consumers have stable preferences and do not 'deviate' wildly from these choices in the absence of appropriate price signals (which are in turn assumed to be the outcome of rational market decisions based on available information). Yet these assumptions are nonsensical, for in the real world individuals make choices which result in 'less than satisfactory outcomes. This seems to be by design rather than anything else. If we always made the choice that ensured constant satisfaction we would soon find that we had no motivation to do anything new' (Pilkington 2011: 2). Marginal utility theory can thus be compared to a belief system (or cult) which 'shuts down' a complex view of the world and subordinates the panoply of possible human actions to the repetitive performance of a narrow repertoire of choices based on given resource endowments.

This theoretical move has major implications for the practice of economics, removing the possibility of critical analysis. Since all societies are considered fundamentally the same, so the 'nature of capitalist society does not have to be examined at all: it is merely a universal, natural system' (Henry 1990: 160). Neoclassicism thus depends on a timeless, 'non-social perspective [...] ostensibly independent of time and place'. Its defenders insist that because it is 'capable of examining economic relations independent of time and place, the theory itself is independent of social foundation' (ibid.: 174). Yet it is marginalism that corresponds to the regressive development of monopoly capitalism in the nineteenth century, leading to extreme concentrations of economic power as anticompetitive trusts restricted output to maintain artificially high prices and eliminate competition while capitalist society displayed increasing inequality. Lacking a critical-historical perspective, neoclassical economics could posit only an imaginary construction of market society based on the myth of free and equal exchange between self-interested agents, and its leading representatives each developed similarly abstract models of a universal market society in which property relations and anticompetitive practices are rendered invisible or irrelevant despite the intensification of class divisions and industrial concentration which characterized capitalism in Europe and North America at that time.

The failure of neoclassicism to grasp the complexity of production, exchange and consumption in capitalism thus lies in its restrictive ontology, which is additionally impoverished by a rhetorical prohibition of normativity. This reflects the impact of logical positivism, which denies the socially constructed character of knowledge, consigning non-tautological statements to the realm of normativity. The issue with MI is not 'how one could give an individualistic explanation of social behaviour, but that of how one could ever give a non-social (i.e. strictly individualistic) explanation of individual, at least characteristically human, behaviour!' (Bhaskar 2015: 28). This concept of rationality leads to functionalism:

> To explain a human action by reference to its rationality is like explaining a natural event by reference to its being caused. Rationality then appears as an *a priori* presupposition of investigation, devoid of explanatory content and almost certainly false. As for neoclassical economic theory, the most developed form of this tendency in social thought, it may be best regarded as a normative theory of efficient action, generating a set of techniques for achieving given ends, rather than as an explanatory theory capable of casting light on actual empirical episodes. (ibid.: 29–30)

For this reason, argues Weeks, nothing resembling

> a Walrasian market exists in any exchange economy, yet such markets are taken as the basis of neoclassical general equilibrium models. The functional role of Walrasian markets in neoclassical theory is clear: these ideal assumptions serve as a superficial justification for the view that economic agents operate with perfect knowledge and foresight of market conditions. [...] Walrasian markets eliminate the possibility of any disruptions due to unforeseen circumstances. Since disequilibrium trades are excluded by assumption, general equilibrium is established by assumption. [...] It is an interesting sociological phenomenon that such a patently absurd view of market operation should be incorporated into mainstream economics and generally accepted. (Weeks 1989: 44–45)

Self-equilibrating markets are thus reduced to successions of conjunctions forming a social system devoid of substantive determining features, obscuring the determination of surplus value in commodity production: 'just as the necessity of the wage-form is its concealment of exploitation', argue Boyle and McDonough (2010: 13), so the 'social function of constant conjunctions is their concealment of structures irreducible to events and societies irreducible to people'. This elides the foundational dependence of market relations on human labour power: to achieve this outcome, 'an atomistic ontology is absolutely necessary as it allows (neoclassical) marginal productivity theory to be contingently conjoined on the basis of their respective productivity [...]. Ideologically, this denial of concrete social relations completely elides the foundational dependence of capital on "dead labour"' (ibid.: 16).

As Özel indicates, however, it is precisely this atomistic ontology that determines the limited capacity of neoclassical economics to establish a viable theory of equilibrium, according to which all market perturbations are deviations from an assumed norm of aggregated individual rational actions. Following Bhaskar (2015), he notes that the 'postulate of rational, optimizing behaviour' is a *normative prescription* and not an explanatory statement: 'to say that people are rational does not explain *what* they do, but only at best *how* they should do it. But rationality, by itself, can explain nothing, even if it is designed to explain "everything"' (Özel 2000: 270). On the contrary, 'rationality is merely an *a priori* presupposition of investigation [...]' (ibid.).

Thus, the atomistic ontology of positive economic science cannot comprehend that there are '*emergent properties* of societies irreducible to the dynamics of individuals' (ibid.: 272). It assumes that no economic state of affairs will lead to a state which is not an equilibrium because agents will defect from a suboptimal transactional environment where more profitable options exist. This produces an idealized picture of social reality which is ultimately based on a value judgement:

> It would seem that the neoclassical theorist needs the postulate of rationality to formulate neat and manageable theories only because human beings frequently make mistakes in their decision-making operations, and often changes their minds, tastes, dispositions in their schedules of choice, even where they accept, in principle, behaviour in accordance with the neoclassical postulate of rationality. But agents could and do sometimes formulate choice schedules at variance with neoclassical theory of rational choice. It is for this reason that the definition of rationality chosen by the orthodox neoclassical theorist must be understood as arbitrarily prescriptive just as ethical definitions of the term 'good' must be understood as being arbitrarily prescriptive. (Keita 1997: 92)

Not only does the assertion of a monolithic conception of individual rationality ignore both the historical genealogy of 'rationality' in economics and the socio-institutional contexts within which embedded individuals act (Zouboulakis 2014), but it also entails a mechanistic view of causality without complexity. Such an ontology is atomistic and simplistic; it is the main reason for the methodological failure of general equilibrium theory because it 'cannot take account of the emergent properties of social structures [...] equilibrium theory cannot explain the aggregate relations which are incompatible with the relations characterizing individual behaviour' (Özel 2000: 276).

The limits of orthodoxy

If neoclassicism fails to explain the dynamic emergent properties of complex systems where continuous conjunctions of events derive from aggregates of individual actions, and where economic disturbances are exogenously determined and short-run, how does its explain cycles of boom/bust that cause capitalist recessions? Which is to say, how do the economists who advise bankers and CEOs apply a model based on rational expectations and price adjustment explain the real world of involuntary unemployment, unpayable debt, monetary easing and market failure? To make sense of macroeconomic theory from a critical perspective, it is necessary to examine the *new neoclassical synthesis* as an attempt to unify and recombine core elements of neoclassicism and Keynesianism into a model capable of explaining short-run fluctuations in markets. While the present crisis has exposed contradictions in orthodoxy (Hart 2010; Keen 2011), which is subject to extensive critique from post-Keynesian and heterodox economics (Lavoie 2013), the new neoclassical synthesis remains the basis for macroeconomic forecasting models like the FRB/US model used by the Federal Reserve, which determine real-world decisions by powerful government officials in advanced economies.[3]

Orthodox new classical analyses of capitalist recessions set out from a basic model of the 'real' business cycle, sometimes defined as the 'neoclassical model of real sector equilibrium plus shocks' – shocks that emanate from the financial sector, technology or another exogenous variables. In this model, four stages of boom and bust are identified, namely expansion, peak, contraction and trough, constituting a repetitive cycle in which lower labour input is seen to account for much of the decline in income and output in advanced economies like the US (Ohanian 2010). Neoclassical theorists assume that booms occur where workers choose to work harder in response to higher wage incentives, whereas recessions occur when workers choose to work less in response to lower wage incentives or to an increase in the marginal utility of leisure. On the basis of these assumptions, they argue that governments need not (and should not) intervene in the 'natural' course of the business cycle because existing allocations of resources are assumed to be Pareto-optimal (efficient such that no alternative distribution could make everyone better off without making someone worse off). Government should restrict itself to promoting productivity, by rewarding competition or lowering transaction costs as demand returns and rising confidence stimulates investment. Ultimately, markets clear of their own accord due to changes in supply and innovation rather than rising demand or government stimulus.

Unlike Keynesian models of real sector disequilibrium, which call for government stimulus to alter consumers' liquidity preferences in order to overcome the 'paradox of thrift' (where consumers save rather than spend under conditions of uncertainty), neoclassical economists insist that demand for money is stable, and (at the risk of exacerbating downturns like that which followed the 'Volcker shock' of 1979–1981) call for counter-inflationary rather than counter-cyclical policies to stabilize prices and bring economies into equilibrium.[4] The assertion that unemployment is voluntary rather than structural allows governments to justify removing welfare entitlements in an effort to 'roll back' the frontiers of the state, satisfying an ideological commitment to austerity in a neoliberal political economy that continues to the present day. Early debates between neoclassicals and Keynesians had revolved around the issue of how quickly prices and wages adjust to market fluctuations. Neoclassicals assumed that markets are self-clearing – that prices (and wages) quickly adjust to changes in demand; markets return to equilibrium independently as workers choose to rejoin the labour force and state intervention is unnecessary. New Keynesians, on the other hand, emphasized market failure, focusing on price rigidities and the inability of firms to synchronize price adjustments. This occurs when firms stagger price changes or fail to anticipate how price changes will affect other firms or the wider economy, and leads to disruptions in demand that perpetuate slowdowns by encouraging consumers to save rather than spend, which in turn discourages firms to invest. Disagreements existed in other areas, such as the link between wages, efficiency and productivity, with neoclassicals advocating wage restraint and Keynesians highlighting efficiency gains obtained from offering higher wages. Yet, in the 1990s, a new synthesis of the new classical and new Keynesian schools emerged in an attempt to bridge divisions, leading some to claim that the discipline had 'resolved' many of its historic issues, leading to a new 'golden era for the [economics] profession' (Hart 2010: 1).

The new classical synthesis had exposed a key contradiction in neoclassical theory, namely the lack of fit between Walrasian microeconomic models based on general equilibrium (market clearing) and Keynesian macroeconomic models with market imperfection (absence of market clearing). Yet modern monetary macroeconomics entails a combination of assumptions and approaches from the new classical and new Keynesian schools. This theoretical convergence centres on a *dynamic general equilibrium model* with microeconomic foundations calibrated to handle short-run disturbances caused by allocative inefficiencies, shifts in demand and changing public policy. The model entails the following:

- Business cycles are driven by shifts in aggregate demand [...].
- Output and employment are affected by fluctuations in aggregate demand because of nominal rigidities that prevent prices and wages from adjusting rapidly.
- The central bank is modelled as actively adjusting the interest rate in response to shocks to the economy so as to achieve its inflation target.
- Aggregate demand fluctuations shift the economy away from the equilibrium rate of unemployment.
- The [equilibrium rate of unemployment] is the outcome of imperfectly competitive labour and product markets [...].
- Supply shocks shift the ERU and institutional and policy differences across countries imply different ERUs. (Carlin & Soskice 2006: x)

Although many neoclassical and Keynesian economists remain committed to their own respective paradigms and disdain attempts at consensus formation, the new neoclassical synthesis tries to bring together important elements of new classical economics (with its emphasis on marginal utility and microeconomic foundations) and elements of new Keynesianism (with its emphasis on aggregate demand and market imperfections). As Rankin argues:

> The seductive beauty of the synthesis of Robert Lucas' new classical economics with Eugene Fama's theory of efficient markets is based on the elegance of the price mechanism in ensuring: that unperturbed markets always clear in the short long-run; that the ensuing price signals lead rational buyers and sellers to allocate resources efficiently; that efficient financial markets rule out substantial economic shocks from the financial sector; and that macroeconomic imbalances self-adjust in the face of a consistent and credible monetary policy. This appeared to be the solution to the holy grail of macroeconomics: deriving a set of macro-truths from micro-foundations. (Rankin 2010: 96)

Its impetus came from a meeting of the American Economic Association in 1997 at a time when the neoliberal consensus was in favour of 'policy restraint', namely that governments should adopt a neutral or 'non-interventionist' position on monetary policy and financial markets in view of the uncertainties arising in the formulation of macroeconomic policies (Hart 2010: 4).

In a paper outlining the basis for a new synthesis, Goodfriend and King set out to locate 'new dynamic microeconomic foundations for macroeconomics' (1997: 232), specifying four elements for a new neoclassical synthesis: intertemporal optimization, rational expectations, imperfect competition and costly price adjustment. An explicit conclusion of their work is that monetary policy is not neutral and can be used to manage aggregate demand 'to deliver efficient macroeconomic outcomes' (ibid.: 256) because monetary policy mimics effects of productivity changes and fiscal shocks. The power of the new synthesis, they argue, 'lies in the complementarity of its new Keynesian and [real business cycle] components, which are compatible because of a shared reliance on microeconomics. The new synthesis allows knowledge gained from New Keynesian and RBC studies to be brought to bear on business-cycle and monetary policy questions in a single coherent model' (ibid.).

Building on new Keynesian theory, the impact of monetary policy is understood to be transmitted to the real economy by altering aggregate demand and influencing the average price mark-up in the economy (ibid.: 259–260). Yet the preference of the new neoclassical synthesis is ultimately to maintain a steady-state mark-up in prices over time through neutral monetary policy aimed at near-zero inflation, because neutral monetary policy 'accommodates shocks that would alter the equilibrium levels of output and unemployment with flexible prices' […] (ibid.: 266). Goodfriend and King consider the possible impact of energy shocks for equilibrium levels of output and unemployment, yet there is no mention of the failure of the efficient markets thesis or the risks associated with financial liberalization and its impact on advanced and emerging economies. While finance cannot explain the occurrence of recession, which occurs where capital is inadequately valorized, causing overinvestment in financial markets offering higher yields, Goodfriend and King ignore the role of money and finance in conditioning 'effective demand' and shaping the real economy, and are oblivious to the effect of shocks on 'real sector equilibrium'. While there is limited acknowledgement of uncertainty in neoclassical theory, rather than being treated as an active variable, the 'supply of money and finance simply "adjusts" inertly to the demand for money, with money and finance impacting on economic activity only to the extent that decision makers are responsive to changes in the cost of finance. In such a setting an explanation of financial instability, and its possible effects on the real economy, is difficult to conceive' (Hart 2010: 9). As we shall see in Chapter 2, it is unrealistic and illogical to separate financial sector instability from real sector equilibrium, as episodes of optimism and pessimism in financial markets 'amplify similar shifts in confidence within the real sectors of the economy. As was most clearly demonstrated in Minksy's (1985) financial instability hypothesis, real and financial sector instability are interconnected and inevitable characteristics of capitalist economies' (ibid.: 10).

A year after Goodfriend and King's paper on the new orthodoxy, the global economy was hit by a wave of extreme financial shocks associated with the Asian financial crisis (1998), the Russian default (1998), the Argentine debt crisis (1998–2001), the collapse of Long-Term Capital Management (1998) and the collapse of the dot-com boom (2000–2001). These events were extreme cases of market failure and systemic contagion risk, highlighting the dangers of global financial deregulation and the rapid acceleration of financial flows. As the subprime mortgage crisis intensified in the US in 2007, the central bank abandoned 'normal' tools of monetary policy for a radically non-neutral strategy to inflate asset bubbles and sustain the illusion of growth and liquidity in the world's leading economy. Yet even after the financial crisis of 2008, which must be understood in the context of unresolved contradictions linked to earlier crises, defenders of neoclassical theory were unrepentant in their refusal to abandon the myths of efficient markets and real sector equilibrium. This dogmatic approach, argues Keen, stems from the 'seductive nature of the neoclassical vision. It portrays capitalism as a perfect system, in which the market ensures that everything is "just right". It is a world in which meritocracy rules, rather than power and privilege as under previous social systems' (Keen 2011: 18). Quite apart from the tendency of the financial sector to create instability endogenously, there are reasons to question the reliability of rational price and investment theory in models used to guide financial decision-making which 'do not survive contact with the real world' (Coleman 2015). Although economists cling to the efficient markets hypothesis (that equity prices are a reliable indicator of the real value of a firm's stock), in the real world of corporate finance the absence of rational pricing and investment decisions is manifest. This is evidenced not only by market turbulence, but by the bounded rationality of decision-making, which tends to produce a 'lengthy catalogue of anomalies, biases and other irrationalities which are traced to psychological or behavioural misperceptions in financial decision makers' (ibid.: 23).

Practical reasons for the devotion of mainstream economics to equilibrium theory are, of course, not difficult to discern. From a sociological perspective, ideological forms of production – including scientific production – are implicated in power relations through processes of professionalization and institutionalization, through which systems of knowledge acquire a durable social basis. Ideological production operates in a 'material matrix of affirmations and sanctions, and this matrix determines their interrelationships' (Therborn 1980: 33). This matrix of affirmations and sanctions operates at a professional level to marginalize intellectual dissent and disruption to the paradigm and all 'institutionalized ideologies tend also to possess an important internal sanction: *excommunication*, often with the support of non-discursive sanctions' (ibid.: 35). Keen highlights further the naiveté of neoclassical economists and their tendency to consider economics a 'positive science'. They tend to treat the methodological foundations of their discipline as 'given', as 'normal science', based on assumptions which are not open to question, still less contradiction. The result is a professional disincentive to criticize the 'gospel' espoused in standard texts, even where the assumptions that underpin 'gospel' are contradicted in empirical research, and even though events like the financial crisis could never be explained (let alone predicted) according to neoclassical theory because not only is finance excluded from the model of real sector equilibrium, but value is determined in a psychologistic rather than material way.

In this sense, a disconnect exists between economic reality and ideology: '*If [...] textbooks gave an accurate rendition of the underlying theory, they would describe an economy that generated cycles, was in disequilibrium all the time, and was prone to breakdown*' (ibid.: 19; emphasis in original). The reason for this lies in MI, which encourages a subjective-psychologistic practice of reducing structural outcomes to an aggregate of individual preferences and actions, even if successful attempts to derive a coherent model of aggregate economic trends or outcomes from the sum of individual preferences and actions are difficult to locate (ibid.). Students of economics are also kept in a relative state of ignorance because the discipline largely avoids any analysis of the history of economic thought: 'Even a passing acquaintance with this literature exposes the reader to critical perspectives on conventional economic theory – but students today receive no such exposure' (ibid.: 21). The absence of any historical or philosophical perspective precludes an adequate understanding of the origins and development of economics in the nineteenth century, the interrelationship between economics and other social sciences (law, sociology) and the theoretical narrowing of the discipline into a standardized orthodoxy supported by econometric methods.

Thompson (1997) also criticizes the preference of neoclassical economics for formal mathematical models which are oblivious to alternative theoretical traditions, lacking in policy relevance and unconcerned with dialogue or intellectual exchange. The result is a perpetuation of ignorance – a refusal to debate the narrow methodological and theoretical assumptions which define the paradigm, which has withered into little more than narrow pedagogy:

> Given the search costs combined with specialisation, there is only so much time to devote to methodological issues. Therefore the dominant paradigm will draw the attention of most scholars. Moreover, the more a system (of thought) is entrenched, and the longer the time it has been operating, the more difficult and expensive it becomes to change that system. Likewise, the more a person has invested in the training required to be admitted to the neoclassical coterie, the more it is in that person's interest to prevent the depreciation of knowledge threatened by alternative modes of discourse. (Thompson 1997: 295)

Parvin (1992) goes one step further and asks whether the prevalent tendency to teach neoclassical economics as *the science* of economics – to the exclusion of other perspectives – is not in fact 'immoral'. Neoclassicism, he observes, 'assumes that the mere existence of a consumer implies autonomous choice. However, when kept in the dark about alternative economic thoughts, do students choose neoclassical theory autonomously? Is not this initiation into neoclassicism similar to being born into it' (Parvin 1992). Parvin argues that the only justification for privileging neoclassical theory would be if *each and every* attribute of neoclassicism could be shown to be 'superior to the corresponding attributes of competing theories' (ibid.: 66), which is clearly not the case. In reality, the privileging of orthodoxy in academia and public life reflects its ideological function, as a vehicle for the political socialization of the next generation of economic specialists and business managers: 'To reproduce an economic structure with the desired property relations', he observes, 'one must ensure that socialization succeeds in varying degrees in embellishing individuals' preference functions with the dominant ideology', defined as the 'invisible guideline by which individuals understand society and participate in it' (ibid.: 66–67).

The result is dogmatic adherence to orthodoxy despite theoretical inconsistency. This is possible not because neoclassicism is superior to heterodox schools of thought but because of a 'lack of research and teaching support for competing paradigms' (ibid.: 74). The parallel with Marxism-Leninism in the USSR could hardly be more apt, for just as Marx would have recoiled at the vulgarization of his critique of commodity society by the 'administrators of historical necessity' in the Stalinist bureaucracy, so the 'founding fathers of modern economics would [...] be surprised to find that a manner of thinking they thought would be transitional has instead become ossified as the only way one can do economics and be respectable' (Keen 2011: 35).

Misreading the crisis

It has become a cliché to say that few economists predicted either the global financial crisis or the long downturn which continues in its wake. One of the chief architects of US monetary policy, Chairman of the Federal Reserve Ben Bernanke, observed in a speech delivered at Princeton University that, despite the 'success' of the Federal Reserve's emergency response to the crisis, the US banking crisis

> as a whole has not been kind to the reputation of economics and economists [who] almost universally failed to predict the nature, timing or severity of the crisis; and those few who issued early warnings generally identified only isolated weaknesses in the system, not anything approaching the full set of complex linkages and mechanisms that amplified the initial shocks and ultimately resulted in a devastating global crisis and recession. (Bernanke 2010: 1)

This is a self-serving fallacy, for not only were there warnings of regulatory failure, unmanageable risk and toxic debt in the Anglo-American financial system from a range of economists and market commentators, but indications were also emerging of deflation in the advanced western economies on the model of Japan. Indeed, Keen (2011: 13) lists a dozen market commentators who did predict the crisis, including Michael Hudson, Eric Janszen, Nouriel Roubini and Peter Schiff. Yet, as Krugman indicates, while the predictive failure of mainstream economics is worrying, a more serious concern is the 'profession's blindness to the very possibility of catastrophic failures in a market economy' (Krugman 2009, cited in Hart 2010: 2).

Bernanke is hardly contrite for failing to identify the warning signs earlier. He insists that although economists have much to learn from the catastrophe, 'calls for a radical reworking of the field go too far' (ibid.: 2). Bernanke blames his critics for conflating economic *science* (theoretical and empirical generalizations about markets) with economic *engineering* (design and analysis of frameworks for achieving policy goals) and economic *management* (real-time supervision of financial institutions). Failure to identify negative trends or to predict the magnitude of the crisis was not a failure of economics as a *science*, but rather a failure of economic engineering and management which limited the capacity of institutions to respond effectively. While he concedes the need for more 'focus on financial instability and its implications for the broader economy' (ibid.: 3), the paradigm of neoclassical theory itself remains intact and continues to help decision makers understand and develop improved responses to market turbulence. Furthermore, although fewer students continue to study economic history, Bernanke claims that economists have as a professional body been able to analyse the dynamics of the present crisis against the experience of previous financial shocks, facilitating a more urgent political response to events, preventing in turn a further catastrophic collapse of confidence. In addition, he argues, research into areas like principal-agent theory in information economics has allowed policymakers to address the issue of moral hazard created by an absence of appropriate sanctions for the incautious exposure of financial institutions to excessive levels of market risk (i.e. unregulated short-term borrowing through the shadow banking system).

Regarding the theoretical and methodological paradigm of neoclassical economics, Bernanke is more cautious in his comments. Criticism of the profession has been intense, and the crisis

> should motivate economists to think further about their modeling of human behavior. Most economic researchers continue to work within the [neo]classical paradigm that assumes rational, self-interested behavior and the maximization of 'expected utility' – a framework based on a formal description of risky situations and a theory of individual choice that has been very useful through its integration of economics, statistics, and decision theory. (ibid.: 6)

Most of these assumptions proved useless in the midst of the crisis given the lack of awareness among decision-makers of the range of alternative courses of action which could be pursued as a result of imperfect knowledge. There also needs to be greater understanding of how speculative bubbles begin and develop, and how investors might be deterred from panic selling in future crisis scenarios, in view of the fact that mass offloading of previously valuable financial assets at fire-sale prices 'contributed to a profound blurring of the distinction between illiquidity and insolvency in the crisis' (ibid.). Finally, Bernanke observes that the standard new Keynesian macroeconomic models employed in neoclassical theory clearly failed to predict the crisis, yet he rejects the idea that they should be abandoned, observing that economic models are 'useful only for the time for which they were designed. Most of the time [...] financial instability is not an issue. The standard models were designed for these non-crisis periods, and they have proven quite useful in that context' (ibid.). Yet this is specious reasoning, as the idea of 'depression economics' is nonsensical: 'do the lessons of economic science drastically change in times of recession? Would it make sense to talk of "depression physics" or "depression biology?" If economics is indeed a hard science, its claims [...] must be universal' (Boettke & Luther 2010: 14).

Bernanke does concede that 'understanding the relationship between financial and economic stability in a macroeconomic context is a critical unfinished task for researchers', as is the task of conducting research with an international-economic (rather than closed economy) perspective (Bernanke 2010: 6–7). As former chairman of the Federal Reserve, however, he is unwilling to criticize publicly the theoretical and methodological paradigm of neoclassical economics of which he is a preeminent exponent. Instead, his focus – like most orthodox economists – is on the extreme nature of financial crises and how deviations from equilibrium might be managed in the future. This is a recurring theme in economics since 2008, as the profession briefly retreated into defensive introspection over its collective failure (Krugman 2009), insisting upon a distinction between the long-term health of capitalism and the temporary instability of the financial system as a result of excessive risk, speculation and leveraged debt, factors known to trigger market turbulence throughout history (Reinhart & Rogoff 2009). Confronted by accusations of intellectual bankruptcy from heterodox economists, orthodox economists continue to defend their efficient market model as appropriate to 'normal' conditions yet deficient in conditions of market turbulence. There has been little attempt to consider the logic of financialization as a mechanism to conceal the underlying structural weakness of advanced economies in which opportunities for profitable investment are in decline due to overaccumulation of capital, the cost of new production technology and the declining share of labour power in the creation of surplus value, creating incentives for restrictive competition, horizontal integration and off-balance sheet accounting as corporations attempt to conceal their exposure to unregulated debt and to 'beat the average' through higher market capitalization (Nitzan & Bichler 2009).

Beyond the official realm of public policymaking, some academic economists have of course adopted a more enlightened perspective on the need for a paradigm shift. The construction of formal models of macroeconomic behaviour using mathematical-deductivist reasoning provide little insight into the workings of actual economies, and this was readily apparent *long before* the present economic crisis and recession. The predictive failure of econometric modelling derives from the fact that the 'twin presuppositions of economic modellers that (i) empirical regularities of the sort required are ubiquitous, and (ii) social reality is constituted by sets of isolated atoms, are simply erroneous' (Lawson 2009: 764). For such assumptions to operate effectively in economic research, there is a need for precise and well-controlled experimental intervention in order to isolate intrinsically stable mechanisms from countervailing factors. Under 'experimental' conditions,

> it is indeed sometimes the case that event regularities are laboriously *produced*, correlating precisely the triggering of isolated intrinsically constant mechanisms and their unimpeded effects. But even in the controlled experiments of the natural sciences, attempts to bring about or reproduce such outcomes are also very often unsuccessful. Economists are thus seen to be rather heroic in assuming that scenarios that are laboured for in natural scientific experimentation [...] occur quite spontaneously in the social realm. (ibid.)

The constituent determinants of economic reality cannot be reduced to systems of isolated atomistic agents, as systems are dynamic and developments in one part have an immediate (and unpredictable) impact on developments in other parts – not least through state intervention, coordinated market actions and 'herd' behaviour among investors. For this reason, he adds, 'we cannot experimentally (or otherwise) isolate markets from monetary systems, from firms and other processes of production, from state institutions including legislative and other processes, etc. Each is constitutively dependent on the others' (ibid.: 765). Echoing (unintentionally) Marxian dialectical theory, Lawson insists that social reality is a *relational totality in motion* with 'depth and structure a world removed from the contrived assumptions of mathematical-deductivist reasoning. The erratic, irrational actions of institutional and individual market actors leading to the financial crisis of 2008 reveal that mathematical-deductivist modelling of (imaginary) regular behaviour patterns is no substitute for patient social-scientific explanation and understanding of what Lawson terms the 'perpetual emergence of novelty' which, 'within a relationally structured, interconnected, totality in motion, is seemingly the essence of any financial system within capitalism' (ibid.: 774).

While it is important to separate analytically the determinants of financial crises and economic recessions, therefore, it is also necessary to identify causal links between the two levels of economic reality in capitalism. Predictably, this is achieved in neoclassical economics by examining the purely surface level of negative transaction costs engendered by financial turbulence, rather than by investigating the structural dysfunctionality and historical pathology of financialized capitalist economies Thus, Reinhart and Rogoff (2009) find that recessions engendered by banking crises are especially damaging for an economy – even an economy as sophisticated as that of the United States: 'Severe financial crises', they insist, 'rarely occur in isolation. Rather than being the trigger of recession, they are more often an amplification mechanism' (Reinhart & Rogoff 2009: 145).

This is especially true in financialized economies which depend on complex financial intermediation to facilitate credit and liquidity and absorb surplus capital, for when banking systems freeze economic growth is 'quickly impaired or even paralyzed' (ibid.: 173). Financial instability is transmitted to the 'real' economy through the mechanism of 'friction', which refers to a 'cost to one side of a transaction that is not a benefit to the other side. A friction usually arises because some intermediary is taking a cut from the transaction' (Hall 2010: 6). This concept derives from Bernanke et al. (1996, 1999), who, while emphasizing the difficulty of including credit-market anomalies in the 'mainstream model' (leaving the field open to financial economists like Minsky [1982]), observe that financial crises 'increase the real cost of credit and reduce the efficiency of the process of matching lenders and potential borrowers' (Bernanke et al. 1999: 1345). Normally frictions in the chain of transactions between buyers and sellers or saver and borrowers are routine and limited, but 'when an adverse shock depletes wealth in many of the links, the frictions can suddenly become large' (ibid.: 7). One of the primary causes of market friction derives from price and wage stickiness, often reflected in labour market distortions and anomalies in credit spreads (variable borrowing costs), which affect purchasing behaviour. Generalizing from the concept of friction, Hall argues that the primary 'failing of macroeconomics in the last few years was not a lack of understanding of what happens in the overall economy when a financial crisis strikes' (ibid.: 17) but in the failure to consider how serious the impact would be of an inevitable price correction in the property market for the stability of the general economy – despite warnings from commentators that an unsustainable investment bubble had been generated: 'We did not consider that, if such a decline occurred, financial chaos would ensue' (ibid.: 18).

Before assessing the financial crisis and recession from the perspective of heterodox economics, it may be useful to consider briefly the redundancy of the efficient market postulate from a market-libertarian perspective, which is critical of the tendency of governments to allow financial crises to occur for political reasons. In the spirit of Von Mises, Hayek and Schumpeter, Austrian economists incorporate a more critical and nuanced vision of the role of the state in modern monetary economies and the dangers of government economic centralization for the productivity and profitability of capitalism (Table 1.1). While Austrian perspectives on 'state capitalism' are theoretically and methodologically distinct from the Marxian critique of 'monopoly capital', there is a broadly shared assumption that the declining profitability of capitalist production and cycles of growth and contraction are caused by a *failure to allow recessions to take their* course, enabling economies to resist pressure for restructuring. Which is to say, Marxian and Austrian approaches conclude, for very different reasons, that for capitalism to evolve and develop new productive forces, states must let unprofitable sectors decline in order to reduce inefficiencies and allow overcapacity to be drained from the system. This, of course, is the precise opposite of actual trends in advanced economies like the UK, where the state allows the financial sector to conceal the wealth of elite investors in the belief that the City of London remains the most efficient wealth-generating machine in the economy – despite alarming evidence that overdevelopment of the financial sector leads to misallocation of resources (Baker et al. 2018).

Both Marx (1954) and Schumpeter (1942) alluded to 'creative destruction' in their work, as a result of which entrepreneurial activity, innovation and new techniques of production facilitate the decay of established economic practices and destruction of unprofitable or unproductive enterprises – though only Schumpeter lived to see the oligopolistic consequences of political failure to sanction this process in deference to the power of corporations that behave like 'self-perpetuating managerial oligarchies' (Carson 2014). Austrian economics differs from neoclassicism in its rejection of equilibrium theory, its focus on growth rather than prices and its substitution of rational decision-making for a dynamic conception of economic agency. Economists rooted in the classical tradition of Adam Smith and Alfred Marshall argue that an alternative to equilibrium theory is required because it 'does not provide us with a good understanding of how the economy works' (Simpson 2013: 1). Although neoclassical equilibrium theory was refined continuously in the twentieth century, this progressive refinement was achieved at the 'cost of such drastic simplifications of assumptions and the exclusion of so many important elements of economic activity that the resulting theory has little correspondence with reality' (ibid.). Markets tend not towards equilibrium but towards *adaptation* and *coordination*, where entrepreneurs (sociological ideal-types as surrogates for optimizing individuals endowed with perfect information) are *themselves* producers of information on future costs and benefits (Huerta de Soto 2008). As a complex social theory of economic behaviour, Austrian theory posits a dynamic conception of competition in which entrepreneurial processes of societal coordination are always necessarily incomplete, that is to say, where the 'creation and transmission of new information […] modifies the general perception of each actor in society concerning potential means and ends' (ibid.: 9).

A seminal work in Austrian economics was published by Von Mises in 1912 (1980) in which he condemned fractional-reserve banking (expansionary creation of credit money unbacked by bank assets) for the instability as a result of

TABLE 1.1 Theoretical approaches to capitalist crisis

Theory	Key thinkers	Cause of crisis	Mode of resolution
Classical liberalism	Adam Smith David Ricardo James Mill J.B. Say	• External shocks/imbalances in supply and demand impede market equilibration	• Market adjustment: balance restored between supply and demand/rate of profit and rate of interest; capital reallocated from sectors with an overproduction of commodities to sectors with underproduction of commodities, preventing partial crises of overproduction becoming general economic crises
Marxism	Friedrich Engels Karl Kautsky Rosa Luxemberg Rudolf Hilferding Paul Sweezy Robert Kurz	• 'Anarchy of production' • Overproduction exceeds demand/underconsumption caused by poverty/falling rate of profit • Falling rate of profit • Inner contradictions of capitalist value form	• Devaluation of capital, destruction of productive capacity/recession and unemployment restore class relations of power • Increasing organic composition of capital
Austrian school	Ludwig von Mises Friedrich Hayek	• Temporary deviation from equilibrium between aggregate savings and aggregate investment	• General equilibrium returns when unemployment and inflation are eliminated
Keynesianism	J.M. Keynes Michał Kalecki Hyman Minksy Robert Sraffa	• Feature of the business cycle; disequilibrium caused by inadequate effective demand/inadequate policy responses	• Appropriate policy changes – deficit spending/stimulation of aggregate demand • State consumes/recycles surplus product
New Keynesianism	Stanley Fischer Paul Krugman Joseph Stiglitz	• Extended deviation from equilibrium between aggregate savings and aggregate investment	• Stimulus/investment needed to restore growth; borrow idle savings to close savings-investment gap (reduce liquidity preference)
New neoclassical synthesis	Paul Samuelson Robert Lucas Ben Bernanke	• Speculative excess of financialized capitalism ('exuberance') • Failure of predictive models in economics	• Stricter macroprudential regulation • Socialization of financial losses • Accommodative monetary policy

its tendency to (a) lengthen the life cycle of production (rendering new production more and more capital-intensive) and (b) encourage malinvestment (poorly allocated investments caused by artificially low borrowing costs and unsustainable expansion of the monetary base) (ibid.: 65). Malinvestment and excessive credit create successive cycles of *increasingly* unsustainable growth, financial instability, market collapse and recession, and the chief culprits in this process are central banks that undermine the postulate of market efficiency by making it more difficult for markets to clear naturally, which in turn prevents or delays a timely transfer of economic resources to new or more productive sectors of the economy. Although financial institutions like the European Central Bank (ECB) are more cautious in their attitude towards credit expansion, as we shall see in Chapter 5, central banks always intervene in markets to stimulate or dampen activity. Regardless of who controls government, the monetary policy of central banks like the ECB and Federal Reserve 'can be characterized as one in which policy is used aggressively to prevent or reverse credit contraction or asset price deflation, but is not used to prevent credit expansion or asset inflation' (Cooper 2008: 24).

In an ideal capitalist economy of efficient markets, central banks would not need to exist and interest rates would fluctuate according to market forces. For the efficient markets hypothesis to hold, the following must be the case:

1. Asset bubbles do not exist; the prices of all assets are always correct.
2. Markets, when left alone, will converge to a steady equilibrium state.
3. That equilibrium state will be the optimum state.
4. Individual asset price movements are unpredictable.
5. However, distributions of asset price movements are predictable. (ibid.: 30)

Of course such conditions never apply, as normally distributed markets are seldom to be found. For this reason Keynes (2017 [1939]) and Minsky (1985) abandoned the efficiency hypothesis in favour of disequilibrium and financial instability, while monetarists like Friedman (1993) continued to search for the origins of inefficiency in state regulation. Cooper finds that although Friedman's call for an end to government manipulation (and central banking) appears naïve in a capitalist credit money system, his position is a 'logical and honest progression that follows from a belief in efficient markets. Today's economic orthodoxy parrots Friedman's reverence of free markets, but does not apply his intellectual rigour in extrapolating what efficient markets imply about the role of central banking' (ibid.: 33).

In political terms, the target of the Austrian critique is fractional reserve banking in fiat monetary systems based on 'arbitrary specification of quantity' (Lapavitsas 2000: 31), where central banks act as lenders of last resort. Although credit money is an essential feature of capitalist exchange economies *and* a precondition for generating consumption-led growth, economies based on credit creation are inherently unstable – even with central banks providing a 'backstop' of unlimited new credit supported by sovereign governments. The paradox is that while central banks were created to stabilize capitalist credit money, by acting as lenders of last resort they exacerbate moral hazard where confidence among investors that investments are protected (by deposit insurance schemes) encourages greater risk-taking as investors place assets in less secure institutions (or firms engage in short-term borrowing from unsecured sources of credit), which offer appreciably higher rates of return. In addition, argues Cooper, the 'presence of a central bank, willing to underwrite all deposits equally, will have the effect of putting safer, less leveraged, institutions at a commercial disadvantage relative to the more cavalier institutions' (2008: 60). This, historically, led to the most profound reform of all, namely centralized money creation by central banks, as a result of which private banks are no longer able to issue gold depository certificates on their own monetary authority. With the demonetization of gold in the 1970s and the switch towards fiat currencies in the advanced economies, the stage was set for limitless devaluation – the only constraint being the consent of citizens to accept worthless paper currency.

As we shall see in Chapter 4, pure fiat money has greatly consolidated the power of unaccountable central banks over national economies by allowing government officials to monopolize the monetary system and devalue their currencies for political reasons. While on the one hand inflation is used as an indirect and invisible form of taxation on spending and saving (counterbalanced by rising interest rates), as Wray argues, the real 'purpose of the tax system is to "drive" the currency' itself. The reason citizens are willing to

> accept the sovereign's currency is that *taxes need to be paid in that currency*. From inception, no one would take currency unless it was needed to make payments. Taxes and other obligations create a demand for the currency used to make obligatory payments. From this perspective, the true purpose of taxes is *not* to provide 'money revenue' that government can spend. Rather, taxes create a demand for the government's own currency so that government can spend (or lend) the currency. (Wray 2015: 5; emphasis added)

In addition, fiat money enables central banks to 'print unlimited currency [which] gives the government the ability to repay *any* amount of debt' (Cooper 2008: 76), albeit at the risk of creating 'irreversible inflation'. As such, modern centralized money creation is simultaneously a licence to lower the cost of borrowing and to increase the supply of currency (through QE) when governments seek to stimulate the economy or counter deflation. From an Austrian perspective, it is this tendency which fuels cycles of excessive borrowing, leading to the accumulation of public and private debt which becomes unsustainable in the contraction phase of economic cycles, or in periods of financial instability. This fuels further financial instability, which in turn exposes not only the fallacy of 'real sector equilibrium' but amplifies underlying structural contradictions in the capitalist mode of production itself.

Conclusion

In a policy paper published by the Federal Reserve Bank of Minneapolis, reflecting the determinedly technical approach of the US financial authorities to understanding the crisis, Christiano (2017: 3) argues that the immediate trigger of the present crisis was the collapse of the US housing bubble in 2007, caused by overinvestment in mortgage-backed securities and the growth of unregulated shadow banking. Before the crisis, he observes, most economists assumed that what happens on Wall Street stays on Wall Street – that is, has as little impact on the economy as what happens in Las Vegas casinos. This idea received support from the US experiences in 1987 and the early 2000s, when the economy seemed unfazed by substantial stock market volatility. But the idea that financial markets could be ignored in macroeconomics died with the Great Recession (ibid.: 4–5).

Indeed, the response of governments to the global financial crisis involved a deviation from the traditional constraints and policy recommendations of neoclassical theory to enable political and monetary authorities to use financial stimulus packages to maintain liquidity in the banking system and prevent a more serious collapse of GDP in the rich economies – albeit at the risk of re-creating the conditions for a repeat of the crisis on a still larger scale.

Cheered on by reformists like Krugman (2009), who sharply criticized the economics profession (and the Chicago School in particular) for its adherence to the 'seductive' elegance of the new neoclassical synthesis, governments have introduced reforms but have refused to abandon their commitment to defend corporate capitalism. Piecemeal changes have been introduced to provide closer scrutiny of the financial sector – for example, new rules on bank capitalization ('stress tests'), but as Mattick (2009) observes it is still 'business as usual'. The main purpose of government policy in the US and EU has been to defend strategic industries (finance, insurance, real estate, automobiles, etc.) while reflating financial bubbles and redirecting capital into the equity and bond markets, and while maintaining near-zero interest rates to ensure public and private debt repayment remain manageable. As a result, reform has been deferred in favour of macroprudential regulation (Dewatripont et al. 2010; Faia & Schnabel 2015), in an attempt to restore trust in the legitimacy and stability of finance among electorates angry at the failure of state managers to manage risk and channel investment into sustainable sources of growth. Yet as Stiglitz notes, while there was resistance to partial nationalization of financial institutions (particularly in the US), 'what we have done [...] has changed the nature of capitalism as we have known it. *We have socialized losses, while leaving profits in the private sector.* This form of ersatz capitalism, or corporate welfarism, call it what you will, is doomed to failure' (Stiglitz 2009: 288; emphasis added). It is this issue that lies at the heart of the present study, namely: to what extent does the crisis testify to an exhaustion of capitalist commodity production; and to what extent does the symbiotic relationship between corporate and political elites testify to the political evolution of advanced economies within or perhaps beyond capitalism towards a coercive form of 'financial socialism'?

In Chapters 2 and 3, we elaborate a critique of Keynesian and Marxist theories of financialization. The present recession in the advanced economies testifies not only to the bankruptcy of neoclassical theory, but to the limits of heterodox approaches which call for demand management and fiscal stimulus – including neo-Marxism, which remains trapped in a class-theoretical critique of capitalism from the standpoint of labour and wedded to a theory of accumulation which limits the possibility of an objective analysis of fictitious capital as an intermediary structure in the reproduction of financialized capitalism. From a normative perspective, heterodox and neo-Marxist economists blame financialization for the crisis, arguing that deregulated finance is parasitic on the real economy of goods and services, and that stable growth can only be achieved through a return to stricter governmental regulation of markets. But while 'casino' capitalism is unstable, the evidence suggests that advanced economies were experiencing declining rates of profitability well before the collapse of the US sub-prime mortgage market in 2007 (Kliman 2012). Commentators on the Left are correct to highlight the dangers of corporate lobbying for the future of democracy (Prasch 2010: 186; cf. Dean 2009; Phillips 2009). Yet there is a failure to develop the full explanatory potential of Marx's theory of capitalist collapse, and to critically assess the interaction between accumulation, value and financialization in advanced post-Fordist economies. Driven by nostalgia for Fordism, many on the Left appear more concerned to repair a dysfunctional system than consider the material origins of this dysfunction in the capitalist form of value. In its present stage of development, capitalism is defined by a contradiction in the valorization process *itself* as capital accumulation takes place without a corresponding accumulation of value. From this perspective, capital is confronted by a crisis of valorization that exists independently of attempts to understand, contain or reverse it; and neither technical innovations in the generation of fictitious capital value in the financial sector nor governmental policies to maintain bank liquidity can resolve this in the long term.

Notes

1 On MI in philosophy of science, see Udehn (2001).
2 See *New World Encyclopedia*, www.newworldencyclopedia.org/entry/Neoclassical_economics.
3 The FRB/US model used by the Federal Reserve

> permits the study of the effects of a broad range of macroeconomic policies and exogenous shocks on real GDP and its major spending commitments. […] FRB has a neoclassical core that combines a production function with endogenous and exogenous supplies of production factors and key aspects of household preferences such as impatience. (Brayton et al. 2014)

4 The Volcker shock was an induced recession in the US which had global implications for developing nations – particularly in Africa. Federal Reserve chairman Paul Volcker advised President Carter in 1978–1979 that high interest rates were essential to counter inflation. At the risk of creating higher unemployment, Volcker tightened monetary policy. This imposed a harsher economic environment on business which in turn used monetary tightening to discipline trade unions and suppress inflationary wage increases as a prelude to the labour reforms imposed by Ronald Reagan in the 1980s.

2

HETERODOX APPROACHES TO CAPITALIST CRISIS

Introduction

If the theoretical and methodological framework of neoclassical theory is of limited utility for understanding the complexity of contemporary financialized economies, to what extent can heterodox approaches offer a more coherent insight into the crisis of neoliberal capitalism? The Keynesian revolution in economics ranks as one of the major intellectual events of the twentieth century, leading to important adjustments in neoclassical orthodoxy by challenging the efficient markets postulate. At the same time, there are important theoretical affinities between heterodox Left-Keynesian economics and neo-Marxist political economy approaches, which share a normative emphasis on the structural link between inequality and demand in capitalist society and a preference for government economic centralization (Sardoni 2015). These currents of thought must be understood before we can proceed towards an assessment of the accumulation crisis of capitalism from a value-critical perspective. While it is beyond the scope of the present study to examine the significance of Keynes' *General Theory* for the theoretical development of the economics discipline, it is necessary to consider some general implications of Keynesian economics for a critical theory of capitalist recessions and the causes of financial instability.[1] In contemporary debates, Keynes' reputation is affirmed less for his refutation of efficient markets theory than for his policy recommendation that governments should use deficit spending to mitigate the effect of recession while using monetary policy to stimulate economic activity and boost consumption. It is clear, however, that the context of Keynes' intervention in the 1930s and contemporary applications of his recommendations differ fundamentally:

> Keynes was writing in the 1930s at the depth of the Great Depression, and was therefore advising the implementation of stimulus policies as a way of

getting out of a depression, that is from a point of already depressed activity. Today Keynesian stimulus is used not to exit depressions but rather to avoid going into recession. The difference between these two applications of Keynesian policy is subtle, but forms an important part of the financial instability story and the story of today's credit crunch. (Cooper 2008: 83)

This is a critical point, for in capitalist societies the notion of 'pre-emptive' stimulus has become routine – a policy tool to prevent even mild contractions in output and GDP which might harm politicians' hopes for re-election. Demand management may be less effective than its practitioners believe – and may be detrimental to the long-term stable development of market economies (cf. Kates 2010), yet fear of financial instability and economic slowdown are such that the routine use of pre-emptive fiscal and monetary stimuli and increasing government economic centralization are unquestioned, even among neoliberals who claim to favour a 'natural equilibrium state' without proactive state intervention.

This does not mean governments have abandoned a commitment to the defence of capitalism, only that part of the price of this defence is recognition among financial and political elites of the increased instability created by financialization. For, while nonfinancial markets are considered to be self-equilibrating, *financial* markets are far more unpredictable because through the twin mechanisms of collateralized debt-leveraged financing and mark-to-market accounting, rising asset prices (e.g. in stock markets) typically trigger more demand based on the expectation among investors that continued upward trends will guarantee future gains. This phenomenon creates a dual tendency towards speculation and price inflation which has the potential to unleash major shocks for the whole economy – particularly following an unwinding of positions in derivatives markets which are dominated by powerful financial institutions like Deustche Bank and JP Morgan. As Lapavitsas notes:

Banks are at the heart of the derivatives markets which have been such a prominent feature of financialization. Derivatives markets rely on banks, in particular on the price-making skills and general organizational capabilities of banks. Indeed, banks are so dominant in derivatives markets that they are even capable of manipulating the key rate on the basis of which derivatives prices are formed. The vast growth of derivatives markets reflects in part the turn of banks toward trading in open financial markets, which is one of the fundamental tendencies of financialization. (Lapavitsas 2013: 10)

The unstable nature of this edifice of claims based on exposure to risk is ultimately a side-effect of continual credit expansion in financialized economies: financial intermediation is an essential and growing feature of capitalism in its present global phase, and it is politically expedient for states to deregulate the financial sector and allow the volume of credit in the economy to grow to accommodate an expansion in economic activity and thus counter rising deflationary pressures.

In significant respects, the *state* form of capital itself is a functional response to the expansion of financial market (commodity) money as a means to *intermediate discontinuities* in the value of capital in the process of accumulation' (Bryan & Rafferty 2003: 12). The temptation to further extend stimulus policies under *extreme crisis conditions* explains the recent pragmatic 'return to Keynes' among policymakers in the wake of the implosion of the new technology boom in 2000–2001, which led to a huge destruction of equity values and intense embarrassment in the economics profession: 'for anyone who had adhered to some form of rational expectations theory', observes Bateman, 'there was no good way to explain all the poor investments that had been made by private agents [...]' (2010: 24). Before 9/11, and long before the crisis of 2008, the Federal Reserve was already using monetary stimulus in a determined (yet unsuccessful) attempt to prevent a slowdown in the US economy; after 9/11, this was extended to include investment in defence expenditure to fund the 'Global War on Terror', an updated form of 'military Keynesianism' which had serious economic and geopolitical consequences.[2] Yet the recent 'return to Keynes' in the aftermath of the financial crisis has proved to be entirely temporary, pragmatic and selective: it did not yield a serious commitment to return to strategic public investment as states reverted quickly to pre-crisis policy perspectives and priorities in a bid to re-establish neoliberal orthodoxy (cf. Seccareccia 2011/2012).

The 2008 crisis raised questions concerning the legitimacy and rationality of global financial capitalism outside the traditional confines of the left-leaning intelligentsia, yet the system of 'embedded neoliberalism' has not (yet) been seriously challenged within the metropole beyond negatively affected countries such as Greece, Spain and Italy. This reflects what Cahill terms the enduring social form of neoliberalism – not as some idealized free market economy envisioned by von Mises, Hayek or Nozick, but as an *embedded policy regime* rooted in three social spheres, namely class relations, social institutions and ideological norms:

> Just as the capitalist economy has always been embedded within social relations and institutions, so too has neoliberalism, an historically specific manifestation of the capitalist economy, been always socially embedded. The institutions, norms and social relations within which neoliberalism is embedded have provided a supportive social structure for its development. (Cahill 2014: 77)

Cahill's model of neoliberalism has similarities with neo-Marxist theories of regime of accumulation and social structures of accumulation, referring to the institutional supports and ideological-discursive practices which make possible enduring forms of market society (cf. Jessop 2000, 2001, 2007; Duménil & Lévy 2001; Kotz 2007). The system remains durable in the near future not because 'there is no alternative', as most neoliberals claim, but because a 'generation of policy makers have only known neoliberalism as the common sense frame for conducting and evaluating policy. The institutional embeddedness of neoliberalism affords it considerable inertia' (ibid.: 81). Yet debate continues between economic historians and sociologists concerning the form of capitalism in the twenty-first century, with some theorists emphasizing the eclipse of the Washington consensus and fragmentation of the liberal international order (Buzan 2011; Zakaria 2011; Hiro 2012; Bello 2013; Wallerstein 2013), and others focusing on the reconstruction of state-democratic capitalism in the advanced economies (Crouch 2013; Hein 2013).[3]

In what follows, I examine historical periodizations of capitalist development in order to contextualize financialization, which has transformed advanced economies since the 1970s, before examining Keynesian and neo-Marxist approaches to financial crisis, recession and unemployment. As Keynes argued in the Great Depression, even where markets do gravitate towards a form of stable equilibrium, this often occurs in the absence of full employment – a phenomenon we see quite clearly repeated in the present crisis of financialized capitalism. The aim is to show how financialization is linked to the functional requirements of capital accumulation and why this process has created deeper instability in capitalist economies, triggering financial crises that amplify underlying structural deficiencies in the capitalist mode of production itself. A secondary aim is to challenge a tendency in radical critiques of neoliberal capitalism to marginalize finance as 'parasitic' on the 'real economy' of goods and services (Hossein-Zadeh 2014; Streeck 2014). This is an understandable perspective given the oligarchic power of financial elites who resemble old-fashioned rentiers (the absentee landlords of Veblen's economic sociology) and who preside over the subsumption of labour to finance capital (Bellofiore 2014). Yet it has no place in a critical theory of capitalism:

> The financial system comprises a set of social mechanisms that emanate from real accumulation, incorporate commercial credit, and mobilize idle funds that are transformed into loanable capital subsequently to be returned to accumulation. The financial system emerges out of capitalist accumulation but also shapes and directs the path of the latter [...] Finance is not a parasitical entity but an integral part of the capitalist economy. Developed capitalism without a developed financial system would be unthinkable. The financial system offers key services to capitalist accumulation and improves the profitability of industrial and commercial enterprises. This is ultimately the reason why financial institutions are able to make a profit on a sustained basis. (Lapavitsas 2013: 122)

Finance is less a 'parasitic' or 'pathological' development in an otherwise *legitimate* commodity society than a necessary consequence of and precondition for the sole logical purpose capital is capable of achieving, namely self-expansion without reason. Popular critiques of finance reflect the delusion of a globalist Left that juxtaposes a 'healthy' form of productive capitalism to the 'anarchic irrationality of the market. Instead of necessarily pointing beyond capitalism, however, such critiques frequently [...] legitimate a subsequent state-centric capitalism' (Postone 2007: 22).

It also reflects a tendency towards historicism in Marxian economic theory which overlooks the significance of Marx's concept of total social capital (*Gesamtkapital*). This category cannot be reduced to a competitive interplay between rival fractions of industrial, commercial and financial capital because *all* branches of capital (including finance) employ labour power to create value. The function of finance in this complex system is to intermediate capital flows 'under particular terms which follow the institutional trends of the capitalist economies. This intermediation is a *sui generis* service itself and therefore a productive activity striving for profit maximization' (Sotiropoulos et al. 2013: 45). In Marx's theoretical scheme the 'circuit of interest-bearing capital does not describe a particular fraction of capital but *is rather the most general and developed form of capital*' (ibid.: 51). This, it is suggested, is the real meaning of Marx's elliptical comment in *Capital* (vol. II) that the '"relations of capital assume their most *fetish-like form* in interest-bearing capital"' (Marx cited in Sotiropoulos et al., ibid.: 52). As we shall see in Chapters 3 and 4, however, it is nevertheless essential to consider the implications of an economy based on *accumulation without value* for the growth of abstract forms of wealth and the expansion of debt which allows capital values to multiply despite internal contradictions in the capitalist value form and the 'speculative excesses' of high finance. 'Financialization' is shown to be a necessary yet insufficient concept for explaining the present crisis, which should rather be understood in terms of the fetishized form of value in capitalist economies where surplus value is determined by average socially necessary labour time. This in turn is determined by changing average rates of productivity in the global economy based on displacement of labour power as the source of value in the production process which lies behind the accumulation crisis of neoliberal capitalism and the desperate search for alternative sources of valorization through the production of fictitious value. This has been and remains a feature of *global* capitalism, for while the crisis of 2007–2009 was a disaster from a *Western* perspective, it should nevertheless be placed in the context of increasing instability in the global economy which led to a succession of deteriorating crises in the late 1990s in emerging market economies before returning to the metropole with the collapse of the dot.com bubble in 2000–2001, after which only a temporary period of economic recovery was achieved.

Financialization

Before examining debates on the interconnection between financialization, financial instability and recessions in heterodox economics, it will be useful to summarize the process through which advanced economies transitioned from Fordist accumulation regimes based on industrial commodity production, universal welfare and demand management towards neoliberal accumulation regimes characterized by financial deregulation, capital market liberalization and the growing power of global finance. This process is depicted as a transition from organized to disorganized capitalism – a useful if simplistic reduction that reflects a widely held view among left-leaning economists and sociologists concerning the salience of *political* regulation in the organization and development of the capitalist mode of production (Offe 1985; Lash & Urry 1987; Harvey 1989). Although this differentiation risks hypostasizing the historically specific regulatory system of the commodity form in capitalism – which 'does not immediately appear as a totality but is mediated by differentiated and apparently autonomous "spheres"', producing a false ontologization of 'politics' and 'economics' as discrete 'social sub-systems' (Kurz 1994: 4) – the transition from Fordist to post-Fordist regulation reflects major changes in the accumulation structure of capitalism which is constitutive of trends towards financialization and a change in the relationship between financial capital and productive capital.

It is assumed in Marxian economic theory that the way in which capital overcomes recurrent crises of accumulation determines the ways in which contradictions giving rise to the initial crisis are displaced and reappear in more serious form at a later stage of development. After the reforms of the Depression era, finance had entered the post-war period subject to stricter legal forms of political regulation. This new environment of reduced competition constrained the investment activities of private commercial banks in particular and limited the influence of financial institutions over corporate decision-making. The new status quo and the agreements signed at Bretton Woods (stable exchange rates monitored by the IMF) favoured currency stability, class compromise and high levels of employment, limiting the power of financial elites who 'fought constantly for the restoration of its privilege and pre-eminence, in particular concerning its international activities' (Duménil and Lévy 2012: 24; cf. Harvey 2005; Jessop 2007). The contradictions of interwar capitalism were essentially displaced by the post-1945 warfare-welfare state (Fordism), a mixed economy based on corporatist management, full employment and universal social security in the 'golden age' of post-war prosperity and stability (1945–1973) in Europe and North America. In the 1980s and 1990s this historical-social formation succumbed to a new hegemonic market-libertarian discourse which limited resistance to the reorganization of productive forces in accordance with the needs of global financial capital, allowing corporations to reduce wages, avoid taxation and relocate production and profits offshore.

As global economic integration advanced in the 1970s and state-democratic capitalism was threatened by 'stagflation', business leaders lobbied for an end to the class compromise of Fordism and a reassertion of the hegemony of the upper fraction of finance capital. This was to be achieved (paradoxically) using the power of the state to oversee the limitation of state intervention in deregulated economies (Gamble 1988). Although the Keynesian national welfare-state, premised on full employment and rising wages, had allowed capitalist elites to avoid a direct political confrontation with organized labour (in Europe and North America, at least), this class compromise became the inevitable casualty of the collapse of Bretton Woods which rendered it 'impossible for money to maintain even the *appearance* of being detached from the basic struggle over wages' (Dodd 2014: 74). An untenable inflationary system had been created where money funnelled into investment was assuming the form of rising wages, as states were transformed into 'lenders of last resort to the capitalist economy *in toto*, forced to run a debt economy to support industry and the public sector' (ibid.). Neoliberalism, in stark contrast, was presented as a sociopolitical order in which liberalization of capital markets, expansion of leveraged debt-financing and deregulation of cross-border investment flows would allow financial institutions to transfer funds across and between markets with fewer constraints, although it was obvious from the outset that a contradiction existed between the political requirement of states for long-term investment and the 'absolute freedom of movement demanded by finance' (Duménil & Lévy 2012: 41). This contradiction had already been diagnosed by post-Keynesians, who noted that 'stable growth is inconsistent with the manner in which investment is determined in an economy in which debt-financed ownership of capital assets exists' (Minsky 1977: 13). The deregulation of financial markets and relaxation of rules on competition increase corporate exposure to debt as firms become more dependent on the 'normal' functioning of financial markets to continually refinance market positions and remain commercially viable.

Using the language of regulation theory, Harvey (1989) evaluates the shift in regimes of accumulation which have taken place since the end of the post-war boom. Harvey observes that

> the virtue of 'regulation school' thinking is that it insists we look at the total package of relations and arrangements that contribute to the stabilization of output growth and aggregate distribution of income and consumption in a particular historical period and place. (Harvey 1989: 123)

This is a reasonable intellectual point, given the complexity of the superstructural forms of capitalism in its modern and late modern forms. Fordism, he argues, was less a

> system of mass production and more a total way of life. Mass production meant standardization of product as well as mass consumption; and that

meant a whole new aesthetic and a commodification of culture that so many neoconservatives, such as Daniel Bell, were later to see as detrimental to the preservation of the work ethic and other supposed capitalist virtues. Fordism also built on and contributed to the aesthetic of modernism – particularly the latter's penchant for functionality and efficiency – in very explicit ways, while the forms of state interventionism (guided by bureaucratic-technical rationality), and the configuration of political power that gave the system its coherence, rested on notions of mass economic democracy welded together through a balance of special interest forces. (ibid.: 136)

Fordism was also racially and culturally specific, privileging unionized white male workers and the educated service class (ibid.: 138), but this social structure became problematic due to rigidities in labour markets, labour militancy and rising inflation which pushed capitalist elites towards a more confrontational approach, abandoning fiscal policy and demand management in favour of monetarism. In effect, the class compromise of state-democratic capitalism ossified into a 'fixed configuration of political power, and reciprocal relations that bound big labour, big capital, and big government into [...] a dysfunctional embrace of such narrowly defined vested interests as to undermine rather than secure capital accumulation' (ibid.: 142). This destroyed the Fordist compromise, accelerating a shift towards flexible accumulation and deregulation, although deregulation itself facilitated more intensive forms of monopolization after a brief period of intensive market activity in the 1980s as the internationalization of capitalist social relations allowed firms in advanced core economies to take advantage of opportunities for cost-saving and outsourcing of production in emerging market economies.

Jessop (2000) argues similarly that the transition from the Keynesian national welfare state to deregulated post-Fordist economic organization reflects the functional requirement of the commodity form for a regulatory regime adequate to the task of securing accumulation in globalizing capitalism – in which finance plays a disproportionate role in the valorization of capital. The constitutive incompleteness of the capital relation means it depends on changing (dynamic) extra-economic factors, including structural contradictions which arise under particular accumulation regimes and conflicts over the regularization/governance of these structural contradictions (Jessop 2000: 325). Accumulation, he contends,

depends on maintaining an unstable balance between the economic supports in the various expressions of the value form and its extra-economic supports beyond the value form. This rules out the eventual commodification of everything and, *a fortiori*, a pure capitalist economy. In other words, capitalism does not (and cannot) secure the tendential self-closure implied in the self-expanding logic of commodification. (ibid.: 326)

Although capital is driven by a logic of maximal self-expansion without reason, it cannot multiply continuously without simultaneously reproducing social-institutional supports and necessary use-values (Kotz 1994, 2007; Westra 2010). Yet as Jessop argues, the system of commodity production constitutive of capitalist society must subsume (or at least achieve 'ecological dominance' over) all other social spheres to ensure the primacy of capital accumulation over alternative modes of societalization.[4] The system of commodity production in pre-capitalist society 'could not have been ecologically dominant [...] Only with the generalization of the commodity form to [include] labour power does the capitalist economy acquire a sufficient degree of operational autonomy' (Jessop 2000: 330).

On this view, capitalism is a complex, dynamic system of production and exchange which manifests a capacity to overcome both internal contradictions and external perturbations through a seemingly perpetual process of spatio-temporal adjustment; and, because it is dynamic (synchronically and diachronically), it is not only co-constitutive of other societal subsystems such as science and law, but also conditions its own immanent self-development. This structuration is extended globally via the internationalization of capitalist relations into the global periphery which (i) increases the complexity of the circuits of capital, (ii) enhances capitalism's capacity to 'defer and displace its internal contradictions', (iii) emancipates the exchange-value dimension from specific constraints, (iv) allows capital opportunity to evade other regulatory systems and (v) reduces the capacity of individual states to 'confine capital's growth dynamic within a framework of national security' (ibid.: 331). This process leads not necessarily to a 'hollowing out' of the nation-state, as critics of globalization insist, but to the 'growth of modes of exercising power which do not depend on imperative coordination by a territorialised state apparatus and that are independent of its borders on whatever scale they exist' (ibid.: 352). For Kurz, this has profound implications for 'politics' organized through the state form of capital as capital seeks 'refuge in the structural "no man's land" of the markets, which act outside of the boundaries of national economies' (Kurz 1994: 32). This loss of control, he adds, 'exhausts and weakens the last energy reserves of "politics"' (ibid.; cf. Streeck 2014).

Viewed from a transnational or macrosociological perspective, it is easy to conclude that disorganized capitalism is chaotic, diffuse and pluralistic, but theorists like Harvey, Jessop and Postone are quick to highlight tensions, discontinuities and anomalies in attempts to construct a neat periodization of capitalist regulatory regimes. The tension 'between monopoly and competition, between centralization and decentralization of economic power, is being worked out in fundamentally new ways', argues Harvey, but this does not necessarily imply 'disorganization'. On the contrary, 'capitalism is becoming ever more tightly organized *through* dispersal, geographical mobility, and flexible responses in labour markets, labour processes and consumer markets, all accompanied by hefty doses of institutional, product, and technological innovation' (Harvey 1989: 159). The real paradox is that in order to manage the 'neoliberalization' of capitalism,

> governments ideologically committed to non-intervention and fiscal conservatism have been forced by events to be more rather than less interventionist. Laying aside the degree to which the evident insecurities of flexible accumulation create a climate conducive to authoritarianism [...], financial instability and the massive problems of internal and external indebtedness have forced periodic interventions in unstable financial markets. (ibid.: 168)

On the other hand, Jessop insists that it is the abstract logic of capital rather than (geo)political strategy which 'remains the best *starting-point* for theorizing capitalist accumulation regimes and their modes of regulation and, a fortiori, for distinguishing and periodizing phases of capitalist development' (Jessop 2001: 299). Only then is it possible to examine the management or displacement of contradictions through 'institutional compromises, spatio-temporal fixes and spatial and temporal horizons of action that help to secure the relative stabilization and structural coherence of accumulation regimes and modes of regulation' (ibid.). In addition, Jessop notes, 'no particular scale or space (such as the national) or particular periodicity (such as long waves, product cycles, or business cycles) should be privileged a priori in analysing phases of capitalism' (ibid.). Finally, it is imperative to avoid a *varieties* of capitalism approach because the

> same abstract logic of capital certainly shapes all forms of capitalism. [...] The dynamic of capital accumulation on a world scale depends on diverse complementarities among accumulation regimes and modes of regulation [...] to respond to new forms of crisis and obstacles to accumulation. (ibid.)

While Postone is himself critical of Harvey's conceptualization of the link between capitalism and postmodernity, he is equally sceptical of simple binary distinctions between organized/disorganized or centralized/decentralized capitalism, observing that a 'contemporary hypostatization of difference, heterogeneity and hybridity doesn't necessarily point beyond capitalism, but can serve to veil and legitimate a new global form that combines decentralization and heterogeneity of production and consumption with increasing centralization of control and underlying homogeneity' (Postone 2007: 22). For Postone, who consistently defends Marx's (1954) definition of capital as an invariant yet socially transformative magnitude of value valorized in circulation (and who is critical of approaches which shift analytic attention towards the contingency of capitalist development on the rise and fall of successive global hegemons), the logical unfolding of capital creates new social forms which *may* point beyond the self-reflexive domination of abstract labour embodied in the capitalist value form. The development of regimes of accumulation is important for the regulation of capitalist economies, but the emphasis on social formation itself should not obscure the historical dynamic of capital which 'entails ongoing transformations of social life that are driven by the essential core of capitalism – a core that is both unchanging and, yet, generative of change' (2007: 15).

It is on this methodological basis that we can begin to contextualize financialization as a core feature of capitalist accumulation regimes characterized by the 'ecological domination of financial capital over other fractions of capital' (Jessop 2007: 84). The term 'financialization' denotes a process of economic transformation based on the expanded and determining role of finance relative to other sectors in modern capitalist economies. On the one hand, heterodox economists see financialization as a negative and destabilizing feature of capitalist modernization in the present era, involving the institutionalization of finance and money capital at the centre of accumulation regimes. Financialization leads not only to a disjunction between productive capital and financial capital, and to regressive forms of 'accumulation through dispossession' (Harvey's rendering of Marx's 'primitive accumulation'), but to the hyperproduction of *fictitious capital* in global financial markets – an abstract manifestation of value generated through the multiplication of paper claims on value in excess of the aggregate surplus value generated in productive activity. Financialization is also identified as a principal reason for the financial crisis and the sectoral imbalances in the advanced economies (Duménil & Lévy 2001, 2012, 2014; Jessop 2007; Fine 2010; Harvey 2010; Dodd 2012; Parenteau 2012; Stockhammer 2012). But while critical theorists concede the destabilizing impact of financialization, they deny that the global downturn can be explained by it. Rather, accumulation crises are linked to internal contradictions in commodity-determined capitalist economies that exist prior to and independently of financialization itself (Kurz 1995, 2010; Postone 2007; Haug 2012; Kliman 2012; Lohoff & Trenkle 2013; Hossein-Zadeh 2014). To understand the logic of financialization, we first have to understand why capitalist commodity production itself is unstable and prone towards stagnation (cf. Brenner 2002, 2006).

Although there is no absolute agreement on the importance (and coherence) of the term, in the most general sense, financialization occurs where finance penetrates 'all commercial relations to an unprecedented *direct* extent' (Fine 2010: 56). In contrast with neoclassical theory – which assumes the existence of a self-regulating financial system quietly and efficiently allocating capital in response to market forces, critical economic thinkers stress the *dynamic* function and power of financial institutions and money capital in the growth (and contraction) of modern monetary economies. In simple market economies, finance plays a largely marginal role, mediating between buyers and sellers of assets; it increases in importance as the supply of credit money grows and as investment requires a larger pooling of capital to intermediate, distribute and manage risk. Keynesians argue that money capital and financial institutions play an increasing role in conditioning demand and shaping the 'real' economy in modern monetary production economies (Bibow 2009), as arbitrary specification of monetary quantity (fiat) and credit become necessary to facilitate accumulation:

> In a [modern] monetary economy, production occurs not to satisfy 'needs', but to satisfy the desire to accumulate wealth in money form. [...] This generates a logic of accumulation: all monetary economies must grow. If they do not, accumulation falters and nominal contracts cannot be met. The logic of monetary production, then, requires nominal economic growth. It cannot be constrained by a fixed money supply, nor by a commodity money whose quantity expands only upon new discoveries. (Wray 1999: 180)

The expanding role of finance in capitalist accumulation regimes is dependent on a general growth in the supply of money and liquidity, a growth in opportunities for the (legal and illegal) international transfer of funds and growing public perception of the continual and immediate interchangeability of assets and money, expressed in terms of nominal growth (real growth plus inflation).

As monetary accumulation regimes develop, restrictions on how financial capital can be employed are relaxed, and financialization allows a growing number of financial institutions (banks, hedge funds, sovereign wealth funds, etc.) to speculate in markets to maximize profit through leveraged risk. The tendency is for banks to take greater short-term risks by borrowing funds rather than using existing money capital. As Tooze (2018) observes, it is in this context of a hunger for short-term profit that major banks in the US, the UK and eurozone became increasingly more dependent on short-term lines of credit than cash deposits, leaving them dangerously exposed to vanishing liquidity when these lines of credit finally evaporated in the 2008 'credit crunch', leading to mass panic selling and a potentially catastrophic devaluation of financial assets.

The continuous growth of finance capital is dependent on what Keynes aptly termed the 'liquidity preference' or 'fetish', namely the expectation that all assets can be transformed into cash which has a premium as a liquid store of value. The financial markets facilitate the continual interchangeability between assets and money by providing lines of short-term and long-term credit:

> If credit is an activity that in any case involves a fundamental uncertainty for the creditor [...] money as a store of value constitutes wealth for its holder with no uncertainty whatsoever. This is why the interchangeability of money and securities at a price expressed by the market rate of interest performs a key role in the functioning of finance as we know it: in the form of the financial market. Interest must be paid in proportion to the degree to which the security is comparatively less liquid than money and therefore represents a *liquidity premium*, in other words a *compensation* for the loss of liquidity incurred by whoever gives money in return for securities. (Amato & Fantacci 2012: 20)

In other words, financial markets are the '*markets of that particular commodity known as saved money*' (ibid.: 27); and, they are a functional prerequisite in capitalism because business cannot invest without first acquiring debt.

Yet the financialization of capitalism accelerates the interaction between money and assets beyond the traditional functional-commercial demand for credit, creating more complex and riskier forms of leveraged credit to sustain unprofitable firms and perpetuate accumulation through the generation of fictitious capital – an abstract mode of valorization which does not correspond directly to the form of surplus value generated through productive investment in commodities. Fictitious capital is generated through the multiplication of new and more complex forms of leveraged debt, extending the expansion of derivative values at higher levels of abstraction. This feature of financialization serves to delay a 'settling of accounts' which otherwise might reveal the decadent condition of a mode of production in which debt repayment constitutes a barrier to the further self-expansion and accumulation of capital without value. As noted in Chapter 1, this unlimited expansion of capital (without value) intensifies a system of valorization in which debts are *never repaid*, only deferred in perpetuity, removing from the creditor-debtor relation that which makes this relation of power 'humanly bearable, namely the end' (Amato & Fantacci 2012: 62).

Heterodox economists stress that overaccumulation of capital in the global economy from the 1990s onwards was fuelled not only by an investment boom driven by the growth of capacity in emerging market economies and deregulation of finance in advanced economies, but by self-multiplication of financial market money through credit expansion and financial innovation to sustain higher-than-average yields. The emphasis is not on greed as such, but on profit maximization: investors 'aim at "total returns", defined as earnings plus capital gains – with increasing emphasis on the latter gains in real estate, stocks and bonds' (Hudson 2010: 27). Short-term gain outweighs the demand for tangible capital formation through the instrumentalization of credit, leading to the creation of the 'financial equivalent of a perpetual motion machine' as firms 'borrow their way out' of debt (ibid.: 27). As a consequence, credit is not 'linked to the shared certainty of a maturity agreed upon from the outset, but to the constantly renegotiated uncertainty of its indefinite prolongation' (ibid.). Financial deregulation merely increases the intensity and velocity of transactions based on credit, facilitated by computer-assisted volume trading using advanced mathematical algorithms. It also allows nonfinancial corporations to reduce their traditional reliance on bank capital by developing financial capacity for themselves, fuelling the rise of 'shadow banking' (short-term unregulated lending by firms and institutions outside the banking sector). In addition, households become more integrated into the debt-credit nexus, sustaining demand as real wages (adjusted for inflation) stagnate or decline (Lapavitsas 2011; Stockhammer 2012). Financializaton, in short, proceeding from the expanding role of credit markets, extends the credit-debt nexus deeper into the fabric of human life, extending indefinitely the maturation of debt to facilitate the continued self-expansion of capital.

In what follows, we evaluate heterodox approaches to capitalist crises. Attempts to theorize the link between financialization, financial instability, globalization and capitalist recession proceed from very different premises. On one side are financial Keynesians who examine the dynamics of financial instability and the transmission of financial instability to the wider economy in periods of crisis: financialization is presented as functionally critical to the development of modern monetary economies based on credit. Neo-Marxists, on the other hand, highlight the parasitic development of finance whose domination of modern capitalist monetary economies exceeds it functional utility for the intermediation of capital flows. Their analyses focus on restricted competition, overcapacity and declining demand in the present phase of monopolistic capitalism, and the negative consequences of financialization for economic stability, investment, GDP growth and living standards.

Financial instability theory

In his defence of Keynes, the economist Hyman Minsky (1977) argued that financial instability is immanent to seemingly stable economic systems due to unpredictable effects of complex financial instruments (financial innovation) and rising debt levels on leverage ratios.[5] Whereas neoclassical economists argue that market economies tend towards equilibrium (bracketing out financial instability), Minsky observed that it does not require exogenous shocks for instability to be generated in conditions of stability because it is *precisely during periods of stability* that financial institutions engage in irrational speculative investment and leverage borrowing as central banks and regulatory authorities relax diligence. Leveraged debt drives cycles of financial market instability, as banks and financial institutions advance from 'hedged' risk, to 'speculation' and, finally, to 'Ponzi finance', where both individual and institutional investors are seduced into the markets by accelerating asset price inflation. This ends when a critical mass of investors either exit the market or can no longer finance loans required to fund their original investments. Non-performing loans (loans that debtors can no longer repay) expose financial institutions to bankruptcy; and, to avoid market contagion, distressed banks must be recapitalized at taxpayers' expense. If a sufficient number of systemically important financial institutions (G–SIFIs) default, the danger of liquidity crisis and systemic collapse intensifies.

Minsky's financial instability hypothesis went out of fashion in the 1990s, but interest in his cyclical theory was revived by the banking crisis of 2008. Minsky's arguments remain valid for analysing contemporary developments, though as Jefferis (2017) cautions, his interpretive scheme should be applied critically rather than adopted as a positive economic science. The methodological innovation of Minsky's financial-Keynesianism was to abandon the naive neoclassical depiction of the market as a 'village fair' where information-rich buyers and sellers exchange goods and to focus instead on the central role of finance and capital assets in monetary production economies. Following Keynes, he argued that 'investment and financing decisions are made in the face of *intractable uncertainty*, and uncertainty implies that views about the future can undergo marked changes in short periods of time' (Minsky 1977: 8). In addition, he observed, the

> financial attributes of a capitalist economy lead to the observed unstable behaviour. In an economy with a sophisticated financial system, the financing veil encompasses many more financial instruments than any narrow – or even extended – money concept includes. [...] This is in marked contrast to the classical and today's neoclassical economic theory, for in both money does not affect the essential behaviour of the economy. (ibid.: 8–9)

Minsky also proceeds from the assumption that the return of financial instability in the US and elsewhere in the 1970s indicated that financial crises are systemic rather than freak events.

This point is well understood by governments that use deficit financing to sustain corporate profitability during market perturbations, which offsets a 'tendency for the debt-sustaining capacity of business to diminish whenever financial market disturbances induce a decline in consumer and business spending' (ibid.: 11). Finally, Minsky observed that financialized economies are additionally vulnerable to destabilization due to the presence of high levels of private debt which tend to increase beyond 'acceptable liability structures' because rational expectations of what constitutes 'acceptable liability' change in periods of relative stability. This leads to increased leverage ratios, as a result of which the cost of debt financing 'raises the market price of capital assets and increases investment. As this continues the economy is transformed into a boom economy' (ibid.: 13). And, once the boom fizzles out, market correction becomes inevitable causing disinvestment, business failure, unemployment and falling demand. In contrast with the 1930s, however, central bank activism is normally adequate to contain financial crises and forestall market collapse. It is difficult to overestimate the role of central banking in modern monetary economies, which 'increases in importance when the financial structure is such that business liabilities need to be refinanced. [...] central banking exists because Ponzi and speculative financing exist' (Minsky 1986: 359).

How relevant are Minsky's observations and how far does his instability hypothesis contribute to an understanding of capitalist recessions? Kindleberger and Alibar (2005) argue that Minsky's model can be used to explain the manias and speculative booms which constitute a 'hardy perennial' of economic history, regardless of the nature of the shock which causes periodic overexpansions of credit. They highlight a pattern where investor optimism ('irrational exuberance') increases alongside credit expansion as firms and individuals invest for purely short-term gain in an attempt to capitalize on rising asset prices before the market collapses. The key to understanding speculation is to recognize that financial institutions buy commodities and assets not for their use-value but for the 'anticipated increases in their prices' (Kindleberger & Alibar 2005: 25).

In the euphoric phase of asset price inflation and credit expansion, as volatility increases sharply, speculation 'leads away from normal, rational behaviour to what has been described as a "mania" or a "bubble"', which the authors define as 'any deviation in the price of an asset or a security or a commodity that cannot be explained in terms of the "fundamentals"' (ibid.). Kindleberger and Alibar acknowledge that there are important historical differences between incidences of speculative mania in history and that there are institutional differences in regulatory systems operating in specific historical periods. They also usefully emphasize the nature of international contagion which led to the transmission of crisis tendencies among major economies between the inflation crisis of the 1970s and the dot-com speculative mania of the late 1990s (Crotty 2009; Arestis 2011). Yet, Jefferis is critical of their attempt to apply Minsky's instability hypothesis as a universal theory of financial crises:

> Kindleberger and Aliber believed that there should be an intellectual division of labour between (a) economists who use models and theory dealing with enduring structural dynamics that shape the economic cycles and (b) historians, who deal with the 'particular' – the ephemera of the past, their perceptions, cultures and institutional forms. However, this stratification that Kindleberger and Aliber posit between the universal and the particular is itself a problem to be studied. History is not just an attempt at realist preservation of the terms and conditions of the past but takes as its subject the interaction between the universal and the particular. In positing this stratification, Kindleberger and Aliber claim an unwarranted universalism for economic crisis theory in general and Minsky's [financial instability hypothesis] in particular. (Jefferis 2017: 3)

This is an important methodological point, emphasizing the dialectical determination of social-scientific concepts and categories and the universal/particular validity of their application in given historical contexts – a perspective traditionally associated with Hegelian Marxism and Critical Realism.[6]

Nevertheless, as we shall see in the next section, there are identifiable patterns in capitalist accumulation crises, the mode of resolution of which tends to determine the form of subsequent downturns (Clarke 1994); and Minsky's approach – although it makes little reference to the underlying causes of declining profitability in capitalist economies – offers a powerful challenge to conventional neoclassical reasoning by reasserting and reaffirming Keynes' focus on disequilibrium as the default condition of unstable capitalist economies. In later works, Minsky rejected the neoclassical view that catastrophic financial events occur once every century and famously posed the question 'can "It" [the Great Depression] happen again?' (Minsky 1982). Echoing earlier critics (Veblen, Keynes, Kalecki), he observed that the 'history of capitalism is punctuated by deep depressions that are associated with financial panics and crashes in which financial relations are ruptured and financial institutions destroyed' (Minsky 1986: 349). These are more serious in sophisticated monetary economies dominated by complex financial intermediation which transmits market perturbance/dislocation more rapidly and unpredictably to other sectors of the economy. But their effects are quickly transmitted to emerging market economies whose spectacular growth in the early 2000s was closely linked to rising commodity prices and to the financialization of commodity markets (Zeremba 2015).

For Vercelli (2001), Minsky's insights can best be understood as a reclarification of Keynes' original conceptualization of the 'structural instability' of market economies, with some modification of terminology. Keynes identified an asymmetry between equilibrating and disequilibrating tendencies:

> The equilibrating tendencies refer to *dynamic stability* – that is to the convergence towards a given short-period equilibrium which does not need to be a full employment equilibrium – while the so-called disequilibrating tendencies refer to *structural instability* – that is, not to a divergent dynamic tendency away from a given equilibrium but to a sudden discontinuous shift of the equilibrium position itself. In logical terms, these shifts do not need to be destabilizing. However, they are in general so because they are triggered by overpessimistic expectations at the beginning of a crisis or by overoptimistic expectations at the end of a boom. (Vercelli 2001: 39; emphasis added)

In effect, Keynes distinguished between *dynamic* stability caused by fluctuating expectations of market behaviour and *structural* instability as a systemic feature of market economies, which Minsky develops in his financial instability hypothesis. Minsky's contribution was to 'rearticulate' Keynes' ideas into a 'coherent conceptual framework for studying economic cycles, updating at the same time the analysis of the institutional environment in order to encompass the sophisticated monetary economies of the twentieth century' (ibid.: 40). The outcome, he concludes, is a 'theory of economic cycles radically different from the main alternative theories that have emerged after Keynes' (ibid.). That is to say, his approach is radically distinct from the 'real' business cycle theories of neoclassical theory considered in Chapter 1 which explicitly exclude endogenous shocks from their elegant mathematical models and focus instead on extreme exogenous events to show why otherwise stable market economies temporarily depart from an expected equilibrium state.

Minsky defined a business cycle as 'the regular repetition of structural states characterized by a different degree of financial fragility which has to be interpreted in terms of structural instability. Both endogenous and exogenous factors play a crucial role and interact in a complex way' (ibid.: 42). Endogenous shocks 'are not grounded in disequilibrium dynamics [...] but in the *intrinsic structural instability of a monetary economy and its evolution*' (ibid.; emphasis added). It is the acceleration of capital investment under conditions of increased risk in business cycles itself, in anticipation of higher profits, which undermines the resilience of sophisticated monetary economies. Focusing on the logic of monetary economies, argues Variato, Minsky's hypothesis takes

> to the extreme the financial characterization of units with the implication that real investment [investment in the real economy of goods and services] is simply one of the possible portfolio choices that agents may undertake; it is the riskiest because most illiquid and most forward-looking. (2001: 91)

This approach is useful to describe 'capitalistic dynamics wherever finance dominates over production' (ibid.), as it indicates the role of the liquidity preference as a factor in determining investment decisions based on expectations of risk.

Heterodox studies of the 2008 crisis from a post-Keynesian perspective emphasize the impact of financial liberalization as a key factor in the subsequent destabilization of the advanced economies – and, as a logical after-effect, in the destabilization of emerging market economies. Sawyer, for example, reports that the crisis originating in the US was 'clearly caused by behaviour, decisions, and actions within and/or involving the financial sector. The precise mixes [sic] of "bad behaviour" is a matter of much debate [...]' (2011: 152), for the negative consequences of human behaviour must be balanced against systemic issues and poor policy decisions (lax regulation). 'One particularly significant element of Minsky's analysis', he argues, 'relates to his attention to different financial relationships and notably the role of Ponzi finance' (ibid.). This phenomenon was especially clear in the overexpansion of credit in the US mortgage market in the period 2003–2007 and the securitization of 'sub-prime' (working-class) mortgage debt into collateralized debt obligations for global investors seeking above average market returns. However, he notes, credit creation is

> *intrinsic to the financial system and always raises issues of sustainability* [...]. Asset price inflation, particularly in the housing sector, plays a role not just in a 'feel-good' sense stimulating aggregate demand but more significantly in the generation of actions based on a belief in the continuous rise in asset prices, and the extension of loans (notably mortgages) underpinned by that belief. (ibid.: 154; emphasis added)

Yet the 'neoliberal atmosphere' prevalent during this period mitigated against effective regulation, based on the belief that self-regulation by rational agents would suffice to prevent excessive risk-taking behaviour, asset price bubbles and rent extraction. This anti-regulatory sentiment was echoed in the general culture of deregulation advanced by governments and international financial institutions identified with the Washington consensus. The result was credit euphoria – the misperception of household credit worthiness which led consumers to spend beyond their means in the expectation of effortless capital gains from leveraged home-ownership, even where the ratio of house prices to earnings were unstable.

Financial authorities were unwilling to recognize the risk, and the consequences of the sub-prime collapse were catastrophic for ordinary working people.

This narrative is well worn, and alongside accusations of greed and corruption, blame is typically laid at the short-sightedness of investors who chose to believe 'this time things are different'. Yet for Crotty (2009) it is the risk-prone structure of the 'New Financial Architecture' (NFA) of financial liberalization itself that created structural flaws which enabled conventional human behavioural pathologies such as euphoria, greed, corruption and short-sightedness to be magnified and accelerated into systemic crisis. The NFA, he urges, introduces 'perverse incentives that induce key personnel in virtually all financial institutions [...] to take excessive risk when financial markets are buoyant' (Crotty 2009: 128). Parenteau (2005) observes similarly that rather than focus on accurate predictions of future value in order to make reasoned investment choices, as a consequence of neoliberal deregulation financial institutions seek only to 'game the future', as a result of which investor behaviour is increasingly governed by 'speculations on the speculations of others'. Under such conditions, 'strategic behavior unfolds to various degrees and a proclivity of bandwagon outcomes can emerge' (Parenteau 2005: 116). This is not simply true of individual investors who 'hop on the caravan to the casino', but of hedge funds that behave as 'rational destabilizing speculators' and institutional investment managers who in the stampede for profit allow investment time horizons to collapse (ibid.: 121–125).

This point is amplified by Henry (2009), who notes that in the marketplace,

> the temptation to take excessive risk, to cheat or to form monopolies is built into the system. As most students of economics will know, when there is anything close to a free market [...] economic profit goes to zero for all firms! (Henry 2009: 79)

The point of business is to beat the average;

> to surpass normal profits or to secure super normal profits, a firm has to engage in some form of risky, non-competitive or even shady behaviour. The firm has to achieve some level of dominance in the market place, such that it does not have to obey the dictates of a perfect market. (ibid.)

This suggests a serious aporia in neoclassical orthodoxy, which ignores the link between *profitability* and *imperfect competition*. It also suggests a failure to consider the determinate role of profit in capitalism: as Mattick comments, this 'is as striking a feature of current economic writing, outside of a handful of left-wing outsiders, as the refusal to recognize the earlier history of depressions' (2011: 35).

Crotty (2009) takes issue with the neoliberal argument that the global integration of financial markets allows risk to be distributed efficiently – an argument voiced by, among others, former US Treasury Secretary Timothy Geithner who insisted that the risk of systemic crisis is reduced where less risk is concentrated in banks and diffused to the markets. The opposite, however, is the case: under financial liberalization the financial institutions inadequately 'hedged' their exposure to risk via credit default swaps (financial instruments which provide a risky form of reinsurance on bonds) and increased aggregate risk. Instead of hedging, they actively accumulated and speculated on high-risk financial assets for clear commercial reasons: first, to 'convince potential investors that these securities were safe, banks often retained the riskiest part – the so-called "toxic waste"'; second, given the 'incentive to generate high profits and bonuses through high risk, they purposely kept some of the riskiest products they created to maximize bankers' compensation by maximizing short-term profits'; third, there was a tendency towards 'warehousing' due to the 'sheer volume of trades and time-lag between purchase and sale [...]' (ibid.: 129). Saleuddin (2015) argues similarly that trading in the securities sector created the basis for dangerous levels of risk not only as a result of 'predatory lending' but because of 'creative compliance' with regulation which led financial institutions to hold leveraged risk within the banking system (Saleuddin 2015: 67).

This was compounded by the failure of ratings agencies which 'strayed away from their long-term business model when they rated tranches of asset pools based on models that estimated not only probabilities of default and recovery, but also, and importantly, default correlation' (ibid.: 79), that is, the probability that a debt-issuing firm will default due to factors affecting other firms' default risk. As a result of this, ratings agencies were responsible for gross miscalculation and a negligence of fiduciary duty, for by 'basing default rates [...] and recovery rates on history (and a benign one at that) and estimating low default correlations, senior tranches of sub-prime originations were viewed as a credit risk remote enough to be rated AAA/Aaa' (ibid.: 80). Crotty concludes that the idea that the NFA served to distribute and/or mitigate risk in the international financial system is simply nonsensical:

> almost all arguments made by financial economists in support of the assured risk-reducing character of innovations in complex derivatives are based on the assumption that distributions of future real sector cash flows are exogenous, unaffected by financial decisions. Transactions in perfect financial markets [...] simply redistribute the fixed volatility of cash flows among agents; they cannot alter its size. However, the degree of system-wide risk associated with any financial regime is endogenous. Financial booms and busts are inherent in capitalist financial markets, but some financial architectures create more volatility than others. (Crotty 2009: 131)

In reality, complex derivative trades do not 'unbundle' risk as defenders claim but 'rebundle' it in 'complicated and non-transparent ways'; and, because the products created are so complex and opaque, they cannot be priced accurately and their values are prone to rapid devaluation during a crisis – as Bernanke (2010) later conceded.

Securitization accelerates and multiplies financial flows while generating fabulous profits but also makes it possible for financial instability to spread extremely rapidly through a globally integrated credit system. By allowing banks to hold risky assets off-balance sheet through 'special investment vehicles', by trusting financial institutions to set their *own* capitalization requirements and by tolerating the growth of an unregulated shadow banking system (although it was the regulated banks which were in fact responsible for the greatest costs to taxpayers), critics argue that the NFA enabled a clique of recidivist gamblers to pretend to act as responsible market actors – a logical impossibility for market operators contractually *employed* to gamble through the securitization and resale of complex debt instruments and *incentivized* to 'front-load' profits to boost short-term performance while concealing downside risks and losses (Admati & Hellwig 2013: 124). Despite the best efforts of campaigners, to assume that self-regulation of the securities markets can work without the unanimous and voluntary cooperation of financial market actors is perhaps as absurd as the decision by President Obama's administration to hand the task of imposing regulatory restraint to a clique of Wall Street financiers who had previously 'spent their entire careers doing just the opposite'. It also explains why financial authorities have 'yet to take, or even express support for, the kinds of effective government intervention [...] required to end the financial crisis' (Crotty 2009: 135).[7]

Contrary to neoclassical orthodoxy, therefore, financialization and uncontrolled credit expansion clearly encourage irrational speculation, creating investment bubbles that not only corrupt the 'information processing ability of financial markets', obfuscate real earnings and create serious moral hazard (Parenteau 2005: 128), but have the capacity to distort and destabilize complex monetary economies. In response to the negative consequences of the crisis, critical economic theorists have thus called for a return to managed capitalism with a 'new Bretton Woods' to stabilize international monetary flows. The latter issue is examined in greater detail in Chapter 6. Here we outline the limitations of reformism, including approaches derived from neo-Marxist political economy which exhibit a nostalgia for the industrial class compromise of Fordism. We will exclude from consideration normative appeals for a shift towards *sustainable* capitalism, tax reform, expanding the commons, maximizing national well-being, etc. (cf. Costanza 2010), as this will divert us from the primary matter at hand, namely the impossibility of returning to 'golden age' capitalism.

Illusions of reformist capitalism

While neoliberal policy regimes have intensified the potential for financial instability examined in the previous section – and are responsible for diverting investment from the productive economy towards financial speculation – financialization itself is not the reason for the downturn of the advanced economies in the last two decades, just as declining real wages have not limited effective demand due to the mass availability of private credit in deficit economies like the US and the UK. In addition, it is clear that emancipation from financialization will not permit a return to 'stable' accumulation as an alternative to liberalization.

Fordism and neoliberalism are historically specific policy responses to the contradictory logic of capital which would otherwise 'purify its environment of non-economic, non-capitalist encumbrances' (Westra 2010: 18). In financialized economies, *money* – as interest-bearing capital – develops a framework through which all phenomena acquire meaning; it is the general equivalent that determines and makes possible all societal relations, dissolving the independent value of things in themselves (Lotz 2014; cf. Marx 1973). How this revolutionary economic formation is historically constituted and mediated is contingent; yet the conditions of possibility which sustain historic regimes of accumulation cannot be re-established by fiat or nostalgia. On the other hand, the self-multiplication of capital cannot expand indefinitely as pure value in the absence of social structures of accumulation, and as Westra reminds us, even in 1900 it was clear that capitalism 'no longer embodied the asymptotic tendency of capital to gravitate towards pure capitalism but rather entailed the maintenance of extra-capitalist excrescences [...]' (ibid.). We will revisit this issue in Chapter 5 and examine the asymptotic logic of oligarchic banking capital as it approaches its maximal level of power.

Neoliberalism is not the *reason* for the failure of capitalist production but a logical *symptom* of the stagnation of 'golden age' Fordist regimes of accumulation following a period of exceptional growth and stability after the total destruction of the Second World War. Through an expansion of credit money, neoliberal accumulation regimes have succeeded in 'buying time', delaying the crisis by effectively borrowing from the future (Streeck 2014: 85). This has involved a supersession of the nation by the market and the victory of 'market justice' over 'social justice' in the post-Keynesian capitalist system. Transnational neoliberalism has made it possible for finance capital to evolve beyond the constraints of a Fordist model of state democratic capitalism and the nationally constituted consumer economy, revealing the 'organizational advantage that globally integrated financial markets have over nationally organized societies' (ibid.: 86). In place of national capitalism, global capital is freed from the 'state-specific' coherence of accumulation in favour of transnationally constituted value chains. This is nowhere more pronounced than the US, where neoliberalism 'attests to an abdication by the US state for performing its historic role as a *capitalist* state' (Westra 2010: 7) – although even here, as a form of 'really existing capitalism', capital requires non-commodity economic supports to maintain preconditions for its self-reproduction and self-expansion.

Nevertheless, by (partially) eliminating 'non-capitalist encumbrances', liberalization advances capital valorization through an increase in the extraction of surplus value in emerging market economies, the self-expansion of interest-bearing capital in financial markets and the circulation of finance in global commodity chains. This comes a step closer to realizing what Hegel termed the Idea of capital:

> as in Hegel where the dialectic closes with the promise of thought divesting itself of all materiality to become pure and objective and thereby reveal itself as the Absolute, so the dialectic of capital is consummated in the category of

interest in which capital appears in the form of M … M' [the self-multiplication of money] and the Idea or 'dream' of capital, in all its cunning, to free augmentation from the labor and production process through its transubstantiation into a commodity or income yielding asset, becomes unmasked. (ibid.: 37–38)

Of course this can never be completed in its entirety, as 'actually-existing' capitalism depends on specific material and human supports which must also be reproduced in pursuit of capital's own self-expansion. Analysing the logical structure of *Grundrisse*, Meaney (2014) notes that for Marx interest-bearing capital, as the Idea of capital, is '"that end toward which all things proceed and produce" in the realm of capitalist production. Interest-bearing capital *structures the whole of reality toward the end of its own self-reproduction*' (Meaney 2014: 47; emphasis added).

Through financialization, therefore, the relative emancipation of interest-bearing capital from 'non-capitalist encumbrances' proceeds in inverse relation to the atrophy of productive capital in the creation of commodities with universal use-value in the golden age of state-democratic capitalism. A global division of labour based on liberalized capital flows (interest-bearing capital in search of profitable investment) and transnational commodity chains (the generation of value in differential quantities in a hierarchy of production and marketing locations) has come into being, rendering superfluous the older logic of protectionism, subsidies and import substitution that temporarily sustained the industrial class compromise of managed capitalism until the 1970s. As Hossein-Zadeh (2014: 18) notes, whereas monetary and fiscal stimuli were used in Fordist state capitalism to maintain full employment and manage demand, such policies are now used to benefit the *financial* sector. In contrast to economic historians like Harvey (2005), who focus on the changes which followed the Volcker Shock of 1979, Hossein-Zadeh traces the political legitimation of finance further back to the 1960s and argues that the liberalization of interest-bearing financial capital was driven not only by high growth rates in the post-war era (leading to a new phase of credit expansion), but by the growth of public finance, the internationalization of the US dollar as a reserve currency and the tendency of the state to use public funds to maintain unstable financial institutions (Hossein-Zadeh 2014: 69–70).

Correspondingly, neoliberalism has negatively affected the performance of non-financial corporations through deregulation and cross-border capital flows. In the 1990s, this signalled the 'end of a commitment by governments to pursue growth through Keynesian policies, undermining the conditions of possibility for stable "corespective behaviour" where firms limit excessive competition in preference for 'co-existence and oligopoly' (Crotty 2005: 80). In addition, through an intensification of competition, financial institutions extract a larger share of non-financial corporate earnings. Prior to the technology boom of the late 1990s,

> it took a precarious and dangerous combination of forces – overinvestment sustained by rising corporate debt and asymmetric management reward structures, consumption drive by rising household debt and enormous stock

market and real estate capital gains, an unprecedented inflow of money from the rest of the world into US financial markets and a sharp fall in labour's share of GDP originating in NFCs [non-financial corporations] – to push NFC profit rates from their low levels in the early 1990s to a two-decade high in mid-decade. The forces supporting this boom were clearly unsustainable. (ibid.: 100–101)

This has led to a financialization of non-financial corporations as firms seek to remain competitive and viable in a global context, by obtaining an increasing portion of their declining profits from financial services rather than the production and sale of goods or services themselves. This process is facilitated by credit expansion and leveraged debt generally, which increases the intermediary power of banks and other financial institutions within the economy while integrating broader sections of society into the debt nexus of finance capitalism in which all values and relations are monetized.

For post-Keynesians and reformist Marxists, the elusive goal is to reconstruct a viable accumulation regime based on adequate financial regulation, limiting the influence of finance over the economy of goods and services, allowing an emphasis on strategic public investment as a tool for growth. This, in turn, would re-establish sustainable income distribution levels as a basis for maintaining stable effective demand (Harvey 2005; Dean 2009; Foster & Magdoff 2009; Florio 2011/2012; Hein 2012, 2013; Streeck 2014; Durand 2017). Yet such policies contradict not only the economic logic of financialization in the reproduction of capitalist sovereignty in the present era of global capitalism, but also the interests of monetary and political elites whose social power ensures their own continuing pre-eminence in a post-recession economy. A decade of near-zero growth since 2008 has failed to persuade political elites to return to a domestically oriented production-centric neo-Fordist accumulation regime and extend neo-Keynesian stimulus policies to the 'real' economy.

Yet it is not only political constraints which militate against reformist demands for a return to state-democratic capitalism but the dialectical contradiction implicit in the idea that the crisis of commodity-determined capitalism can be resolved by artificially re-creating in post-Fordist societies a mode of regulation appropriate to a historically redundant phase of industrialism. While post-Keynesian and heterodox critiques of financialization elucidate the contagion effect of financial innovation for economies, the utopian assumption that a hypermonetized society based on the expansion of credit can be reformed in a grand voluntarist gesture to control 'parasitic' finance is illogical and absurd. The fact that such a high proportion of the total surplus-product of capital is invested in the financial sector testifies not merely to credit expansion but to the declining profitability of a stagnant productive economy characterized by excess capacity and competition. A distinction is continually made between the real economy and the financialization sector, but as Lotz argues 'capitalist social relations cannot exist without the fundamental role of credit, debt, interest, fictitious capital, etc.' (2014: 80). The growth of finance capital in advanced capitalist economies is not an anomaly: 'it is a fundamental characteristic of an advanced stage of capitalism. Finance capital is the ideal and quintessential form of capital, or capitalist property – independent of physical forms of value, or of the often cumbersome processes of producing goods and services' (Hossein-Zadeh 2014: 86). Whereas in earlier phases of capitalist development firms relied on simpler forms of credit to invest, at higher stages in the development of productive forces financial institutions acquire more market power and play a more active and determinate intermediary role. Overcapacity and overproduction create a tremendous surplus of accumulated capital which cannot be invested profitably in conventional ventures and must be valorized through more advanced forms of financial speculation as abstract or fictitious value.

The predictable failure of governments in the advanced economies to moderate the market-distorting power of high finance *before* the 2007 banking crisis erupted in the US indicates the extremely low probability that a self-expanding system of fictitious wealth creation based on limitless credit creation and abstract value can simply be reformed by legislative fiat. This reflects not only the oligarchic power of financial institutions in the state circuits of capital (where the state creates moral hazard by acting as lender of last resort) but the political redundancy of post-Keynesianism as a positive alternative to financialization which, by extending the complex intermediary channels and financial flows through the magnification and intensification of the liquidity preference (retaining value in the form of money capital), financialization creates a more advanced structure of dissociated sociality than was possible in earlier stages of capitalist development.

We can understand this more clearly if we consider the 'progress' of advanced economies in terms of the distinction between Hegel's affirmative dialectical thought (elaborated in *Science of Logic*) and Marx's critical dialectical thought (elaborated in *Capital*): 'In stark contrast to Hegel's *affirmative* systematic dialectic, in which later levels overcome fundamental contradictions and shortcomings [...], in Marx's *critical* systematic dialectic more complex and concrete theoretical levels reproduce and deepen the initial contradictions and shortcomings' (Smith 2014: 32–33). More specifically, adds Smith, 'Marx's concept of capital does not overcome the fetishism that was a special feature of the initial level of Marx's theory; the concept of capital is the concept of capital-fetishism' (ibid.: 33). A 'return to Keynes' (monetary stimulus/demand management, etc.) cannot resolve the central contradiction of the capitalist mode of production in which creative powers of labour are alienated and appropriated as surplus value as a condition for the reproduction of capital: whereas for Hegel contradictions were overcome in an idealist sense through the *advancing logic of the Concept* (world-spirit), for Marx 'these contradictions are *repeated* in successively more complex and concrete ways' (ibid.: 34). They are never resolved because the material conditions for their sublation cannot be realized without dethroning capital as an 'Absolute Subject' constituted through the impersonal self-reflexive domination of social necessary abstract labour (Postone 1993).

This suggests irreversible consequences for the development of human subjectivity. Capital, argues Lotz, constitutes the social totality of capitalism as a 'real Universal', namely, the force which drives forward all social processes (Lotz 2014: 9). Capital

> establishes a horizon of meaningfulness that regulates our access to entities in our world [...] this schema establishes itself independent from the will of individuals and the will of groups, as the social synthesis is established *prior* to individuals and groups that are living within this synthesis. (ibid.: 27)

Following Haiven (2010) and Stiegler (2011), Lotz insists that the schematization process established by capitalism enframes the human sense of self *itself*, as a result of which

> all functions, places and activities are now subjected to money in general, but also, especially recently, to money in a special temporal sense: credit and debt. With this comes a new form of de-possession [sic], namely, the de-possession of the life of individuals, by the transformation of personal horizons into economic investments. (ibid.: 80–81)

Subjectivity is thus shaped by the logic of money capital as individuals conceptualize *their own lives* as competitive conduits for investment. While it is tempting to retreat from this deterministic conclusion back towards voluntarism – to reconstitute state-democratic capitalism and mitigate rising social inequality, Lotz observes that human imaginative capacities are themselves constituted by and functional to the cognitive and societal reproduction of the capitalist schema, as a result of which 'imagining alternatives [...] is no longer possible. For as life becomes financialized money, it is not only the form of social relations, but also the "medium of thought through which we come to imagine social relations"' (ibid.).[8]

Conclusion

In Chapter 4, we will return to the ontological form of capitalist money as a 'universal and abstract constitutive moment of sociality'. It will suffice to conclude here that absent from reformist narratives of regulated capitalism are, first, a recognition that the logical self-expansion of capital is contingent on expanded opportunities for accumulation, which accelerate the global concentration and combination of capitals (and destruction of superfluous capitals) through the overdevelopment of global finance (Sawaya & Garlipp 2011). Secondly, there is a failure to perceive that a level of accumulation necessary for the development of productive forces under capitalism exists, beyond which additional accumulation yields diminished returns, leading to economic stagnation in advanced capitalist economies and overinvestment in unproductive sectors (cf. Onishi 2011). Third, reformist narratives overlook the structural and historical causes of the declining profitability of commodity production in advanced economies (and the absence of new commodities with universal use-value validity to overcome the disappearance of human labour power from the generation of surplus value). Fourth, speculative finance is clearly *not* a pathological 'false-turn' in an otherwise rationally constituted market system but rather a complex moment of the capitalist abstraction of value – and hence a logical and necessary feature of the *acceleration of capital* in financialized economies where self-multiplication of money capital through credit expansion and value abstraction becomes an end in itself (Fuchs 2014; Manzarolle & Kjøsen 2016). Finally, there is a failure to recognize that the acceleration of financial capitalism constitutes a specific form of *temporalization*, which monetizes the future, altering the framework through which humans cognize their world, as a result of which even human traits such as trust and benevolence are 'framed by monetary relations' (Lotz 2014: 89). The schematization process established by financialized capitalism enables the capital relation to penetrate further into all areas of human existence, via a 'world-embracing matrix of signals that allows for a form of synthetic comprehension of social totality and futurity' (Haiven 2010: 93).

These issues are explored further in subsequent chapters in an attempt to theorize the developmental trajectory of financial socialism. Our thesis is that the finitude of fictitious capital as self-expanding form without content is determined by a crisis of valorization derived from a contradiction in the value form. This is intensifying the decadence of accumulation without value in commodity-determined societies which can only be sustained (but not overcome) through a continual expansion of the credit-debt nexus. Private ownership of the means of production has thus finally evolved from a catalyst for progress to a cause of 'degradation and bankruptcy' (cf. Kautsky 1914), placing in question the very rationale of exchange society. In this context, financial socialism indicates the pathology of postliberal capitalism as a temporary resolution of the crisis: as one possible direction for the accumulation of capital and monetary power *where decadence itself becomes institutionalized*. The historical development of capital through fascism in the mid-twentieth century illustrates the potential power of capital to overcome barriers to its own further self-expansion through massive investment in *non*-productive sectors of the economy, leading to financial repression, militarism and world war. As the power of a non-productive international banking oligarchy intensifies, financial socialism suggests the potential exhaustion of private ownership as means for wealth creation and the erosion of traditional liberal conceptions of right as the requirement for government economic centralization intensifies and Western economies assume characteristics traditionally associated with authoritarian accumulation regimes.

Notes

1 Keynes's (1936) argument stressed the importance of 'effective demand'. Demand is said to be effective when consumers' income is used to purchase consumer and investment goods. In contrast with neoclassical theory, Keynes held that that aggregate supply and demand are only equal where effective demand is equal to the aggregate supply price of output. On the Keynesian revolution, see Cord (2013) and Goodspeed (2012). On the connections between Marxian and Keynesian theories of demand, see Sardoni (1987).

2 'Military Keynesianism' is a term used to denote the positive impact on employment of increasing military expenditure in peacetime. See Cypher (2007, 2015). The term was popularized among anti-war activists during the global wars of the US under Bush and Obama. At the outset of the US banking crisis in late 2008, at least one *Wall Street Journal* writer (Feldstein 2008) argued that increased military expenditure offered an additional potential form of stimulus to stabilize the US economy.

3 On the Washington consensus, see Williamson (2004).

4 Jessop uses this awkward word as an equivalent for the German *Vergesellschaftung*, which refers to the transformation of extra-societal concepts, ideas or practices into societally functional/legitimated structures and forms. The concept is often linked to the economic sociology of Georg Simmel.

5 Leverage ratios are measurements which indicate how much debt is present in financing for capital assets and levels of risk in lending to clients.

6 On Hegelianism in Marx's method, see the essays in Moseley and Smith (2004); on Critical Realism, see Lawson et al. (1998).

7 Saleuddin (2015: 13) comments that if reform of the securities markets were to work, then 'design of any regulatory regime should provide at the very least the potential for a lasting contribution to the funding of the real economy without unduly risking the stability of the financial system as a whole and, often by extension, end borrowers (bank clients) and taxpayers.' We will examine the evolution of banking regulations in relation to depositors in Chapter 5.

8 Lotz lists Haiven's paper on financialization as Haiven (2011), but the actual date of publication is 2010.

3

CRITICAL VALUE THEORY

Introduction

Neither orthodox nor heterodox approaches provide an adequate basis for grasping the structural contradictions in commodity-determined societies which contribute to capitalist breakdown. Here we survey the Marxian theory of crisis in greater detail, looking beyond the financial instability thesis in an attempt to grasp the origins of capitalist recessions in the inner contradictory development of the capitalist value form. Our first task is to differentiate traditional Marxist and value-critical approaches to the crisis of accumulation in capitalism, which set out from similar premises, yet adopt distinct and incompatible analytical frameworks for explaining the failure of capitalist production – both historically and in the present conjuncture of economic stagnation and political instability. While Marxist political economy provides an important corrective to main-stream economics, critical value theory (*Wertkritik*) dispenses with two fallacies in traditional Marxism:

1. The tendency to define Marxian economic theory in a *formalist* sense as a 'positive economic science'; and
2. The tendency to conceptualize capitalism (and hence the struggle against capitalism) from the sociological standpoint of labour.

Marxian critical value theory represents a radical departure from the positivist tendencies of orthodox Marxism (Marxism of the Second International led by Engels and Kautsky, superseded by Marxism-Leninism and later Eurocommunism) towards a critique of contradictions in the capitalist value form.[1] Central to this critique is the assumption that if modern monetary economies are constituted precisely through a continual expansion of interest-bearing capital, finance is a necessary indispensable feature of complex commodity societies. Although finance constitutes a global, denationalized force that transcends sovereign economies, it must nevertheless be sustained through state and transnational circuits of capital. Hence the stability and functionality of modern monetary economies founded on the accumulation of fictitious value is unsustainable without a significant extension of administrative power over the global monetary system.

Not only must we discard dubious concepts of 'deviant' finance, therefore, but should also rethink twentieth-century notions of 'postliberal'/'state' capitalism for a twenty-first-century context. The state form of capital has evolved under changed historical-social conditions, not spontaneously, but in response to fiscal and monetary contingencies in advanced capitalist economies and the sociopolitical interests of capitalist elites. The apparent 'neutrality' of state power, argues Clarke, 'is not an essential feature of the state, it is rather a feature of the fetishized form in which the rule of capital is effected through the state' (2001: 3). Unlike in the 1950s, however, the contemporary state form of capital is mediated via national *and* transnational networks of regulatory control which stand above the particularistic interests of individual national capitals, forming an indispensable regulatory superstructure of legal and administrative power in the reproduction of total social capital. To understand this regulatory superstructure it is necessary to distinguish system-functional and system-disabling dimensions of an accumulation regime based on fictitious value as we approach the fourth industrial revolution in which digitalization renders significant numbers of intellectual workers economically redundant and as value acquires complex forms in circulation sphere. Under the rubric 'neoliberalism', this global accumulation regime is constitutive of a coercive form of postliberal capitalism which hints at the emergence of a new form of 'financial socialism'. Financial socialism is driven by the contradictory relation between variable and constant capital in the valorization of surplus value, and by the limits imposed on accumulation by the intensification of competition and declining profitability of invested capital as debt becomes simultaneously a system-functional and system-limiting feature of economic development.

Theorists associated with value-critique, in both German and Anglophone scholarship, are concerned with the dialectical character of structural social change – that is, with a 'mode of understanding empirical socioeconomic phenomena as *necessarily* yet *contradictorily* interrelated' (Appelbaum 1978: 76). Marxism in its traditional guise is methodologically flawed, not simply for its formalist tendencies but for ascribing an unrealizable deterministic potential to collective human agency. Marxism from the standpoint of labour is less relevant in the present era because

> categories of class opposition cannot provide a basis for any adequate conception of the extreme growth in social inequality, nor are the oppositions and conflicts between social interest groups resulting from such inequality simply recurrences of what [...] were once accurately conceived as instances of class struggle. (Trenkle 2006: 201)

Writing immediately prior to the implosion of the US sub-prime mortgage market in 2006–2007, Trenkle critically assesses the redundancy of traditional Marxism and the absence of meaningful class resistance to capital in the 'currently unfolding' crisis. The modernization and atomization of capitalist societies in the twentieth century reveal the opposition between capital and labour incubated in the nineteenth century to be an 'immanent conflict between social and economic interests internal to capitalism. [...The] conduct of labor struggles today is no longer premised on the irreconcilability between the interests of the sellers of labor power and those of capital' (Trenkle 2006: 201). He attributes this to four dynamics.

First, in contemporary capitalism labour applied directly in the production process has been dramatically reduced in favour of 'capital-intensive technologies of automated oversight and control and of pre- and post-production functions' (ibid.: 204). This has resulted in the effective declassing of the proletariat through the disappearance of a 'value-producing industrial workforce' and the growth of differentiated varieties of unproductive wage labour which cannot produce or sustain a coherent class identity. Second, through the continual circulation of workers between temporary or short-term positions of employment, the relation of workers to their socioeconomic location has 'ceased to be in any way anchored in their biography or environment' (ibid.: 205). Third, he observes,

> new hierarchies and divisions cut across the categories of capitalist function rather than overlapping with them. [...] they are not determined by the opposition between wage labor and capital, for the social differential is just as steep within the category of wage labor as it is in society as a whole. (ibid.: 205–206)

Finally, declassing means more individuals fall through the 'grid of functional categories', finding that there is no place for them in a commodity-determined society which productively exploits 'less and less labor power' (ibid.: 206). In post-Fordist economies, increasing numbers of manual and non-manual workers sit precariously above a 'social nothingness', reduced to the function of proletarianized consumers whose de-skilling and consequent loss of *savoir-faire* augments their purchasing power while further extending into leisure activity the 'expropriation of human time submitted to commodity time' (Stiegler 2011: 27; cf. Debord 1994).

Postone also criticizes the normative critique of capitalism in traditional Marxism as a positive critique which hypostatizes the category *labour* into a transhistorical form:

> 'Its standpoint', he suggests, is an already-existing structure of labor and the class that performs it. [...] rather than pointing beyond the capitalist social formation, the traditional positive critique, made from the standpoint of 'labor', hypostatises and projects onto all histories and societies the forms of wealth and labor that are historically specific to capitalism. (Postone 1993: 66)

Traditional Marxism, which in its classical form privileged the collective agency of industrial workers, proceeds from the *standpoint of labour*. Yet a more profound contradiction in capitalism lies not in class conflict, but in the existence of surplus-labour (labour power required to create surplus value) as a functionally necessary yet socially redundant category:

> Although capitalism tends to develop powerful forces of production whose potential increasingly renders obsolete an organization of production based upon direct labour time expenditure, it cannot allow the realization of these forces. The only form of wealth that constitutes capitalism is one based upon direct labour time expenditure. Hence, value, despite its growing inadequacy as a measure of the material wealth produced, is not simply superseded by a new form of wealth. Instead, according to Marx, it remains the necessary structural precondition of capitalist society [...] although capitalism is characterized by an intrinsic developmental dynamic, that dynamic remains bound to capitalism; it is not self-overcoming. What becomes 'superfluous' on one level remains 'necessary' on another: in other words, capitalism *does* give rise to the possibility of its own negation, but it *does not* automatically evolve into something else. (1993: 34)

Unlike traditional Marxism, capital-theoretical approaches 'avoid the unhistorical position that the ideals of bourgeois society *will be realized in socialism*, as well as the antinomic opposite – the notion that the ideals of bourgeois society are all shams' (ibid.: 67; emphasis added). What is required is a critique of the specific character of labour in capitalism, focusing on the determinate structuring (and structured) forms of social practice that constitute modern society. As Smith notes, Marx's dialectic social theory

> consists of a progression of social forms defining the 'inner nature' of capital, that is, social forms in place in any given period of capitalism. In themselves, these social forms tell us what capital is, but not what it might become. (Smith 2003: 26)

As noted in the previous chapter, capital constitutes the 'social totality of capitalism as a "real Universal" – the force that drives all social processes' (Lotz 2014: 9). All of the wealth capital which creates is 'incidental to the only purpose capital is capable of recognizing according to its concept of itself, namely the accumulation of value, a one-dimensional purely quantitative measure of its achievement which negates all content' (2002: 141). Capitalism is not a 'system' as such – reducible to an economy of firms, workers and machines; it is, rather, *money in perpetual motion* – a dynamic historical-social synthesis which develops structural forms with systemic properties. Capital – like the nation-form in which it expanded – predates and exceeds real historical individuals incorporated in it, whose operativity for the generation of value is determined by their functional utility as productive labour in contingent structures of accumulation. Lotz argues that capitalism 'appears to standard economic theory and the public mind as a static system that circles around itself and can go on forever' (Lotz 2014: 105). This illusion is achieved only through the expansion of monetary values created by capital as *credit money* – the aggregate of commercial and monetary credit relations in exchange societies (Lapavitsas 1991). It is through the expansion of the credit-debt nexus that the 'violent core of the commodity subject' (*Vernichtungslogik*) is revealed in its modern financialized form – that is, as financial 'violence becomes *the* driving force and effect of the capitalist scheme, even if this violence, due to capital fetishism, remains hidden behind the surface of commodity exchange and the surface of what most still call "market economy"' (Lotz 2014: ibid.; cf. Lohoff 2003).

In Marxian value-critique, capital is understood to be approaching its vanishing point because in the competition to maintain profitability, total social capital can no longer maintain a level of productive living labour necessary to create surplus value. The intensity of competition between firms for a declining share of relative surplus value increases inexorably (yet invisibly, from the perspective of individual capitals) as productive living labour is displaced from the output of commodities and not redeployed as productive labour in new growth sectors driven by real innovation and/or new commodities with universal use-value which establish profitable value chains, in turn stimulating investment in related sectors. 'Neoliberal' capitalism represents an accumulation regime augmented by an unprecedented expansion of fictitious value: an 'abstract form of valorization', defined as money capital that does not correspond to value generated by productive investment. Profitable investment in commodity production is problematic outside low-wage economies like China, Vietnam and Indonesia where intensive exploitation of labour power (based on an increase in the production of *absolute* surplus value through a de facto extension of the working day) is permitted. For this reason nonfinancial corporate profitability has been in decline in advanced economies since the late 1960s – not simply because the bargaining power/wage share of productive workers has grown but because the wage share of *unproductive* labour relative to productive labour has declined (Mejorado & Roman 2014: 167; cf. Moseley 1988, 1992).

In the advanced economies the declining rate of profit has resulted in a search for new modes of valorization in the sphere of circulation, encouraging a trend for capital to shift from the nonfinancial to the financial corporate sector and for investment in manufacturing industries to transfer from high-wage to low-wage economies. From the 1980s onwards,

> financial sector expansion required nonfinancial corporations to distribute an increasing share of profits as dividends. They did so pressed by stockholders needing funds to speculate in financial markets in search of higher yields. In the event, the emergence of new financial opportunities allowing

corporations to reverse past profitability woes absorbed a growing share of nonfinancial corporate funds to the detriment of nonfinancial investments. (Mejorado & Roman 2014: 229)

The attraction of the financial sector lies not only in a reduced requirement for capital intensity but in the range of sophisticated investment instruments – such as financial market derivatives – which allow investors to store value for fixed periods and to commodify risk. The early twentieth-century economist, Rudolf Hilferding (1981), viewed financial market derivatives as a representation of money which measures the value of underlying commodities, wrongly predicting that in monopoly capitalism futures markets would become redundant. In contrast to Hilferding, Sotiropoulos et al. (2013) define derivatives as 'financial contracts that bear a money price':

> Hilferding was not able to clearly see this dimension because [...] he erroneously thought that derivatives markets totally annihilate risk. In that case, derivatives might be considered forms of money because they would bear a price without trading something. Nevertheless, derivatives markets do not eliminate risk. They commodify and trade it: risk is singled out of the underlying commodity, sliced up, and repackaged into a new commodity form which now acquires a price. (Sotiropoulos et al. 2013: 77)

As will become clear in Chapter 4, financial market derivatives 'set up the dimension of abstract risk by making different concrete risks commensurable' (ibid.; cf. Bryan & Rafferty 2003, 2006). Derivatives facilitate the emergence of a 'production process within the circulation process', enabling capital to overcome barriers to accumulation by magnifying the nominal market value of global securities and futures – estimated at $1.4 quadrillion – far beyond the combined value of global GDP.[2]

Nevertheless, as Lebowitz (1976) observes, while Marx recognized that circulation is critical for the realization of value in commodity exchange, the more lengthy and more complex this process becomes, *the more it potentially constrains* the self-expansion of capital in commodity production itself. Marx outlined this point clearly in *Grundrisse*, remarking that:

> Circulation time in itself is not a *productive force* of capital, but a *barrier to its productive force* arising from its nature as exchange value. The passage through the various phases of circulation here appears as a *barrier to production*, a barrier posited by the specific nature of capital itself. All that can happen through the acceleration and abbreviation of *circulation time* – of the circulation process – is the reduction of the barrier posited by the nature of capital. (Marx 1973: 545)

For Marx, the sole logical purpose of capital is self-expansion; yet in its attempt to transcend finitude, capital must continually overcome the contradiction between this tendency to expand and a contradictory tendency to create barriers to its own self-expansion by displacing living labour in the valorization process. The question then becomes whether the *barriers* capital creates to its own continual self-expansion can be overcome indefinitely (through a continual augmentation of fictitious value), or whether some insurmountable *limit* exists between capital accumulation and the self-expansion and valorization of abstract value (cf. Harris 1983).

Financialization results not merely from the creation of state-controlled fiat money and credit money to fuel market speculation (creating the illusion of liquidity, rising prices and growth), but from a logical contradiction in the capitalist value form and the uncontrolled self-expansion of capital as a magnitude of value abstracted from real objective social needs. Financialization intensifies the growth of fictitious value through the multiplication of complex financial instruments to leverage capital value; yet the present crisis derives not from financialization *per se* but from the tendency of the general rate of profit to fall over time as a result of a displacement of living labour power from commodity production, the consequences of which are disguised (to a large extent) by a severing of the link between productivity growth and real wage growth and the ideological abandonment of full employment as an economic priority in advanced economies in the 1980s (cf. Palley 2013a). Although Marx (1959: 232–240) observed the importance of 'counteracting influences' to the tendency of the rate of profit to fall – principally, the capacity of industrialists to intensify labour exploitation to increase the effectivity of given quantities of invested capital, the origins of the present downturn, triggered in the short-term by an excessive growth of debt and the insolvency in the banking system, lie less in neoliberalism as a deregulated global accumulation regime than in the hyperproductivity of advanced commodity societies in which valorization depends on a paradoxical displacement of human labour power as the real substance of commodity value. Which is to say, it is precisely because labour is the '*only element* that takes on the form of value whilst it is not produced within the capitalist sphere of production that it potentially creates value-added' (Reuten & Williams 1987: 69; emphasis added). Intercapitalist competition accelerates advances in productivity by forcing firms to continually invest in new techniques of production in a race to remain competitive; yet the technical means of production themselves (no matter how advanced) 'provide no value-added because they have been *produced previously* within a valorization process, and as such represent previous value-added' (ibid.). This point is essential for understanding the relevance of labour-power for profitable accumulation, for the value of constant capital 'is *not* derived from the ideal value of the output of the production process in which they actually figure as means of production, but from the process of production in which *they* were actually produced' [...] (ibid.).

Growing limits on the capacity of firms to realize increased relative surplus value through the valorization of capital in productive investment do not necessitate capitalist breakdown, therefore; they necessitate, rather, that unlimited credit expansion becomes necessary to compensate for a crisis of valorization caused by the paradox of *accumulation without value* (Lohoff 2014). The result is the growth of fictitious value assisted by central bank activism (quantitative easing, interest rates below the zero lower bound) and fractional reserve banking: capital becomes fictitious when failed loans are concealed and paid off with new loans, and where asset values are leveraged through complex derivative trades which have a nominal value that dwarfs the value of the original assets traded. While this process appears *prima facie* potentially limitless, it is built on continual multiplication of debt and exposure to this multiplying volume of debt creates perilous levels of risk and instability in all but the most disconnected financial institutions. More than a decade has now passed since the most serious debt crisis in modern economic history, which was ultimately resolved only through the accumulation of more debt to appropriate value from the future to fund liabilities in the present. The possibility of a second transnationally coordinated stimulus programme on the scale of that undertaken by G20 economies after the 2009 London Summit is extremely difficult to envisage.

The roots of the present crisis thus lie not simply in the limited capacity of state interventions to drain excess capital from the system and reboot accumulation – as if financial crises could be manipulated at will and devaluations controlled to order; rather, fictitious capital has become a core defining feature of capitalism in its *decadent* form, increasing the violence and intensity of successive financial events following the economic crisis of advanced economies in the 1970s, while reducing the time interval between destabilizing moments. It is important to recall that while the 'global' financial crisis was indeed a defining event from a *Western* perspective, it gathered pace as a succession of similar lesser financial catastrophes occurred in emerging market economies in the late 1990s. These were followed in the metropole itself by the emergency bailout of Long-Term Capital Management in 1998 and the abrupt end of the new technology equity bubble between 2000 and 2001, after which a very short period of recovery was engineered as mobile interest-bearing capital flooded into US and UK housing markets, the Chinese economy, financial derivatives and other boom sectors. This decade-long period of market turbulence announced the end of the final phase of the 'long boom' in the global economy (1980s–2006), a global financial super-cycle ending in an extended 'bust', partial recovery from which has been achieved *only* through expanding 'central bank and Treasury deficits that are unprecedented in size and impose other challenges for long-term financing of governments' (Allen 2016: viii).

While the creative destruction of capital and relocation of valorization from the realm of production to circulation enabled capitalist economies to sustain the illusion of innovation, liquidity and rising prices, the wealth of financialized capitalism is maintained by *stealing value from the future*. For some, accumulation is sustainable assuming state intervention – or, more precisely, faith in the efficacy of central bank activism to support overvalued markets. Marazzi (2010), for example, argues that the profits fuelling financialization are possible because new processes of accumulation come into being that compensate for declining rates of surplus value. Accumulation no longer consists *exclusively* of direct investment in constant capital (technology) or variable capital (labour power) in commodity-producing industries, but in the manipulation of financial instruments and investment in *biocapitalism* to exploit multiplying sources of 'free labour' (unpaid labour that creates value in the sphere of circulation). For others, however, it is only a matter of time before this edifice of leveraged value tumbles, triggering a potentially catastrophic devaluation shock (Lohoff & Trenkle 2012). New sources of fictitious value may be possible now and into the future; but accumulation is less stable when based on derivative values, which – supported by coordinated market intervention – magnify and distort the real earning power of equities and other traded assets, requiring central banks to ease monetary policy and generate liquidity to support investors. The ever-present risk remains that leveraged values magnify gains and equity prices; but in the real world of uncertainty, costs of debt-servicing and risk of default threaten to evaporate overpriced non-productive assets as markets seize, causing investors to flee back into cash and new sources of credit to dry up.

The question of the *limits* to capital, which cannot be answered without considering the intermediary function of the state form of capital in modern monetary economies, is addressed briefly in the final section – ahead of the analysis of financial socialism and managed consumerism in Chapters 5. Two outcomes are considered. On the one hand, capital is understood to be approaching its vanishing point as opportunities for profitable exploitation of productive labour decline and the accumulation of fictitious value through credit expansion and derivatives trades become precarious. On this view, capitalist breakdown becomes more likely because the ontological substance of capital (social necessary labour) 'cannot acquire a new lease of life' (Feldner & Vighi 2015: 18), which threatens not just another recession but an 'ontological break' in human civilization. Following Kurz (1995), Feldner and Vighi argue that the

> present crisis gives us an indication of the extent to which the compensatory mechanism of external and internal economic expansion, which in previous crises prevented the relative fall in the rate of profit from turning *irrevocably* into an absolute fall in the mass of profit, has ground to a halt. (2015: 20)

The impoverishment caused by the crisis in core and semi-peripheral economies also 'provides a stark reminder that the right to exist under global capitalism hinges for the vast majority on the dubious fortune of being utilized on profitable terms' (ibid.).

On the other hand, a decadent or suboptimal form of capitalism may persist as Western countries, following the example of Japan, avoid restructuring in preference for 'utilizing non-productive sectors' more intensively to sustain the existing structure of power relations (Onishi 2011: 27).[3] This attempt to defer a catastrophic unwinding of market values has an obvious appeal for both state and corporate actors: it delays the terrifying moment of debt-deleveraging which might otherwise annihilate the fictional market values which sustain the advanced economies. Investment in non-productive sectors also goes beyond finance: it potentially includes sectors such as construction, infrastructure, transport and defence, which absorb huge amounts of excess capital and maintain unprofitable strategic industries through using generous state subsidies and public-private partnerships (PPPs), and which depend – as we shall see in Chapter 5 – on a continual flow of government contracts to remain economically viable.

Scholars in Marxian IPE rightly emphasize the internationalization of capitalist social relations as a response to the accumulation crisis of metropolitan economies, which in turn leads to the growth of emerging market economies whose competitive potential, rapid growth and resulting financial instability tend to trigger renewed crises in the metropole itself. As Sawaya and Garlipp (2011) observe, the economic integration of post-communist states (and the modernization of China in particular) have enlarged the potential for accumulation but have not solved the problem of expanded capital. Capitalist globalization incorporates new opportunities for the expropriation of local producers and the acquisition of resources but intensifies contradictions in capitalism by accelerating structural changes in global labour markets as core metropolitan economies strive to become more competitive while managing unprecedented levels of debt. China's breathtaking economic modernization has disguised contradictions in global capitalism as Chinese capital seeks new avenues for investment in Asia and Africa, fuelling a commodities boom and rising property values in key global cities. This has, at the same time, ignited a massive credit expansion in China itself where monetary authorities are now following the Western example by classifying systemically vital banks 'too-big-to-fail' (Wildau 2018).

Despite growth in emerging markets, the global economy – and G7 economies in particular – has witnessed a declining rate of profit on capital invested. This can be resolved only if accumulation is artificially limited and unproductive sectors of the economy are 'allowed' to fail, re-establishing the conditions for a new phase of dynamic accumulation. While South Korea, Thailand and Indonesia went through extremely painful restructuring after the Asian crisis in 1997–1998, elites in the US, the UK and EU have striven by all means possible to limit social and political unrest and stabilize neoliberalism since the 2008 crisis, suggesting a move towards financial socialism based on increasing government economic centralization. Supported by centralized money creation and managed consumerism, structures of national and transnational economic governance sustain corporate oligopoly, mediated by financial institutions with increased powers of dispossession of depositors' assets. But while a concentration and centralization of capital provide respite from intercapitalist competition (which causes the organic composition of capital to rise), it does so at the price of retarding economic and technical modernization (Reuten & Williams 1987: 132), making Western corporations less competitive in relation to emerging market corporations in the long term.

Marxian economic theory

Marx defined value in qualitative terms as the 'productive expenditure' of human physical and mental capabilities: value 'becomes a commodity when its direct utility is denied and [...] can be exchanged for other commodities in the abstract quantity of labour' (Amorim 2014: 96). Marx (1954) argued that the capitalist mode of production is a *relative* rather than *absolute* historical form for the development of the productivity of labour and that commodity production is best understood as the organization of social labour for the reproduction of its own material conditions of existence in private property-owning societies. In the early texts, Marx noted the paradoxical societal form of capitalism embodied in the contradiction between the societalization (*Vergesellschaftung*) of social relations and the egoism of liberal political theory:

> It is a curious thing that a people which is just beginning to free itself, to tear down all the barriers between the different sections of the people and to found a political community, that such a people should solemnly proclaim the rights of egoistic man separated from his fellow men and from the community [...]. (Marx 1970: 230)

To overcome the contradiction between societalization and the multiplication of egoistic capitalist interests, material reproduction is driven by the dialectical principle of 'unity-in-difference', through which the constitutive and contradictory moments of the commodity form of value are realized and institutionalized in a self-reproducing social totality (Arthur 2002; Ahumada 2012). Marx noted further that barriers to capitalist development are internal to capitalist production itself 'as distinct from an external [i.e. exogenous] barrier arising from presumably "natural" causes such as were to be found in classical political economy' (Harris 1983: 311). Capitalism emerged in the early modern era in response to the stagnation and overpopulation of agrarian economies in Europe, inaugurating an unprecedented burst of industrial power and emigration which fuelled the rise of mercantilist colonial trading empires and the expansion of capital outside the metropole. Yet the point of departure for the rise of capitalism was neither mercantilism itself nor the primitive accumulation afforded by imperial plunder but the *commodification of labour power*, which transformed existing patterns of labour exploitation through a new concentration of productive forces in factories under the surveillance and control of capitalists. The wealth generated by this historic transformation was thrown back into the production process, reinvested in machinery (constant capital), enabling capitalists to 'set in motion' new quantities of labour power (variable capital) in the new factory system. As productivity gains were generalized across national economies, it was possible to generate more surplus value by introducing additional quantities of constant capital into the labour process, increasing output while using the *same* quantity of variable capital. This growth of constant capital in proportion to labour power in production accelerated the emergence of a detailed division of labour (division of labour functions into multiple minute tasks). Supported by automation, this raised productivity beyond previously imaginable barriers, while generating new and unprecedented profits for capitalists whose political power developed alongside that of landowners. The commitment of the latter towards political liberalization was always moderated by parochial and conservative beliefs in rank and status, yet the reformist impulses and competitive zeal of the new capitalist class were also balanced by a preference for oligopolistic anti-market practices (Braudel 1982), in addition to a general disinterest in developing civil society beyond an aggregation of egoistic 'partial beings'. This tendency was reflected in the rise of classical political economy which 'grasps bourgeois social relations to a certain degree, but only in order to declare them unceremoniously a part of the natural order' (Trenkle 1998: 7).

It is assumed by orthodox economics that the process of economic rationalization set in motion by capital is potentially infinite – up to the point of eliminating human labour power from whole areas of production through automation. In critical value theory, by contrast, capital is conceptualized in dialectical terms, that is, through a consideration of the multiple ways in which the components of productive systems interact, combine and recombine to constitute a unity: the realization of universal social production entails a conceptualization of the 'concrete-universal', in which the constituent forms of production, distribution, exchange and consumption are not simply a 'chaotic sum' but rather 'objective members of a totality [...,] distinctions within a unity which is established by the overarching moment of production' (Schmidt 1981: 39). Although Marx conceptualized capitalism in the later texts *synchronically* as a fully functioning 'system', which serves 'as a principle of explanation of its own past as well as future development and hence also explains precisely those driving forces which undermine its systematic character' (ibid.: 53), the tendency to view capitalism as historically given – as a fully formed 'system' – negates its *diachronic* movement towards financial and monetary complexity where value is increasingly realized through extended structures of circulation and exchange. This illusion derives, in part, from the fact that the reproduction of capital is obscured by the complexity of its phenomenal forms (commodity, value, surplus value, etc.). As a *contingent* historical-social synthesis, capital appears contrary to its own nature – a nature concealed from immediate view. This results in a failure to recognize that, as a *relative* historical form for advancing the productive forces of society, capital is a ceaselessly self-expanding value which stimulates labour productivity while simultaneously creating barriers to the realization of this productive potential in society. This leads to periodic crises of accumulation which undermine the stability of the capitalist mode of production as an economic model for satisfying human needs – a dynamic that assumes heightened intensity in advanced monetary economies.

Employing a dialectical-critical methodology, Marx entirely rejects the tendency to view capitalist commodity society as a naturally occurring 'system'. Instead, he identifies how, under 'specific historical conditions, a single subset of human social relations came to manifest an ontological structure of "Absolute-like" logical interrelations amenable to dialectical exposition' (Westra 2010: 17). Not only is the historical-social form of capital dynamic and unfolding, but the scientific categories used by economists to comprehend it are *themselves* rooted in commodity abstraction through 'reification', where the autonomous power acquired by the value of commodities and abstract market relations is reflected back into human cognition through a process of abstraction. The abstraction of commodity exchange, as it develops in monetary economies, leads necessarily to the 'historical formation of abstract cognitive concepts able to implement an understanding of primary nature from sources other than manual labour' (Sohn-Rethel 1978: 75). This rationalizing force of abstraction constitutes the real critical significance of *capital* as a refutation of philosophical idealism based on the insight that intellectual labour – and thus the scientific categories of thought – are 'historical by origin and social by nature'. For Sohn-Rethel, it is necessary to 'proceed from commodity abstraction to the source from where the abstraction emanates and [. . .] carry through a painstakingly accurate and detailed analysis of the formal structure of exchange as the basis of its socially synthetic function' (ibid.: 9). In this way, the materialist critique of political economy challenges the epistemological immediacy of naïve empiricism (attributing primacy to surface phenomena over logical or systemic interconnections), making possible the critical-realist postulate that knowledge of intransitive (independently existing) objects is always – and must necessarily be – cognized through or mediated by transitive forms of knowledge.[4]

Wertkritik takes as its theoretical starting point the contradiction in the value form, according to which capitalist crises result from a tendency towards the generalized overproduction of commodities: competition for market share and profit drive capitalists to expand the production of exchange values without limit, leading to an increase in the ratio of constant capital (machinery/raw materials/ energy) to variable capital (labour power) in production:

> The valorization process, and not the technical process of production, is the characteristic driving-force of capitalism. Wherever valorization falters the production process is interrupted, even if from the standpoint of the satisfaction of needs production as a technical process may be desirable and necessary. The existing literature has totally ignored the fact that the process of setting free labour that Marx describes in the chapter on accumulation, and which is reflected in the formation of the reserve army, is not rooted in the technical fact of the introduction of machinery, but in the imperfect valorization of capital specific to advanced stages of accumulation. It is a cause that flows strictly from the specifically capitalist

form of production. Workers are made redundant not because they are displaced by machinery, but because, at a specific level of the accumulation of capital, profits become too small and consequently it does not pay to purchase new machinery and soon profits are insufficient to cover these purchases anyway. (Grossmann 2005: ch. 2: 15)

The purpose of capitalist commodity production is to generate profit – to valorize the capital invested in a concern, and no capitalist will continue to invest once imperfect valorization becomes unprofitable. Although productive labour is not the only source of the value realized in the extended reproduction of capital, it is the shift in the 'organic composition' of capital (quantity of constant capital required per employee) which has a tendency to reduce the proportion of variable capital employed in production, which in turn reduces the quantity of surplus value (and thus profit) generated, resulting in crises of valorization.

The social form of capitalist value is determined by abstract labour, a historically specific category distinguished from naturalized or anthropological concepts of work as the employment of human vital energy to reproduce the material conditions of existence. Abstract labour, argues Trenkle, depends on

> a highly specific rule of time that is both abstract-linear and homogeneous. What counts is objectively measurable time – in other words, the time that has been separated from the subjective sensations, feelings, and experiences of working individuals. Capital has rented them for a precisely defined time-period, in which they have to produce a maximal output of commodities or services. Each minute that they do not expend for this purpose is, from the standpoint of the purchaser of the commodity labor power, a waste. Each and every minute is valuable, in so far as it, in the literal sense, presents potential value. (Trenkle 1998: 5)

The commodification of abstract labour power in conditions of temporal abstraction is a precondition for 'socially necessary labour' – that is, the expenditure of a socially average measure of labour power adequate to generate surplus value by producing commodities, whose value is realized through exchange. Abstract labour constitutes a

> reduction of all the different forms of commodity-producing labour to a common denominator. It makes them comparable and as a result capable of being exchanged for one another, by reducing them to the pure abstract reified quantity of elapsed time. As such, it forms the *substance of value*. (ibid.: 6; emphasis added)

Trenkle is critical of Sohn-Rethel's mechanistic categorial identification of *actually existing abstraction* (the a priori structure of social synthesis that presupposes and determines thought and action) with the *act of commodity exchange*. In his view, this reduces all values to a common equivalent regardless of their qualitative distinctions. However, he is more critical of Heinrich (1991), who separates the *form* of value constituted through commodity exchange from the *substance* of value constituted through the appropriation of surplus value in the labour process:

> in the capitalist mode of production, it is not the case that products are innocently created and only arrive on the market a posteriori; rather, every process of production is from the outset oriented toward the valorization of capital and organized accordingly. That is to say, production occurs already in the context of a fetishized form of value, and products must fulfil a single purpose: to represent in the form of value the amount of labor time necessary for their production. (ibid.: 9)

Although time spent in the sphere of circulation is a seen as a barrier to valorization, circulation is at the same the space in which the homogenized or fetishized form of capitalist value is realized in commodity exchange. This is particularly the case in advanced economies where funds are typically invested in complex financial instruments which realize a form of production in circulation. Were it possible, which logically it is not, capital might attempt to dispense with the requirement for concrete use-value entirely and exist only in the sphere of production because – recalling Trenkle's apt expression – 'each and every minute is valuable' for the generation of surplus value as a basis for profitable accumulation.

In fact, the sphere of circulation (and the barriers to self-expanding value this entails) is itself a critical moment in the valorization process of capital, and to dispense with use-value is logically impossible because value must have a 'material bearer' to be viable – even if given commodities are themselves intrinsically worthless or socially useless. What matters is that value expands, for the self-expansion of value is a prerequisite for accumulation, which is the sole logical purpose capital is capable of following as a directionless yet irrational universal subject (Arthur 2002). The inner contradiction of capital lies in its possession of 'false infinity' – in its compulsive self-augmentation through appropriation of surplus value in commodity production, as a result of which *capital always returns to its original form as augmented value in search of material substance.* Proceeding from Hegel's *Science of Logic*, Marx concluded that the drive for infinity compels capital towards a circular condition of 'eternal return' rather than transcendence. In Hegel's method, unilinear progress is defined as something 'finite (at any given time) and infinite (in tendency) for there is always something beyond the finite' (Arthur 2002: 139). But while this unilinear progression is always incomplete, circular repetition 'has no beyond because the movement stays within a set of points defined by it. It is complete in itself. So the movement always returns to itself and abides with itself' (ibid.).

This observation goes some way towards explaining the compulsive cycle of capital as a ceaselessly repetitive mode of value-augmentation whose social form evolves continually but whose *telos* remains identical. This seems to be the intended meaning of Benjamin's (2004) oblique assertion that there is 'no day that is not a feast day' in capitalism'. As Hamacher observes:

> The permanent holiday of capitalism consists in the ritual efforts to celebrate this holiday always once again and at the same time ever more festively. Capitalism's ever-lasting Sunday is the perennial workday of surplus value and surplus labor. The time of capital, thus characterized, extends the end of history into the dead eternity of surplus time. In the time of capital, there is no 'now' that might not be simultaneous with any other 'now'; there is no 'now' that would not be intent upon its return in another, none that would not itself stand under the law of returns and appear as the mere revenant of another 'now'. (Hamacher 2002: 89)

In this sense, capital is movement without direction or, more precisely, *money in perpetual movement*, achieved through an eternal return to itself in an augmented form. Its restlessness is driven not merely by the compulsive nature of its circular logic but by the continually increasing productivity of average socially necessary labour time as a measure of value. This measure of value is not subjectively determined (as price or marginal preference); rather, it derives objectively from the tendential development of the productivity of society which 'assumes power in this [economic] process as a merciless sovereign' (Trenkle 1998: 10).

This perception of capital is entirely missing from traditional Marxism, which depicts socialism as a planned allocation of resources rather than the abolition of socially necessary labour. The mistake of Marxism-Leninism in the USSR and eastern Europe was to emulate the growth-at-all-costs logic of market society and attempt to 'nail down' an empirical determination of value, turning the Marxian critique of political economy into a positive science. This resulted in misguided attempts to develop a 'scientific' form of socialism geared towards the logic of plan fulfilment, but in the absence of real economic actors, the hierarchical structure of the planned economy yielded a neo-estate society based on *self-co-opting* political power as a substitute for functionally differentiated class society (Staniszkis 1992). It also resulted in futile attempts to theorize science as a productive force in the 'scientific-technological revolution' and an alternative ideal of 'socialist efficiency' based on the adaptation of capitalist labour practices, supported by an ideology of 'technical humanism' which promised emancipation through planned scientific progress. Rather than assert the autonomy of science, Marx attempted to overcome the dualism of subject/object and his appropriation of the Hegelian idea of 'totality' illustrates this most clearly (Jay 1984). As Murray observes, even as Marx adopted the tools of modern science, he also demanded that science 'submit the question of the *relation* of "facts" and their logical reconstruction itself to empirical scrutiny. This critical approach to concepts and their interconnections is one feature which sets Marx's theory of knowledge apart from positivist understandings of science' (Murray 1988: 41;

cf. Schmied-Kowarzik 1981). This leads to a technocratic misconception, where 'revolution' becomes the task of a class vanguard – a 'trained minority ruling by authoritarian measures', sheltering beneath a 'mechanistic' determinism of historical materialism (Wellmer 1971: 75).

Yet it also distinguishes critical value theory from modern 'Frankfurt School Marxism', whose leading theorists separate technical-instrumental labour (*poesis*) and social interaction (*praxis*) as distinct fields of human activity (Habermas 1987; cf. Arendt 1958), eliminating from Marx's category 'social labour' (*gesellschaftliche Arbeit*) the possibility of overcoming the abstract violence of socially necessary labour (*gesellschaftlich notwendige Arbeit*). That is to say, it negates the possibility of an 'objectively-communicative action of relations based on the division of labour' to overcome the senselessness of abstract labour as a condition for the self-expansion of the capitalist value form and 'real subsumption' of labour (Krahl 1984: 394).[5] Social labour intends a dialectical supersession of Aristotelian dualism, and attempts to construct a critical theory of interaction distinct from actual technical progress are utopian because they reconstruct idealized categories of *poiesis* and *praxis*. These categories are already superseded by the de facto conditioning of social labour (Rüddenklau 1982), which in advanced economies combines the limited capacities and knowledge of individual actors to create otherwise unattainable collective outcomes. This is not to rehearse the naïve eulogization of industrial labour in Marxism-Leninism or the autonomist delusions of 'workerism' (*operaismo*), but only to indicate the historical specificity and interdependence of technical and human development and the possible transformation of objectively communicative action in societies based on a complex social division of labour.

In a general sense, the accumulation and valorization of capital is interrupted not only by the requirement for commodities to have use-value, but by a variety of exogenous factors, including constraints of supply, disappearing credit, negative ecological costs, ageing populations or even the declining 'libidinal energy' of the consumer in late capitalism (Stiegler 2011: 25). Yet beyond these factors, the real limits to the self-expansion of capital lie in the capitalist reproduction scheme itself, for if 'the barrier to the continuation of the capitalist process is *internal to that process*, to its own inner drive for expansion, then it follows that the capitalist process is inherently self-limited so as to drive its own internal transformation' (Harris 1983: 312; emphasis added). But are these barriers to accumulation surmountable, or does some *limit* exist beyond which self-valorization is impossible?

For Marx the contradiction of capitalism begins with the relentless drive of capital to expand through commodity exchange: capital is valorized in production by siphoning off 'surplus value' from workers who sell their labour power below market value; once wages are paid to ensure the physiological reproduction of their labour power, they are obliged to work 'for free' for a (variable) portion of the working day. Excess unpaid labour (socially necessary labour time) is accumulated through the production of commodities with exchange value, sold at a profit to realize the value of the capital invested. In Marx's scheme, capitalist crises result from a tendency towards the *generalized overproduction of commodities*: competition drives capitalists to expand production of exchange values without limit (without respect for the utility of or demand for a commodity), which leads to a tightening of wages and an increase in the ratio of constant capital (machinery, raw materials, energy) to variable capital (labour power) in production. This alteration in the organic composition of capital (the quantity of capital required to fully exploit the labour power of each worker) tendentially reduces the proportion of abstract labour employed in the production process, which in turn reduces the quantity of surplus value generated. The result is a crisis of accumulation, as declining profits discourage entrepreneurs from reinvesting accumulated surplus value in production. As a result, even where unsatisfied demand exists (irrespective of whether this demand is effectively backed by purchasing power), and where essential human needs are unmet, enterprises close, factories stand idle and economies fall quickly into incrementally deeper recessions. Marx theorized this process in broader terms as the tendency of the rate of profit to fall over time as the organic composition of capital increases; and while some Marxists have tried to develop this insight into an 'economic law', the tendency towards falling profitability is best understood as a *potential immanent in the trend towards* increasing organic composition which gradually displaces the *primary* source of surplus value (socially necessary labour) from production in the relentless urge of capital towards self-expansion.

Reflecting the orthodox Marxism of the Second International, Kautsky (1914, 1937) argued that recession is caused by a failure to realize surplus value in the circulation stage: the anarchy of the market (unplanned/uncontrolled production of commodities for profit) leads to a production of exchange values *without limit* and a resultant contraction of wages as a consequence of attempts by firms to remain competitive. Declining wages in turn reduce the purchasing power of workers as consumers, reducing (in the absence of credit) aggregate demand for capitalist goods. This was summarised as the 'chronic inability' of the workforce to buy back the commodities produced in capitalist factories, creating a periodic vicious cycle of factory closures, redundancies, falling demand, impoverishment and unmet needs. This insight – which informed the agenda of the German labour movement in the late nineteenth century, was developed in a different direction by Luxemburg (1913), who observed that in a 'pure' capitalist economy composed of capitalists and proletarians, the expanded reproduction of capital is unfeasible without the addition of 'third consumers' (petty-bourgeoisie, colonial subjects, peasants, artisans) to compensate for inadequate demand. In Luxemburg's scheme, capital reaches barriers to its own self-expansion as demand from these strata is exhausted and a significant portion of society is pauperized. The result, to paraphrase Keynes, is declining *effective* demand, leading to underconsumption and recession, exacerbated by anticompetitive practices of monopoly capital as firms price themselves out of markets. Despite an excess of credit, this erodes the ability of middle-income workers to enjoy the material benefits of compensatory consumption, threatening the welfare of 'aristocracies of labour' with competition from foreign workers in the capitalist periphery.

Alternative Marxist approaches have focused on a range of other factors that inhibit capitalist expansion, leading to crises and recessionary downturns. Famous for his theory of finance capital, Hilferding (1981) argued that in contrast to equilibrium theory, which assumes dogmatically that markets efficiently allocate capital to new or 'dynamic' sectors of the economy, the *anarchy of production* causes booms in some sectors which absorb disproportionate quantities of investment capital. This leads to crises of overproduction in some sectors and underproduction in others, creating an imbalance between the capital goods sector ('Department I') and the consumer goods sector ('Department II'), itself exacerbated by the formation of anticompetitive trusts (cartelization). Hilferding's approach appears less relevant in contemporary capitalist economies which exhibit a far higher level of economic diversification, but as we saw in the previous chapter post-Keynesian economists continue to highlight sectoral imbalance in financialized economies where underinvestment in the 'real' economy is blamed for stagnation, and where financial deregulation is blamed for triggering the recession. Sectoral imbalance is blamed for speculative bubbles, malinvestment and excess debt, while global finance is considered parasitic on 'real' economy of goods and services (Foster & Magdoff 2009). Financialization leads to a massive expansion of credit and financial innovation which create an illusion of wealth supported by fractional reserve banking, accommodative monetary policies and a massive growth in financial market values.

A further group of critical economists seeks to explain the tendency for accumulation crises in theories of profit squeeze and class struggle. Capitalism is prone to crises of valorization due to supply-side constraints caused by insufficient production of surplus value at the M–C stage of production (the transformation of money into capital), and inadequate factors of production (notably labour power), which in different ways act to inhibit investment and limit the expansion of production to meet rising demand. On this view, an overproduction of capital ensues, that is, capital which cannot be valorized. Alternatively, accumulation crises may develop in the production stage, particularly due to class struggle, labour shortages or solidarity between the employed workforce and the 'reserve army' of unemployed workers – an alliance (typically short-lived) which can increase the bargaining power of labour leading to rising wages and declining surplus value. This line of reasoning is advanced by Cleaver, who suggests that

traditional Marxist approaches to the issue of secular crisis need to be explicitly resituated within the fundamental class forces at work at the heart of the system. For example, it is common in many Marxist theories of secular crisis (or of more cyclical crises for that matter) to treat class struggle as one force among others driving (overdetermining) the development of the system toward crisis. They fail to see that if the self-activity of the working class (both negative and positive) is the fundamental force opposing capital's set of rules/constraints on social life, then avoiding fetishism means that the other, supposedly distinct, forces can and must be rethought as particular moments or aspects of the class conflict. (Cleaver 1992: 2)

This reflects the perspective of Bell and Cleaver who see accumulation as the growth of a class relation particular to the capitalist mode of production. Accumulation, they argue, is growth. However,

> expanded reproduction is not simply something added. It is a necessary characteristic of capitalism. The source of this necessity of growth lies in the dynamic of the class struggle itself. Basically it is only through growth that capital can maintain control. (Bell & Cleaver 2002: 23)

Yet while Bell and Cleaver are correct to argue that labour struggles force capital to raise productivity, that new forms of labour organization, surveillance and control are necessary to limit workers' capacity to push up wage costs and thus limit profits, and that growth is a precondition for subduing class struggle, there is evidence to suggest that declining profitability in the global economy exists alongside falling real incomes as inflation reduces demand and workers are collectively disempowered through the political marginalization or active suppression of organized labour, rendering labour struggles essentially *defensive*. This phenomenon can be seen across the capitalist metropole, most obviously in Germany where workers' pay has been stagnant since the late 1990s under a succession of centre-right and centre-left governments (Jones 2016; Springford 2018). Class struggle may help to explain the political strategy of neoliberalism, but the logic of capitalist crisis lies in the accumulation of capital *without* value, a consequence of the displacement of labour power from commodity production rather than a direct outcome of political class struggles.

Accumulation without value

Formal models of capitalist development possess explanatory utility, but for Trenkle the

> empirical foundation of the critique of value in general and the theory of crisis in particular cannot in any way [...] be carried out in a quasi-scientific, mathematized form. Wherever this methodological criterion is applied a priori [...] the concept of value and the entire framework constructed around it is already fundamentally flawed. (1998: 13)

Critical value theory must be concerned therefore with the reified social relations mediated through commodity abstraction. From this perspective, the sphere of commodity production is neither distinct from nor contradictory to the sphere of circulation; it is, rather, *mediated through it*. There is little to be gained from attempts to quantify the precise relation between abstract labour, surplus value and the price of assets in advanced monetary economies based on the expanding role of fictional capital where value is increasingly reproduced and augmented in a complex sphere of circulation and exchange separate from traditional commodity production. Value is irreducible to an 'empirical category that can be positively determined by calculating the number of hours of socially useful labor that are embodied within any particular product' (Larsen et al. 2014: vvii). It follows that naïve attempts to

> found a society on the principle that the price workers should be paid for their labor should justly be determined by its (notionally calculable) value will necessarily reaffirm the fetish on which capitalism is based rather than moving beyond it. (ibid.)

Instead, value-critique stresses the importance of relative surplus value, which, rather than lengthening the working day, allows for a reduction in socially necessary labour through the introduction of new methods of production and the 'real subsumption' of labour – that is, in addition to assuming control of labour processes which exist prior to the capital relation embodied in wage labour, the generation of value in commodity production is fully reorganized internally in response to the functional requirements of capital. As Kurz notes, even if the 'world economy turns into the world-political phenomenon that takes on a dynamic of its own and engenders its own laws, the fundamental economic movement of the accumulation of relative surplus value ultimately remains the determining factor' (Kurz 1986: 45). For Kurz, an increase in accumulation facilitated by relative surplus value 'consists in the increasing tendency of the individual product to lose value – that is, in this interminable process, mediated by competition, of the development of the productive forces, the products decline in value' (ibid.: 46; emphasis added). The implication of this critique is clear: despite an increase in relative surplus value, the displacement of socially necessary labour from commodity production leads to a decline of surplus value, and, irrespective of its precise quantitative measurement, to a tendential decline in the profitability of commodity production.

This value-critical conception of the displacement of human labour as the authentic substance of value is criticized by Brenner (1998), who rejects the thesis of a long-term tendency towards a falling rate of profit as nonsensical in view of the fact that socially necessary labour is quite clearly no longer the unique source of surplus value (profit) in commodity capitalism. Brenner is right to reject simplistic theories of profit-squeeze and underconsumption which directly attribute crises of accumulation to class struggle; and he is correct to stress the generation of value in non-productive contexts. Yet, as Kliman astutely observes, his suggestion that falling profitability is 'intuitively illogical' is itself nonsensical: the tendency for the rate of profit to fall appears to 'fly in the face of common sense'

> because it seems intuitively obvious to many people that a more productive capitalism is a more profitable capitalism. This intuition is reinforced

by the fact that technologically advanced companies are more profitable than backward ones – an individual company does raise its rate of profit by adopting techniques of production that are more advanced than those of its competitors. However, to assume that this implies that the economy-wide rate of profit will also rise when productivity rises throughout the whole economy is a logical error, the fallacy of composition. Here are a couple of analogous cases: if you are in a stadium and you stand up, you can see better; but if everyone stands up at once, you will not all see better. If you get a master's degree, you will get a better job and make more money; but if everyone has a master's degree, you will not all get better jobs and make more money. (Kliman 2012: 15)

This phenomenon is inescapable due to the inevitability of emulation and competition where any gains achieved in productivity by one firm are rapidly universalized across sectors and whole economies such that any hard-won initial advantage is quickly lost. Short-term gains in productivity which enable individual producers to outmanoeuvre their competitors (and reduce the power of labour) are commonplace, yet the gains realized are always lost as incremental changes in the organic composition of capital (the ratio of productive technology to labour power) are generalized societally via diffusion, imitation and improvement. This feature of capitalism may accelerate innovation and improve the quality of commodities, but the impact on profitability (and thus commercial viability) is negative.

The assumption, therefore, that profitability can be sustained in the long term ignores the point that accumulation is based on the extraction of surplus value in relation to socially average labour time. To assume an individual marginal gain in productivity means the 'economy-wide rate of profit' as productivity gains are generalized is thus absurd. As productivity rises, so inevitably more commodities and services can be produced per socially necessary labour-hour. Kliman observes that rising productivity

> does not cause more new value to be created. The same amount of value is 'spread out' among more items, so the increase in productivity causes the values of individual items to decline. In other words, things can be produced more cheaply. And because they can be produced more cheaply, prices tend to fall. (ibid.: 16)

Hence the law of the tendency of the rate of profit to fall should be understood as an indirect rather than proximate cause of capitalist crises, one which creates the structural conditions for downturns. This is necessarily the case, for

> if a fall in the rate of profit has led to an average rate of profit that is relatively low, many more low-profitability businesses will find themselves in serious trouble, because their rates of profit are now less than the minimum needed in order to survive. (ibid.: 17)

From this perspective an already unprofitable economy will be more susceptible to economic downturn and more firms and households will go bankrupt, increasing the probability of new deflationary crises linked to falling asset values. Low interest rates and monetary easing may sustain the illusion of stability in the short term, but it is only the availability of cheap credit that allows the system to continue expanding in the absence of new sources of value.

While it is instructive to theorize long-term cycles of capitalist development, writers like Brenner, whose formal-analytical approach entails the adaptation of equilibrium theory from orthodox economics, rehearse errors in the theory of overproduction which fail to comprehend that the contemporary crisis – as Clarke observed two decades ago – is not just a crisis of manufacturing production but a crisis of capital, that is, 'of the production, appropriation and realisation of surplus value' (Clarke 1999: 5). Downturns may be affected by a glut of investment in fixed capital and overproduction, yet the tendency towards overaccumulation is inherent in the self-expanding logic of the value form itself, which, quite regardless of the subjective motivational states of individual capitalists, must continually overcome barriers to its own self-expansion, facilitated by the growth of credit money to sustain investment, leveraged buy-outs, oligopolistic practices and financialization, as well as to overcome the inevitable gap arising between the oversupply of new goods and services in a consumer boom and long-term effective demand for them (Suarez-Villa 2015). In addition, the growth of credit reflects the disproportionality between fixed capital and the diminishing quantity of socially necessary labour as the organic composition of capital increases, introducing new technologies into the process of production (Kurz 1995: 7). Commodity-producing capital, argues Kurz, 'vampirizes' its own future,

> prolonging its life on a meta-level beyond its now-visible internal limit. This mechanism only functions as long as the mode of production continues to expand [...] and only to the extent that the fictitiously anticipated mass of future value is effectively realized. (ibid.: 8)

As we shall see in more detail in Chapter 4, in modern monetary economies the historically critical form of capitalist money is not state-issued fiat currency, but interest-bearing capital (financial market money derived from deposits) traded in financial and currency markets, as a result of which socially necessary labour largely disappears into an abstract 'form without a content' (Kurz 1995: 3). This quantity of 'form without content' – driven by financial innovation and the growth of nominal market values with 'no expression outside circulation' (Bryan & Rafferty 2010: 113), expands without explanation, creating the appearance of a direct movement of M–M' (money augmenting itself) in place of the traditional reproduction scheme M–C–M' (money augmented through its assumption of the form of a commodity). Which is to say: a new sequence of valorization based on the self-augmentation of money substitutes itself for the traditional sequence money → commodity → augmented money (M–C–M′). In contrast to simple commodity exchange, where money plays a functional role as a universal equivalent mediating between buyers and sellers – a stage along the way towards the final goal of consumption, in a credit-based modern monetary economy 'money and capital markets can be seen as commodity-producing markets. For the commodity money capital, the market is not only an instance of realization, but simultaneously its sphere of production' (Lohoff 2014: 33).[6] The securities and derivatives which facilitate the growth of fictitious capital in financial markets 'deconstruct' money into its constituent attributes and commodify value, giving value a specific materiality 'not in terms of what it symbolically represents, but in terms of what it, itself, is and does' (Bryan & Rafferty 2010: 107).

The growth of financial derivatives permits 'replication (unbundling and rebundling) of security payoffs and hence the commodification of the "risks" associated with the ownership over capital' (Sotiropoulos et al. 2013: 54). But that which can be commodified, the authors add, can also be priced, which reveals the dynamic role of finance as a technology of power, which organizes capitalist power relations through risk management in deregulated markets, which in turn limits resistance from labour (ibid.: 54). Yet the continual expansion of fictitious value in the financial markets also necessitates continuously expanding liquidity, which calls into play the state circuits of capital connecting banking and public finance:

> this is precisely the fundamental contradiction of contemporary capitalism. The rise of finance makes capitalist exploitation more effective but heavily reliant on market liquidity. When the latter evaporates, the whole setting quickly becomes deranged. In other words, the demand for more discipline for the capitalist power relations makes the economic milieu more vulnerable and fragile. This is an unavoidable trade-off, the root of the financial instability of our contemporary capitalist societies. (ibid.)

The result of financialization is that interest-yielding capital becomes separated from the real process of valorization, resulting in 'disembodied M–M′ – making money from money itself in a sterile "zero-sum" transfer payment' (Hudson 2010: 8). Fictitious capital is therefore money disconnected from labour where 'there is no longer even the appearance of real commodity production', and where the logic of the sequence M–M′ 'grows so strong that compared to the speculative increase in the value of stocks, real dividends are insignificant' (Kurz 1995: 4). This results in a situation where the ratio of asset prices to profits 'grows entirely out of all proportion […] speculative bubbles, the fruit of the fictitious increase in value of titles to property, witnessed on innumerable occasions in capitalist history, always and inevitably terminate in a great financial crash' (ibid.).

Clarke notes that credit has the 'magical power of suspending altogether the barriers to the accumulation of capital, providing finance for new ventures, and sustaining unprofitable capitalists through periods of difficulty. The only limit to accumulation appears to be the availability of credit' (1999: 9). Credit booms end as debt spirals out of control – extending to a fiscal crisis in the state circuit of capital caused by the socialization of private losses to government – not just from failing banks but from industrial concerns – as witnessed with the insolvency of the UK construction firm Carillion in 2017.[7] Yet financialization facilitates cooperation between capitalists and the expansion of markets beyond previously given limits by aggregating savings, structured deposits and debt instruments through securitization. 'Whatever triggers the crash', argues Clarke,

> it will gain momentum as the contraction of credit precipitates defaults that spread through the financial and productive system in a destructive spiral. In the crisis the overaccumulation of capital suddenly appears in the form of a mass of worthless debt and an enormous overproduction of commodities, leading to the massive devaluation of productive capital and destruction of productive capacity, and an enormous increase in the reserve army of labour, in a cumulative spiral which will only be checked when the conditions for profitable accumulation have been restored. (ibid.: 10)

The question is whether this constitutes a secular process of boom/bust, as orthodox and heterodox economists assume, or whether the deepening crisis of neoliberalism – which has its roots in the failure of Western economies to recover adequately from the accumulation crisis of the 1970s (Kliman 2012) – indicates the moribund state of capitalism after the new technology boom of the late 1990s and the 'exuberance' of the financial markets prior to 2008. This leads to a further question, namely, whether potential sources of (fictitious or non-fictitious) value exist which can be valorized adequately through the production of new commodities with a universal use-value adequate to sustain the consumption necessary to reproduce financialized economies founded on 'endless competitive maximization of profit' (Haiven 2014: 3; cf. Hudson 2014). Or, are we witnessing the self-annihilation of the commodity form through a growing disconnection between socially necessary labour and value as a result of planned obsolescence and 'total disposability', where constant supersession of products, technologies and media forms is presented as economic 'improvement' rather than a marketing tool to keep consumers in a general state of dissatisfaction and indebtedness? (Tischleder & Wasserman 2015).[8]

Financialization, and the production of fictitious capital based on the appropriation and valorization of future value, recreates capitalist societies through the destruction and transformation of social forms and social relations by the disciplinary mechanism of finance. As we have seen, financialization is not a historical aberration but a core element of capitalist accumulation relative to a specific stage of development of global capital – which is to say, a mechanism through which structural contradictions of capital are displaced, extending and expanding the reach of money as interest-bearing capital into the lives of ordinary individuals as consumers/debtors. The so-called 'transformation problem' in Marxian political economy (the absence of a direct quantitative link between socially necessary labour time and prices) may not in fact be a problem after all but simply a *dialectical heuristic*: 'It is not a flaw in Marx's logic that leads to the irreconcilability of real value and price', argues Haiven, 'it is that these two are *never* reconciled under capitalism' (Haiven 2015: 30):

> The reasons why capital never accurately measures the value of labour as embodied in commodities are varied, but one key reason is the tremendous influence of finance and banking over the value and quantity of money. At no moment has finance failed to produce fictitious capital – that is, freely circulating claims to future surplus value that *act* as money and so distort the ideal capitalist economy. The result is that, for this and other reasons, there is always more capital than value to which it has a claim, and this excess fictitious capital, while to a certain extent necessary to overcome certain crises in capitalist economies, fundamentally and essentially skews capital's reckoning of value. [...] capital consistently mis-imagines [sic] value. Price is an inherently flawed means of measuring underlying value. (ibid.)

Financial crises thus occur as the disconnection between fictitious capital and the 'real value it claims to represent becomes too great' (ibid.: 31). The term 'fictitious' should be understood here to denote 'imaginary' *only* in the sense that finance makes possible a generalized myth of rising wealth among ordinary individuals incorporated into the spectacle of commodity capitalism through their own performance of reified market relations.

Productive and unproductive labour

Financialization is thus not the cause of the present crisis but a symptom of it – of the growing dependence of productive capital on the expansion of interest-bearing capital to compensate for the declining substance of productive labour in the valorization of capital and the tendency of the rate of profit to fall over time. Before examining the evolution of modern monetary economies in Chapter 4, it will be useful to consider briefly the distinction between productive and unproductive labour for valorization in advanced capitalism as traditional forms of commodity production are overshadowed by tertiary economic-technical processes which attempt to realize an equivalent (or higher) rate of surplus value from a declining quantity of socially necessary labour. Just as secondary circuits of the state form of capital (expansion of the public sector) were necessary in the twentieth century to compensate for the 'asocial sociality' of commodity society and render labour power 'fully accessible to the market' through the provision of vital health, education and welfare services at non-market prices (Lohoff 2009), so continued reproduction of the productive form of socially necessary labour that drives the process of valorization remains essential to compensate for the growing proportion of unproductive labour in advanced economies dominated by tertiarization, finance and speculative investment. Following the crisis of Fordism which undermined the viability of state-democratic capitalism in the 1970s, the share of productive labour in the creation and valorization of value has been in decline – masked, if not entirely concealed, by a diminished welfare system oriented no longer towards a reproduction of socially necessary labour but towards the management of social distress and exclusion (ibid.). It is here, argues Lohoff, that we can see most clearly the financial logic of fictitious capital as *stealing value from the future*, a feat made possible via the 'profitable utilization of future labor' to serve as a 'substitute fuel for the flagging exploitation of actual, present-tense labor [keeping] the valorization machine running and, in appearance, moving forward' (ibid.).

In what sense, however, is labour 'productive' or 'unproductive', and why is this distinction critical for the profitability and viability of commodity society? First, the term *productive* does not mean 'material' or 'concrete' as such, specifying the unique quality of creating physical objects. Rather, productive labour is simply labour that makes possible the valorization of capital through the creation of revenue over and above the cost for the employer of purchasing labour power – in other words, labour which generates surplus value and hence profit. Unproductive labour, on the other hand, is labour which,

> although carried out in exchange for monetary remuneration and within the context of money-oriented reproduction, [...] does not itself produce commodities (that is, it does not as such take part in the production of commodities), or when the quasi-products it creates assume only a formal and insubstantial commodity character. (Kurz 1995: 10)

It is not the physical use of productive labour or its products which matters, then, but its role in the reproduction of the commodity form, which in turn constitutes the most primary structural condition for the reproduction of capitalist society. Unproductive labour is not valueless in a commercial sense, only unproductive when considered in isolation from socially necessary productive labour:

> On the plane of the particular capital, the unproductive character of this kind of labor does not manifest itself in an absolute ('in itself') sense, but only relatively, insofar as the 'overhead costs' of an enterprise can appear as a substantial production of commodities or services on the part of a second enterprise, which specializes in providing them to other enterprises (a firm, for example, which employs janitorial personnel and offers this 'janitorial product' to other firms). From the point of view of the commercial economy, the labor of cleaning, unproductive in an auto factory, constitutes in turn the productive labor of the janitorial company, and thus enters into its substantial commodity production, while the labor of the accountants in the cleaning company forms part of its unproductive 'overhead costs'. It is possible, however, that a third firm would carry out the accounting for every kind

of enterprise, this being the specialized commodity-service which it offers: in this case, for the providers of these specialized services, even accounting itself becomes productive labor in the commercial sense. (ibid.: 11)

In a general societal sense, however, this process of tertiarization – which displaces older forms of private commodity capitalism by dispersing non-productive labour functions across extended commodity chains, is commercially significant because it represents a *subtraction from total surplus value*. Unproductive labour is categorized as such precisely 'because it does nothing but mediate commodity-money relations, without itself being a substantial production of commodities' (ibid.). It is subsidiary to productive labour *not* because it is unworthy or irrelevant commercially (as some critics of Marxian theory assert), but because its 'products (as well as its reproduction costs) return to the capital accumulation process', and because this consumption of productive labour 'is recovered again in expanded reproduction' (ibid.: 13).

This leads Kurz to the conclusion that capitalism is only

> possible if a sufficiently expanding part (which grows with capital accumulation) of 'employment' is capable of producing [...] a self-mediated identity of 'productive consumption', in which the production and consumption of value interact, so as to make the fetish-form and the fetish substance sufficiently coincide in amplitude market. (ibid.)

He concedes that Luxemburg touched on this theme in her own discussion of 'third consumers' who compensate for inadequate demand (but whose economic means exist outside the immediate context of the real productive reproduction of capital). Yet Luxemburg failed to note that the

> limit of capital might consist in the very fact that its dynamic creates an increasing number of unproductive sectors and 'third persons', whose revenues and consumption become a growing burden which the reproduction of capital will ultimately be unable to support. (ibid.: 14)

The accelerated growth of fictitious capital in finance becomes necessary to offset the atrophy of commodity capitalism by countering a negative drainage of value imposed by the growing proportion of the labour force whose economic utility lies largely or exclusively in mediating commodity-money relations, and whose own contribution to the valorization of capital is overshadowed by the increasing centrality of advanced technology in the advanced societies – which in itself has done remarkably little to remedy the 'fundamental systemic dysfunction of over-accumulation' (Lohoff & Trenkle 2013; Suarez-Villa 2015: 94). Financialization thus facilitates the development of markets beyond preconceived limits; and derivative values, in a system founded on credit, dramatically supersede (but do not entirely replace) the traditional dependence on state circuits of capital to facilitate deficit spending and the absorption (through infrastructural spending, defence and securitization) of accumulated surplus capital which cannot be invested profitably. This can be seen in the unproductive growth of security as a feature of contemporary capitalism, which highlights the *'complicity* between security and capital, a complicity in which the security state and security industry collide and collude in a mutual bid to reinforce a political agenda structured ideologically around the security fetish' (Neocleous 2008: 144).

Financialization is thus a reflexive symptom of the inner contradiction in the value form which creates a tendency for the rate of profit to fall, leading to a search for new sources of value in non-labour-intensive tertiary and financial sectors, a further increase in the proportion of productive capital per unit of labour, and the offshoring of production from core to peripheral economies. This is made possible not only by the relocation of factories but by the emergence of 'postnational' forms of contemporary mobility featuring 'de-localized virtual environments enabling information, money, trades, images, connections and objects to move digitally as well as physically [...]' (Urry 2014: 9). It is not simply the diversion of capital from productive investment towards 'parasitic finance' or 'casino capitalism' which causes the rate of profit to fall – as critics of neoliberal 'excess' insist (Hudson 2010, 2014; Lapavitsas 2013), but the decline of productive employment in relation to the accumulation and valorization of fictitious capital, which is in turn linked to the revolution in digital communications technology and the valorization crisis caused by the acceleration of 'planned' obsolescence in advanced consumer economies (Kliman 2012: 123; cf. Tischleder & Wasserman 2015). For Marx, *accumulation of capital is equivalent to the growth of the labour force*, until the decline in full employment leads to recession which produces greater slack in labour markets (cf. Cockshott 2013: 324). The outcome of stagnation and slow growth in productive employment is *accumulation without value*, where opportunities for the realization of profits decline and capital seeks respite or immediate gains through high-risk investment and rent-seeking. Although the advanced economies expanded rapidly in the decade prior to 2007 (despite growing instability in the financial system), the long-term economic trend has been one of stagnation and decline.

For Kliman, the tendency of the rate of profit to fall is likened to an 'increase in the ratio of advanced capital to employee compensation' (2012: 128). Using the US economy as an example, he finds that the technical and organic composition of capital have risen consistently since the 1940s – on average 1.5 per cent per annum, in contrast with the value composition of capital (average 0.1 per cent per annum since the 1960s) (ibid.: 133). This evidence is consistent with Marx's general theory of accumulation, but it does not necessarily verify the existence of a universally applicable theory of the falling rate of profit. What can be said, however, is that the

> rate of profit that existed at the start of the post-war boom fell, and had to fall, because it was unsustainably high. And it was unsustainably high because, throughout the entire six decades that followed, the rate of return on new investments [...] was too low to allow it to be sustained. (ibid.: 136)

This, he suggests, is hardly surprising: 'the rate of profit fell because new investments of capital failed to generate enough additional employment of living labour to sustain the rate of profit at its current level' (ibid.: 138). This trend reflects the depreciation of capital assets and the growing obsolescence of commodities produced by communications technology which have made it increasingly difficult for firms to realize and sustain a profitable accumulation of capital value.

Conclusion

Marx did not argue that a falling rate of profit would lead directly to collapse, only that the intensified competition and productivity of capitalism would indirectly and inexorably weaken the capitalist mode of production as a system for generating and valorizing surplus value as the organic composition of capital led to the growing displacement of labour from the production of surplus value. This trend is a major feature of the present stage of capitalism, as automation, robotization and artificial intelligence (AI) presage a structural crisis of technological displacement through continual innovations and new technologies which replace productive labour. As Collins (2013) observes, the accelerating technical composition of capital through the application of automation and artificial intelligence is displacing not only productive labour from the generation of surplus value, but is also eliminating a wide range of skilled administrative labour functions, indicating the growing redundancy of the tertiary service class as a key sector of employment among intermediate strata in the advanced economies. Opportunities for the redeployment of this army of white-collar workers are blocked for several reasons, notably:

1. New technology does not create sufficient new jobs in new sectors of the economy to absorb redundant workers from other sectors;
2. New markets for expansion are declining: the limits of the capitalist periphery are being reached rapidly, as communications technology is spreading cultural capital globally, undermining skilled labour functions;
3. Financialized capitalism is unstable and the prosperity illusion it creates will not compensate for the structural displacement of skilled labour: not everyone can be a networked entrepreneur; technological displacement will eventually limit employment opportunities in the financial sector itself;
4. Public sector employment is in sharp decline with the fiscal crisis of the state caused by neoliberal austerity politics; and
5. Education as insurance against unemployment is no longer affordable or viable due to credential inflation, though education itself employs and preoccupies a large number of people who would otherwise look for skilled jobs, and government subsidization of education is therefore a form of hidden Keynesianism. (Collins 2013: 39)

While the technological leap forward of the 1990s prepared the ground for a 'third' industrial revolution or 'information age', simultaneously displacing living skilled labour power from production and accelerating the accumulation of fictitious value, this breakneck development of productive forces induced a metaphorical 'heart attack' in advanced capitalist economies leading to a massive overaccumulation and eventual devaluation of fictional monetary assets (Kurz 1995, 2012; Lohoff and Trenkle 2013).

Yet automation and digitization are understood as primarily beneficial for advanced capitalist economies due to cost savings implicit in the elimination of routine labour functions. To read confident predictions of the 'tech invasion' in mainstream corporate media is to experience the full force of this delusion as self-proclaimed entrepreneurial visionaries forecast a future of subsidized consumption in fully-automated societies. Although automation may bring benefits (abolishing, for example, certain degrading or stressful forms of physical labour), the accelerated process of digitization also dramatically undermines social cohesion in advanced economies based on credentialism, social mobility and the capacity of individual subjects to consume and acquire debt – activities which in turn depend on access to skilled employment and the material rewards this brings. As one recent OECD report concludes, while young unskilled workers are those most at risk of economic redundancy as we approach 2020, as many as 14 per cent of skilled labour functions are likely to disappear in the next decade as the range of tasks which robots and AI cannot do 'shrinks rapidly' (OECD 2018: 1). A similar report published by PWC (2017) predicts that more than 30 per cent of jobs are likely to be lost to automation in the UK. This would stimulate productivity in certain sectors but would simultaneously increase inequality and condemn millions of citizens to economic marginalization and poverty. According to PWC, automation will eliminate employment opportunities in three waves:

1. An 'algorithmic wave' (early 2020s) based on automation of simple computational tasks and data analysis;
2. An 'augmentation wave' (late 2020s) characterized by 'dynamic interaction with technology for clerical support and decision making';
3. An 'autonomous wave' (into the mid-2030s) featuring 'automation of physical labour and manual dexterity', and 'problem solving in dynamic real-world situations that require responsive actions, such as in transport and construction'. (PWC 2017: 2)

In this brave new world, the threat of profit squeeze presented by rising labour costs might hypothetically be reduced or temporarily overcome, but this gain would come at the price of displacing the *real* substance of value in commodity production, namely, productive labour – even if a higher proportion of capital value can now be generated in the sphere of circulation and through the exploitation of intangible assets in the 'knowledge economy'.

Entrepreneurial visionaries typically predict a post-material future for capital where value is extracted from data, ideas, information and culture. In the new 'knowledge economy', it is claimed, value will be derived more intensively from *immaterial* labour – which is to say, intellectual labour that provides informational and creative content for new commodities. This perspective is shared (for different reasons) by post-Marxists such as Lazzarato (1996) and Hardt and Negri (2000), who erroneously accord subjective autonomy to 'emancipated' workers with new-found powers over information flows and ideas in post-Fordist societies. On this view, 'immaterial' labour requires new subjective skills distinct from conventional labour functions in manufacturing (reduced to machine operation and surveillance). But while it is obvious that the *concrete* nature of work evolves to include more ideational/creative labour functions in the production of intangible commodities, it is a fallacy to assume that, with the eclipse of Fordism, changes in the materiality of production obviate the requirement for average socially necessary labour time to valorize the capital invested in commercial enterprises. It is also a fallacy to believe such changes necessarily bring in their wake new and progressive forms of social and political organization in 'knowledge-based' economies where, as a result of automation and AI, workers gain more control over the labour process and/or more free time to engage in critical praxis. And, finally, it is a fallacy to believe that these emancipated forms of labour will conjure into being a new and revolutionary form of productive labour to compensate for the rising organic composition of capital which drives the tendency of the rate of profit to fall over time.

Labour is if course never *actually* immaterial for it is not the 'content of labour but its commodity form that gives "weight" to an object or idea in a market economy. Its physicality or otherwise is wholly irrelevant' (Thompson 2005: 41). As Amorim correctly observes, 'all human activity, whether under capitalism or other production forms, depends to some degree on intellectual labour', and the notion of immaterial labour is based on a conflation of the materiality of labour with its physical form (2014: 93, 95). In Marx's theory of labour, he notes,

> all human activity is a process of objectification of human subjectivity, that is, of putting oneself in the world, in a repeated historically-determined synthesis, theoretically fracturing any methodological duality between subject and object. [...M]anual and intellectual labour are concepts that express a contradictory reality. In terms of an analytical process of conceptual determinations, they allow a dialectical analysis of living labour, which is done by taking into account the predominance of manual or intellectual activities depending on the way they appear. (ibid.)

Amorim makes the additional point that it is capital *itself* which promotes the 'proliferation of professional qualifications' required in knowledge economies where the

> intrinsic character of labour *as labour* is not constituted by [...] particularities but by common characteristics. Marx called this common element, which is present in all labour in capitalist society, *abstract labour*, defining this as the average working time socially necessary for the production of commodities. (ibid.: 94)

To enforce a qualitative distinction between 'crude' manual and 'creative' immaterial labour is thus to resort to a vulgar theory of political economy which, in the final analysis, 'detaches the production of intangible commodities from the forms of production that are typically capitalist (ibid.).

Clearly, the historic confluence of high-tech capitalism and the expansion of fictitious capital associated with financialization has allowed advanced economies to temporarily conceal stagnation and evade some of the more painful consequences of economic restructuring. For emerging economies in Asia and elsewhere in the periphery, on the other hand, the new technology boom of the 1990s stimulated economic growth while creating new forms of labour exploitation and new forms of accumulation by dispossession which enable value to be exported to metropolitan economies while reproducing global economic dependency in underdeveloped nations such as India where routinized ICT jobs outsourced from Europe and North America comprise a major form of employment. The development of global value chains in the information economy has also been accompanied by new forms of de facto slavery in commodity-producing economies of Africa which supply raw materials and labour for the ITC and telecommunications sector (Fuchs 2014). While many routine ITC jobs have been abolished in core economies, allowing technology firms in California to concentrate on brand identity and product development, key stages of the labour process in the 'knowledge economy' have simply been offshored to peripheral economies integrated with the capitalist metropole through global value chains where precarious and/or dangerous forms of labour are socially and politically tolerated. As Amorim observes, the majority of ITC-related jobs outsourced to peripheral nations like Brazil are characterized by 'precarious contracts with poor working conditions and high rates of staff turnover. In relation to their scope for creativity or control over their labour processes, there is little or no difference between these workers and Fordist workers' (Amorim 2014: 96).

In a hypothetical society without human needs, capital could reduce to a minimum or even eliminate the time spent in the sphere of circulation entirely, and thus eliminate the time wasted outside production. Yet the capitalist mode of production cannot exist as a 'bourgeois utopia' of seamless valorization in the absence of non-commodity social supports and mass popular consumption of commodities with universal use-value (Westra 2010). As Marx argued:

> Capital exists as capital only in so far as it passes through the phases of circulation, the various moments of its transformation, in order to be able to begin the production process anew, and these phases are themselves phases of its realization – but at the same time [...] of its *devaluation*. As long as capital remains frozen in the form of the finished product, it cannot be active as capital, it is *negated* capital. (Marx 1973: 546)

Nevertheless, as we have seen, to exist as a purely fictitious magnitude divorced from concrete economic processes, capital is reduced to a self-valorizing value without the utility obtained through the exchange of commodities with universal use-value; it becomes, in effect, a self-expanding value *pure propter* – a 'pure' quantity of value existing for its own sake, detached from material wealth. As opportunities for *profitable* accumulation diminish, and as the ratio of productive to unproductive labour shrinks, the power of interest-bearing capital over economic systems grows exponentially through the self-expanding growth of fictitious financial values which are continually threatened by the spectre of devaluation.

Lohoff and Trenkle (2013) attempt to answer the question of capital's limits by examining the relative role of fictitious capital in the economic history of capitalist development. In contrast with the industrial revolution and the Fordist age, when the functional importance of financial investment to the development of an advanced industrial infrastructure was critical yet strictly limited, through the anticipation of future value finance has become an *essential* 'motor of accumulation' in advanced economies. In the absence of avenues for productive investment outside the 'fire-insurance-real-estate' economy, fictitious value is vulnerable to devaluation pressures and shocks which threaten to undermine this motor of accumulation at precisely the moment when automation, digitization and artificial intelligence are replacing human productive labour. At the same time, public finances are threatened by the transfer of devalued assets from corporate balance sheets to the state circuits of capital, while the escalating magnitude of private and public debt is dependent on a continual expansion of new credit money and maintenance of low or negative interest rates. In this respect, the escalation of the crisis in 2008 was a truly explosive moment, one which revealed not only a structural crisis in the valorization of capital but also the defective form of fictitious capital as a motor of accumulation based on the anticipation and capture of future value. This expansion of fictitious capital was necessary not only to sustain an illusion of growth but to temporarily restore employment to pre-crisis levels – as occurred after the stock market collapse of 1987 and dot-com crash of 2001 (Palley 2013b). Yet as Stiegler (2011) notes, the consumer model upon which capital presently depends is itself no longer sustainable; and, while systemic collapse has been averted through central bank activism, the continual expansion of new debt since 2008 indicates not only the exhaustion of the 'libidinal economy' of hyperconsumerism in the advanced economies but the escalating risk of devaluation inherent in the accumulation of capital without value.

As we shall see in Part II, a potential solution to the crisis lies in the development of *financial socialism*: to compensate for the impact of declining surplus value and the logic of exchange-value based on the competitive overproduction of commodities for profit, monetary and political elites will be forced to limit systemic risk through capital controls and restrictions on the preservation of wealth outside banks. This amounts to the use of financial repression, where banks become

> vehicles that allow governments to squeeze more indirect tax revenue from citizens by monopolizing the entire savings and payments system, not simply currency. [...] This allows the government to finance a part of its debt at a very low interest rate. (Reinhardt & Rogoff 2009: 143)

Financial repression may also be used to prevent investors indulging a preference for liquidity (where yields are low increasing demand for cash and other 'liquid' assets whose value can be realized quickly) and divert investment from highly liquid assets into bond markets to stabilize the edifice of leveraged value. This consideration has informed government policy in advanced economies since the global financial crisis, namely to control the bond markets through expansionary monetary policies (low interest rates/quantitative easing), creating a 'risk-free' rate of return and a baseline against which other asset classes can be valued. This has led to an expansion of secondary price bubbles in the equities, commodities and real estate markets, leading in turn to unstable price bubbles in the tertiary sphere of 'free money' trading, including volatility-linked trading strategies which constitute 'one corner of a complex and expanding "volatility ecosystem" that has evolved over the past decade' (Wigglesworth 2018: 1). If financial repression is intensified in the interests of maintaining the status quo, this suggests that a coercive form of *postliberal* capitalism could be sustained in a suboptimal state through a continual expansion of the capitalist credit system, although 'growth' would no longer be linked to human development or 'creative destruction' of overaccumulated capital. Stability would be achieved at a high cost, however, for productive investment would be entirely superseded by rent-seeking and oligarchy. A provisional stabilization of postliberal capitalism might thus be possible *without* a catastrophic devaluation of capital value in the manner of previous recessions like the early 1980s, when market collapse created opportunities for new investment and innovation to compensate for the tendency of the rate of profit to fall. As we shall see in Chapter 4, however, this may be feasible only if we assume a change in the form of capitalist money as a means to stabilize dysfunctional accumulation regimes; and this begs the question whether a market economy based on financial repression is possible without a significant change in the political-ideological form of capitalism itself.

Notes

1 For a critical survey of competing schools in Marxism, see Kołakowski (1978).
2 $1.4 quadrillion is *ten* times the value of global GDP. For a systematic visual representation of the value of financial assets in the global economy (date = 2017), see money. visualcapitalist.com.
3 On parallels between Japan after the collapse of its property bubble in the 1990s and the US after the collapse of its sub-prime bubble in 2007, see Koo (2015). Koo observes that unlike after previous recessions, when increased liquidity (expansion of the monetary base through central bank bond purchases) was accompanied by equivalent increases in the money supply and bank lending, after 2008 this failed to occur, retarding any stimulus effect. This paradox, and its relevance for the argument of the present text, is discussed in more detail in Chapter 4.
4 This insight provides the starting point for the critical-realist epistemological distinction between transitive and intransitive knowledge, examined in depth by Bhaskar (1975).
5 'Real' subsumption of labour indicates the subordination of labour to a process of production materially shaped by capital, that is, by the sole and exclusive aim of

realizing surplus value, rather than merely the production of simple commodities. Marx observed that capital cannot expand confined within the limited framework it finds in already existing productive processes: a *real* capitalist labour process can only be achieved/organized by capital itself.

6 'Bei den Geld- und Kapitalmärkten handelt es sich dagegen um Warenerzeugende Märkte. Für die Ware Geldkapital ist der Markt also nicht nur Realisationsinstanz, sondern zugleich ihre Produktionssphäre Aber nicht nur ihre Geburt verschiebt sich bei der Ware Geldkapital in die Zirkulation hinein, sondern auch ihr Tod'.

7 See Chapter 5.

8 On the development of consumer ideologies in the US, Germany and Japan, see the collected essays in Berghoff and Spiekermann (2012).

PART II
Financial socialism

4

ACCUMULATION AND MONETARY POWER IN POSTLIBERAL CAPITALISM

Introduction

To understand the logic of postliberal capitalism in a period of deepening economic stagnation, it is necessary to investigate the phenomenology of capitalist money and identify more clearly the changing forms of commodity money, fiat money and financial market money as bearers of value and means of exchange in the advanced economies. In Marxian theory, capital is understood as 'money in perpetual motion', facilitated through an expansion of the sphere of circulation as an integral moment in the expanded reproduction of total social capital. Central to this socioeconomic formation is the state form of capital itself, which issues currency on the basis of 'arbitrary specification of quantity' (Lapavitsas 2000), providing a material basis for valueless fiat-backed credit money characteristic of advanced capitalist economies. But while statist theories of money are correct to highlight the apparently infinite elasticity of fiat currency in the present epoch (and the logical imperative of accommodative monetary policies), and although the value of capitalist money is determined by its de facto acceptance and function as a unit of account, means of exchange and store of value, statist theories of money in heterodox economics are vulnerable to critique from both Austrian and Marxian economics. A consequence of financialization in the advanced economies is the rapid expansion of interest-bearing capital in the form of financial market derivatives and other forms of fictitious capital, the growth of which raises serious questions concerning the structural interrelation between *sovereign* fiat money and *private* bank money created endogenously in capitalist economies.

To identify potential barriers to the growth of interest-bearing capital in capitalism – and the capacity of capitalist money to expand indefinitely – it is essential furthermore to examine the phenomenological development of these twin dimensions of the money form of capital as they mutually condition each other through the intermediary structures of state and market. On the one hand, it is evident that a logical consequence of state-issued 'elastic' money will be further government economic centralization – the increased nationalization of money and credit and the effective takeover of private financial institutions by central banks using draconian forms of intervention (Schlichter 2014: 221). This will certainly increase the tendency towards financial socialism as governments seek to acquire still more drastic powers to stabilize the financial and monetary system in periods of market turbulence. On the other hand, however, it is clear that statist approaches like modern money theory fail to account for the multiple ways in which pre-existing categories of money and money creation are *themselves* transformed by capital (Jessop 2013: 249–251), placing in question the real source of monetary sovereignty in advanced economies.

Here it is useful to recall that capitalism is a dynamic historical formation in which categories and concepts used to explain commodity society are *themselves* subject to continual modification by the contradictory development of the value form itself: the self-expanding logic of capital is determined by systematic properties and historical contingencies, and the categories used to explain capitalist development are subject to continual redefinition in response to changes in the material basis of commodity-determined societies. Once the creation of money from money becomes the defining feature of capitalist economies,

> attempts to comprehend generalized commodity production as a system designed to meet human needs must be abandoned. The valorization imperative – money must beget money! – is the dominant principle of this system, and the satisfaction of human needs occurs only in so far as it is compatible with this dictate. (Smith 2003: 25)

Recognition of this feature of capital necessarily modifies our perception of the real nature of 'market society', placing in question supply- and demand-based notions of production, consumption, growth and contraction. A critical social science must be alert to categorial complexity and must recognize the epistemological limits of established paradigms – including formalistic models favoured by neoclassical economics discussed in Chapter 1. From a critical-realist perspective, social science comprises an extensive body of transitive knowledge (*Wissenschaft*) which transcends specific sociohistorical conditions, *and* a temporally constituted mode of intellectual production using empirical and analytical methods to identify underlying structural features and interconnections in capitalist society. These dimensions are mutually determining, and the application of dialectical reason to understand the systematic properties and historical dynamics of capitalism can seem like trying to board a moving train: capital is a 'totality in motion', and it is essential to reject the ahistorical bias and unreflective craving for conceptual stability of conventional social science (cf. Ollman 2015).

Our second task is to investigate the limits of fictitious capital in the reproduction of total social capital, and the complex forms of commodity exchange,
derivatives and futures trading which allow investment banks and hedge funds
to trade *exposure* to the performance of assets (or liabilities) without trading the
underlying asset (Bryan & Rafferty 2014), and which facilitate capital accumulation in financialized market economies. Any investigation into the future of
capitalism which seeks to identify the putative barriers or limits to capital must
account for the resilience of the value form as a material basis for the objective
structure of economic domination in commodity-determined societies based
on the appropriation of socially necessary abstract labour *and* the extension of
production into the circulation process. The self-expanding logic of interest-
bearing capital is sustained not only through labour intensification or the expansion of global markets, but through the extended reproduction of value in the
disembodied forms of fictitious capital that constitutes financial market money
('commodity money'), which in turn provides the liquidity necessary for high-
volume computerized trading in the financial markets and to synthesize incommensurable systems of value (Bryan & Rafferty 2003, 2006a). This disembodied
bearer of value, supported by state-issued fiat money created *ex nihilo*, is a specific
articulation of monetary abstraction in advanced capitalism. It assumes additional significance in financialized economies that depend disproportionally on
the appropriation of *future* value to sustain *present* accumulation. Anticipating the
discussion in Chapters 5 and 6, our purpose in what follows is to consider the
implications of monetary abstraction for the structural development of financial
socialism, an accumulation regime that depends on the survival of systemically
important banks (G-SIFIs) whose security and monetary power as the nerve
centre of the international monetary system is organized in accordance with new
macroprudential regulations introduced by G20 economies since 2009.

Before assessing the evolution of money in capitalist economies it is first
necessary to examine the specific character of the capitalist credit money system, which exists to overcome barriers to the continual self-expansion of value.
Ingham (2004a) argues that in capitalism the debt of central banks is turned into
legal tender, for the payment of all other debts. There is also a hierarchy of debt,
with central bank debt (which doesn't have to be repaid) at its base:

> In a capitalist economy, money is essentially legal tender issued by the cen-
> tral bank. [...] It is the fact of being declared legal tender that makes money
> a store of value, and hence a form of wealth, a commodity that is able to be
> indefinitely accumulated. In capitalism, money is demanded not because
> it has an intrinsic value but because it is a store of value. [...] The non-
> payment of debts becomes ever more clearly the foundation of capitalism.
> (Fantacci 2013: 139–141)

States are of course the primary beneficiaries of this condition, which facilitates
refinancing through the capital markets. As we have seen, a basic assumption of

capitalism is that capital is invested to realize a profit through the production and exchange of commodities. The expansion of capitalism begins with local market economies in which roughly equal producers have an incentive to invest and compete; the aim of realizing a rate of return is enough for entrepreneurs to take risks with their own capital. Market economies of this type depend on the creation of surplus value through the exploitation of labour power and the partial reinvestment of profits in the form of constant capital (production technologies). They function most efficiently where the distorting effect of oligopoly is limited by effective legal rules, although such rules are variable and subject to political influence.

The evolution of modern credit money reflects the transition from competitive capitalism, where similar-sized producers compete for market share, to postliberal corporate capitalism, where large firms restrict competition and are largely content to 'beat the average' (Nitzan & Bichler 2009). Corporate capitalism is a postliberal accumulation regime with oligopolistic tendencies in which capital is not routinely invested by risk-taking entrepreneurs but lent by financial corporations as interest-bearing capital. Competition exists in a *managed* form – between global corporate actors supported by sovereign states with a strategic investment in the success of firms headquartered in their respective jurisdictions. In this globalized system, successful capitalists no longer take risks with their own money. Rather, they either lend funds (as investors) or borrow funds (as entrepreneurs) through the capital markets. This enables corporations to expand either by absorbing subsidiaries or acquiring competitors' businesses, increasing the quantity of credit money in the economy while limiting unwanted competition. An important distinction between simple commodity capitalism and corporatism is that wealth is not directly invested as such but loaned into the economy as interest-bearing capital. To accommodate the expansion of credit and digital payments, capitalist money becomes an abstract representation of value issued by central banks and private banks to facilitate wealth expansion through credit, or to be multiplied by financial institutions using complex leveraged transactions as myriad forms of fictitious capital.

As the recent monetary history of the advanced economies attests, the state form of capital increasingly plays an *unmediated* role in sustaining a pyramidic edifice of denationalized credit money and fictitious capital which enables global investors to capture value from the future and sustain capitalist class relations, reproducing a suboptimal global market economy in which the productive allocation of capital is overshadowed by rent-seeking and transnational oligopoly. In this hypertrophied financialized order, characterized by an excessive accumulation of abstract value, two levels of monetary power coexist: on the one hand, an international monetary system composed of financial market money priced in globally traded currencies and supported by the IMF, BIS and a network of G-SIFIs; on the other hand, territorially bounded currencies which function as national units of account supported by leading central banks. These levels of monetary power are interdependent yet their precise interrelationship is unclear. As we will see in Chapter 6, the IMF is positioning itself as a key transnational monetary actor by recalibrating its 'special drawing right' (SDR) international reserve system as a global unit of account to regulate currency and trade balances between sovereign states – a potentially postcapitalist system of international central banking which recalls Keynes' ill-fated 'bancor' model rejected by the US Treasury at Bretton Woods in 1944. What is clear is that both levels are fundamental for preserving a dysfunctional global accumulation regime in which a hypertrophied quantity of financial assets and liabilities comprising fictitious capital is stabilized by profligate issuance of sovereign currencies ensuring the paradoxical expansion of state-based monetary power as a functional prerequisite for global financial capitalism.

This raises the question whether capitalist money is state- or market-created – that is, whether capitalist money comes into existence as the product of sovereign states or whether, once created, independent monetary forms effectively exceed the legal and political jurisdiction of territorially bounded entities while remaining (particularly in periods of market turbulence) functionally dependent on their monetary support. For advocates of modern money theory, it is a largely unquestioned assumption that a hierarchical relation of power exists where state-issued money presides over bank-created credit money, determining the nature and extent of 'valid' or 'legal' money in society. The 'superior' status of state-issued fiat is typically viewed as an institutional fact, yet neo-chartalists overemphasize a single institutional monetary function of the state, namely the 'establishment and maintenance of the unit of account' (Beggs 2016: 464). Although this is a critical function of the state circuit of capital, which enables the state to tax the population and modify the quantity of money in circulation at will, for Beggs it is 'not the same as "creating money" as such. It is only part of the relations through which money is reproduced' (ibid.). Although fiat money represents a highly advanced monetary technology, key dimensions of money in capitalist economies are in fact determined not by states but by markets. As such, the assumed position of the state 'at the top of the national monetary pyramid cannot be taken for granted' (ibid.). Indeed, it might be argued that the

> *very structure of politics has been shaped by engagement with money.* From the rise of the central bank to the evolving norms of fiscal policy, monetary aims profoundly form and constrain the modern capitalist state. The state is a creature of money as much as the reverse. (ibid.: 465; emphasis added)

It also raises a further question whether a coercive political economy characterized by the entrenchment of oligopoly is feasible without a *concomitant alteration in the political form of capitalism.* If the structures of corporate power and financial manipulation continue to defend G-SIFIs – whose power over markets is sustained by central bank activism and the regulatory effect of international financial institutions, how far can this model proceed before it clashes not only with the competitive logic of capital as a means of private wealth creation, but with the imperatives of *national* (and, by logical extension, regional) economic policy pursued by states, exposing contradictions in transnational neoliberalism as a global accumulation regime while intensifying precisely those contradictions it was designed to resolve?[1] Government economic centralization problematizes the normative ideal of monetary pluralism analysed by economic sociologists like Dodd (2014): although interest in alternative and local currencies has exploded since 2009 – offering individuals and communities means for organizing trade and settling payments outside the banking system, as the dramatic collapse of Bitcoin in 2018 testifies, these monetary technologies are vulnerable to commodification and speculative excess once powerful financial actors enter the market. This not only limits their utility as 'secure' means of payment/stores of value but also their potential uptake outside niche groups of well-informed investors.

In terms of reversing the tendency for the organic composition of capital to increase as living labour is edged out of production, state institutions have the power to create legal frameworks for more efficient labour exploitation and financial deregulation. And they can seek to satisfy the demand for a global liquidity preference through the issuance of new money to purchase distressed financial assets, thereby ensuring (ideally) that regardless of the timing of their sale the full value of financial assets can be realized (Lozano 2014: 18). Whereas in productive economies states act *indirectly*, attempting to increase market efficiency via public-private partnerships and market deregulation, in financialized economies monetary elites intervene *directly*, fuelling liquidity through fiat issuance and central bank purchases of corporate and sovereign debt. The most egregious example of this is the underreported figure of $16 trillion transferred by the US Federal Reserve Bank to distressed banks between 2008 and 2018 – an incomprehensible sum (Greenstein 2018).[2] Yet this liquidity transfer has done little to address contradictions in the value form which limit the valorization of capital by driving the tendency of the rate of profit to fall over time. The capacity of states to limit the tendency of capital to autonomously undermine valorization by removing living labour from production has been shown to be as ineffectual as the power of a 'child sitting behind the wheel of a toy fire engine to determine the direction of his vehicle' (Lohoff 2016: 9). In 'financial market socialism', he adds, capital is entering a period of latency, suggesting discontinuity in the sequence of capitalist development while some sectors of the economy spin out of control as others lie dormant. This dysfunctional latency period might also be defined as *wasted time*: an extended period of unproductive development as gains accrued through the anticipation of future value are concentrated in fewer hands while elites search for new methods to ward off deflation through expansionary monetary policy, asset price inflation and increased debt accumulation. This strategy, as economists at BIS themselves note, is hardly cost-free, since all 'monetary and fiscal expansions work to a considerable extent by borrowing demand from the future. And when the future becomes today, there is inevitably a price to be paid' (BIS 2018b: xiii). But if intervention cannot stabilize accumulation through an *infinite* expansion of fictitious capital, strategies have been adopted in an attempt to determine '*which* dimension the accumulation of fictitious capital assumes, *how long* the devaluation of unsecured accumulated claims on future value can be delayed, and *which* forms these eventually take' (Lohoff 2016: 10; emphasis added).

Towards a theory of capitalist money

A category error in mainstream political economy derives from the *naturalization* of the capitalist money form, as a result of which the function of money as a general equivalent in commodity exchange and the historical specificity of capitalist credit money are obscured. As Dodd rightly observes, for Marx 'money's broader role in capitalism is to conceal its most basic contradictions by making their effects seem both *natural* and *just*' (Dodd 2014: 72). It is a major strength of Marx's general approach, he adds, that it 'seeks to penetrate behind the veil of apparently objective, quasitechnical aspects of money to uncover the social relations that underpin its circulation and accumulation' (ibid.). The naturalization of money in mainstream political economy is responsible not only for the false reduction of modern credit money to a means of payment and store of value, but for a failure to comprehend the phenomenology of interest-bearing capital as the motor of accumulation in global financial capitalism. It is also necessary to distinguish capitalist and postcapitalist money forms, focusing on the role of the state form of capital in the reproduction of capital values in the postliberal phase of contemporary global capitalism. This requires a reassessment of modern money theory, which posits fiat money as an 'infinitely elastic' quantity. On this view, there are, and can be, no limits on the power of sovereigns to issue currency within their 'monetary space' because money is what governments say it is. In fiat monetary systems, money *has* neither intrinsic value nor *acts* as an indicator of value, for the nominal value of currency is set by central banks or may be subject to a predetermined rate of devaluation to deter hoarding of idle capital outside the banking system (and thus stimulate consumption and investment). For post-Keynesian economists, this has the virtue of maximizing the utility of money as a means of payment, increasing the velocity of money in the economy; for libertarians and some Marxian economists, the shift from commodity to fiat money is indicative of *fascism*, as a consequence of which commodity money is withdrawn from circulation (Jehu 2017). In its place valueless tokens (physical currency/digital representations of currency) become the exclusive means of payment for goods and services, circulating as means of exchange where traditional forms of commodity money no longer exist. This leads to monopolization of exchange relations by states and the loss of money's residual status as a bearer of intrinsic value.

In classical political economy, 'quantity theory' stressed the harmonious equilibration of the total output of commodities and the total quantity of commodity money (Itoh & Lapavitsas 1999). The theoretical foundations of quantity theory held that the stock of money = price × real income. In quantity theory, money is understood as a *secondary* dimension of exchange, a so-called 'veil' disguising underlying economic relations which may be exposed to disturbances created by the inflationary effects of monetary expansion. This perspective grew to prominence among neoclassical and monetarist economists, who favour restrictive monetary policies to control inflation, and it remains influential in contemporary economic theory. Keynesians largely concur with quantity theory in its principal assumptions, though heterodox approaches sometimes proceed beyond orthodoxy to examine the hierarchy of sources of monetary value and the primacy of state-issued fiat currency as a unit of account and means of settlement in capitalist monetary economies. Building on early studies by chartalists,[3] modern money theory emphasizes the unlimited capacity of sovereign governments to dictate the nature of a currency within a territorial space, rehearsing the Thomist view that money exists not by nature but by law.[4]

Wray (2014) traces the history of chartalist approaches to state-issued money, starting with the work of Knapp (1973) who rejected 'metallism' which holds that currencies can be conceptualized *without reference to states*, and that money should be based on a commodity – the exchange value and purchasing power of which determine the value of currency itself. From this perspective, argues Wray, it is

> not simply a 'legal tender' law that makes state notes acceptable in private transactions, but [the fact] that the state first decides what it will use or accept as money in its own transactions, and that this must then be acceptable as means of settlement of private debts. (Wray 2014: 6)

Innes (1914) also examined state-issued money but widened his analysis to include its parallel development alongside credit money – commercial money created by banks, which is not merely a 'veil' concealing underlying economic relations, as classical economists assumed, but constitutes the *real* basis for credit-debt relations in modern monetary economies. As states spend, he argued, they too become debtors through the issuance of state money: 'even state money is credit money, however, it is a special kind of credit, "redeemed by taxation"' (Innes 1914, cited in Wray 2014: 12). Contrary to orthodox thinking, argues Wray, the appeal of state-issued money is determined not by intrinsic value but by the 'nominal value set by the state at its own pay offices' (ibid.: 13). The fact that state money is backed by legal tender laws is largely irrelevant:

> It is certainly true governments [...] adopt legal tender laws, but these are difficult to enforce and hence often ineffective. The power of government to impose a tax and to name what will be accepted in tax payment is sufficient, and trumps legal tender laws. (ibid.)

Despite the power of sovereign states to determine what constitutes money, chartalists do recognize de facto limits to the power of states to determine *quantity*, challenging monetarist notions of exogenous control of the money supply with an emphasis on endogenous money creation through commercial transactions and credit expansion. This takes place through routine economic activity as new debts are brought into existence and the quantity of credit money in the economy expands, enlarging the 'pyramid of liabilities' – at the apex of which stand the liabilities of central banks themselves (ibid.: 19). Capitalism also depends fundamentally on the existence of private banks which maintain the power to create credit-money and finance enterprise outside the state's monopoly of currency issue:

> With this change the private capitalistic financing of enterprise on a large scale became a possibility. Eventually, such signifiers of debt became completely 'depersonalised' (payable to *x* or bearer) and were issued as bank money; that is to say, the promises to pay drawn on banks became a widely accepted means of payment. In a second and related major structural change in early modern Europe, some states began to finance their activities by borrowing from their wealthy merchant classes. Their promises to repay these 'national debts' became the basis for public credit money that existed in an uneasy and uncertain relationship with the coinage. (Ingham 2004b: 187)

Yet modern monetary theorists nevertheless insist that this is only possible due to the existence of sovereign territorial states, for until the historic moment when credit money was 'incorporated into the fiscal system of states which commanded a secure jurisdiction involving extensive legitimacy, it remained, in evolutionary terms, a "dead-end"' (ibid.: 202). Backed by state-issued fiat, money has acquired a purely nominal value, and the state retains (or *attempts* to retain) political control over the 'functionality' of public finance with a view to meeting its fiscal commitments in accordance with (or in spite of) targets set by international financial institutions like the IMF or debt-to-GDP ratios policed by credit ratings agencies.

In contrast to modern money theory, Austrian economists criticize the concept of immaterial fiat money as conducive to economic and financial stability, and there remains a preference among economic libertarians for 'stable' monetary systems such as the gold standard which link the value of currencies to commodities. Austrian theorists question the presumption in favour of infinite elasticity in the money supply and the assumption that money is created by law not nature. State-issued fiat plays a unique indispensable role in the regulation of currency as the principal means of exchange in modern monetary economies, but chartalism is really a theory of *how* money achieves societal validation rather than what money is and why it comes into existence. Although the residual historic link between currency and gold was eventually severed in 1971, many investors continue to view possession of (physical) precious metals as a reliable means for preserving wealth outside the banking system; and – as we shall see in Chapter 5 – the preference for bullion is also shared by central banks which publicly criticize private hoarding of gold yet remain by far the largest institutional purchasers of bullion as an asset with no counterparty liability.

Which is to say, the value of gold as a financial asset is not dependent on the actions of central banks or national treasuries: bullion cannot 'default', or manipulate its own value or mislead markets through dishonest accounting (although the value of bullion can of course be leveraged many times by leasing the metal to governments on a temporary or semi-permanent basis, or its fictitious value can be traded in the derivative form of 'gold paper'). Given its unique form and limited supply, bullion is used by governments to support national currencies by maintaining a stable gold-to-GDP ratio (Rickards 2014, 2016b; Middelkoop 2015). As Rickards observes, if

> we take GDP as a metric for the economy, and gold as a metric for real money, then the gold-to-GDP ratio tells us how much real money is supporting the real economy. It is the inverse of leverage through government debt. (Rickards 2017: 2)

This measure is critical for emerging economies like Russia, where the gold-to-GDP ratio is a massive 5.6 per cent, compared to the US where the ratio stands at 1.8 per cent.[5]

Following Rothbard (1963), Austrian economists hold that the primacy of state-issued money intensifies state economic centralization, a form of 'monetary totalitarianism' characterized by the de facto nationalization of money and credit:

> A system of elastic money is suboptimal, unstable and ultimately unsustainable. Nevertheless, it has its defenders, apologists and enthusiastic advocates. It is unlikely to disappear quietly. The measures by which the state will try to uphold it will most certainly become more aggressively interventionist and even draconian as the inconsistencies and instabilities become more apparent and pervasive. (Schlichter 2014: 221)

Viewed through the prism of economic libertarianism, argues Schlichter, 'free market endeavour is impossible in a system of state-controlled fiat money. Ultimately, banks become the protectorate of the state and the extended arm of its central bank' (ibid.: 222). Although modern central banks act as a 'backstop' in the financial system as 'lenders of last resort', the modern state is 'structurally incapable of living within its means', finding itself instead 'in deadly embrace with the overstretched financial industry, which it needs to protect from market forces and on which it equally depends for its own financial survival' (ibid.: 222). On this view, the private banking system becomes a de facto extension of the state and instruments of state economic policy, even if systemically relevant financial institutions benefit from direct access to the spigot of cheap money during periods of financial instability and expansionary monetary policy. Although the libertarian critique risks inverting the *actual* hierarchy of power relations between private banks and central banks (that is, between financial market money and fiat money), it does succeed in capturing a basic contradiction in capitalist monetary systems, namely the historic decline over the course of the twentieth century of money as a stable bearer of value and indicator of private wealth independent of state-regulated banking systems. Austrian theorists also reveal the reality of finance as a 'public-private partnership' between banking capital and the state in which the banking system becomes the 'private beneficiary of a public service' (Wolf 2018), yet where risk multiplies exponentially and depositors' assets are liable to confiscation by predatory global financial elites during periods of extreme market volatility.

In further contrast to modern money theory, economic sociologists are also critical of the notion of state-controlled money, identifying the decline of 'state monopoly currencies' and a new age of 'monetary pluralism'. Drawing on classical economic sociology, Dodd (2014) returns to Simmel's (2004 [1907]) definition of money as a 'claim upon society', according to which the existence of monetary forms depends on the extent to which society — defined as a negotiated *process* based on association and exchange between agents rather than a 'bounded' jurisdiction — reproduces levels of trust necessary for the monetization of social relations. For Simmel, money embodies abstract economic value and can therefore be substituted for every economic value:

> If the economic value of objects is constituted by their mutual relationship of exchangeability, then money is the autonomous expression of this relationship. Money is the representative of abstract value. [...] This ability of money to replace every economic value — because it is not connected with any of these values but only with the relation into which they may enter — assures the continuity of the series of economic events. This series exists in both the production and consumption of goods. (Simmel 2004: 120, 124)

The significance of money results from its objective interchangeability and 'lack of specific qualities', as a result of which 'all things receive their meaning through each other, and have their being determined by their mutual relations' (ibid.: 128–129). Yet it is the irrelevance of intrinsic value which once again stands out in contemporary capitalism because

> commerce tends to more and more to eliminate money as a substantial embodiment of value, and this trend is unavoidable because, even if the production of precious metals were increased to the utmost extent, it would still be inadequate to allow all transactions to be conducted in cash. (ibid.: 143–144)

An alternative approach to capitalist money builds on Marx's critique of political economy. The development of money as a 'general equivalent' becomes functionally necessary where a

> *specific* type of commodity with whose *natural form the equivalent form* coalesces socially becomes the *money-commodity* or functions *as money*. Its *specific social function* and hence its *social monopoly* becomes the playing of the role of general equivalent *within the world of commodities*. (Marx 1978: 136; italics in original)

As 'pure quantity', money plays a unique role in capitalism since the labour time incorporated into a money commodity is the most accurate measure of the social value of the necessary labour time contained in other commodities. The universality of money is derived from its capacity to relate through exchange a particular use-value to all other possible use-values as elements of abstract total social wealth. Marxian theory also highlights the dynamic nature of capitalist money as a universal equivalent based on its fungibility:

> [1] As the general equivalent money can buy *everything*; [2] money is constituted by its *social externality*; [3] as this external force, money can 'modify' […] all properties inherent in things; [4] money *transforms* everything into an instrumental thing that exists, for the self-interest of individuals; [5] money contains a *violent* aspect; money becomes the new *untouchable* ('holy') thing in capitalism, its new God. (Lotz 2014: xvii)

Here the most powerful feature of capitalist money is its capacity to transform all pre-existing forms of production, exchange and human interaction, and thus determine the '*form* of all accessible objects in a capitalist universe' (ibid.: xvi). On this view, for anything meaningful to *exist* in capitalism it must be expressed in a monetized form. Capital, in turn,

> establishes a horizon of meaningfulness that regulates our access to entities in our world. In addition, this schema establishes itself independent [sic] from the will of individuals and the will of groups, as the social synthesis is established *prior* to individuals and groups that are living within this synthesis. (ibid.: 27)

A modern systematic Marxian account of capitalist money is offered by Lapavitsas (1991), whose studies of monetary political economy highlight the inner contradiction between exchange-value and use-value in the determination of monetary forms. He suggests that the functions of money for Marx are: (i) unit of account; (ii) means of circulation (universal equivalent for buying/selling commodities); and (iii) 'money *as money*' (bearer of value/means of deferred payment, implying ability to differentiate itself and stand above simple commodity exchange) (Lapavitsas 1991: 298–300). It is the latter which is characteristic of advanced economies in which a complex network of deferred payments transcends the spatio-temporal context of real-time exchange. Fiat money has a unique and privileged point of entry into the general circulation of money, namely the state, which pays for what it needs using money created *ex nihilio*.

Yet this money is worthless outside circulation because its tokens lack any intrinsic value. Fiat money is quickly superseded by endogenously created credit money in capitalism, as a consequence of two historical trends:

1. Generalization of commercial credit relations – *the advance of commodities rather than money against a promise to pay*;
2. Generalization of monetary credit relations – *lending money for the purpose of earning interest (the special function of interest-bearing capital)*. (ibid.: 304)

These monetary credit relations 'materially influence the endogenous character of the monetary mediation of capitalist exchange' (ibid), which is to say, in non-technical language, they facilitate and mediate the commercial transactions which comprise the private business economy where the quantity of money is determined not simply by the supply of new money from central banks but by the inflationary dynamics of commerce. As Lapavitsas observes, in capitalist monetary systems

> commercial credit connects the circuits of different capitals without the intervention of money. [...] circulation time is reduced and the completion of the circuits of individual capitals is accelerated. Marx identified the speeding up of the circuits of individual capitals, and thus of the total social capital, as the social role of commercial credit in capitalist exchange, such credit becoming a condition for rapid accumulation. (ibid.: 305)

The point is, he argues, that the 'elevation of means of payment into the dominant function of money corresponds to the emergence of specifically capitalist money, credit money' (ibid.: 306). Modern capitalist monetary systems multiply the scale of this credit money through the growth of 'hoards' – deposit money that corresponds to the function of money as a store of value which Marx theorized as an excess of profit above that which needs to be invested, and which increases as circulation time in the process of accumulation is reduced. Hoards are turned by banks into 'interest-bearing capital', a structural feature of capital accumulation which leads to a supersession of *banknote* credit money by *deposit* credit money in the financial system.

Marx observed that the social relations of capital eventually assume their most 'fetish-like' form in financially sophisticated economies as interest-bearing capital, where the value of financial market money is continually augmented through circulation and exchange:

> Capital appears as a mysterious and self-creating source of interest – the source of its own increase. The *thing* (money, commodity, value) is

now capital even as a mere thing, and capital appears as a mere thing. The result of the entire process of reproduction appears as a property inherent in the thing itself. It depends on the owner of the money, i.e., of the commodity in its continually exchangeable form, whether he wants to spend it as money or loan it out as capital. In interest-bearing capital, therefore, this automatic fetish, self-expanding value, money generating money, are brought out in their pure state and in this form it no longer bears the birth-marks of its origin. The social relation is consummated in the relation of a thing, of money, to itself. Instead of the actual trans-formation of money into capital, we see here only form without content. As in the case of labour-power, the use-value of money here is its capac-ity of creating value – a value greater than it contains. Money as money is potentially self-expanding value and is loaned out as such – which is the form of sale for this singular commodity. It becomes a property of money to generate value and yield interest, much as it is an attribute of pear-trees to bear pears. And the money-lender sells his money as just such an interest-bearing thing. But that is not all. The actually function-ing capital, as we have seen, presents itself in such a light, that it seems to yield interest not as a functioning capital, but as capital in itself, as money-capital. (Marx 1959: 392)

It is interest-bearing capital that generates the growth of financial market money in advanced economies, which in turn forms the basis for fictitious capital, the nominal value of which rapidly dwarfs the monetary base of national economies derived from fiat issuance and private fractional-reserve banking (credit creation).

As a general principle, then, the 'form' money assumes in distinct historical periods is explained by the *'adequacy of each particular form for the functions which money is called to perform in capitalist exchange.* Performing these functions encour-ages the evolution of money's form, leading to the emergence of several types of non-commodity ("valueless") money' (Lapavitsas 2000: 631; emphasis added). In contrast to modern money theory, which assumes infinite elasticity as a pre-rogative of the sovereign issuer, fiat money

cannot adequately preserve value outside the sphere of exchange because it neither possesses value nor is it organically connected with the process of real accumulation through the credit mechanism. The mere word of the state is good enough to enable mediation in the process of circulation, but it is not good enough to preserve value, or satisfactorily to settle past obli-gations and transfer value at all times. To secure a valueless money adequate for these functions, what is necessary is, above all, connection with the credit system. (ibid.: 646)

This does not deter monetary and political elites from attempting to manage financial crises through central bank activism, however, indicating the utility of

elastic money creation for financial and monetary authorities who are unconstrained by traditional attachments to 'sound money' or currencies pegged to
the nominal value of a rare commodity like gold. Since the Second World War,
governments have consistently sought to manage market economies through
an expansion of state credit, for as long as 'central banks can create acceptable
hard cash in times of crisis, and sufficient quantities of liquidity ease the process
of capital restructuring, they can also limit the extent to which prices must fall
in a slump' (ibid.: 654). While modern money theorists believe state-issued fiat
can eliminate unemployment and exploit available resources more efficiently,
there are problems with the paradigm of infinitely elastic money as a basis for
maximizing social resources and addressing gross inequality in capitalist class
societies. As Buick notes, approaches of this type appeal to 'those who think that
capitalism can be reformed to work to everyone's benefit. But there's nothing
"modern" about it. It's an old illusion of those who see unemployed workers
and idle resources alongside unmet needs and think that the obvious solution
is simply for the government to create and spend more money' (Buick 2017: 1).
This illusion is, he adds, a feature of 'various schools of currency crankism […]
this since the first capitalist economic downturn in 1825' (ibid.).

Why is this illusion so pervasive? Buick insists that such approaches 'ignore
the reason why these resources and people are unused in the first place, which is
that the market does not recognize any profitability in employing them' (ibid.).
It reflects a reformist tendency to believe that demand management can effectively
compensate for cyclical downturns by utilizing slackness and stimulating consumerism, without calling into question the defunct industrial consumerist model
itself (Stiegler 2011: 4). In the real world of commercial logic, capital must leave
resources unused and labour unemployed because it is uneconomic to invest when
firms cannot beat the average rate of return and satisfy demand for shareholder
value. This explains not only the periodicity of recessions which destroy accumulated capital which cannot be invested profitably, but the trend towards corporate
oligarchy as financial institutions intensify their power of disposal over interest-
bearing capital, 'creatively obstructing' the rational reallocation of resources in
society (cf. Wasserberg 2013). 'Looking at the commanding heights of financial
capitalism', observes Tabb,

> it is really a very small club. More than half of all the debt of households,
> non-financial companies, and government in the United States is held by
> the top fifteen institutions, and among them there is a tremendous concen-
> tration of assets in the top five and even the top three mega banks. (Tabb
> 2012: 182)

Chartalism also fails to address the functional necessity of historically evolving
monetary forms, which develop so that the 'limits to capitalist expansion set by
commodity money could be broken' (Jessop 2013: 259). The credit-money system alters the circuits of capital: credit, 'reduces the need for productive capital to

hold reserves, lowers the socially necessary turnover time of capital, and changes the temporary structure of the circuits of capital' (ibid.: 252). Specifically, Jessop notes:

> As Marx moves from the functions of the money-form in simple commodity circulation (where he assumes that money is also a real commodity) to the forms and functions of money in a fully developed [capitalist mode of production], he makes three crucial conceptual moves. First, he unfolds its forms and their relation to credit, seeking to show that in a fully developed capitalist economy money must take the form of increasingly complex forms of credit. Second, he distinguishes (1) real commodities, real money and real capital from (2) fictitious commodities, fictitious money and fictitious capital. And, third, he distinguishes money as functioning capital from money as property. Unsurprisingly, given the logical-historical method adopted by Marx, these categories are interconnected both conceptually and in their historical movement. (ibid.: 252)

On this view, financial market money becomes a representation of value as fictitious capital emerges as a representation of debt. Returning to Marx's original formulation, Jessop concludes that interest-bearing capital is the

> most fetish-like form of money because interest makes it appear that capital, not labour power, creates surplus value, rather than interest being taken from the value created in production (ibid.: 258). This leads to 'increasing reliance on leverage unrelated to the real movement of value', although the real movement of capital will sooner or later re-impose itself. (ibid.)

Jessop is correct to highlight the risks of unregulated credit expansion and 'Ponzi finance',[6] yet is quick to remind us that in structural terms fictitious capital *had* to advance to its present scope so that 'limits to capitalist expansion set by commodity money could be broken' (ibid.: 259), allowing new (abstract) iterations of value to be incorporated into total social wealth. The growth of derivatives markets has become indispensable because these play a 'key role in the tendential completion of the world market in transforming future incomes streams (profit, dividend or interest) into tradable assets and also change the dynamics of competition on a world scale' (ibid.: 262). Derivatives enable financial institutions to achieve gains that would otherwise be impossible, which suggests that attempts to legislate against their routine use by banks is likely to fail once periods of volatility have subsided: 'Because individuals and firms could not obtain the payoffs of derivatives efficiently by manufacturing them on their own, derivatives make markets more complete – that is, they make it possible to hedge risks that would otherwise be unhedgeable' (Stutlz 2004: 180). This circulation of ethereal capital is entirely dissociated from actual social relations and conducted using complex mathematical algorithms in corporate trading rooms where the 'emotional focus is on the means rather than the actual content of the trade' (Ailon 2013: 614; cf. Li Puma & Lee 2004).

As noted in Chapter 3, the nominal value of global derivatives ($1.4 quadrillion) is so vast that one decade after the global financial crisis, insiders are warning that renewed instability is inevitable as governments led by the US begin to relax macroprudential regulations (Chu 2018; Rappaport & Flitter 2018) and raise interest rates.[7] Yet the sheer scale of fictitious capital in circulation – exceeding the combined value of global currencies, stock markets, real estate and debt – requires us to consider the problematic nature of interest-bearing capital as endogenously created financial market money and the status of financial derivatives as representations of value. It also requires us to consider the supplementary function of state-issued fiat money in the process of monetary easing which allowed the advanced economies to transcend the immediate threat of collapse after 2008 by creating new money to purchase high-risk debt instruments and bonds, enabling banks and non-bank financial institutions ('shadow banking') to return to pre-crisis levels securitization and lending practices in the race to develop new high-risk financial innovations including exchange-traded funds, algorithmic trading and volatility trading which take advantage of the (false) stability created by central bank intervention (Das 2018).

Yet a more fundamental question remains, namely why there has been no return to profitable accumulation despite all of the money pumped into the banking system and bond markets by central banks. In the present post-euphoric phase of globalization, as the limits of government stimulus programmes become evident, collapse has been averted by artificially magnifying capital values across a range of asset classes, as a result of which property and equity markets are systematically overvalued as debt levels increase and banks securitize greater quantities of debt. When central banks have used forward guidance in recent years to signal an intention to raise interest rates above historically unprecedented low levels, market commentators quickly warn of dire economic consequences (Elliot 2018). This indicates that despite proclamations of 'recovery' since 2015, it is obvious that the structural causes of capitalist decline in advanced economies have been neither addressed nor resolved. A return to 'normal' monetary policy is always deferred to an unspecified future date while the goal of synchronized global growth is overshadowed by protectionism, geopolitical rivalry and competitive devaluations as political and monetary elites in the principal centres of capital adopt neo-mercantilist strategies to outmanoeuvre rival centres. This leads us towards a fundamental question for international political economy, namely whether monetary and political authorities are establishing *their* hegemony over global finance through accommodative policies – with a view to imposing future controls over the financial and monetary system, or whether banks are asserting *their* hegemony over monetary and political authorities in order to re-establish conditions for increased profitability. To answer this question, it is necessary to consider not only the ontology of fictitious capital as a form of global capitalist money contingent on yet functionally independent of territorially demarcated sovereign monetary forms, but the broader social and political impact of financial socialism as a 'public-private partnership' between monetary and political elites as a new phase in the accumulation crisis of postliberal capitalism unfolds.

The dialectic of fiat and commodity money

As one economist argued during the recession of the 1970s which laid waste to America's industrial base, corporations have only *two* strategies: 'They must restore competition in the labor market in order to ease labor scarcity and undercut labor strength. And they must find new ways to make more efficient use of their workers. When booms persist, they can accomplish neither' (Gordon 1975: 1). This statement reflects an established class-theoretical perspective prevalent among heterodox and Marxist scholars, namely that periodic recessions are indispensable to return capitalist firms to profitability. Recessions do not just 'happen'; they are determined by the mode of resolution of previous capitalist downturns (Clarke 1994), the causes of which are forgotten or dehistoricized by the tendency in mainstream economics to reduce capitalist recessions to simple 'downswings' in the 'normal course' of the business cycle. This obscures not only the mode of resolution of capitalist crises through the search for alternative sources of value and macroprudential regulation (discussed in more detail in Chapters 5 and 6), but the disciplinary dimension of market contractions and falling production as profits are squeezed by competition, overproduction and an absence of slack in labour markets:

> With a rise in unemployment, labor 'discipline' improves. As output falls, the razor of market competition trims worker power and pares away inefficient operations. Recessions restore the basis for capital accumulation. 'By momentary suspension of labor and annihilation of a great portion of capital', Marx wrote 125 years ago, production for profit can resume. (Gordon 1975: 1; cf. Harvey 2005)

Yet, as we saw in the previous chapter, the logic of recession in capitalism derives less from the class conscious agency of investors and financial managers than from the inner contradiction in the value form: capital may be approaching its 'vanishing point' not simply because economic repression is more difficult to enforce, but because, in the competition to maintain profitability, capital can no longer maintain a level of productive living labour necessary to create a requisite quantity of surplus value at profitable rates. This is not the trigger for recession itself, but an underlying cause of structural weakness in low profit economies with high levels of debt (Kliman 2012). Recession becomes inevitable as the intensity of competition between firms for a declining share of relative surplus value grows, and as productive living labour is displaced from the output of commodities and not redeployed as productive labour in new growth sectors driven by innovation or in the production of new commodities with universal use-value adequate to establish profitable value chains in a globally organized economy. Financialization is not the *cause* of the accumulation crisis afflicting the advanced economies of the US, EU and Japan but a *logical correlate to* declining real sector profitability and the search for new forms of (fictitious) capital gains through the anticipation and capture of future value.

We have also seen that 'neoliberal' capitalism is an accumulation regime augmented by an unprecedented expansion of fictitious value as an abstract form of valorization: money capital that does not correspond to value generated by productive investment. The primary arena for the circulation of fictitious capitalist money is the financial markets, or more precisely, the derivatives markets and foreign currency exchanges where computer-generated volume trading takes place one step removed from routine trade and investment decision-making in corporate boardrooms in the leading centres of global capital. In no previous phase of capitalist development, argues Lohoff,

> has the accumulation of fictitious capital played such an important role as the present epoch. Contemporary capitalism cannot be understood without a deeper appreciation of this form of capital formation, while the consequences it engenders remain inexplicable. As a self-sustaining end-in-itself the capitalist valorization of value had already reached its historical limits with the crisis of Fordism in the 1970s. New possibilities for development became available only because it was able to transform itself, in ever more monstrous dimensions, into a system for anticipating future value. Since the 1980s the production of fictitious capital came to replace a system based on the production of value through the exploitation of living labour as a motor for accumulation. In this way, a kind of *inverse capitalism* was constituted in which the traditional relation between the financial sector and functioning capital was stood on its head. Paradoxically, this financial superstructure has become the 'foundational industry' of capitalism while the accumulation of productive capital can only continue to function as side-show to the generation of fictitious capital. (Lohoff 2016: 13)

As financial innovation has accelerated and financial markets have intensified inter-capitalist competition by dispersing capital globally, fictitious capital has evolved not only to compensate for a relative decline of profitability in productive sectors of advanced economies but to facilitate the development of an internationally commensurable form of commodity money which transcends nation-state money. This does not mean profits obtained through derivatives trades are 'real', however. Gains made through financial speculation are entirely fictitious and 'will never be paid out of the value creation process. From a Marxist perspective, no value has been created' (Cooper 2014: 23). The opposite is in fact the case, for a financial market derivative whose 'value is purely speculative and not underpinned by the value creation process demeans money as a store of value' (ibid.). What derivatives allow for is a transfer of risk to counterparties that are 'more willing or better able to assume that risk' (Rechtschaffen 2014: 148), either to realize an immediate financial gain or to manage their own exposure to risk more effectively in the future.

Yet, derivatives *do* overcome barriers to the global integration of capital because they 'reinforce the separation between the general movement of capital based on valorisation and the fluctuation of money prices and profit and, in this way, facilitate financialization and the rise of finance-dominated accumulation' (Jessop 2013: 264). Despite their association with market volatility, 'toxicity' and extreme risk, to reduce derivatives to financial speculation obscures their vital commensuration function in the operation of global financial markets. This rhetorical strategy shuts down an inquiry into the way in which money and commodity production may be transforming within capitalism. By historical analogy, the formation of the joint-stock company as a fictional legal person in the mid-nineteenth century was often seen at that time mainly as a device to permit speculation on an expanded scale. We now know that the joint-stock company has been a critical way that capital as a social relation and as a value in movement has been able to expand under changed, and changing, conditions of accumulation (Bryan & Rafferty 2003: 10).

This commensuration effect operates at two levels: on the one hand, derivatives overcome discontinuities of measurement between monetary units, without rendering currencies equivalent; on the other hand, derivatives overcome discontinuities in the measurement of value across the continuum of space-time: 'So long as there is no single global currency and global central bank (an abstract notion that is associated with particular idealised notions of competition and money anyway)', argue Rafferty and Bryan, 'derivatives markets are the primary means to provide continuity to global financial markets' (ibid.: 11).

Notwithstanding their appearance as a fetishized articulation of fictitious capital, therefore – whose nominal market value bears no relation to the value of tradeable commodities, equities or other assets – derivatives can be defined more precisely as a form of 'denationalized capitalist money' which is irreducible to national currencies or other simpler monetary forms. This dialectic of *supranational* and *national* monetary forms reflects a contradiction in transnational capitalism in which the interests of globalizing capital transcend the interests of individual national capitals in international political economy. This, in turn, indicates a geopolitical contradiction between capitalist sovereignty and national sovereignty which has been traditionally resolved by the preponderance of US military and monetary power and the political willingness of American elites to play the role of the 'indispensable nation' serving the interests of transnational capital rather than the US economy itself (cf. Robinson 2004). For this reason it is necessary to be wary of restrictive conceptualizations of Western hegemony and adopt a more critical, geocentric perspective – even if the 'hegemonic stability' of the US-centric global order is challenged by the impatience of rising powers like Russia, China and India who question the leadership of Western elites in international politics (Hiro 2012).

In international financial terms, the dissonance between functionally and spatially demarcated monetary forms is partially resolved through derivatives as instruments that go beyond the simple 'intermediation' function of finance, allowing transnational investors and financial managers to maximize shareholder profit by 'hedging' the future value of currencies, commodities and equities:

> In order to circulate on a global scale, money has to keep converting between different national currencies, and facing unwelcome changes in the rate of conversion. The global money system thereby embodies implicit risks for participants. But these risks, while not entirely avoidable, are manageable. [Derivatives] perform this function: they unify the money system and, in the process, they are a form of asset holding and even a means of current and deferred payment. They are, in important respects, money. (Bryan & Rafferty 2006a: 135)

This argument has implications for state theories of money which artificially separate national and international monetary flows to defend a nationalist vision of monetary sovereignty in which money 'is' whatever the state considers to be money – namely an 'institutional fact' which exist only in virtue of their collective recognition and validation by social actors (Beggs 2017). That states 'nominate' what serves as money means that money is a creation of states; yet this only applies in the case of *currency* – the 'monetary base' of national economies (the total sum of money held by depositors and banks within a territorial unit) rather than the complex structure of denationalized monetary forms which constitute total global capital. As we have seen, neo-chartalist approaches entail an arbitrary assertion of sovereign prerogative, for while states intervene in the functioning of money, this 'does not mean that money is logically anchored on the state. An extra-market authority would have to possess extraordinary omniscience and power arbitrarily to determine the basis of commodity value measurement' (Lapavitsas 2013: 78).

It also has implications for the concept of 'moneyness' – that is, for a definition of the essential qualities money assumes either as credit money or commodity money. 'Moneyness' connotes the 'property of any financial asset that is not money, but is capable of being used as a medium of exchange' (Lozano 2014: 6). The capacity of a synthetic financial asset to assume the functions of money – and to be recognized as such – may be durable or transitory; but Lozano adds, if

> money is the first financial asset, perhaps it should not surprise us when, acting as an image of value for an economic object, money now seeks out an object in its own image *capable of acting as an image for its own object*. (ibid.: 7)

In reality, derivatives are a logical extension of the idea of commodity money as a monetary instrument defined by its inherent 'moneyness': like all monetary forms in capitalism, commodity money retains a connection with state money; it also depends on the willingness and capacity of central banks to increase the supply of state-issued money and to inject capital or coordinate private capital injections to stabilize distressed financial institutions. Yet commodity money cannot be reduced to purely numerical state money because it is fungible, assuming manifold forms through division and multiplication. Following Deleuze (1994), Lozano observes:

> The historico-ontological progressive differentiation of synthetic finance signals the coming-into-being of a series of qualitative multiplicities [which change in kind through their division], such as credit derivatives and other synthetically structured assets (e.g. synthetic CDOs), which now enjoy this double property of both transcendence and immanence in relation to the pre-existing, actualized set of numerical multiplicities [which do not change in kind], which in turn populate the domains of action, or markets, comprising the system of exchange we call finance capitalism. (2015: 102)

As synthetic financial market assets, derivatives are essentially *banking instruments* which exist beyond the grasp or control of sovereign monetary power in the global banking system. These complex financial assets employ to great effect the 'price-making skills and general organizational capabilities of banks [and] the vast growth of derivatives markets reflects in part the turn of banks toward trading in open financial markets, which is one of the fundamental tendencies of financialization' (Lapavitsas 2013: 10).

Lapavitsas remains sceptical of conceptualizations of financial market derivatives as 'commodity' money: while they are used effectively as money in global trading, derivatives contracts have no intrinsic value and do not constitute (as commodities hypothetically do) the abstract value of the labour of financial intermediation and cannot therefore be defined as commodity money. For Bryan and Rafferty (2006b: 76–77), however, *derivatives are themselves commodities*: 'They are produced and traded, not just as titles to ownership, but as packaged systems of conversion between different forms of assets'. Derivatives as such are 'distinctively capitalist money, and a recognition of their role serves to transform debates about Marxist theories of money' (ibid.). They assume this role because they exist as a 'production process within a circulation process' (Bryan & Rafferty 2006a: 153). To understand this claim, and its implications for our discussion of capitalist money, it is important to recognize that all commodities are forms of capital, and that similar to traditional forms of commodity money like gold, derivatives facilitate *synonymization* and provide a means for producing equivalence in which incommensurable values are interchanged and rearticulated. From this perspective, it is not simply the exchange value of derivatives in financial market exchange but their functional dynamics which determine their utility as commodity money, the logic of which lies 'not in the reduction of money to some other commodities, but the commodified role of commensuration that derivatives perform' (ibid.). This commodification function operates in a deregulated sphere of circulation *rather than in production*, enabling interest-bearing capital to predict and expand future values to maximize investment gains. This commodification of risk in the sphere of circulation, utilizing 'value-at-risk' models to estimate probability distributions for the future value of investments (Olson & Wu 2015), is a key aspect of financialization which is inextricably tied to capital ownership as a class relation, a means of determining where interest-bearing capital is invested and thus an economic means to discipline labour (Sotiropoulos et al. 2013: 54). Derivatives are in this sense a logical response to and insurance against intensifying risk, for in a 'world where risk exposures are [...] measured relative to rate of return on capital, hedge funds and investment banks find readily available tools of risk diversification and opportunities for trading in trends in risk perception' (Bryan & Rafferty 2014: 892).

Sovereign states thus have the power to determine that which counts as money within territorially bounded jurisdictions, yet *cannot* determine to the same extent or with the same authority the value of that money (Beggs 2017: 472), and certainly cannot control the relative exchange value of national currencies if they operate floating exchange rates. By extension, governments cannot, even with a legal mandate from citizens in the wake of financial crises, control financial derivatives markets which allow investors to revalue/reprice all assets including the future value of currencies and sovereign bonds – although the 2010 Dodd Frank Act in the US does allow the US Congress in theory to impose greater transparency on the derivatives markets in the interests of reducing systemic risk (Rechtschaffen 2014: 218).[8] Financialization in effect creates a transcendental realm of fictitious value through futures, options, credit default swaps and other financial derivative trades which determine the price of actual assets but which elude sovereign regulatory control. As Beggs notes, it is thus more logical to posit the state a 'creature of money' rather than the other way around:

> By treating 'the state' simply as a sovereign force with the power to declare what will function as money, [neo-chartalism] explains neither how the state gets this power nor why it makes the choice it makes. A more sociological and historical treatment would discuss the state within the context of its evolving social environment. In doing so, it would find the power of the state to nominate money both constrained by the strategic situation, and only one aspect of the state involvement with money. It would need to treat the state not as a unitary actor, but as a complex of institutions with different powers and agencies, and within a world of many states and many currencies. And it would need to take the economic sphere of production and market exchange seriously. (ibid.: 473)

For Beggs, legal and political institutions are themselves shaped by the evolving form of money in capitalism. This phenomenon is replicated globally, as new transnational institutions evolve in response to demands for regulation of commodity and derivatives markets which multiply forms of money as leveraged synthetic financial assets detached from (yet dependent on) fiat currencies as numerical quantities of state-issued elastic money.

It should be clear from this analysis that a blind spot exists in statist theories of 'elastic' money, namely that in modern capitalist economies a large proportion of the task of creating money is delegated, to privately owned fractional-reserve banks which, under normal circumstances, determine the scale and value of credit money in circulation independently of sovereign monetary authorities. While fiat monetary systems are organized and managed through continual interactive feedback with the wider economy in which they operate; and while central banks (as we shall see in Chapter 5) intervene coercively to induce specific forms of market behaviour through quantitative easing and other 'open market' interventions, as commercial banks issue new loans to individuals and firms, they themselves are effectively creating new money and – by definition – new obligations to repay debt. This delegation to private commercial banks by sovereign monetary authorities of the right to create money (and debt) is a core constitutive element in the financial architecture of capitalist monetary economies which facilitates the continual expansion of debt and debt-based consumption, consolidating the real subsumption of commodity-determined societies to the power of interest-bearing capital. This process operates at a still higher level in the financial markets, where derivatives function as denationalized commodity money that facilitates the 'synonymization' of a complex array of value-bearing assets in the sphere of exchange, creating a 'production process within the circulation process' that magnifies the total nominal value of market trades far beyond the modest value of sovereign economies.

Subsumption of commodity society to interest-bearing capital

The dialectic of fiat and commodity money thus underlies a dynamic in contemporary capitalism towards financial market socialism, which – through the scale and power of financial markets – necessarily transcends territorially bounded state money as a unit of account, means of exchange or store of value. The transnational state form of capital is thus integral to the reproduction of total social capital where exchange value determines the emergence of money as a universal equivalent mediating and aligning incommensurable leveraged values. It is here the conditions of possibility for the emergence of fungible forms of global commodity money take shape, that is, for the prolific global expansion of interest-bearing capital as a self-valorizing value distinct from state-issued fiat money and the contingency of commodity circulation mediated by territorially bounded currencies. Marx indicated what capital might become if it existed unconstrained in accordance with its own immanent principles – namely *pure quantitative structure without substance* as 'finite' forms of capital (wealth) cease to exist as barriers to 'capital's drive towards infinity, its *telos* as absolute wealth' (McNally 2003: 6). As the real subject of modern monetary economies, interest-bearing capital rationalizes inchoate social, economic and cultural forms to appropriate the results of human labour, yet this appropriation is *unstable* in the absence of corporate organization and *defenceless* in the absence of its state form. In this sense, the dialectical relation between global disembodied money and its national-state form as a means of payment and unit of account is only one component in the global reproduction of total social capital as a self-constitutive dynamic mode of power in which all aspects of human society and culture become structurally embedded. This reciprocal relation between corporate and state power is a generic feature of contemporary postliberal capitalism as oligopoly replaces competition and derivative market values overshadow state circuits of money capital yet paradoxically remain dependent, in periods of extreme turbulence, on state-issued fiat to sustain liquidity in the financial system through public acquisition of distressed private bank assets.

Before proceeding to examine the evolution of monetary power in financial socialism as a logical extension of postliberal capitalism, it is worth considering the broader social implications of the growth of financial market money and the unprecedented expansion of credit markets in commodity-determined society. The power of capital, argue Bryan and Rafferty, derives

> not just from the extraction of a surplus, but also from the capacity to shift financial and other risks onto other people. Perhaps people's subordination to capital comes not just from the extraction of a surplus in the workplace, but also from holding illiquid assets (jobs, houses, health) in a world of liquid assets, leaving workers (households) as systemic 'shock absorbers' in global financial markets, itself a variation on 'surplus' extraction. (2014: 891)

An essential feature of neoliberal financialization is the transfer of risk, not merely *within* the financial system in the form of speculative trades, but disproportionately *across* society as a whole. This is no more apparent than in the collapse of working-class households following the implosion of the US mortgage market in 2007, which reflects the real subsumption of commodity-determined society to the logic of capital in advanced economies. As a result of the multiplication and repackaging of mortgage debt as 'mortgage-backed' securities, the contagion effect of non-performing loans in the retail property market escalated rapidly under conditions of crisis. This led the US federal government to intervene to prevent the collapse of government-sponsored mortgage agencies while allowing banks to sequester properties from impoverished families as collateral against failed loans.

The consequences of 'sub-prime' suggest that the concept of *ownership* itself must be reformulated as ownership of 'exposure to the performance of capital' – that is to say, as a disciplinary mode of power: individual 'market actors' must now assume personal responsibility for the failure or success of market outcomes – irrespective of their own agency. Financialization thus provides a mechanism to 'break the link between political rights and citizenship and the idea of the common or public good' (Lazzarato 2009, 2012; Birch & Tickell 2010: 47). As argued throughout the present study, this indicates not the degeneration of 'stable' managed capitalism but a dynamic inherent in the logic of interest-bearing capital, which further intensifies the real subsumption of human life by capitalist relations of power. For Lazzarato (2015), 'stable' managed capitalism (Fordism) is *itself* the real historical exception: capital has historically pushed the barriers of interest-bearing capital into all areas of human life, only acquiring an ideal 'managed' form for a very brief interlude in Europe, North America and Japan after 1945 as the great industrial corporations dominated post-war economic development.

The disciplinary logic of financialized capitalism is reflected in a practical sense in the use of 'zero hours contracts' in advanced economies, legal instruments that shift the risks of contracted employment from firms to workers; it is also reflected in the development of social investment vehicles ('social benefit bonds') which transfer the risk of public investment from the state to investors whose rate of return is 'contingent on the extent to which the programme or intervention achieves its stated aims' (Bryan & Rafferty 2014: 895–897). At issue here is not the strategic calculus of derivative capital as a device for hedging risk – creating secondary markets linked to the performance of assets and trades on fluctuations in the relationship between present and future values – but the long-term implications of transferring fiduciary responsibility for the performance of financial market money away from corporate-state actors to individuals with lower risk tolerance. Not only are pension funds and other structured investment vehicles vulnerable to the market uncertainty created by debt-leveraged trading, but debt itself has become infinite and unpayable, articulating a social relation of subjectivation which powerfully transcends the original economic function of debt as an instrument of finance (Lazzarato 2015). As noted in Chapter 1, an extreme articulation of this phenomenon is the renewed expansion of credit markets in the US and the UK since the 2008 crisis, which has led to a mushrooming of debt among workers and students who are vulnerable to tiny upward movements in interest rates as the Federal Reserve and Bank of England attempt to tighten monetary policy in a vain effort to return to a 'normal' monetary policy cycle without causing a new downturn. Although declining demand in itself cannot explain the incidence of capitalist crises, the desire/capacity of firms and consumers to acquire additional debt is central to understanding not only the growth of credit markets and the disciplining of labour through debt-financed acquisitiveness, but the continuous calibration of finance as a technique of government (ibid.). It is also leading to a deterioration of underwriting standards which may be rational during market upswings but constitute a dangerous folly as recessionary pressures reappear (Rennison & Smith 2019).

There are multiple additional ways to demonstrate this phenomenon of transferring risk. Our example in Chapter 6 will be the legal status and financial security of depositors' investments in the banking system and the capacity of states to manage risk and underwrite the liquid assets of ordinary individuals in the event of bank insolvencies and renewed market turbulence. In critical political economy, neoliberalism is typically conceptualized as a means for establishing 'mechanisms of security for property, financiers and investors, shielding them from consequences issuing out of democratic processes deemed out-of-synch with the imagined or expressed interests of powerful economic interests' (Schneiderman 2013: 1). Yet in postliberal capitalism, not only are financial risks of corporate elites and investors socialized and the assets of small investors appropriated, but the principle of value-driven investment is effectively replaced by the logic of financial economics, that is, by an abstract calculus linked to the performance of synonymized derivative market values. As we shall see in Chapter 5, from a value-critical perspective financial socialism defends an accumulation regime which incorporates subjects into a hegemonic logic of financial literacy, commodifying and objectifying human social relations in accordance with abstract market valuations (Bryan & Rafferty 2014). From an Austrian perspective, on the other hand, financial socialism seems to erode the concept of ownership while delegating entrepreneurial agency from individuals to financial markets which acquire the power to determine optimal resource allocations via the implementation of value-at-risk models founded on standardized models of diversification under normal distributions. Viewed from either of these distinct yet complementary perspectives, financial socialism raises profound questions about the development of capitalism in its postliberal phase as resource allocation is increasingly subsumed under the logic corporate-state power, and as central banks assume a dominant role in the management and planning of the advanced capitalist economies.

Conclusion

When investors borrow on credit markets to maximize their financial leverage power in derivatives markets they magnify possible gains of fictitious capital at the risk of catastrophic losses as market volatility eventually undermines confidence in inflated asset bubbles, leading to price corrections. Since the end of Fordism, capitalism has become unstable, unprofitable and risk-prone, yet through deft central bank activism defies doom-laden predictions from Austrian economists in favour of 'sound money' and Marxian prognoses of overproduction and profit squeeze. Yet the self-expansion of capital is not accidental: the phenomenal accumulation of fictitious capital without value in modern monetary economies has been sustained and supported by state circuits of capital employing accommodative monetary policy to funnel new money capital into the banking system and reduce the threat of large-scale corporate debt default and fiscal collapse. As Dodd argues, in contemporary global financial capitalism,

> money socializes not only risk but, through inflation as well as austerity, the very destruction of capital itself. [...In] a system of fiat money, the ultimate consequence of this scramble is inflation, fuelled by the efforts of monetary authorities to prevent the credit system from collapsing altogether. (2014: 99)

For Rickards (2014), this is leading to far-reaching changes in the structure of capitalism which *no longer operates* without unlimited money creation. For Wray

(2015), on the other hand, it is evidence of a transition to a *total fiat monetary system* where governments spend and lend money into existence regardless of debt inflation or fiscal deficits, and where money may ultimately lose its vestigial status as a store of value. Yet the reality of capitalist money is more complex. Although the present crisis has irreversibly intensified central bank activism in advanced capitalist economies, fiat money is only one part of the overall monetary structure of global capitalism as the total value of currencies is dwarfed by the vast edifice of fictional capital articulated as commodity money in financial markets.

The primary question, however, is not simply the ontological limit of fictional capital (accumulation without value) but the political limit to financial repression as a means to defend G-SIFIs and prevent an inverted pyramid of debt from destabilizing the international financial and monetary system. This raises two questions, namely: (i) at what point does the expansion of fiat money and sovereign debt become so extensive that it crowds out private entrepreneurial capital, instrumentalizing and appropriating non-governmental wealth as banks become vehicles for states to 'squeeze more indirect tax revenue from citizens by monopolizing the entire savings and payments system' (Reinhardt & Rogoff 2009: 143); and (ii) if sovereigns continue to sustain the liquidity illusion by issuing additional fiat currency (in part to monetize their own debt), at what point will monetary expansion debase currencies and induce inflation, driving investors from bond markets? The prospect of financial socialism suggests a partial recognition of this contradiction and the potential repression of independent capital to defend corporate financial power, pointing towards a 'postcapitalist' monetary system where money as 'stored value' may become unredeemable – that is, where the positive interest function of money as a means to prevent asset devaluation is eroded through rising taxation, negative interest-rates and bank resolution schemes which 'bail-in' depositors' assets to defend the global banking system.

Yet these complex developments cannot be explained in isolation from the proximate impact of underlying stagnation in the advanced economies where the tendency of the profit rate to fall and rising barriers to entry in oligopolistic markets mean productive investment and the creation of new surplus value are in decline – thereby reducing the scope for and possibility of a 'creative destruction' of capital and the cultivation of entrepreneurial dynamism. As Marx argued:

> A fall in the rate of profit and accelerated accumulation are different expressions of the same process only in so far as both reflect the development of productiveness. Accumulation, in turn, hastens the fall of the rate of profit, in as much as it implies concentration of labour on a large scale, and thus a higher composition of capital. On the other hand, a fall in the rate of profit again hastens the concentration of capital and its centralization through expropriation of minor capitalists, the few direct producers who still have anything left to be expropriated. This accelerates accumulation with regard to mass, although the rate of accumulation falls with the rate of profit. (Marx Capital vol. III; ch. 15/1)

In addition, it is important not to lose sight of the additional accumulation of debt since the financial crisis, which threatens to capsize an already unstable financial system. Although the accumulation of private debt noted above is hazardous for workers, unlike the bubble in the US sub-prime mortgage market in 2006–2007, the next collapse in credit markets is more likely to come as investors flee low-grade debt in the bond markets. This in turn would reflect a loss of confidence in corporate incomes and – more seriously – the capacity of sovereign governments to defend the global economic system and guarantee the rule of law in the credit markets, as well as a loss of faith in financial institutions and unprofitable companies.

Economists agree that G20 governments papered over the 2008 financial crisis by printing money and accumulating debt to compensate for and disguise the mountain of debt in the banking system. As we shall see in the next two chapters, regulations introduced since 2009 to prevent insolvency may prove inadequate in future market disturbances (Chu 2018), leading to more open forms of financial repression to defend and maintain G-SIFIs in their present role as the primary institutional determinants of resource allocation in the global economy. This would drastically accelerate trends towards a postcapitalist monetary system based on generalized acceptance of the notion that a positive balance (credit) is not an entitlement to store value but really only an entitlement to acquire goods and services (Fantacci 2013). In a cashless economy with negative interest rates, money could no longer function as a store of value and depositors would be forced to accept non-monetary financial compensation with few alternatives for preserving wealth outside the official system. Regulations might also include proscription of precious metals and/or virtual currencies which threaten the monopoly of state-issued fiat money by allowing individuals to evade surveillance of their assets and private transactions, and could even be extended to capital controls on financial assets that allow independence from expanding structures of corporate organization and state control.

Notes

1 On the interrelationship between national and transnational power in global corporate capitalism, see Robinson (2004, 2007, 2011); Carroll (2010); Miller (2010); Picciotto (2011).
2 See Chapter 5.
3 A school of monetary theory associated with Knapp (1973 [1924]).
4 Thomist refers to the economic ideas of St Thomas Aquinas. For a discussion of the philosopher-saint's relevance for modern debates on the evolution of capitalism, see Scheler (1964).
5 Rickards (2017) notes that 'Russia's strong gold position combined with a very low amount of external debt leaves Russia in the best position to withstand economic distress without default or a funding crisis in the future. This is one reason US economic sanctions have been relatively ineffective at hurting the Russian economy despite a slowdown and recent recession'.
6 This is any pyramidic financial market fraud which pays older investors with funds gained from newer investors who are tricked into believing that they too will make

easy gains. Such schemes promise to return high yields with no risk, yet the cash is never actually invested but used instead it to pay off those who joined at the beginning.

7 See money.visualcapitalist.com.

8 Rechtschaffen notes further that Dodd Frank

> subjects derivatives to a bifurcated regulatory system, in which standardized derivatives contracts with sufficient liquidity must be cleared by a clearinghouse and traded on an exchange, whereas customized derivatives contracts are exempt from the clearing and exchange mandates but are nonetheless subject to capital and margin requirements. (2014: 221)

5
POSTLIBERAL CAPITALISM

Introduction

While the structural causes of the present economic crisis are glossed over by policymakers and corporate media, concerns about the economic stability of the advanced economies and solvency of systemically important banks after the financial crisis have generated a shift away from the so-called 'new monetary consensus' of the 1990s which claimed to offer an neutral 'rules-based' monetary policy regime targeting inflation in place of a 'discretionary' regime aimed at anticipating shocks and other pressures emanating from macro-environments within which central banks operate (Pilkington 2014: 23). The global financial crisis – and the failure of economists to predict it using 'dynamic stochastic general equilibrium' models – has not only exposed the myths of 'neutrality' and 'transparency' popular within monetary policy circles in the 1990s but has led to the development of *hyper*-discretionary monetary policies designed to create inflation, using QE, bank recapitalization and zero interest rates to prevent a post-crisis recession deteriorating into a 'Great Depression 2.0'. The crisis of 2007–2009 also stimulated a new consensus on the need for intensive coordination between central banks and international financial institutions to manage global financial turbulence, leading to the establishment of new rules on capital-to-lending ratios (Basel III) and solvency resolution aimed at protecting the financial system from contagion during future financial shocks. Through sustained pressure on political and monetary elites in all G20 economies, financial corporations have succeeded in legitimizing the idea of transferring significant systemic risk from the private to the public sector; and, while banks continue to expand their holdings of liabilities (supported by mildly improved capital-to-lending ratios in accordance with new Basel rules), governments have dutifully provided liquidity for the financial system and desisted from fiscal expansionary policies in order to manage a dramatic expansion of sovereign debt in the advanced economies after the crisis. The social impact of this assault on public services has been immense as the shift in emphasis from public provision to defence of the market has further distorted the functional role of government, reinforcing the idea of the 'competition state' in which public services continue to be funded yet are 'refunctionalized' to render society fit for 'market competition' (Genschel & Seelkopf 2015).

Yet it is possible to frame this process another way, namely as a core component in a broader strategy of corporate risk management which entails not only the erosion of public fiduciary accountability but an increasing trend towards government economic centralization. This phenomenon is examined here under the rubric 'financial socialism', the chief architects of which are central banks. To understand financial socialism, and its role in global capitalism, it is necessary to appreciate the determining force of *oligarchy* in the silent yet relentless corporate reorganization of liberal-democratic states (Wolin 2010). In postliberal oligarchic capitalism, economic elites representing major financial and nonfinancial corporations exert a disproportional impact on the determination of public policy, while citizens and broad-based civil society groups (NGOs) have token influence. The latter provide, at best, a legitimizing narrative of 'democratic pluralism', preserving a limited competitive exchange of ideas and a semblance of participatory activism while financial institutions and 'big tech' firms increase their control over flows of capital and data while cementing a symbiotic relationship with state elites (Fleming & Fox 2018; Levine 2018). At its core is a network of corporate-state actors who intermediate the financial, political and legal systems of society via a revolving door of insider patronage and cronyism, collectively transforming the concept of public service into a commercial system of private gain and privilege.

The 'winners' in oligarchic capitalism are financiers, bankers, rating agencies, intelligence officials and political insiders whose strategic decisions determine the allocation of capital through public-private partnerships, as well as corporate contractors who have replaced government agencies in the supply of many public services. The 'losers', on the other hand, are taxpayers and indebted consumers who have no access to the revolving door between corporate and political power which ensures private sector profits are augmented by public subsidies while losses are compensated through the state circuits of capital as sovereign debt. The actions of corporate entities before, before, during and after the crisis, have contributed to an unprecedented destruction of wealth among intermediate strata, transferring resources to elites to ensure the stability and continuity of elite accumulation (De Graw 2010). Oligarchic capitalism depends on the corporate model of economic organization which survives because it is part of a

> coercively maintained system in which the state intervenes in the market with subsidized inputs, coercively enforced monopolies and entry barriers, regulatory cartels, artificial scarcity rents, and state enforcement of labor discipline and other restrictions on the bargaining power of labor. (Carson 2014: 90)

These structures insulate corporate elites from what Carson terms the 'competitive effects of inefficiency'. However, he notes, this model of corporate oligarchy is 'unsustainable for the same reasons as the Soviet command economy. The demand for subsidized inputs grows exponentially, and the growing socialization of corporate costs drives the state to bankruptcy' (ibid.: 92).

As a direct result of the global financial crisis, corporate oligarchy and the socialization of corporate failure have been further institutionalized in advanced economies. Financial socialism can be distilled into the following principles for the organization of monetary political economy:

1. *Socialism for the investor class* (which benefits from the issuance of new central bank money and whose corporate interests are protected by monetary easing and new 'macroprudential' regulatory frameworks); and
2. *Darwinian capitalism for the masses* (who must compete for the right to retain meagre assets and survive in a harsh economic environment characterized by inequality and risk).

As Tabb argues, after the crisis of 2007–2009 only a fraction of the funds transferred by the Federal Reserve to financial corporations found its way into productive economic investment, as the government chose 'too-big-to-fail' banks to be its 'primary social partner, to use the European term for class interest and hegemonic bloc formation' (ibid.: 186–187). 'Implicitly or explicitly', he observes, a 'decision had been made to encourage the biggest banks to get bigger still, making it far more difficult to think of ever winding them down in the case of a subsequent failure' (ibid.: 187). This development must be understood in the context of the broader structural evolution of the capitalist mode of production in its postliberal trajectory and the development of advanced economies beyond the constraints imposed by the logic of commercial competition and private production for private gain. In this sense, the forces driving social change in advanced economies are *immanent to the logic of capital itself*, irrespective of international class struggle or movements for global justice.

From an Austrian economic perspective, the postliberal evolution of capitalism reflects the accelerated decline of the liberal concept of *right* embodied in concrete form in the principle of exclusive ownership of property and individual entrepreneurship. This school of thought, which holds that only a 'free' economy can achieve a coherent set of value interconnections between market actors, is critical of what it sees as 'global socialism' – defined as a corporate global system administered by unelected transnational elites which overshadows the historic operation of competitive market capitalism in a drive to reduce international economic imbalances and promote 'synchronized global growth'. For libertarians, corporate globalism is 'clad in free trade garb' but through the destruction of borders and identities 'applies a broad economic brush to varying problems and economic conditions of differing regions and as a result […]

tends to exacerbate economic problems rather than fixing them, and hinders free trade by distorting market responses' (Carlson 2017: 1). It is an extension of 'political capitalism' in a national context, where economic and political elites cooperate for mutual benefit (Holcombe 2018). This reflects not only libertarian distrust of transnational liberal elites who populate governance institutions such as the IMF or WTO but a *conservative* antipathy towards the rationalizing mono-cultural tendencies of globalization and the levelling impact of transnational corporate power on sovereign nation-states (Saul 2009). Although corporate media habitually fail to link the rise of right-wing populism to anti-corporatist sentiment in western democracies (particularly in the US), astute writers have made a clear, if not irrefutable, connection: 'The problem is not Trump', argues Hedges;

> it is a political system, dominated by corporate power [... Trump] tapped into the hatred that huge segments of the American public have for a political and economic system that has betrayed them. He may be inept, degenerate, dishonest and a narcissist, but he adeptly ridicules the system they despise. (Hedges 2018: 1–2)

From a Marxian perspective, on the other hand, it reflects a contradiction in the capitalist form of value discussed in Chapter 3, revealing the barriers to profitable accumulation within the framework of neoliberal globalization which, by suppressing wages despite continually rising productivity, prohibits effective demand management by national governments and fails to comprehend the limited economic value of new technologies for the generation of surplus value. Although it has failed to overcome the economic stagnation and disinflation caused by the bursting of investment bubbles in the US technology sector (1999–2001) and US housing market (2002–2007), the logic of financial socialism (thus far) appears to lie in the stubborn determination of existing monetary and political elites to forestall a more serious devaluation of fictitious capital values in the global markets and to return the global economy to some form of 'profitable' accumulation – although there is clearly a distinction between profitability in the financial sector and the rate of profitable accumulation in the wider economy stimulated by productivity gains and investment in capital and consumer goods using state-of-the-art technologies (AI, robotics, etc.). Such products appeal to sophisticated consumers yet lack *universal* use-value and depend less on the generation of surplus value through employment of productive labour. As Patnaik argues:

> [A] dollar shifted from the poor to the rich, even if it generates the same consumption expenditure, entails expenditure on very different sets of commodities. Typically expenditure by the rich is on goods and services which are much less employment-intensive than those which the working people demand. This is because technological progress under capitalism in

the form of process and product innovations has the character generally of economizing on labour [...] and the rich demand more up-to-date goods than the poor. (Patnaik 2016: 10)

Although it is widely assumed that new technologies feed directly into the production of new commodities with universal use-value, 'progress' is usually achieved at the price of excluding productive labour from employment to create goods and services for which there is a paucity of demand. At the same time, capital is 'impelled to bring the state and superstructure back in to manage an expanding array of externalities or facets of human economic life which its inner logic is incapable of handling' (Westra 2010: 74). The political-economic evolution of capitalist society in this respect reflects the *concretization of the contradiction between value and use value*, which is to say, the concretization of the logic of capital as it is refracted by the recalcitrance of its stage-specific use values (ibid.: 76).

Understood in this sense, financial socialism portends a postliberal-capitalist socioeconomic formation in which central banks not only tax the population indirectly by reducing the rate of interest on savings below the rate of inflation (Hoda 2016) but also assume increasing control over the strategic direction of the economy. In centrally planned capitalism, maintaining interest rates at or near the zero lower bound means that money effectively loses its historic function as a store of value, as economic and monetary elites coerce institutions and investors into bond markets to finance an expanding inverse pyramid of debt. The growth of central bank control over the monetary system, to stimulate consumer spending by reducing private hoards and accelerating the velocity of money in the economy, exerts a stabilizing effect on the financial system yet crowds out independent capital, while destroying through negative real interest rates and rising taxes the financial position of intermediate strata who can no longer finance or reproduce the class privilege of property ownership.[1] The aim of financial socialism is not simply to prevent a recurrence of the financial crisis – which forced states to shoulder the liabilities of insolvent banks – but to maintain an exhausted accumulation regime in a suboptimal condition of *latency* while compensating for the limited stimulus effect of investment in financial and information technologies designed to secure new sources of wealth through the anticipation of future value and exploitation of financial data as a secondary – or proxy – form of capital.

As we have seen, given the scale of additional debt accumulated since 2008, global liquidity is the main policy priority of global elites because monetary collapse would result in a catastrophic destruction of value harming not just elite institutions but *entire* economies. This would potentially limit the capacity of investors to appropriate the surplus product of the global economy, undermining the hidden structural influence of banking elites. Despite clear evidence of declining asset values in the economically critical technology sector – after market leaders Facebook, Amazon, Apple, Netflix and Google combined lost more than $1 trillion in market capitalization during 2018

(Wigglesworth et al. 2018), political and monetary elites continue to believe with sublime confidence that the illusion of rising asset values can (and will) be maintained indefinitely. The alternative presumably entails an unacceptable loss of economic influence and power over capital, for if prices fall precipitously then major global institutional investors who purchased equities, commodities and financial derivatives at already inflated prices after the Wall Street 'recovery' of 2015–2017 will be confronted by ruinous losses. Yet the potential for deteriorating systemic stability is increasing steadily – not simply due to the contradiction between global capital mobility and national monetary governance (which requires ill-equipped *national* reserve banks to take responsibility for the resolution of failed *international* financial institutions operating within their jurisdictions) (Schoenmaker 2013) – but because declining profitability has led to the stagnation of Western capitalism. In addition, stagnation in the West is exacerbated by slowing growth and declining profitability in China (Watts 2019).

To combat this, monetary and political elites have opted for a latter-day version of Ricardo's 'stationary state': a centrally planned yet stagnant capitalist economy sustained by central bank activism and government conservatorship (partial nationalization), where profits and wages flatline as government-backed financial corporations accumulate capital without value. Dependent on government bond purchases and public-private partnerships (PPPs), financial socialism can be compared in key respects to economic fascism – that is to say, a corporatist model of political-economic management to stabilize capital and deflect anti-globalist pressures. As Schumpeter (1942) observed, the development of corporatism *both announces yet defers the decadence of capitalism*; it coincides not only with a declining 'entrepreneurial function' and 'hollowing out' of private property (Swedberg 1992), but with the triumph of state-issued (fiat) money and the intensification of financial repression to appropriate the private wealth of citizens. Fascism is typically associated with radical right-wing political movements, and there are indeed strong similarities between these currents – especially in the EU (Eatwell 2004; Norris 2005). Yet as Marxists emphasize, fascism emerges *wherever capitalist hegemony is placed in question* – that is, wherever employers lose control over the political agenda or can no longer manage workers using the normal levers of economic repression. Economic fascism leads to new forms of state intermediation, as a result of which private financial institutions and corporations become partially or wholly subject to state direction. PPPs exemplify this model, imposing state controls over the allocation of private capital. At the same time, financial repression implies not simply negative real interest rates but hidden forms of taxation which favour corporations yet penalize small firms and middle-income households. It also implies the legal marginalization of alternative currencies and the removal of physical money from circulation on the grounds that cash held outside banks (particularly high-value bills) increases transaction costs and facilitates organized crime and terrorism (Sands 2016; Rogoff 2016).

In what follows, we examine the function of central banks in global finance and their role in the process of government economic centralization. In the final chapter, we will then examine the new framework of bank resolution and elite attempts to reform the institutional architecture of global capitalism without recognizing the declining power of G7 economies. Although the supersession of the G7/8 by the G20 in 2009 marks a tacit acceptance of new growth poles in the global economy, Western elites still dominate the primary institutions of international financial regulation and capital still remains relatively concentrated in financial centres of North America, Europe and Asia. Compliance with financial regulation is uneven, reflecting the relative importance of finance capital in specific national economies. Yet there is increasing awareness of the weakness of 'recovery' in advanced economies and the growth of financial risk as investors continue to leverage profits through the accumulation of debt. There is also growing awareness of the risks of returning to 'normal' monetary policy after a decade of low interest rates accompanied by record equity prices in a market led by a handful of financial corporations and 'big tech' firms whose market valuation has pushed global share indexes to historically unprecedented highs.

Central bank activism

To understand how monetary policy has evolved, and how it influences the wider economy, it is necessary to consider the economic function of central banks in postliberal capitalism, before examining the limits of state-issued fiat money as a means for stabilizing the edifice of fictitious capital in advanced economies. Our thesis is that while elites saw few other options than to use monetary policy after September 2008 to defend their economic power and limit political unrest, the acceleration of central bank activism has become a policy option which *cannot now be unlearned or reversed*: it has made the advanced economies more rather than less dependent on banks of last resort and has increased the moral hazard of sustaining giant financial institutions; and it has – despite public mistrust of bankers – made it more difficult for people to imagine alternatives to capitalist central planning. Although a future devaluation of leveraged asset values in financial markets cannot be deferred indefinitely – particularly if interest rate increases lead to debt-defaults or price corrections in equity markets – central bank activism reflects a deeper transformation in the political organization and legitimation of capitalist accumulation based on government economic centralization. Shielded by the veneer of 'independence', which is always contingent (Singleton 2011), and the symbolic performance of 'stability cultures' in monetary policy discourse (Tognato 2012), central banks have assumed a leading role in managing the self-expanding logic of capital. It is no exaggeration to say that the increasing use of open market operations and recapitalization by central banks to stabilize the financial system and defend distressed banks are unprecedented in modern economic history (Prins 2018).

Central bank authority is tied to public expectations of prudence, yet the monetary authority of the ECB, the Federal Reserve and the Bank of England depends less on the economic literacy of the public than on shared value-orientations, where a preference for price stability is linked at a deeper level to concepts of identity (Tognato 2012). Central banks serve as backstops in the financial system with the authority and might to respond to *force majeure*; they have the perceived authority, as quasi-independent institutions, to respond decisively to irresistible and/or unforeseeable actions which necessitate a rapid change of policy or cancellation of obligations for which no agency can ultimately be held accountable. Their actions possess, in this sense, a *force higher than law*, an exceptional or 'sovereign' quality which enables them, with the backing of national governments and transnational financial institutions, to impose emergency measures to contain market contagion and quell financial panics. The changing role of central banks in advanced economies in recent decades reflects the rapid evolution of the global financial system, which has increased the scope and pressure for radical forms of market intervention to engineer economic expansion, combat the threat of deflation – which increases the actual burden of debt over time (Hoda 2016: 64) – and shore up the financial system during periods of credit contraction.

It is the basic function of central banks to use monetary policy to manipulate the economy by persuading consumers to borrow money and purchase goods and services. This is achieved, argues Hoda, through an elaborate 'bluff' – that is, by assuming a posture of absolute confidence about future prosperity in order to increase the willingness of consumers and investors to take risks in the present:

> by lowering interest rates [central banks] can propel the public into economic activity that leads to greater prosperity characterized by more jobs and wages. At the outset, investors are lured into risky financial investments such as stocks, corporate bonds and real estate by cheaper borrowing costs and the promise of higher wages that will ultimately provide the buying power to sustain these asset prices. At the same time, an inadequate return on savings in interest-earning bank accounts or via risk-free investments in government securities in the face of inflation gives investors a further prod to invest in risky assets. (ibid.: 9)

However, she observes:

> The thrall of the apparent wealth created by a rush to invest generates a tremendous 'feel-good' factor, but it does not necessarily serve as a conduit for higher wages. In the absence of higher wages, asset prices and higher levels of indebtedness can be sustained only by lower and lower risk-free interest rates, and the illusion that greater prosperity is just around the corner. Both of these factors act to continually make risky investments attractive. The downside is that these assets then become vulnerable to

investors' changing perceptions, as well as any appreciable rise in the cost of borrowing. (ibid.)

This bluff works only if rising inflation and falling interest rates threaten consumers with the reality of declining purchasing power; it is, in effect, a form of intimidation, always followed by a reimposition of financial discipline as prices rise and new asset bubbles are created, leading banks to raise rates to reduce the amount of money chasing goods and services to prevent economic 'overheating'. As long as central banks maintain their aura of invincibility to prevent deflation and limit the damaging effects of periodic economic downturns, it is a bluff that the public (and investors) always fall for because no one wants to miss out while others take advantage of cheap money and while banks effectively charge customers to keep their money 'secure' by offering negligible interest on savings.

The ultimate functions of central banking are thus to manage the quantity and stability of money in a particular jurisdiction by issuing new money (liquidity), influencing the velocity of circulation of money in the economy and managing inflation using interest rates, which affect the price of borrowing across the economy and encourage entrepreneurs to borrow and invest (Chorafas 2013b: 57–58). Monetary policy is normally conducted in tandem with fiscal policy, which may also be expansionary or restrictive, and the two processes are coordinated between central banks and finance ministries to reduce the potential for contradiction. The core aim is to maximize the velocity of money while maintaining price stability, though it is not always clear how the actions of central banks directly or indirectly affect the circulation of money in an economy given the scale of credit money created by fractional reserve banking (creation of money by banks through issuance of credit) and the growth of fictitious capital (commodity money) in financial markets. In addition, one must factor in the impact of foreign exchange markets which are responsible for trillions of dollars in currency trades daily.[2] Yet, as Chorafas reminds us, the key issue is 'rapid monetary growth, which typically flows first into the prices of financial assets and then spills over into other commodities' (ibid.: 68). Directly or indirectly, 'the loosening of monetary policy can trigger inflation in financial markets and thereafter in other commodity prices. Nobody has yet disproved that in the long run inflation is primarily a monetary phenomenon' (ibid.).

In the short- to medium-term, however, the abiding concern of central bankers is to avoid the 'liquidity trap', where each additional unit of new money capital created has a diminishing economic return:

Conventionally, the expansion of the money supply will generate inflation as more money is chasing after the same amount of goods available. During a liquidity trap, however, increases in money supply are fully absorbed by excess demand for money (liquidity); investors hoard the increased money instead of spending it because the opportunity cost of holding cash – the forgone earnings from interest – is zero when the nominal interest rate is zero. Even worse, if the increased money supply is through LSAPs [large scale asset purchases] on long-term debts (as is the case under QE), investors are prompted to further shift their portfolio holdings from interest-bearing assets to cash. (Arias & Wi 2014: 1)

Although low interest rates have become the 'new normal', accommodative monetary policy exercises a deflationary effect as *each new monetary unit generates less economic activity* (Minerd 2016). The lag between central bank actions and changing prices/market outcomes obscures the long-term dynamics of monetary easing on consumer behaviour *and* the moral hazard implicit in the (false) self-assurance of G–SIFIs who assume that risk-prone market action will be compensated for by public assistance or – as we shall in the next chapter – a 'bail-in' of depositors' assets.

While the scale and scope of central bank activism have both grown since the late nineteenth century, the logic of emergency market intervention is the same, namely *price discovery*: to determine the correct price of commodities/securities by evaluating supply and demand and associated factors. In normal circumstances, price discovery is achieved by the market, where the greater the number of participants, the faster the rate at which prices are determined. This process is assisted by algorithms that efficiently calculate expected outcomes for a range of assets. In conditions of financial panic, on the other hand, bank runs, capital flight and credit contraction lead to a general breakdown of market calculation, making it more difficult to determine prices. The creation of the US Federal Reserve Bank in 1913, which handed the power to print the nation's money to a clique of private bankers, was a direct result of the Panic of 1907 when markets collapsed and flows of credit dried up, leading to a near meltdown of the US financial system. This was the fifth in a series of escalating banking crises dating back to the panic of 1873, triggering a recession in Europe and North America ending the long boom of the second half of the nineteenth century and ushering in a new age of protectionism. To counter the deterioration of financial stability, an elite group of bankers convened to resolve the crisis informally by establishing valuations of troubled bank assets and identifying insolvent institutions.

The creation of the US Federal Reserve formalized this arrangement, though in the modern era insolvency resolution has become more complex, extensive and prolonged, facilitated by procedures with long acronyms like the US Troubled Asset Relief Program (TARP):

Today markets are global; assets held by financial institutions, including mortgage-backed securities and asset-backed securities are more complex; and there are numerous categories of debt and derivatives. Nevertheless, the principle of price discovery as a way to gauge financial institutions' exposure to bad debt is essentially the same for the Great Credit Crisis of 2007–2009 as was for the Panic of 1907. The main difference is that [...]

we may need more sophisticated techniques – among them public-private investment programs (PPIPs) or perhaps an equivalent private sectors solution in which hedge funds or private equity groups buy troubled securities from banks at a substantial discount, allowing some form of market-related price discovery for toxic illiquid mortgage-related assets to be achieved as they are removed from bank balance sheets, and enabling financial institutions to accurately determine their balance sheet capacities and new capital needs. (Jones 2014: 17)

In exceptional conditions, once price discovery is achieved it becomes possible through emergency funding through the 'discount window' (providing liquidity at preferential rates for depository institutions and the banking system as a whole through backup funding via state circuits of financial capital) to ring-fence and dispose of 'toxic' assets and liabilities, allowing private investors to return to the market and resume speculation.

Singleton (2011) observes that banking crises became more frequent as the deregulation of finance and banking intensified. As we saw in Chapters 2 and 3, precedents for the 2008 meltdown were already clear in the series of deepening crises which hit Asia, Russia, Latin America, the US hedge fund Long Term Capital Management (LCTM) and finally the new technology sector between 1999 and 2001:

> Lacking experience of managing risk in a deregulated environment, banks and financial institutions often made unwise lending decisions to clients wishing to buy property and financial assets at inflated prices. Prudential policy was weak in this phase, as central banks and other supervisors struggled to develop and implement new procedures. When the asset bubble burst banks were left with non-performing loans on their books. (Singleton 2011: 226)

The Greenspan years at the Federal Reserve became synonymous with liberalization and a new culture of risk and inflated asset prices, and despite Greenspan's 'deft touch' the period is remembered for escalating instability fuelled by accommodative central bank policies – defended for public consumption as 'light touch regulation'. This trend was mirrored in the UK where the Bank of England concluded that the banking system was 'resilient' thanks to 'strong and stable macroeconomic and financial conditions' (*Bank of England Financial Stability Report* April 2007, in Singleton 2011: 278). Fuelled by jubilation among global elites over the institutionalization of the European single currency and the creation of the ECB – reflecting a German-oriented *ordoliberal* preference for economic decision-making liberated from political interference (Feld et al. 2015), this period may be viewed historically as a highpoint in central bank autonomy before the abrupt intrusion of government into the rarefied world of monetary political economy in the global financial crisis (ibid.; cf. Buiter 2009).

If, in addition to political interference, the independence of central banks is defined in terms of their proximity to financial markets (where central bankers attempt to deliver as close as possible a monetary regime that the markets expect, adopting in the process the short-termism so characteristic of investors), then it is clear the financial crisis 'created a new avenue along which markets can influence the monetary authority – namely their impact on central bank attempts to mitigate the prospects of future financial instability' (Siklos 2017: 186). This is exemplified by controversy over the controversial use of 'forward guidance' – the attempt by central banks to sustain confidence and steer economies by influencing market expectations of future interest rate movements through pre-planned statements. While forward guidance is used in the interests of communication, in the attempt to promote financial *certainty* a new type of *uncertainty* is created, namely whether central banks can actually fulfil the measures entailed in their own forward guidance statements (Rickards 2014: 66). This point is voiced by other observers, who argue that central banks are taking forward guidance too far, leading central banks 'to hint at steps they are unable to carry out or to engage interventions that are outside their remit, with the consequence that monetary authorities end up taking on burdens beyond their normal role' (Siklos 2017: 188).

A dramatic escalation of capitalist central planning through central bank activism occurred in the wake of the financial panic of September/October 2008 caused by the collapse of Lehman Brothers which threatened to trigger a more general collapse of the US banking system, and which had serious implications for the international financial system. Unique in the official response to the crisis, however, was not price discovery or emergency recapitalization, but the response of the authorities to the initial failure of accommodative policies to stem rapidly deteriorating financial conditions. This forced the Federal Reserve – followed by other central banks – to deploy *unconventional* large-scale easing through a massive increase in the long-term purchase of distressed assets, securities and government bonds. For some observers this extension of central bank activism was little short of heroic; whether one takes the US or Europe as an example, argues El-Erian,

> central banks have essentially been the only policymaking entities consistently willing and able to take bold measures to deal with an unusually complex set of national, regional, and global economic and financial challenges. In doing so, they have evaluated, to use Federal Reserve Board Chairman Ben Bernanke's phrase, an 'unusually uncertain' outlook; they have confronted some unknowable cost-benefit equations and related economic and political trade-offs and, in some cases, they have even had to make things up as they went along (including moving way ahead of other government agencies that, frustratingly, have remained on the sidelines). (El-Erian 2012)

After the Lehman collapse, however, central banks led by the Federal Reserve effectively abandoned their carefully nurtured reputation for prudence and caution to defend favoured banks and allow the collapse or takeover of weaker institutions, extending elite control over the entire banking system *without* extracting a 'quid-pro-quo and without proportional and appropriate pain for shareholders, directors, top managers and creditors of the institutions that benefited' (Buiter 2008: 103). In the US, 'access to Fed resources was extended without a matching expansion of the regulatory constraints traditionally put on counterparties enjoying this access'. As a result, Buiter notes, 'it is difficult to avoid the impression that the Fed [was] too close to the financial markets and leading financial institutions, and too responsive to their special pleadings to make the right decisions for the economy as a whole' (ibid.: 104). In the EU, meanwhile, the indebted states of Greece, Portugal and Ireland were required to take on more debt to remain in the eurozone and to ensure the continued solvency of German, French and British banks, leading the three weakest EU economies to become by far the largest borrowers of emergency funds from the IMF (Evans-Pritchard 2016).

The 2008 crisis was accompanied by high drama, as US Treasury Secretary Paulson, acting on behalf of Wall Street, threatened congressional leaders with dire consequences should they reject the second attempt by the federal government to pass the Emergency Economic Stabilization Act (EESA) authorizing more than $700 billion in emergency public capital transfers to private US banks facing imminent collapse – the initial stage of what quickly became the largest central bank recapitalization in history. The House of Representatives had initially rejected Paulson's bank bailout legislation on 29 September 2008 but after a further collapse of markets and dark warnings of political chaos, the EESA was deviously reintroduced in Congress and passed by the Senate, attached to a bill already being debated, effectively sidelining opposition in the House of Representatives where financial legislation is normally introduced first. Congress finally approved the bill on 3 October 2008 and it was instantly signed into law. Some observers liken this train of events to a financial state of emergency or even a 'stealth coup d'état' where 'the machinery of governance grinds through a simulacrum of democracy, but it's all for show' (Smith 2010). Yet the EESA and Troubled Asset Relief Program (TARP) were only the start of a long-term transfer of public funds, according to a 2018 audit which media have largely ignored (Greenstein 2018). This 2018 audit was without precedence in the history of the Federal Reserve, revealing that 'over $16 trillion [had been] allocated to corporations and banks internationally, purportedly for "financial assistance" during and after the 2008 fiscal crisis' (ibid.).

To place this event in context, De Graw suggests that the 'financial coup' of September 2008 made possible in the capitalist metropole something which financial elites are normally able to achieve *only* in peripheral or semi-peripheral economies through agencies like the IMF, which provides emergency lending to insolvent governments and arrives in Third World capitals to take control of fiscal and monetary policy: 'When financial coups are carried out in [poor] countries', he notes, 'they call it a structural adjustment program (SAP). The end result is the theft of working class wealth, the privatization of public functions and resources, rising unemployment, the elimination of the middle class and increasing taxation and debt [...]' (De Graw 2010: 1). Since 2008, the official name for structural adjustment in the West has been 'austerity', which the IMF concedes has failed to resolve the underlying structural problems afflicting developed capitalist economies (McDuff 2017).

The criminal nature of this wealth transfer notwithstanding, bank bailouts in the US and the UK created a serious problem of moral hazard which Woll (2014: 67) defines as the 'undesirable side effect of insurance: an individual who knows that the costs of his or her actions will be borne by someone else has a greater tendency to engage in risky behaviour'. The author cites an apt comment in the *New York Times* in August 2007 before the crisis intensified, namely that 'capitalism without financial failure is not capitalism at all, but a kind of socialism for the rich' (Grant 2007, cited in ibid.: 65). This perspective correlates closely with the argument outlined above, namely that corporate power has accelerated a shift from competitive market capitalism to financial socialism. Although the socialization of financial losses in the US and the UK has assumed different forms (nationalization *versus* conservatorship), events on both sides of the Atlantic demonstrate 'how little the liberal market traditions and the importance of the two financial centers in the overall economy shapes government crisis management' (ibid.: 111). This approach was also adopted, if on a less spectacular scale, in Germany and France where collective action by the financial sector induced monetary and political elites to intervene to forestall liquidity crises and recapitalize financial institutions which dominate the highly concentrated banking sector in both states, allowing some banks to exploit the crisis to further consolidate their market position by acquiring others (ibid.: 122–138).

The use of quantitative easing and forward guidance by central banks to steer capitalist economies has fuelled rising equity prices and distorted term premiums on government securities (higher yields paid on longer-term government bonds), inverting yield curves and threatening instability as investors seek higher returns from riskier assets (potentially reducing liquidity in 'safer' bond markets).[3] Since the 1990s, central banks have graduated from 'neutral inflation targeting' towards driving the asset-price transmission mechanism (the link between monetary policy and aggregate demand) to induce depositors and investors to engage in more risk-prone activity in the belief that economic growth and rising prices will inevitably push up the value of their investments. Yet they have achieved financial repression at the price of creating a counter-narrative to the official discourse on economic growth and rising asset prices. This counter-narrative is distilled in an intuitive suspicion among depositors and investors that the long-term resort to monetary easing and low interest rates to sustain credit creation indicate that 'something [is] seriously wrong with the economy, which will not permit the central bank to normalize the situation [...]' (Hoda 2016: 91).

It is this dilemma which confronts political and monetary elites in low-growth G7 economies in which intermediate strata face financial ruin while central banks transfer bad debts to their balance sheets (El-Erian 2012;

Singh 2017), and while QE has become *conditio sine qua non* for encouraging financial corporations to lend.[4] Writing in 2015, Grant argues that after an extended period of QE and near-zero rates, the long-term consequences of central bank activism are unknown. 'The virus of radical monetary intervention has entered the world's political bloodstream', he observes: 'in the US, the UK, the EU, Japan and Switzerland, QE and zero per cent interest rates now pass for mainstream central banking doctrine' (Grant 2015: 2). As an insider, however, Grant questions not the logic of central bank intervention (a 'necessary' measure to deter financial panic) but its *scale* and *duration*: how long is it feasible to maintain the illusion of recovery through accommodative monetary policy; and how great a distortion of asset prices is permissible before the reality that issuing new money to aid insolvent banks and saturate bond markets creates only a short-lived blip in economic activity followed by a debauching of currency?

Conventional wisdom states that accommodative monetary policy can be used effectively to address short-run cyclical problems yet cannot resolve underlying structural contradictions (Minard 2016). Critics *outside* the investor class, on the other hand, question what insiders prefer to ignore, namely the unviability of an economy based on the continual reflation by central banks of asset classes in the absence of an equivalent rise in wages – all to support credit creation and sustain the illusion of prosperity. They also reject the conventional wisdom that booms are investor-led – natural or inevitable consequences of irrational exuberance. Instead, financial excess is seen as a consequence of economic failure: the status quo is determined by the stagnation of capitalism and the one-dimensional outlook of monetary and political elites whose motive is to prevent a devaluation of leveraged market values leading to a destruction of accumulated wealth (Lohoff & Trenkle 2013).

Others even suggest that the failure to exit the crisis by normalizing monetary policy and return economies to growth indicates that we are approaching the limits of liquidity finance itself: 'Alarming as it may be to admit it', argue Amato and Fantacci, 'there can be no getting away from the fact [that] since 2007, the world has been in a state of crisis from which there is no turning back. The deluge is not "after" us. All that was to happen has happened, what was to finish is over and there is no *belle époque* to return to' (Amato & Fantacci 2014: 18). While there is rarely any public recognition of this denouement – the official posture is always a return to 'business as usual' (Mattick 2011) – the emphasis in international monetary political economy is on *governance*, based on the assumption that new forms of macroprudential regulation are adequate to compensate for systemic risk created by financialized capitalism. This moves the discussion away from the 'crime scene' of the banking crisis in the US and the UK and the sovereign debt crisis in the EU to the problem of managing systemic risk created by international financial liberalization and allocating responsibility for insolvency resolution in the future.

Unstable equilibrium

As noted in Chapter 3, it is the mode of resolution of earlier capitalist cri-ses which creates necessary preconditions for the unfolding of future crises. The consequences of monetary easing and government stimulus in advanced economies created a shallow recovery driven by historically low interest rates. This regime was adequate in the short-term to promote interbank lending and forestall sovereign default, yet elites are careful to play down the longer-term risk of systemic failure (MacKinnon 2017). New sources of instability became clear as in 2017 as central banks tentatively began to tighten mon-etary policy (only to decelerate this trend again as financial instability resur-faced in late 2018). Excessive monetary easing and government stimulus led one commentator to observe in February 2018 that because 'policy has been "ultra-easy" for many years […] it is now caught in a debt trap of its own making. Continuing on the current monetary path is ineffective and increas-ingly dangerous. But any reversal also involves great risks' (White 2018: 1). The author adds that:

> inflation is not the only danger. First, debt ratios have been allowed to rise for decades, even after the crisis began. Moreover, whereas before the crisis this was primarily a problem of the advanced economies, it has since gone global. Second, tolerance of risk-taking threatens future financial stability, as does the narrowing of the profit margins for many traditional financial institutions. Third, the misallocation of real resources by banks and other financial institutions is encouraged by this monetary environment. With markets unable to allocate resources properly, due to the actions of central banks, the likelihood that rising debt commitments will not be honoured has risen sharply. (ibid.)

In this precarious environment, critics argue that capitalism faces a 'bifurcation moment': a point in the development of complex socioeconomic systems where changes in the *qualitative* orientation of existing structures become possible or necessary for the existing system to continue to function. Such changes may take the form of a loss of stability in *existing* modes of functioning, regulation and control, leading to their eventual supersession by new modes of function-ing with altered or new system properties. The nature of these new systemic properties 'is as yet undetermined and, in principle, impossible to predeter-mine, but one that is open to human intervention and creativity' (Wallerstein 2000: 251).

Wallerstein is correct to argue that a 'bifurcation moment' might create open-ings for a new critical praxis – a radical oppositional strategy, for example, based on *inoperativity* (unilateral withdrawal of workers from socially necessary labour) in defiance of the 'project-oriented vision of human existence' entailed in the capitalist *Arbeitsgesellschaft* (Prozorov 2014; cf. Eisenberg 1999; Watkin 2012).

This highlights the potentially disruptive effects of what Agamben terms 'destituent power': a radical oppositional strategy to render systems of law *inoperable* by negating the 'anarchy of power' that seeks to govern disorder in the modern surveillance state (Agamben 2014). As Wolters argues:

> If the fundamental ontological question today is not work but inoperativity, and if this inoperativity can, however, be deployed only through a work, then the corresponding political concept can no longer be that of 'constituent power' [*potere constituente*], but something that could be called 'destituent power' [*potenza destituente*]. And if revolutions and insurrections correspond to constituent power, that is, a violence that establishes and constitutes the new law, in order to think a destituent power we have to imagine completely other strategies, whose definition is the task of the coming politics. A power that was only just overthrown by violence will rise again in another form, in the incessant, inevitable dialectic between constituent power and constituted power, violence which makes the law and violence that preserves it. (2014: 1)

Theorists of destituent power in constitutional sociology have attempted, with mixed results, to relocate the role of the people – not as a unitary or collective actor but as a countervailing 'constitutive mechanism which assumes a particular function in relating the political to the legal system and vice versa' (Möller 2018: 35). Although initially promising in its attempt to develop a critical constestary logic within the realm of constituent power by establishing a 'particular latency of revocatory scenarios which indirectly inhibits constituted powers from carrying out their hegemonic basis' (ibid.: 51), if this countervailing force fails to apply the negative implications of destituent power *to itself*, it risks challenging institutional patterns only to substitute these for alternatives which rapidly congeal into a new hegemonic claim on society that 'immunises itself against critique and reflexivity' (ibid.: 55).

Extrapolating from present conditions it seems another outcome is more probable, namely a further usurpation of power from above and rearticulation of capitalist hegemony through the coercive disciplinary effects of financial socialism. To understand why, it is necessary to theorize financial socialism as a transitional moment in the postliberal evolution of capital which preserves the economic power of the investor class at its present level – which is to say, at its *highest ever historical level*. This reflects the 'asymptotic' nature of power, which escalates continually yet cannot logically reach its own upper limit without unleashing negative consequences:

> The reason can be explained in reference to the following dialectical progression: capitalists cannot stop seeking more power: since capital is power, the drive to accumulate is a drive for more power, by definition; however, the closer capitalist power gets to its limit, the greater the

resistance it elicits; the greater the resistance, the more difficult it is for those who hold power to increase it further; the more difficult it is to increase power, the greater the need for even more force and sabotage; and the more force and sabotage, the higher the likelihood of a serious backlash, followed by a decline or even disintegration of power. [...] The problem that capitalists face today [...] is not that their power has withered, but, on the contrary, that their power has increased. Indeed, not only has their power increased, it has increased by so much that it might be approaching its asymptote. And since capitalists look not backward to the past but forward to the future, they have good reason to fear that, from now on, the most likely trajectory of this power will be not up, but down. (Nitzan & Bichler 2012: 4–5)

Like a decadent empire faced with the inevitability of its own decline, asymptotic logic suggests that to reproduce an oligarchic system at or near to its maximal level of power, monetary and political elites must impose higher levels of financial and political repression and actively restrict public access to (and public awareness of) alternative scenarios for postcapitalist development. In theory, this can be achieved through financial socialism, that is, by aligning the contradictory imperatives of production for private profit and capitalist central planning, leading to de-democratization of advanced western economies and a further mystification of capitalist ideology.

Confronted by financial socialism, the question arises whether capital can continue to expand if the social and material conditions of its reproduction through the valorization of value are undermined by the erosion of dynamic forces (productive labour/competition/profitability) which drive risk-taking and investment. Capital reinvents itself yet remains fundamentally the same: a self-expanding substance derived from surplus value which subsumes economic and cultural processes into the logic of the commodity form, the function of which is to valorize value and transcend an immanent contradiction between new productive forces and decadent relations of production. 'The normal state of capitalism', argues Žižek, is the

permanent revolutionizing of its own conditions of existence: from the beginning, capitalism 'putrefies', it is branded by a crippling contradiction, discord, by an immanent want of balance: this is exactly why it changes, develops incessantly – incessant development is the only way for it to resolve again and again, come to terms with its own fundamental, constitutive imbalance, 'contradiction'. Herein lies the paradox proper to capitalism, its last resort: capitalism is capable of transforming its limit, its very impotence, in the source of its power – the more it 'putrefies', the more its immanent contradiction is aggravated, the more it must revolutionize itself to survive. (1989: 53–54)

Orthodox Marxists traditionally theorized the 'inevitable' supersession of capital through the technical advancement of productive forces, anticipating a revolutionary society based on planned economic development and egalitarianism. Yet this vision of progressive societal evolution failed to take into account precisely the disintegrative tendencies in capitalism which enable capital to continually postpone the moment of its own sublation (*Aufhebung*) by overcoming instead barriers to its own self-expansion, driving the mode of production beyond its present constitutive imbalance through a judicious recalibration of technological and political-institutional supports.

The historical development of capitalism is characterized by cycles of growth, contradiction, collapse and recalibration which Wallerstein (1974) theorizes in terms of Kondratieff 'long waves' – after the eponymous economist whose research into capitalist 'super cycles' was denounced in the USSR but championed by political economists like Schumpeter. Super-cycles last 40–60 years and are influenced by new technologies, by war and revolution, and by the conquest of new territories which facilitate the global expansion of capital (Kondratieff 1979: 538–540). Although the duration of recent cycles has been shorter than historical precedents, long waves are characterized by 'A-phases' (upswings linked to sectoral growth) and 'B-phases' (downswings linked to stagnation). The most recent 'B-Phase' commenced in the 1970s with the crisis of Fordism, followed by a growth phase driven by communications technology and financialization, culminating in the 'sixth' Kondratieff boom of the late 1990s (Nefiodow & Nefiodow 2017). As we have seen, however, the 'new economy' boom was in fact sustained only by central bank activism – principally through the accommodative policies of the Federal Reserve under Alan Greenspan, who repeatedly used monetary policy to combat deflationary pressures and sustain a wealth apparition which finally burst with the dot-com crash of 1999–2001.

As the B-Phase of the cycle unfolds, stagnation has deepened despite central bank activism, leading central banks to prime new asset bubbles to sustain the illusion of rising prices, while fuelling short-run cycles of overinvestment and overselling. Yet Wallerstein's *real* insight is that B-phases of a systemic movement *never end where the A-phases began*. Which is to say, 'there is always a systemic price to pay for renewing the upward phases of cycles. The system has always to move just a little further from equilibrium' (Wallerstein 2009: 2). In other words, the re-establishment of equilibrium is always more unstable in each successive cycle, as new growth sectors provide ostensibly promising yet ultimately inadequate bases for a further development of the commodity form as a vehicle for profitable accumulation. This phenomenon is apparent in the present period as a new generation of entrepreneurs search for 'dematerialized' commodities with universal use-value like AI and fintech to drive a new upswing. In the absence of a hyperinflationary expansion of asset values, however, deflationary pressures suggest a continual shortening of the growth cycle as an exhausted mode of production approaches its asymptotic limits, which is to say, as *further* accumulation becomes impracticable without undermining systemic coherence. The key question, argues, Wallerstein is not 'how will the capitalist system mend itself, and renew its forward thrust. The question is *what will replace this system?* What order will be chosen out of this chaos?' (ibid.; emphasis added).

It is equally apparent that financial socialism in advanced economies coincides with a power transition in the international system. On the one hand, stagnant G7 economies remain in limp mode, sustained by central bank activism and low interest rates to maintain financial market capital by stimulating credit creation and debt-leveraged investment in sectors like energy, student loans and automobile finance. Although 'recovery' in the EU and the US was officially declared in 2015–2016, prospects for a normalization of monetary policy are doubtful in G7 economies marked by excess liquidity, asset price inflation, increasing levels of non-performing loans (Borak 2019) and a doubling in the size of the leveraged loan market to $1.2 trillion as financial investors seek higher returns (Rennison & Smith 2019). On the other hand, global trends suggest a decline in the commercial and geopolitical pre-eminence of G7 economies as emerging market corporations generate higher rates of growth (Lin & Dailami 2011):

> Most agree that its critical Western core is weakened and multilateralism is challenged. As a result, the system is likely to struggle to (i) accommodate the development breakout phase in systemically important emerging economies and (ii) absorb the deleveraging of finance-dependent advanced countries. What is yet to be seen is whether the outcome will be a bumpy transition to a more multipolar global system or the healing and reassertion of a unipolar one. (El-Erian 2012: 3)

For the first time in the economic history of the modern world-system (1500 onwards), *non*-Western corporations are increasingly succeeding in their own industrial sectors, placing pressure on advanced economies to adapt to a more multilateral framework for cross-border trade and investment. Although emerging markets are vulnerable to fluctuations in demand in core capitalist economies (witness growing instability in BRICS economies since 2015), despite rising indebtedness they are also quicker to return to growth. Added to this convergence in economic trends, there is a dramatic divergence in demographic factors among ageing and equally indebted Western economies with declining birth rates and rising pension costs – including the UK which faces a potential retirement savings shortfall of $33 trillion by 2050 (Mauldin 2017).

Wallerstein imagines a pluralistic decentred globalism in which major economies and regions determine which type of globalization is appropriate for *their* national interests (cf. Buzan 2011). The issue is not the 'West versus the rest', but the future spatial form and distribution of capital in a globally constituted system of commodity production: it is not just a question of rivalry between great powers, but which regional economic formation in a decentred global growth system can achieve relative preponderance, and which model of capitalism will assume pre-eminence in a post-US-centric order. For transatlantic elites, two strategic policy options exist:

1. Maintain an oligarchic global economic order *in cooperation with* non-Western elites, creating the conditions for a multipolar global growth system; or
2. Maintain an oligarchic global economic order *in conflict with* non-Western elites to preserve a unipolar world order, creating the conditions for war.

The former is the preferred option of geoeconomic realists influenced by a perhaps inevitable shift in the balance of global economic power towards a Eurasian bloc of state-capitalist economies led by China – a partial consequence of the 2008 crisis. This reflects a belated realization that the *sovereign* economic interests of the US have been neglected amid the eagerness of the US to maintain preponderance in an international security system led by the Anglo-Saxon nations who maintain economic superiority through the Echelon intelligence-gathering system (Burghardt 2013). Adopting a neo-mercantilist stance, Trump does not eschew globalization but *does* reject imbalances which favour authoritarian state-capitalist economies like China, Russia and Iran whose illiberal political systems are characterized by more extreme forms of oligarchy.

Contradictions between globalizing capital and national capitals notwithstanding, capitalist accumulation remains a self-propelling end in itself (Trenkle 2006), and if barriers to capital's self-expansion through 'free' trade are approached, accumulation may be sustained by *dirigiste* means, namely government economic centralization, restrictions on property rights, controls on the freedom of citizens to hold wealth outside banks, and a further erosion of civil liberties through state surveillance and police violence. Elite responses since the 2008 financial crisis and its political aftershocks indicate that there are potentially *no limits* to what transnational elites, supported by sovereign governments, are prepared to do to maintain system-stability and preserve their prerogative right to appropriate the surplus product of the global economy. As Robinson argues:

> The [transnational capitalist class] and state apparatuses at its disposal attempt to resolve both the economic crisis of overaccumulation and to manage the political conditions of that crisis, that is, the spread of global revolt and the potential – not yet realized – of that global revolt to overthrow the system. As digitalization concentrates capital, heightens polarization, and swells the ranks of surplus labor, dominant groups turn to applying the new technologies to mass social control and repression in the face of real and potential resistance. The new systems of warfare, social control and repression made possible by more advanced digitalization include global electronic surveillance that allows for the tracking and control of every movement. (Robinson 2019: 162)

This includes control over movements of money in advanced economies through capital controls as financial surveillance becomes more advanced. In the US, de facto capital controls have already been unveiled in the Bank Secrecy Act to prevent depositors removing money from accounts, while the Financial Crimes Enforcement Network monitors movement of funds to foreign accounts. Similar controls exist in the EU and elsewhere.

As we shall see in Chapter 6, events in the eurozone indicate that monetary elites, confronted by bank insolvency, will resort to extraordinary measures to sequester funds from depositors using 'bail-in' resolutions – even if the capacity of large-scale bail-in procedures to replace conventional bailout procedures is untested (Buccuzzi & De Lisa 2017). To ensure the continuity of accumulation and prevent a change in the juridical framework of corporate power, the solvency of GSFIs must be defended in order to maintain a system of wealth transfer to the investor class. Yet while elites tried in 2008–2009 to 'keep the collaborators on board as the ship sank' (Buck 2008), as the next downturn approaches it is inevitable that the independent wealth of intermediate strata will be viewed as an additional potential source of liquidity to pre-empt insolvency in the banking system and prevent a deleveraging of capital value. For elites, financial socialism offers a means to stabilize accumulation through capture of idle capital, extension of capital controls, manipulation of demand, and the promotion of continuous consumption through universal credit schemes. Although opposition to such measures is inevitable, it is unlikely to deter elites whose power depends on the capacity of the banking system and tax system to transfer wealth upwards. As such, financial socialism will accelerate the present decline of intermediate strata – not just in the US, where trends are already pronounced (Desjardins 2017) – but globally.

To illustrate this point, a report by McKinsey Global (2016) found that median incomes have declined as 70 per cent of households across 25 advanced economies saw earnings fall in the decade 2005–2015, compared to 2 per cent over the previous 12 years (Matthews 2016). This decline has been fuelled not only by the disappearance of secure employment opportunities (as Buchheit [2016] observes, 'high-salaried jobs in technology still exist, but they are available to fewer people as machines get smarter'), but by *falling real* incomes across OECD nations (Donnan & Fleming 2016). As one study indicates, this is highly pronounced in EU states, measured not simply in absolute terms but as a function of the probability that intermediate groups will fall back into poverty despite education and other advantages:

> using a poverty line of $21.70 per day (in purchasing power parity terms), which has been suggested for high-income countries, the income threshold above which one belongs to the middle class – meaning they have a sufficiently low probability of falling into poverty – was about $34 per day in the EU from 2005 to 2008. In less than a decade, this threshold has increased 20 per cent, to $40 per day. (Bussolo et al. 2018: 2)

The authors interpret this rising threshold as 'an "insurance premium" necessary to mitigate the risk of falling into poverty' (ibid.). It is a premium increasingly beyond the reach of the petty bourgeoisie and 'new middle class' whose ability to secure self-employment or gain access to white-collar employment have both declined sharply in recent decades revealing the contradictory class location of intermediate strata in late capitalism (Wright 2015).

To focus on one example, a major cause of income inequality in the UK is the wealth transfer effect caused by unequal access to property and the financial leverage which asset bubbles in the property market created by central bank policies afford to rentier elites with access to revenues from property. Asset price inflation in the property market is closely correlated with income, age and social inequality, creating a specific type of economic pathology:

> The profit accruing to the owner of an asset from the appreciation in its value depends to a great extent on how long that asset has been owned. The old owner therefore benefits most from an appreciation. The housing market then redistributes income and wealth from young people earning less at the start of their careers and indebting themselves hugely in order to get somewhere decent to live, to people enjoying the highest earnings at the end of their careers. But housing inflation is also like a pyramid banking [Ponzi] scheme because it requires more and more credit to be put into the housing market in order to allow those profiting from house infla-tion to be able to realize their profits. (Toporowski 2014: 102)

Macfarlane identifies structural reasons for the impoverishment of households who have no opportunity to achieve property ownership:

> Whereas in the mid-1990s low and middle income households could afford a first timebuyer deposit after saving for around 3 years, today it takes the same households 20 years to save for a deposit. Many have increasingly found themselves with little choice but to rent privately. For those stuck in the private rental market, the proportion of income spent on housing costs has risen from around 10% in 1980 to 36% today. Unlike home-owners, there is no asset wealth to draw on to fund new cars or holidays. (Macfarlane 2017: 1)

In the UK, he concludes, 'we have yet to confront the truth about the trillions of pounds of wealth amassed through the housing market in recent decades: this wealth has come straight out of the pockets of those who don't own property' (ibid.). To fuel price inflation and sustain rising asset values, the continuity of elite accumulation depends on supply-side constraints, price inflation and credit expansion which facilitate economic inequality and the continuous capture of wealth from intermediate strata and poor households. There is also a demonstrable link between inequality, asset price inflation and monetary easing, which privileges lenders and propertied elites while excluding low income strata from the advantages of ownership. This wealth transfer effect is directly enhanced by new money creation, and has led to a 22 per cent rise in property prices and a 25 per cent rise in equity prices in the UK in the present period (Lanchester 2018: 7).

One response to the wealth transfer effect would be to increase supply, enabling low-paid workers to remain in urban centres – although this in itself will not resolve the issue without a cap on market speculation (Pettifor 2018). Yet trends indicate that not only are price inflation and market speculation intensifying, but that in the case of construction (a sector of the UK economy that thrives on public contracts and lax planning laws) 'social cleansing' of cities is already advanced, transferring municipal assets to developers using PPPs and other financial investment vehicles to maximize corporate value-capture at the expense of taxpayers. PPPs are a technical term for corporate subsidies issued by governments to facilitate sales of public assets below market value, allowing corporations access to public revenue streams. While the contradiction between unaffordable housing and corporate value-capture is partially mitigated by reduced requirement for skilled manual and non-manual workers in deindustrialized urban centres (revealing a contradiction between de-skilling and oversupply of educated workers), as the disconnect between falling real incomes and spiralling housing costs accelerates, the result is de facto gerrymandering: the legal removal of urban poor from subsidized housing in potentially lucrative city centre districts and the irreversible dislocation of poor communities who can no longer justify their presence in the capitalist metropole.

In the absence of alternative profitable investment options, financial socialism is fuelled by the use of public funds to refinance insolvent financial institutions and the institutionalization of PPPs. The latter are used for a variety of purposes, including raising finance for ostensibly progressive public projects. However, their primary function in financial terms is to defend corporate power and mitigate financial risk in large-scale investment ventures where financial investors are offered highly beneficial terms to commit their capital. As Hall argues, PPPs are in effect shadowy forms of privatization which

> hide behind confidential negotiations to protect commercial secrecy. There are no public consultations, lots of false promises, and incredibly complex contracts, all designed to protect corporate profits. There is also a fair amount of bribery, as privatisation contracts can be extremely valuable. [...] For the private companies involved – the banks, the builders and the service companies – they represent an extremely attractive business opportunity. A single contract gives them a flow of income for 25 years or more – usually underwritten to a great extent by the government itself. The companies can lobby politicians to ensure that governments create PPPs, and renegotiate them as necessary during the long years of the contract. From the outset,

the PFI was criticised from both right and left for being far more costly than using public finance, undermining services, and a 'scam' to conceal real public borrowing and expenditure. (Hall 2014: 2, 8)

PPPs reinforce corporate oligarchy because only a small number of big corporate entities – financial or non-financial – can provide government with the technical and strategic capacity to manage risk in state-led projects – most obviously in the defence sector, but also in construction, engineering, data management and energy. Where only a limited number of private entities that can assume this role, competition is irrelevant and government is placed at a disadvantage, particularly in relation to the initial anticipation of costs which inevitably escalate beyond early projections.

To take one example, selling off public assets below market value is the essence of the US government's recently announced $1 trillion stimulus package to revive America's collapsing infrastructure using 'private sector investment' (Dolack 2017). The scheme is similar to private finance initiatives used in the UK, Germany and Canada, where consortia of banks and construction firms use their influence within government to finance, operate and lease property back to taxpayers at variable prices for long-term periods. This strategy makes 'no sense as public policy' (ibid.) but is perfectly consistent with the logic of elite accumulation. Its goal is to extract profit from *all forms of human activity*:

> Similar to governments handing over their sovereignty to multinational corporations in so-called 'free trade' deals that facilitate the movement of production to locales with ever lower wages and weaker laws, public-private partnerships represent a plundering of the public sector for private profit, and government surrender of public goods. All this is a reflection of the imbalance of power in capitalist countries. (ibid.: 3; emphasis added)

As noted in Chapter 3, the collapse of the UK firm Carillion in 2017 also exemplifies the transfer of public wealth to corporate insiders and the transfer of corporate risk to taxpayers. Despite repeated profit warnings, the UK government continued to offer new contracts to the firm in 2017, including a £1.4 billion contract for HS2, until Carillion went into receivership in 2018 aided by a government rescue package. As the *Financial Times* reported in January 2018, when the firm finally went into compulsory liquidation, it was because there 'was nothing worth buying' for investors (Vincent 2018: 1). As an empty investment shell, which the UK government was forced to disguise, Carillion had nothing of economic value except its privileged access to lucrative government contracts which it needed to create the public impression of operating as a viable concern. As Vincent argues, Carillion effectively became 'a lawful sort of Ponzi scheme – using new or expected revenues to cover more pressing demands for payment' (ibid.).

Continuous consumption

There is evidence to suggest that the consumerist model of industrial society has reached its potential limits because it has become 'systemically short-termist, because it has given rise to a *systemic stupidity* that *structurally prevents the reconstitution of a long-term horizon*' (Stiegler 2011: 5). At the same time, systemic stupidity and alienation have intensified what Stiegler (2006) terms 'uncontrollable societies of disaffected individuals' – where nihilism and disenchantment among disintegrating communities increasingly exceeds the capacity of integrative structures in the state and economy to absorb or displace anti-systemic pressures. The legitimacy of capitalism is thus overwhelmingly tied to continued popular belief in consumerism. This belief enables individuals with disposable income or access to credit to benefit materially from commodity production oblivious to the social imaginary of consumerism and its 'totalitarian character' as it operates through colonization of the lifeworld and 'progressive conquest of the whole of society, effected through [capital's] logic of reification and commodification' (Xavier 2016: 208). This mode of subjectivation and legitimation is augmented at a higher social register through the massaging of positive sentiment among investors: 'the prices of financial assets and commodities', argues Martenson, 'become political and propaganda tools. [...] All prices have to send the "right" signals at all times, in the same way that certain news outlets pump a point of view endlessly'. Repetition, he argues, 'creates its own intended reality in the minds of consumers and market actors' (2018a: 2). Rational evidence of system-reproducibility is irrelevant: what matters for consumers and investors is, respectively, belief in the perpetual multiplication of choice and faith in the inevitable return of upward sentiment in markets. These convictions solidify the assumption that quasi-natural market forces create boom-bust cycles from which markets always recover: prosperity may be elusive now, but it *always* returns along with job security as new growth sectors absorb unemployed workers. While these assumptions are clearly naïve, their prevalence helps explain the powerlessness and fatalism of individuals who cannot comprehend the forces (central banks, capital flows, insider manipulation) that shape their lives, as well as the bullish optimism of investors who 'play the system' with varying degrees of sophistication.

The mythic force of capital is further valorized and legitimated in consumer economies by the 'fetish' character of commodities referred discussed in Chapter 1. As Xavier observes, consumerist ideologies conceal the 'irrational, immaterial, artificial fetish manufactured and attached to the commodity'. This entails 'elaborations of sign-value – social signification artificially attached to some form of consumption or commodity – as fetishized narratives and imagery that articulate cultural fantasies and desires, and determine the commodity-forms that promise to satisfy them' (Xavier 2016: 209). For Žižek, the commodity fetish is integral to valorization: capital is valorized not only via production and circulation, but through the symbolic power of the commodity form as a determinant of 'misrecognition':

> The *value* of a certain commodity, which is effectively an insignia of a network of relations between producers of diverse commodities, assumes the form of a quasi-'natural' property of another thing-commodity, money. [...] the essential feature of commodity fetishism does not consist of the famous replacement of with things ('a relation between men assumes the form of a relation between things' [Marx]); rather it consists of a certain misrecognition which concerns the relation between a structured network and one of its elements: what is really a structural effect, an effect of the network of relations between elements, appears as an immediate property of one of the elements, as if this property also belongs to its outside in relation with other elements. (Žižek 1989: 19)

The peculiar effect of the commodity fetish is to structure social relations beyond the process of exchange in economic life, for example, power relations and identities where particular social forms are determined by networks of structured relations. This leads not only to the dehistoricization of the capitalist mode of production as a variant form of 'market' society, but to cognitive repression of actual relations of domination and servitude which persist in capitalism behind a carefully nurtured myth of 'free' exchange between individuals with equal property rights (Žižek 1989: 22). It also obscures the proletarianization of the consumer herself, that is, the organization of consumption through the *'destruction of savoir-faire with the aim of creating available purchasing power*, thereby refining and reinforcing that system which rested on the *destruction of savoir-faire with the aim of creating available labor force'* (Stiegler 2011: 27; italics in original).

Here we can begin to approach a clearer understanding of financial socialism as a hegemonic articulation of capital in its decadent iteration – a mode of production in which the concept of private ownership for private gain and acquisition for use-value are degraded, suggesting movement beyond the existing framework of accumulation. The degraded character of value in late capitalism is reflected in commodity aesthetics as a principal source of misrecognition. Research into commodity aesthetics has been advanced by Haug (1983), who observes its particular salience in fascism, a compulsive and irrational political force which he defines as 'pseudo-socialism'. Pseudo-socialism creates an aesthetic copy of the original, superimposing this onto stratified class society: 'It is not the technical apparatus which creates a medium of expression for the masses; it is effective only where a mere aesthetic copy exists as a kind of amplification of the original' (ibid.: 132). Fascism is not an ideological revolution, as Griffin (2007) suggests, but a 'revolution *in* the ideological; not a revolution in the framework of society but a revolution in the experience of this framework; not a revolutionization of domination, but a stabilisation of domination' (Haug 1980: 74). Fascism is also a response to the 'organic' crisis of capital at a particular stage of economic development (Robinson 2019). In the 1930s, this involved a fusion of reactionary political power and *national* capitals; in the present period, it involves the fusion of *transnational* capital with an emerging global police state to suppress opposition to globalizing capital by misrepresenting the *specific* class project of transnational elites as conducive to the *general* interest of citizens – even if the 'discourse of national regeneration' so popular among right-wing demagogues sharply contradicts the 'transnational integration of capital and a globally integrated production and financial system upon which hinge the class and status interests of the major capitalist groups and state elites' (Robinson 2019: 170).

Historical fascism provided legitimacy for a state-capitalist regime of accumulation and destruction in National Socialist Germany, where aesthetic politics functioned to implicate declassed subjects of capital in an objective structure of domination, disciplining sense perception through the anaesthetizing force of popular-cultural imagery, consumerism and organized mass tourism. As Koepnick (1999: 53) argues, interwar fascism announced the moment when politics itself became a commodity, accelerating the erosion of traditional authority in modern class society. Political authority was swiftly replaced with naked violence and sophisticated political manipulation to promote regime loyalty and consumer satisfaction, encapsulated by the equation:

$$\rightarrow \text{spectacle / acclamation} + \text{privatized mass consumption}$$
$$= \text{new dominative rationality}$$

In historical fascism, the symbols of collective existence appear as so many commodities: the leader-image, flags, national myths, hate-figures, uniforms, ritual and so on; each is integral to the reproduction of a commoditized political culture, and each can be reproduced or finely tuned to reflect changing political conditions, supported by a new consumer culture tailored to the private fantasies of atomized subjects (ibid.: 53–54). On the other hand, historical fascism also reveals the essential destructiveness of capitalism – a system based on wasteful expenditure of resources. Overaccumulation leads to periodic downturns, interimperial rivalry and war: in the absence of recovery, the destruction of capital becomes a condition for its own self-renewal. This was the conclusion of critics in the interwar period, who observed the compulsive nature of a mode of production which reduces the price of war while increasing the possibility of intercapitalist competition (Harrison 2014). Rearmament and war enable the elimination of overaccumulated capital that cannot be invested profitably through investment in military capacity, the destructive consequences of which create conditions of possibility for a future self-expansion of capitalist value in peacetime.

In the present epoch of global corporatism the anaesthetizing force of the commodity form overwhelms subjects at an ever more intense level through the abstraction/relativization of social and cultural forms and production of planned obsolescence masquerading as novelty, innovation and progress. In globalizing capitalism, the function of commodity aesthetics has evolved in more sophisticated and complex ways, moving beyond the traditional political or cultural reference points of the nation-state and its real or imagined enemies. This promotion of global cosmopolitanism erodes or disqualifies special claims to entitlement among indigenous strata yet constitutes a major source of dissonance – one which finds logical articulation in support for right-wing populism. Yet the commodity retains its unique force, as the signs of hyperconsumerism constitute 'creative acts' shaped by 'fictional moments' in commodity-determined societies no longer justified by considerations of use-value, durability or necessity (Ulrich 2008). Not only is hyperconsumerism driven by libidinal attachment through (ironic) manipulation of emotion, but by a continual intensification of marketing and advertising in a multiplicity of media formats where superficial innovation is misrepresented as 'inevitable' and 'fascinating':

> The illusion is maintained that it is the *things* as such which change by themselves. [...] The aesthetically differentiated generations of commodities replace one another, as if from natural causes, like changes in the weather. From the standpoint of the capitalists, the process looks completely different. For them, it belongs to the realm of *natura naturata* [nature already created], of their capital, which it is their business to produce amid anxiety and high risk. They require that the social 'necessity' – for such is the use-value of their commodities – be sanctioned again and again to achieve the determining aim of the valorisation standpoint. (Haug 1983: 42)

As a structuring principle of postliberal capitalism, the commodity operates at an aesthetic level as a hegemonic articulation of value in its decadent form, where capital inadequately valorized through productive labour fails to find productive outlets. This further intensifies the compulsive logic of consumerism as a simulation of productive economic development in stagnant economies dependent on accommodative monetary policies and credit expansion.

As argued in Chapters 3 and 4, a core feature of financialization is the expansion of fictitious capital: derivative multiplications of value which constitute financial market money. Abstract value captured from the future provides liquidity to facilitate computer-assisted trading in currencies, equities and derivatives which synthesize incommensurable systems of value (Bryan & Rafferty 2003). Its legacy is a fantastic edifice of leveraged value masquerading as wealth – a directionless self-expansion of the capitalist value form without reason. This constitutes an immense spectacle of wealth and power which at once dwarfs and obliterates alternative narratives of social and political organization, fragmenting yet coordinating the atomized mass of individualized consumer desires which sustain capital. Above all, however, the abstraction of capital value – which supersedes all social and cultural forms, appears as a 'haunting', that is, where exchange-value weighs on use-value through a transformation of singularity into equivalence, imposing a schematic logic on subjectivity via a compulsive and dreamlike reconstruction of consumer fantasy as reality (cf. Derrida 1994).

Yet the question remains whether continuous consumerism, assisted by vast data extraction industries, monetary easing and credit creation, is viable in the long term or whether the next recession will lead to debt deleveraging, devaluation and the delegitimation of capitalism. This would have unpredictable consequences, disrupting passive acceptance of consumerism in advanced economies. The answer for monetary elites surely lies in a reconfiguration of the system of payments which enables uninterrupted consumer spending, and here it is essential to recall the functions of money as *unit of account*, *means of exchange* and *store of value*. It is the last of these that financial socialism places in question:

> Modern banknotes, even though they have ceased to represent a given quantity of metal, still embody the unit of account. Indeed, all the means of payments that are currently in use, whether coins, banknotes or electronic currencies, bear a fixed relationship to the unit of account. Therefore, they are a store of value. And, as such, they are liable to be withheld from circulation and accumulated, effectively obstructing the circulation of goods that they are intended to facilitate. (Fantacci 2013: 126)

Fantacci attempts to understand how postcapitalist money might resolve this problem, which perplexed earlier thinkers like Einaudi and Keynes. He defines postcapitalist money as a 'non-reserve currency', where the 'nominal value is set by authority [fiat] or is subject to a predetermined rate of devaluation' (ibid.: 127). An example is redeemable 'scrip' which employs a technique known as an 'ambulatory tax' payable to the issuer. This is designed to prevent hoarding of assets by charging account holders a periodic holding tax to incentivize spending, which in turn accelerates the velocity of money in the economy: it cannot be hoarded without incurring a loss. Einaudi posited the formal separation of money as unit of account from money as means of exchange: this involves (a) 'ideal' money as an abstract unit of account to denominate prices and debts; and (b) 'real' money as a means to pay for goods and debts (ibid.). In this system, argues Fantacci, the relation between ideal and real money is fixed, as with the gold standard; it is set by a monetary authority (ibid.: 130).

In 1944 Keynes developed a comprehensive programme for postcapitalist money based on the 'bancor' – a plan for the international monetary system rejected by the US at Bretton Woods in favour of the dollar as an international currency of reserve. Keynes (1936) believed that the rate of interest in an economy was determined by the demand for money as a store of value, which is of course a hedge against political and financial uncertainty favoured by those endowed with some wealth. Keynes did not agree that the true function of money *should* be as a store of value, only that this is what it had *become*. As Fantacci argues, the

> reason why money is hoarded lies in the fact that it is a store value, that is, it has a fixed value in terms of the unit of account, unlike all other assets which are subject to costs, losses or unpredictable depreciations. (ibid.: 132)

The bancor would have been a non-existent bank money operated through an international 'clearing union' where each state would start with an initial balance of zero bancor and have an overdraft facility in line with its balance of trade: 'Thanks to the centralization provided by the Clearing Union', notes Fantacci,

> bilateral credits are thus monetised: in exchange for its goods and services, the exporting country receives a credit in bancor that it can spend in any other country [...]. Symmetrically, a deficit country can repay its debts by exporting to any other country. In this respect, the Clearing Union acts like a bank. (ibid.: 135)

The point is, however, that 'bank money' cannot be redeemed: a positive balance does not constitute 'savings' (hoard), only an entitlement to purchase commodities encouraged by the use of charges on both negative and positive balances. It is therefore not a traditional form of capitalist money because it removes the positive interest function of money which depositors seek to prevent devaluation of their personal wealth or to enjoy the privilege of obtaining interest. In theory, a model like the bancor allows sellers to sell more and buyers to purchase more than if using traditional money, for 'where money is not a store of value, credit is essentially an anticipation of goods in view of receiving other goods in the future' (ibid.: 139). A postcapitalist monetary system would therefore be one based on the idea of non-monetary compensation; consumers would have to accept that a positive balance (credit) is not an entitlement to money as wealth but an entitlement to acquire goods and services (possibly within fixed-term periods).

Little discussed outside banking and finance, negative rates are now a feature of monetary policy in post-crisis monetary political economy as governments consider new methods to stimulate spending and combat the threat of deflationary recession. Elite economists like Haldane suggest that negative interest rates could offer central banks greater power to stimulate spending in a recession by incentivizing depositors to purchase rather than hoard (Spence 2015). Just as banks might be charged to 'park' their assets with central banks (thus incentivizing them to issue loans), so depositors confronted with a predetermined rate of devaluation that skims value from savings would logically seek to maximize the value of their assets and avoid hoarding in favour of continuous consumption. This, it is argued, could limit fluctuations in consumer spending and prevent a rapid return to recession, avoiding the normal course of the credit cycle by countering deflationary tendencies where consumers opt to deleverage or defer spending in anticipation of future price reductions. To imagine the impact of a predetermined rate of devaluation, it may be useful to consider the effect of a negative interest rate of a −2.0 per cent on the savings of a worker totalling £40,000. After six years, the worker's savings would be worth only £35,430, coercing him or her to spend the balance or lose it. This effect is achieved most easily by transgressing the zero lower bound, where banks charge depositors for the right to deposit. Such rates are in use in countries such as Sweden, where the authorities might wish to normalize bank rates above zero (giving the central bank greater room to manoeuvre), but are deterred by concerns over falling asset prices (Martin 2018).

The fragility of the advanced economies is demonstrated most forcefully by the reversal in December 2015 of monetary policy by the US Federal Reserve after its ultra-cautious 0.25 per cent rate increase – an almost imperceptible tightening after seven years of easing – and the tapering of 'QE3' in the autumn of that year which terrified markets. The Federal Reserve always issues secondary justifications for its failure to tighten monetary policy (China's slowdown, Brexit, etc.), but the motive is to defend bond markets and minimize the burden of interest repayments on corporate and public debt. Although further rate rises were planned for late 2019, at the first sign of stress, central banks in the US and Europe are again returning to accommodative monetary policy to offset price instability in equity markets and fears of a global slowdown (Strauss 2019). While indebted economies like the UK have endured a decade of near-zero rates – placating overmortgaged householders while hurting depositors and people on fixed incomes – the stimulus function of interest rates has been destroyed as governments 'run out of ammunition'. This is indicative of the moribund nature of financial socialism, which privileges banking elites who have an opportunity to invest newly created money early *before* monetary expansion inflates prices for everyone else, while stripping wealth from middle-income groups. In financial socialism not only do banks enjoy privileged access to new money, but they also pass on the cost of negative rates to customers by introducing charges on deposits and cash transactions. In addition, they can rely on government to suppress access to alternative monetary commodities like precious metals, as evidenced by the closure in July 2016 of accounts belonging to Tavex Guld & Valuta, a well-known Swedish bullion dealer. This followed a surge in demand for allocations of bullion as a hedge against currency instability after Brexit, creating a precedent for similar moves in the US and other EU states where depositors question the security of their life savings.

The use of negative interest rates to penalize hoarding of idle capital may indeed stimulate consumption, yet it is a subtle form of economic *predation* which expropriates wealth from depositors and can reduce productive investment:

> It has long been recognized that the absence of secure property rights can severely affect economic decisions. A particular emphasis has been put on the effects of weak property rights on investment and, as a consequence, on economic growth […] the mechanism that relates weak property rights and intertemporal economic decisions is quite obvious. If an agent is not sure that she will enjoy tomorrow the returns from her investments today, she is likely to reduce investment and increase her current consumption. (Chassang & Padró i Miquel 2010: 645)

Breaking through the zero lower bound also necessitates the transition to a 'cashless' society based on electronic bank-controlled money – a trend led by EU economies like Sweden which operate exclusively electronic payment systems (and where the use of cash is regarded as suspicious). 'Cashless' consumerism is glamourized through slick marketing campaigns which depict banknotes as anachronistic compared with the immediacy and convenience of electronic payments or which emphasize the security of phone-based contactless payment methods as the 'new normal' for a younger generation accustomed to cashless transactions.

The real motive for withdrawing cash from society – and for the disappearance of ATMs from towns and small communities (Brodbeck 2019) – is the determination of banks to encourage consumers to 'navigate the broader economy through their systems'; which is to say, the disappearance of cash payment in retail and service outlets is neither an accidental nor random process. As Scott argues, financial institutions

> are trying to nudge us towards a cashless society and digital banking. The true motive is corporate profit. Payments companies such as Visa and Mastercard want to increase the volume of digital payments services they sell, while banks want to cut costs. The nudge requires two parts. First, they must increase the inconvenience of cash, ATMs and branches. Second, they must vigorously promote the alternative. They seek to make people 'learn' that they want digital, and then 'choose' it. (Scott 2018: 1)

Negative interest rates and electronic money are interlinked because if bank notes cease to exist or cease to be accepted as means of payment, then it is impossible for individuals to remove their assets from banks during banking crises (such as the one that led to the collapse of Northern Rock in 2008) or extended 'bank holidays' (such as the one imposed on Greece in July 2015). It is therefore in the interests of monetary authorities to devise means to coerce depositors into digital payments: having 'chosen' such payment methods, and accepted negative bank rates, depositors will then have no option but to pay a bank tax or spend their money to avoid a loss of purchasing power. They will also be vulnerable, as we shall see in Chapter 6, to regulations agreed by the G20 in 2014 which will enable banks to engage in economic predation and to acquire depositors' funds ahead of public bailouts that socialize private losses and place the financial burden on all taxpayers.

There are strong reasons for political and monetary elites to eliminate the zero lower bound, in particular the need to find alternatives to existing forms of economic stimulus such as quantitative easing or fiscal expansion. Yet simply eliminating cash or banning physical cash withdrawals is likely to be counterproductive given that consumers might then choose not to spend, harming sales and depressing profits. Other proposed strategies for breaking through the zero lower bound include modern versions of 'stamped money', adapting

Silvio Gesell's idea from the 1930s. According to this proposal, currency only retains its value if is officially stamped on a routine basis at a cost to the holder 'roughly equal to the excess of the money-rate of interest [...] over the marginal efficiency of capital corresponding to a rate of new investment compatible with full employment' (Kimball 2013: 4). The aim is to penalize hoarding and incentivize savers to consume continuously. Another tactic would be to use an updated version of Eisler's 'depreciating paper currency' idea, where two types of currency coexist: 'current money' for small-scale purchases and 'bank money' as a unit of account for major transactions. This idea has never been fully developed, however, in part because Eisler did not 'fully recognize that in such a system, to the extent possible, it is important to treat the units of the bank money as the unit of account for all purposes' (ibid.: 5). Perhaps the only way to eliminate the volume of physical money held outside the banking system – which limits the potential for expanding electronic money payments and breaking through the zero lower bound – is to introduce a time-varying deposit fee beginning with private bank deposits at central banks, extending later to retail customers. This would create an effective exchange rate between paper currency and electronic money, encouraging consumers to identify with the goal of creating a largely electronic monetary system.

Monetary and political elites are all-too-aware of the political problems entailed in reducing rates below the zero lower bound and the associated problem of supporting this by removing cash from society – a move which is bound to create distrust – even if many consumers are attracted to the idea of immaterial electronic money or accept that there is no a priori reason why paper currency has a special historical status or why a paper dollar or euro should always be worth the same amount as an electronic dollar or euro. As a recent *Economist* report notes:

> Though some central banks experimented with sub-zero rates over the last decade, few ventured far into negative territory. So long as holding cash (which has a nominal yield of zero) remains an option, negative rates can only be used sparingly, lest depositors take their money and run. Indeed, an analysis of negative rates post-crisis by Gauti Eggertsson of Brown university and colleagues found that banks generally do not reduce the rate paid on deposits below zero, presumably because they fear cash withdrawals. A radical monetary reform could solve this. But sucking money from bank accounts would have unintended consequences and would be unpopular. (Economist 2018: 11)

The absence of public debate on these issues makes it hard for ordinary people to understand the changing nature of electronic money and the potential vulnerability of their deposits in the banking system. It also makes it virtually impossible for people with modest assets to see what lies ahead, rendering them liable to a loss of wealth in future crises – as happened to both wealthy and low-income depositors in Cyprus in 2013, as well as poor US pensioners in the Detroit bankruptcy of the same year (Brown 2013). Depositors will become still more vulnerable – particularly in the eurozone – once state-funded depositor protection insurance is withdrawn and retail customers discover how difficult it has become to withdraw significant quantities of physical money from their accounts.

Conclusion

'Escalating inequality is the work of a global elite that will resist every challenge to its vested interests', argued Milne in the *Guardian* in January 2015. Notwithstanding the impact of the Federal Reserve's short-lived decision to finally begin 'tapering' its programme of asset purchases and to raise interest rates in the second half of 2018 – precipitating an increased flow of US dollars back to American markets, exacerbating liquidity issues for weakened emerging economies (El-Erian 2018; Engdahl 2018) – a decade of monetary easing and central bank activism have transformed the landscape of global monetary policy in advanced capitalist nations, enabling financial and nonfinancial entities to resume tightening their hold over the global economy through leveraged buy-outs where the debt component in corporate acquisitions is serviced by the profits of purchased firms. Concentrations of market power in advanced economies have reached new and alarming levels, leading even establishment commentators to question whether oligopolistic trends in the US corporate sector are allowing cash-rich predators to sustain profitability by expanding without investing (Wessel 2018).

As we have shown in this chapter, the collapse of Lehman in 2008 threatened a complete collapse of the US financial and monetary system, with serious potential implications for the stability of the international financial system. Yet unique in the response of economic elites to the crisis was not the use of price discovery or emergency recapitalization, but a dramatic escalation of accommodative policies to save the 'too-big-to-fail' banks and prevent a serious challenge to the vested political interests of the corporate oligarchy. The US Federal Reserve and other central banks deployed large-scale easing through a massive increase in the purchase of distressed assets, securities and bonds designed to force down interest rates, restore liquidity to credit markets and defend banks holding large quantities of leveraged debt. Yet financial socialism is determined in the final resort by the definition of capital as power: elite accumulation has seemingly reached asymptotic limits where further increases can be achieved only through a further intensification of violence and repression (Nitzan & Bichler 2012). Although the productive social basis of capitalist accumulation is inadequate to sustain the valorization of surplus value necessary to maintain profitability, financial socialism offers an authoritarian means to secure the stability of critical financial institutions and defend the agglomeration of fictitious capital in financial markets and banks. The upward movement of equity values testifies to the short-term success of this policy, providing a mythic backdrop of perpetually rising prosperity misrepresented to the public as evidence of 'recovery'. This conceals not only the escalating scale of corporate share buybacks as cash-rich corporations purchase back rather than issue new stock to raise money for investment (or where corporate executives limit their own tax-exposure by increasing earnings through share dividends rather than pay increases) (Cox 2018; Girouard 2018), but also the dominating presence of a clique of financial corporations, energy and technology firms in the global economy and their close proximity to governments.

While sustaining corporate income, financial socialism has undermined growth in advanced emerging market nations and failed to stimulate a surge of new business development (Schumpeterian 'creative destruction') in core economies due to an absence of wage growth and long-term investment in productive sectors. At the same time, the discretionary monetary policy of central bank activism has – as Higgs (1997) observed – increased economic uncertainty concerning the future purchasing power of money, which in turn undermines an essential property right associated with capitalism (Dorn 2018). Critics have therefore questioned the rationality of central bank activism itself:

> Thanks to the trillions of dollars of liquidity that major central banks have pumped in to the global economy over the past decade, asset markets have rebounded, company mergers have gone into overdrive, and stock buybacks have become a benchmark of managerial acumen. By contrast, the real economy has spluttered along through ephemeral bouts of optimism and intermittent talk of downside risks. And while policymakers tell themselves that high stock prices and exports will boost average incomes, the fact is that most of the gains have already been captured by those at the very top of the pyramid. (Kozul-Wright 2018: 1)

The extent to which quantitative easing and central bank asset purchases have become the 'new normal' remains to be seen, and there are suspicions that interest rates were allowed to rise in 2018 not only to calm inflationary pressures but to enable central banks more policy scope to ease monetary again when the *next* financial crisis occurs. The evidence suggests that financial socialism has become a de facto policy-tool for preserving fictitious capital while staving off a deflationary recession exacerbated by unmanageable levels of debt, not only in moribund consumer economies in North America, Japan and the EU,[5] but in emerging economies like Turkey, Argentina and Brazil whose capacity to weather financial turbulence is more limited, threatening market contagion and the reverberation of financial instability in the metropole itself.

In Chapter 6, we examine the response of monetary authorities (central banks, transnational financial institutions) to the accumulation and transmission of risk in the global financial system since 2008. As a result of inadequate capital-to-lending ratios and excessively leveraged/collateralized liabilities, financial corporations in the US, the UK, EU and Switzerland have utilized their political influence to socialize losses through state circuits of capital and recalibrate bank insolvency rules to ensure that the interests of creditors are not harmed in order to prevent a collapse of confidence in the global banking system. Monetary elites have developed new strategies for containing systemic risk reflecting changes in the organization of postliberal capitalism itself. At the centre of corporate risk management strategies are new regulations on bankruptcy resolution to be deployed in the event of bank failure. These rules attempt to determine the legal status of deposits in the hierarchy of assets and liabilities in the banking system. To understand this subtle yet significant shift in macroprudential regulation as a feature of financial socialism, it is necessary to consult documents published by key IFIs, whose policies constitute a direct yet unpublicized response to the present crisis.

Notes

1 According to the Institute of Fiscal Studies (2018), the probability of young adults on middle incomes owning a home in the UK has halved in the past two decades due to falling real incomes.
2 There is some dispute about the value of the currency markets. The accepted estimate was that forex trading is worth more than $5 trillion per day (Scutt 2016). However, more recent estimates lower this figure to $3 trillion (Reuters 2017).
3 Pento explains that an inversion of the yield curve in bond markets inevitably indicates a recession if central banks begin to tighten monetary policy, leading to a contraction of credit:

> The reason is because the fuel for asset bubbles is monetary creation, a boosting booming money supply which we don't have any more. And the reason why the money supply gets shut off when the yield curve inverts is because banks' loans are earning less than their liabilities, which are deposits. So when your assets are earning less than your liabilities, you don't make any more loans. You don't want any more assets. That's a great way to make your bank insolvent. (Pento 2018: 1)

4 At its peak in 2015, the value of troubled assets transferred to the Federal Reserve reached $4.5 trillion (Federal Reserve Bank 2019).
5 Unsecured consumer debt in the UK reached more than $205 billion in 2017 (Inman 2018). Anti-poverty groups argue that this unsustainable figure is due not simply to consumer profligacy but to fall real wages which have led the poorest 10% of households to spend two-and-a-half times their disposable income annually.

6

MONETARY INTERNATIONALISM

Introduction

After the global financial crisis and public outcry at excessive government largesse towards the banks, transnational economic elites – principally from G7 nations – were forced to consider new strategies for containing future systemic risk in the global financial system. The financial crisis revealed how 'rapid financial innovation during an era of prolonged macroeconomic stability had resulted in a highly complex and interconnected system that was inadequately understood by regulators' (Gai 2013: 1). Financial systems manifest what Gai terms a 'robust-yet-fragile' constitution: 'while the probability of contagion may be low, the effects can be extremely widespread when problems occur' (ibid.: 11). But while the detail of new regulation regimes must be understood and evaluated, a deeper issue also concerns us here. It is the thesis of the present study that risk management strategies developed since 2008 reflect not only the issue of systemic risk but also a more fundamental change in the *legal organization of postliberal capitalism itself.* This in turn reflects, at a broader level, the ongoing development of global governance as an elite response to the structural crisis of globalizing capital which has, since the financial crises of the late 1990s, led to a major consolidation of transnational co-governance in elite forums like the G20, the Financial Stability Board (FSB) and the Basel Committee on Banking Supervision (BCBS), the functions of which are to stabilize rather than transform a global finance-led accumulation regime (Decker & Sablowksi 2017). The strategic intention of the new regulatory framework is to mitigate risk and address instabilities created by contradictory pressures in transnational capitalism between global integration and the fragmentation/hierarchization of the international economy into segmented networks of capital flows, information flows, commodity and value chains connecting financial centres and consumer markets in G20 economies with low-wage manufacturing and commodity-rich zones in the periphery.

At the centre of risk management strategies are new international rules on bankruptcy resolution to be deployed in the event of future bank failures – rules which have major implications for the legal status of deposits in the hierarchy of financial assets and liabilities that comprise the global banking system. As the official publications by international financial institutions reviewed here suggest, these regulations are a direct response to the meltdown of 2008 which revealed 'substantial weaknesses in the banking system and the prudential framework, leading to excessive lending and risk-taking unsupported by adequate capital and liquidity buffers' (BIS 2018a: 1). Their function is to manage instabilities in the growth cycle and reduce or (in limited crises) obviate the requirement for *public* solvency support in the event that financial institutions face a sudden loss of investor confidence. But while proposed changes are presented in suitably anodyne language as measured and timely – in the best interests of the global economy – they also indicate a controversial dimension of neoliberalism after the crisis, namely a drift towards *coercive* capitalism where losses of private financial institutions are transferred to the public not only through the state circuits of financial capital (public bailouts) but directly to citizens (depositor bail-ins) whose assets may be locked into the banking system.

As noted in Chapter 5, our concern is not the efficiency of the banking system, but the consequences of transferring fiduciary liability from corporate-state actors to ordinary individuals with lower risk tolerances and financial security. Although banks have historically sequestered depositors' assets in banking crises, this new erosion of private property rights by financial corporations represents a significant and deeply disturbing shift towards financial socialism. As we have seen, financial socialism assumed new extremes in the aftermath of the Lehman collapse as G7 governments extended public insolvency support to distressed banks, state-backed corporations, insurance firms and other commercial entities on an unprecedented scale, ensuring financial institutions would receive 'more for their assets when public entities purchased or ensured them than the market thought they were worth' (Tabb 2012: 178). Yet a new global framework has been implemented by Western governments since 2010 (adopted by all G20 economies in 2014), the purpose of which is to manage instabilities in the global growth cycle and reduce/mitigate the requirement for *public* solvency support in future crises by making management and shareholders (depositors) legally culpable. Although the present crisis demonstrates the fragility and limitations of global management of economic and monetary policy (*Economist* 2018), this system for managing failed financial sector firms – placed on a statutory basis by the Bank Recovery and Resolution Directive (BRRD) in the EU, the Dodd Frank Act in the US and the Special Resolution Regime (SRR) created by the 2009 UK Banking Act – forms a central pillar of the legal-regulatory architecture of global financial socialism in developed economies. The implication is that emerging economies will eventually follow suit and introduce similar rules on bank recapitalization and insolvency resolution within their own jurisdictions.

Through this new regulatory framework, monetary and political elites are confident disorderly bank failures can be prevented in future crises, enabling them to defend and consolidate their control over the international banking system and their power to appropriate the surplus product of the global economy by mitigating financial risk and *bailing-in* depositors' funds to maintain liquidity. To cite one report by the Federal Deposit Insurance Corporation (FDIC) and Bank of England, under new bail-in regulations

> [a] resolution authority could intervene at the top of the [banking] group. Culpable senior management of the parent and operating businesses would be removed, and losses would be apportioned to shareholders and unsecured creditors. In all likelihood, shareholders would lose all value and unsecured creditors should thus expect that their claims would be written down to reflect any losses that shareholders did not cover.. [...] legal safeguards ensure that creditors recover no less than they would under insolvency. (FDIC & Bank of England 2012: 3)

Observers argue that this regulatory framework could extend to financial martial law to freeze funds inside the global financial system through emergency bank holidays ('resolution weekends'), facilitating closer surveillance of and control over financial assets in a bid to defend G-SIFIs and impose a more centralized system of global financial governance (Rickards 2016). Whether such a radical change in the governance of global finance is possible at this juncture is open to question, and certainly the legality of asset seizure or even temporary asset sequestration is doubtful. What is clear, however, is that the historic long cycle of capitalist growth and recovery experienced since 1945 is in jeopardy, leading even market-fundamentalists at the *Economist* (2018) to reassure readers that central bank activism – fortified perhaps by the issuance of time-delimited free money ('universal basic income') for consumers – should be adequate to manage the financial and political fallout of the next global downturn.

In this final chapter we focus primarily on the new model of banking regulation in the eurozone, which Streeck (2014: 174) defines mordantly as a 'frivolous' monetary experiment to create a 'political jurisdiction close to the ideal of a market economy freed from politics by politics itself'. The emerging global architecture of financial socialism indicates the determination of political and monetary elites to avoid a repetition of the political crises which erupted in the eurozone in 2010 as bankrupt governments in Portugal, Italy, Ireland, Greece and Spain queued for emergency lending from the ECB/IMF and investors pleaded for reassurance that the ECB would purchase eurozone bonds if necessary to sustain the single currency. 'Within our mandate', declared Mario Draghi in July 2012 at the depths of the Greek crisis, 'the ECB is ready to do *whatever it takes* to preserve the euro. And believe me, it will be enough'

(Draghi, cited in McCrum 2017). As is now well understood, the financial crisis undermined overleveraged 'Club Med' economies, which surplus economies in the eurozone (Germany, the Netherlands, Finland, Austria) were reluctant to bail out by issuing further eurozone debt.

The eurozone crisis indicated the fiscal vulnerability of eurozone economies, forcing international regulatory authorities to consider alternative avenues for maintaining the liquidity of the banking system: funds must come from somewhere, and it was decided by the Eurogroup in 2013 during the crisis in Cyprus that depositors' assets could legitimately be used to prop up distressed banks in order to limit financial risk and market contagion, thereby reaffirming the principle of monetary *nationalism*: despite the supranational profile of the eurozone as a shared currency unit, it fell to local monetary authorities/depositors to resolve a crisis within their own specific jurisdiction, revealing the institutional inadequacy of the eurozone as a coherent monetary bloc. The decision by Eurogroup finance ministers to lock Greece in a perpetual debtor's prison in order to immunize the eurozone from the Greek crisis were seen as a necessary step to defend Franco-German banks from the consequences of debt default (Varoufakis 2015). This reflects the complexity and unpredictability of market contagion which creates vulnerability in the initial phase among 'clusters' of adjacent banks. The probability of contagion is 'directly linked to the size of the vulnerable cluster' (Gai 2013: 19). Once contagion spreads through a vulnerable cluster (as in the eurozone in 2011), even secure banks become 'susceptible to default and contagion can spread well beyond the vulnerable cluster to affect the entire connected component of the network' (ibid.).

Yet, if we consider the way in which the new regulatory architecture has been devised and implemented since 2010 (following detailed and precise policy recommendations by the FSB and BIS to G20 finance ministers), then developments in this direction might also be reframed as evidence of a new monetary *internationalism* where core capitalist economies synchronize monetary strategies through global co-governance systems, including 'single point of entry' (SPE) bankruptcy resolution, the aim of which is to resolve the insolvency of highly integrated G-SIFIs at a global level – at the level of transnational corporate holding companies rather than at the level of individual national subsidiaries. Although international cooperation on global issues has declined since 2014 amid rising geopolitical tensions, rising protectionism and other pressures towards deglobalization, behind the nationalist and mercantilist rhetoric, financial structures are being erected not only for SPE resolution regimes to limit risk for G-SIFIs but for a currency unit based on the IMF's Special Drawing Rights (SDR) facility to mediate international payments. Following its own mandate, this drive towards monetary internationalism – a supra-sovereign monetary unit to facilitate global market exchange – is proceeding without public discussion in advanced economies where opposition to globalization among the anti-globalist right, as witnessed by the rise of populist economic nationalism, increasingly drowns out support for globalization among the globalist left. James observes that a lack of democracy 'has been at the heart of anti-globalization critiques of multilateralism in rich countries' (2017: 7; Subacchi & Pickford 2011). This is an important point, and popular perceptions of the legitimacy deficit of global governance have intensified in the decade since 2008. Yet it is the hegemonic *rearticulation* of this critique which is more significant, leading one German commentator to observe that the 'social costs and economic limitations of the growth path of globalizing capitalism are leading to the emergence of new domination projects within the elite' (Decker 2018: 2). Such projects, he suggests, channel discontent with globalizing capitalism into 'national resentments' (ibid.). This creates the conditions of possibility for the stabilization of capitalist accumulation regimes in advanced economies, positing a dialectical antithesis to transnational neoliberalism in the form of anti-establishment populism (cf. Woodley 2013).

Since the 2008 crisis, critical economists have suggested that, despite the continued strength of the US dollar as a currency of reserve – and its utility as a source of US economic power[1] – a *multipolar* international monetary system could compensate for deficiencies in the *unipolar* monetary system which ultimately failed to guarantee liquidity in 2008 crisis until G20 government leaders agreed to coordinate monetary easing at the 2009 London summit (Dailami & Masson 2009). Here it is possible to detect signals of a new drive by global financial elites to redevelop and augment the IMF's existing SDR facility beyond its existing *official reserve* function (providing liquidity to central banks) to become a denationalized market-traded currency ('M-SDR') alongside the US dollar and other leading currencies (IMF 2018a). Clearly this ambition may be opposed by nationalist forces in the US reluctant to allow either EU and BRICS economies to challenge America's 'hegemony of initiatives and power' in the global monetary system (ibid.: 3).

As America's trade deficit and national debt continue to escalate without limit, however, and as growth in equity markets and corporate debt run dangerously ahead of underlying growth, the present dollar super-cycle – supported by the radical discretionary policies of the Federal Reserve – may be approaching its end phase, as evidenced by pressures towards de-dollarization among BRICS economies and the abortive tightening of US monetary policy by the Federal Reserve in 2018. Any attempt at de-dollarization by emerging powers will of course invite immediate financial or even military retaliation from Washington, as evidenced by the fate of Iraq in 2003 and Libya in 2011 whose governments had proposed selling oil in alternative currencies (Clark 2005; Wile 2011). Yet, the declining use of the dollar for trade settlement has led some commentators to suggest that a formally constituted multi-reserve global currency system (governed by appropriately strict monetary rules) could in the event of a further weakening of the dollar provide a more secure medium of exchange than a globally traded national currency which is inherently vulnerable to debasement by its issuing central bank (Wilson 2018).

To assess these issues, and their implications for financial socialism, it is necessary to decipher the dialogue between global elites, national governments and bankers over the future of the international financial system. Behind contemporary narratives of deglobalization and geopolitical crisis, the institutional structure of the international economic order created under US leadership after 1945 has always been more likely to *evolve* than simply *disappear* as the US enters a period of introspection. This reflects the continued relevance of arguments by neoliberal institutionalists, namely that the international system created after 1945 designed to encourage 'rule-taking' behaviour by emerging nations retains a capacity to evolve and survive in revised forms. While IR theorists like Ikenberry (2018) concede that liberal features of the post-1945 global order are increasingly vulnerable – criticized by non-liberal states and dispossessed voters in the West – institutions of global economic governance and financial regulation have successfully encouraged emerging powers to adapt to the capitalist world-system rather than challenge it, leading to calls for recalibration rather than full-scale transformation. Evidence of this can be seen in the fact that China – despite tensions over trade policy with the US, favours the IMF's SDR system as a unit of account for global trade as an alternative to the US dollar – a reserve currency which renders all states vulnerable to economic warfare from Washington.

It should be noted here that a potential contradiction exists in plans by global elites to reform the international monetary system. Until recently it was possible for rising powers such as China, Russia, India and Iran to adapt to the 'Washington consensus' while reserving the right to pursue their own agendas through alternative geopolitical strategies. This enabled them to conform to norms of international economic cooperation (through the WTO, for example) while looking beyond the present US-centric order towards a multipolar global growth system. In recent years, however, this approach has collided with a dangerous new direction in US foreign policy as neoconservative hawks in the US conclude that competition from rival economic blocs (or, more seriously, cooperation *between* rivals, is not in America's interests). This explains the intensification of sanctions on rivals such as Russia, particularly on firms in the defence and energy sector which provide unwanted competition for the US military-industrial complex and liquified natural gas industry within the EU (Savitsky 2018). It also explains US support for regime change in Eurasian states (Iraq, Georgia, Ukraine, Libya, Syria, etc.) and the catastrophic wars that have ensued. That Western opposition towards power transition in the international system is exacerbating global conflict is hardly in question: for those economies with the most to lose from power transition (the US, the UK, Israel, Saudi Arabia and Japan) there is no appetite for a reordering of the international system which recognizes or formalizes the rising power of China, Russia, India and Iran. What *is* in doubt, however, is the capacity of the US to coerce allies like Germany into accepting that *their* national interests lie in forestalling the rise of emerging economies which are, at the same time, *their* most important future trading partners. Not only has Germany rejected American efforts to bloc Russia's strategic Nord Stream 2 pipeline (Reuters 2018), but belated recognition of this contradiction finally led EU leaders in September 2018 to launch a new 'special purpose vehicle' (SPV) as an alternative means of payment 'to facilitate legitimate financial transactions with Iran [...] in accordance with European Union law' ahead of the new US sanctions regime imposed on Iran in November 2018 (Escobar 2018). A balanced assessment of Western attitudes towards monetary internationalism must conclude that transatlantic elites are deeply divided in their estimates of the advantages/disadvantages of global economic convergence and the consolidation of denationalized monetary institutions which could significantly limit their prerogative power to control capital flows, manipulate financial markets and refinance their continually expanding public debt (Rickards 2014).

Macroprudential regulation

With their phenomenal capacity for leveraging asset values, banks 'have incentives to take on excessive risks from the perspective of the financial system as a whole' (Smith et al. 2012: 337). 'What makes sense for a given financial institution may not', they add, 'make sense for the financial system, or the exposure of taxpayers who may be called upon to rescue the institutions that have triggered the systemic risk' (ibid.). Although radical sceptics might disagree, for monetary elites a culture change has taken place in global finance since 2008:

> The decade since the onset of the global financial crisis has brought about significant structural changes in the banking sector. The crisis revealed substantial weaknesses in the banking system and the prudential framework, leading to excessive lending and risk-taking unsupported by adequate capital and liquidity buffers. The effects of the crisis have weighed heavily on economic growth, financial stability and bank performance in many jurisdictions, although the headwinds have begun to subside. (BIS 2018a: 1)

This assessment by economists at BIS typifies the outlook of international financial institutions, which assume the present crisis is a *cause* of low growth and 'real' sector instability rather than a *reflection* of underlying structural weaknesses in financialized economies characterized by declining profitability and malinvestment. Yet the message is clear: despite radical central bank intervention, as a proportion of wealth-production the banking sector is in relative decline; banks are switching to more complex activities to generate revenue; bank profits are lower; and banks have been forced to improve resilience by strengthening capital and liquidity buffers to satisfy new Basel regulations (ibid.: 2). In addition, banks face greater competition from new financial technology firms ('fintech') which have lobbied to reduce banks' monopoly on the use of customers' data, and from a shadow-banking sector which remains largely unregulated. Low profitability (the 'new normal') reflects not only a weaker business outlook but also the costs of new capitalization rules which impose additional costs in a 'post-crisis macro-financial environment' (ibid.: 7).

In the world of global monetary governance, risk is defined in systemic terms as the threat or existence of 'widespread disruption to the provision of financial services that is caused by an impairment of all or parts of the financial system, and which can cause serious negative consequences for the real economy' (IMF/BIS/FSB 2016: 4). Financial risk has two dimensions:

1. *Time dimension*: Vulnerabilities related to the accumulation of risks over time;
2. *Structural dimension*: Vulnerabilities linked to interconnectedness and distribution of risks across the financial system. (ibid.)

In addition, the risks faced by individual financial institutions, which are considered solvent if the total value of their assets exceeds the value of their liabilities (Singh 2012), can be further subdivided into:

1. *Diversifiable risk*: Where asset portfolios held by financial institutions consist of assets whose returns are not correlated; and
2. *Non-diversifiable risk*: Where additional bank capital/liquidity is required to ensure solvency. (ibid.: 15)

Here our task is to investigate the response of international monetary authorities to the accumulation and transmission of risk in the financial system where, as a result of inadequate capital-to-lending ratios (a structural weakness of fractional-reserve banking) and excessively leveraged/collateralized liabilities, financial corporations in the US, the UK, EU and Switzerland have exploited their political influence to negotiate a socialization of losses through the state circuits of capital. That is, the losses of 'too-big-to-fail' banks were socialized to protect creditors and prevent a loss of confidence in the banking system. This phenomenon is less significant for major state-capitalist economies like China and Russia because their banking systems, while notionally competitive, are *already* subject to more extreme government controls to limit capital flight and mitigate global systemic risk.

A turning point in the regulation of global banking arrived with the request by G20 leaders at the St. Petersburg summit in 2013 to the FSB to develop new rules to govern the loss-absorbing and recapitalization capacity of systemically important banks. This resulted in a set of agreements formalized at the G20 Brisbane Summit in 2014, which was overshadowed by a diplomatic dispute between Russia and the West over Ukraine. Although international financial institutions charged with developing new rules on capital adequacy and insolvency resolution are staffed by transnational elites, inspiration for the new regulatory framework advanced by the IMF, BIS and the FSB can be found in the Dodd-Frank Act passed by the US Congress in 2010. This Act (elements of which were recently repealed in May 2018 at the insistence of Trump) created a Financial Stability Oversight Council to 'police' Wall Street and enforce bank reserve requirements, and to ensure observance of the 'Volcker rule' which prohibits banks from using hedge funds to enhance their own profits and from using depositors' assets to trade on their own accounts. In addition, the Act was designed to oversee the activities of credit ratings agencies and regulate high-risk derivatives markets (GAO 2012). The new rules on capital adequacy and insolvency resolution also formalized procedures employed by the ECB to resolve the crisis in Cyprus in 2013 when 'bail-in' measures were used in a major way for the first time to recapitalize insolvent banks. These regulations, giving monetary authorities powers over depositors' assets in the event of bank failure, are detailed and extensive, and build on the evolving Basel framework (I/II/III) authored by BIS since the 1980s.

The purpose of bank regulation is to limit risk. More specifically, however, it is often argued that the aim of *bank capital* regulation is 'not to increase bank capital per se, but to limit risk exposures relative to the bank's capital' (Gleeson 2012: 22). The ability of banks to maintain capital adequacy (to attract capital which might otherwise flow to competing corporate entities) depends on their monopoly right to accept deposits, and monetary authorities reserve the right to impose

> almost any level of capital requirement which they choose […] provided they are prepared to cooperate in ensuring that banks are able to charge their customers sufficient to enable them to raise that capital. Thus the idea of meaningful capital requirements is inextricably connected with the idea of a protected statutory monopoly. (ibid.)

The reason why governments have historically tended to support failing banks is due to their public function as a conduit for payments – as well as the fear that bank closure will result in financial dislocation. Hence the traditional view that central banks, as the principal monetary authorities empowered to regulate banking within specific jurisdictions – in partnership with national treasuries, as principal architects of fiscal policy – should have full *statutory* powers to manage both the assets and liabilities of distressed banks as well as broad *discretionary* powers to vary existing contracts in accordance with financial markets law (ibid.: 30–32).

The first international protocol authored by the Basel Committee on Banking Supervision at BIS for managing bank capitalization was the Basel Capital Accord of 1988, which standardized rules on capital holdings and established minimum capital 'tiers' based on risk-weighted asset values. This accord was revised in 2004 ('Basel II') and subsequently superseded by Basel III in 2013. The logic of these revised rules is laid out on the first page of a BIS communiqué from 2010:

> One of the main reasons the economic and financial crisis, which began in 2007, became so severe was that the banking sectors of many countries had built up excessive on- and off-balance sheet leverage. This was accompanied by a gradual erosion of the level and quality of the capital base. At the same time, many banks were holding insufficient liquidity buffers. The banking system therefore was not able to absorb the resulting systemic trading and credit losses nor could it cope with the reintermediation of large off-balance

sheet exposures that had built up in the shadow banking system. The crisis was further amplified by a procyclical deleveraging process and by the interconnectedness of systemic institutions through an array of complex transactions. During the most severe episode of the crisis, the market lost confidence in the solvency and liquidity of many banking institutions. [...] Ultimately the public sector had to step in with unprecedented injections of liquidity, capital support and guarantees, exposing taxpayers to large losses. (BIS 2010: 1)

The document lists priorities of supervision as: (i) raising the quality, consistency and transparency of the capital base of banks, ensuring they hold 'comparable' levels of Tier 1 capital (see Table 6.1); (ii) augmenting risk coverage of the capital framework, given that 'failure to capture major on- and off-balance sheet risks, as well as derivative related exposures, was a key destabilising factor during the crisis' (ibid.: 3); (iii) supplementing risk-based capital requirements with new leverage ratios in response to a build-up of 'excessive on- and off-balance sheet leverage in the banking system' (ibid.: 4). This excess leverage was, BIS notes, a feature of previous financial disturbances:

> During the most severe part of the crisis, the banking sector was forced by the market to reduce its leverage in a manner that amplified downward pressure on asset prices, further exacerbating the positive feedback loop between losses, declines in bank capital, and the contraction in credit availability (ibid.);

and (iv) reducing procyclicality and promote countercyclical buffers to limit amplification of financial shocks in the wider economy (ibid.: 5).

TABLE 6.1 Simplified summary of Basel III capital adequacy rules[2]

Status	Types of capital	Characteristics
Tier 1	Shareholders equity; retained earnings; preferred stock; reserves created by appropriation of retained earnings; share premiums; minority interests	• No contractual obligation to pay dividends or interest to Tier 1 holders • Tier 1 should be able to absorb losses before, or instead of, general creditors
Upper Tier 2	Perpetual deferrable subordinated debt (including debt convertible into equity); revaluation reserves from fixed assets and fixed asset investments; and general provisions	• Perpetual, senior to Tier 1 preferred and equity • Coupons are deferrable and cumulative • Interest/principal can be written down
Lower Tier 2	Fixed-term preference shares; long-term subordinated debt; fixed-term subordinated securities	• As for Upper Tier 2, but repayment dates fixed

Reference in the Basel communiqué to the 'September 1998 crisis' concerns the panic over Long Term Capital Management (LTCM) which followed the Latin American, Asian and Russian financial crises of 1997–1998. LTCM was a giant hedge fund which acted as a counterparty in an interlocking web of complex financial trades, and which went into receivership after billionaire investors initially refused to step in to provide liquidity to the fund whose potential default threatened a collapse in global equity and bond markets (Rechtschaffen 2014: 148–151). A consortium of banks was eventually formed to maintain the fund in receivership while its derivatives trades were unwound and the risk of contagion limited. Rickards argues that the lessons of LTCM were clear: the density and opacity of financial market derivatives 'meant neither regulators nor banks knew where the risk lay. Derivatives allowed massive leverage because the collateral required was minute relative to their gross value' (2016: 142). Although awareness of the aggregate effects of complex risk has grown since the global crisis, Rickards insists that few experts fully understand the nature of complexity in the modern financial system, preferring to rely on older concepts such as 'gross notional value' (total value of a trading position) rather than recognize that in complex counterparty trades involving multiple agents the accumulation of risk proceeds in nonlinear ways. 'Put plainly', he observes,

> if you double derivative gross notional value, you do not double the risk, you increase it by a factor which can be ten or one hundred times depending on specific system characteristics [...] derivatives risk increases exponentially as a function of scale measured by gross notional value. (ibid.: 145)

In addition, systemic risk is 'much more than just the composition of individual types of risks affecting financial institutions' (Smaga 2014: 3). Before the crisis different components of risk tended to be considered separately or in isolation, but there is now greater recognition that interaction between these risks 'leads to undesired and unexpected consequences [...]' (ibid.).

This means even minute changes in initial systemic conditions can lead to divergent or chaotic outcomes. There are in reality no black swan events: 'crises emerge because regulators don't comprehend the statistical properties of the systems they regulate' (ibid.: 148). Gleeson highlights a similar misunderstanding of risk among banks and regulators in the 2008 crisis, where risk-modelling failed 'spectacularly' because sophisticated statistical techniques used to assess risk began to be used by

> structured product engineers to create securities with defined risk characteristics. [...] these structures reversed the ordinary process of risk analysis – instead of starting with a portfolio of risks and assessing its riskiness, they started with a target level of riskiness and structured the portfolio to deliver it. (Gleeson 2012: 25)

As noted in Chapter 2, these high-risk financial instruments (CDOs) entered the market to be exchanged with AAA-rated assets with a lower built-in risk component, causing chaos as once prudently managed institutions struggled to quantify hidden levels of systemic risk entailed in the accumulation of derivative value in multiple classes of leveraged assets. Ironically, it is precisely the activities of hedge funds in derivatives markets which deepened and intensified systemic risk in the global financial system by increasing levels of opacity and leverage in the markets, leading to anxious discussions among international monetary elites in the years immediately prior to the global financial crisis concerning (ECB 2007).

To create an adequate capital buffer against unexpected losses in the event of a crisis on the scale of 1998 or 2008, Basel III rules require that total Tier 1 capital must be at least 8.0 per cent of risk-weighted assets to be considered 'adequately capitalized' and 10.0 per cent to be considered 'well capitalized'. If banks fail to meet either of these requirements, they are considered undercapitalized and 'mandatory restrictions are placed on its activities that become increasingly sever as the bank's capital ratios deteriorate' (Gleeson 2012: 95). It is important to note here that once an international agreement like Basel III is reached, because the task of actually implementing and enforcing the rules falls largely to *national* regulatory authorities (including rules on bank liquidity coverage), deviations from standardized procedures are inevitable. Liquidity risk in the banking sector emanates from three sources: systemic market-wide factors (financial dislocation/loss of investor confidence), idiosyncratic factors (internal institutional dysfunction), and technical factors (timing of cash flows, etc.) (Adalsteinsson 2014: 43). Liquidity regulation has become a topic of heated debate since liquidity risk is an unavoidable outcome of *maturity transformation* – the process through which banks borrow notional capital from the future to spend in the present. It is also controversial because Basel III regulates liquidity at the level of *qualitative* rather than *quantitative* holdings of the type outlined above (ibid.: 350). It is necessary to deal with these points before examining the further development of macroprudential regulation after the Brisbane Summit in 2014, where elites endorsed new regulations to manage the financial system in a future crisis.

A traditional orthodoxy in financial economies states that every asset has a price and that all assets will find a buyer. This, argues Gleeson, is a

> manifestation of the well-known economic error – the idea that a market asset has a true value which is somehow different from the price which a market purchaser is able and willing to pay for it. During the crisis [...] portions of banks' traded asset books were discovered to be illiquid at any price. The reinvention of the liquidity regulation as a separate discipline in itself was therefore one of the most significant features of the post-crisis Basel settlement. (ibid.: 362)

This settlement imposed two requirements: the Liquidity Coverage Ratio (LCR), which requires banks to hold 'high quality liquid assets' to cover potential cash outflows over a period of 30 days; and the Net Stable Funding Ratio, which requires banks to balance short- and long-term funding. But these rules still permit banks to model their own liquidity position autonomously which creates anomalies and irregularities by defining liquidity ratios in 'broad-brush classifications' which lack the detailed specificity of capital adequacy requirements (ibid.: 363). On the one hand, the rules can be seen as *less* restrictive, allowing deposits to be covered by liquid securities; on the other hand, they can be seen as *more* restrictive as reserve requirements because they apply to a wider range of bank liabilities and try to limit maturity transformation – that is, where banks fund long-term lending on the basis of short-term loans with the assumption that the risk of creditors suddenly withdrawing deposits is low. Yet, as the world saw in September 2008, this assumption is hardly warranted as individual bank runs escalate rapidly into systemic panics, leading to system-wide demands on the financial architecture which destabilize indebted sovereign governments.

According to the Basel Committee, the LCR – defined in terms of high-quality liquid assets (HQLA), requires that, under normal market conditions, banks maintain the value of the ratio no lower than 100 per cent (i.e. the stock of HQLA should at least equal total net cash outflows) (BIS 2013: 9). In periods of financial stress, on the other hand, 'banks may use their stock of HQLA, thereby falling below 100 per cent, as maintaining the LCR at 100 per cent under such circumstances could produce undue negative effects on the bank and other market participants' (ibid.). Two categories of assets make up HQLA, namely level 1 cash and assets which can rapidly be turned into funds in periods of credit contraction; and level 2 assets likely to yield at least 85 per cent of their value in a crisis, including bonds and securities. The latter (level 2 assets) should not exceed 40 per cent of the total HQLA held by a bank. Although this rehearses the myth that assets have a 'true' value distinct from the price a buyer might actually pay for them in an *actual* liquidity crisis, the document states further that regulators should (a) assess conditions at an early stage, and take actions if deemed necessary, to address potential liquidity risk; (b) allow for differentiated responses to a reported LCR below 100 per cent [...] supervisory responses should be proportionate; and (c) assess firm- and market-specific factors to determine appropriate responses and other considerations related to both domestic and global frameworks and conditions (ibid.: 10).

The implication of these rules is that all financial firms must consider their liquidity coverage ratio requirements and access to capital to cover their changing exposure to risk. This requires banks to plan far ahead to integrate this requirement into the institution's decision-making structure to enable it to manage liquidity and align it to capital and earnings targets (cf. Accenture 2016). Yet researchers have examined how Basel III rules have actually been implemented in the US and EU, noting that they contain many 'untested and difficult to quantify provisions', which raises not only the 'costs of bank compliance but also the cost of enforcement to authorities' (Fratianni & Pattison 2015: 11). They also report major differences in the way rules are applied between jurisdictions, reflecting asymmetric preferences among national regulators. More seriously, however, while the LCR is designed to make banks *more* stable in crises, the rules can in fact lead to a 'snowballing' of borrowing requirements as firms engaged in maturity transformation struggle to borrow enough funds in an emergency to comply with regulations such that the ratio 'operates as an effective "tax" on the liabilities of banks in the form of higher funding requirements for debt borrowed at short terms and debt that shows instability in past crises' (Hartlage 2012: 470; cf. Lindblom & Willesson 2013).

Although banks can in theory respond by deleveraging liabilities and funding liquidity through issuance of equity rather than debt, Hartlage argues that this is unrealistic because few firms would willingly choose to raise funds through the sale of equity (ibid.).[3] Comparing the implementation of prescriptive liquidity rules in South Korea in the Asian crisis with conditions in the US, he concludes that liquidity requirements exacerbate instability by creating more competition for the types of funding required by the rule. This point is reiterated by Hummel, who argues that 'by hobbling a bank's discretionary control over its balance sheet, the rule may well exacerbate the crisis' (2015: 2). More broadly, a binding rule of this type simply '*increases the government's central planning of the allocation of savings*. [...] it is another futile attempt to use prudential regulation to overcome the excessive risk taking resulting from the moral hazard created by deposit insurance and too-big-to-fail' (ibid.; italics added).

It is clear from this analysis that new capital adequacy rules open the door to further economic centralization by imposing a cost on higher funding requirements for certain types of debt and by creating competition for types of funding imposed by the rules. In this sense, it may be the case that rules conceal a subsidiary function distinct from the stated goal of limiting systemic risk, namely to employ macroprudential regulation not only to compensate for the erosion of an entrepreneurial risk-taking culture by financial socialism, but to centralize resource allocation by extending the mediational power of state circuits of financial capital. If so, it may alter the *legal structure of capital allocation* in postliberal capitalism by rendering the commercial investment decisions of private firms more contingent on state mediation. Taken to a logical conclusion, this suggests that the legal basis of capital ownership in postliberal capitalism is becoming attenuated: monetary policy is evolving to favour too-big-to-fail financial institutions which enjoy generous – if not unconditional – state support or which possess the financial power to engage in regulatory arbitrage (complying with competing regulations depending on their relative costs/benefits), as well as elite employers' organizations and PPPs whose economic power is manifest in the policy process, and whose actions inhibit the claimed ameliorative effect of 'ordered risk-taking' in market economies in favour of capitalist central planning.

Insolvency resolution

To understand the new regulations for managing G-SIFIs, it is necessary to recall the institutionalization of the Financial Stability Board in April 2009, which replaced the Financial Stability Forum (FSF) created in 1999 after the Asian financial crisis. The agency behind this supervisory body was the G7, led by Hans Tietmeyer, former head of the Deutsche Bundesbank. With the eclipse of the G7 by the G20 in November 2008, however, the FSF was given a new mandate with a stronger institutional basis and broader membership reflecting the new balance of geoeconomic power after the global crisis. The mandate of the FSB, as a transnational supervisory body, was to strengthen the global financial system and increase stability in markets by developing policies to be implemented by international and national financial authorities. It was established – in theory, of course – to coordinate the regulatory work of national financial authorities and international standard-setting bodies in order to improve oversight and pre-emptive intervention, and thus increase financial stability. As one FSB report from 2009 states, the goal is a more 'disciplined and less procyclical financial system that better supports balanced sustainable economic growth. This system will not allow leverage to increase to the extent that it did. Nor will we allow risks to be taken where profits accrue to individual actors but ultimate losses are borne by governments and the wider public' (FSB 2009: 1). Its remit was to end the uncertain status of government responsibility for 'too-big-to-fail' banks by assessing their capacity for 'supervisory intensity, for more effective resolution, and stronger financial market infrastructure' (FSB 2015: 3). The aim was to ensure that distressed G-SIFIs would be resolvable 'without exposing public funds to loss', ensuring that such banks have the capacity to absorb financial losses before and during resolution (ibid.). Implicit was the assumption that regulators should have the authority to prevent crises from spreading by using their powers to *quickly* 'write down, modify the terms of, cancel completely and/or convert into equity the liabilities of a failing bank *before* it becomes insolvent [to] protect "good liabilities" at the expense of those holding "bad liabilities"' (Sullivan & Worcester LLP 2016: 1).

This mandate was reaffirmed at the G20 summit in St Petersburg in 2013, leading to the publication of a key document calling on advanced economies to translate FSB policies on G-SIFIs into new legislation binding in national jurisdictions: 'national authorities, in consultation with standard-setting bodies [... will] determine which institutions will be designated as G-SIFIs. The methodologies to identify G-SIFIs need to reflect the nature and degree of risks they pose to the global financial system' (FSB 2013: 8). Using indicators developed by the FSB, G20 finance ministers were asked to determine which institutions in their jurisdiction should be classified as G-SIFIs, based on five measures of systemic importance, including size, global activity, interconnectedness, complexity and substitutability. This list is updated annually and originally included 28 banks ranked in accordance with desired levels of additional loss absorbency. The updated list (FSB 2017) includes 30 global megabanks deemed critical to the functioning of the global financial system. This is not an exhaustive list of systemically important institutions, for it excludes powerful asset management firms and other market actors which might also be subject to specific regulations in a financial emergency (Rickards 2016). However, regulators seek to ensure these global banks *in particular* maintain 'sufficient loss-absorbing and recapitalisation capacity available in resolution to implement an orderly resolution that minimises any impact on financial stability, ensures the continuity of critical functions, and avoids exposing taxpayers to loss with a high degree of confidence' (FSB 2015: 5). This, the authors assert, is the 'guiding principle from which the other principles flow. Instruments or liabilities that are not eligible as [total loss-absorbing capacity] will still be subject to potential exposure to loss in resolution, in accordance with the applicable resolution law' (ibid.). Financial regulators must ensure 'early intervention' and 'continuity of critical functions' after resolution, in order that the entity emerging from resolution meets 'conditions for authorisation, including any consolidated capital requirements, and be sufficiently well capitalised to command market confidence' (ibid.: 5–6).

This document insists portentously that 'resolution is not resurrection [...] nor is it insolvency' (ibid.). It is, rather, a form of financial restructuring designed to ensure that regulators (central banks) have the statutory authority to *require* the bailing-in of creditor funds and liquidation of bad liabilities to ensure that creditors in general do not suffer worse losses than would occur through liquidation:

> Given that TLAC-eligible instruments [funds] will need to absorb losses and contribute to recapitalisation needs in order for an orderly resolution to take place, there is a particular need to ensure that authorities possess the necessary legal powers to expose the TLAC-eligible instruments to loss and that they can exercise their powers without material risk of successful legal challenge or giving rise to compensation costs under the 'no creditor worse off than in liquidation' (NCWOL) principle. Similarly, authorities must be confident that the holders of these instruments are able to absorb losses in a time of stress in the financial markets without spreading contagion and without necessitating the allocation of loss to liabilities where that would cause disruption to critical functions or significant financial instability. TLAC should not therefore include operational liabilities [current liabilities and costs arising from the business operations of a firm that are non-interest bearing] on which the performance of critical functions depends [...]. (ibid.: 6–7)

The question *who* is liable for *which* losses clearly also requires clarification, and the authors demand that 'investors, creditors, counterparties, customers and depositors should have clarity about the order in which they will absorb losses in resolution. This requires disclosure of information on the hierarchy of liabilities on a legal entity basis' (ibid.: 7). This should apply to

> all resolution entities and each legal entity that forms part of a material subgroup and issues internal TLAC to a resolution entity, so that there is as much clarity as possible ex ante about how losses are absorbed and recapitalisation is effected in the resolution of cross-border groups. (ibid.: 7)

How, therefore, is this hierarchy of liabilities in insolvency resolution determined, and what is the legal status of depositors' assets in the (likely) event that distressed banks succumb to market contagion and are confronted by the threat of a bank run? To answer this, it is necessary to examine the impact of the BRRD, which came into effect in eurozone economies in January 2016, and which has since led to litigious exchanges between the EU and national governments in the banking union (Khan 2015). According to the ECB, to 'credibly remove the implicit state guarantee upfront for all banks, it must be possible to effectively resolve banks without public support and to do so without significant contagion risk' (ECB 2017). But is it possible to avoid a socialization of bank losses and limit the pain of recapitalization for creditors and depositors? And, how much responsibility should the latter be required to assume for the risk-prone behaviour of banks to safeguard funds in accounts which no longer offer interest above the rate of inflation and which open the door to predation? This leads to a further question, namely can bail-in regimes work at all if depositors know they can withdraw their funds in anticipation of an impending loss?

Guidelines published by the European Parliament's Directorate-General for Internal Policies reaffirm that the purpose of prudential regulation is to end the moral hazard associated with excessive risk-prone actions in the banking sector and to shift the burden of bank rescues from taxpayers to creditors/depositors. To this end, resolution authorities have the power to allocate losses to shareholders and creditors (BRRD Article 43) in line with the valuation of the entity and in accordance with Article 48. Shareholders/creditors should be able to absorb losses for at least 8.0 per cent of liabilities, including their own funds, before they are entitled to resolution funds. As bailing-in some liabilities may be legally *difficult* (for example, those issued in foreign jurisdictions), or potentially *disruptive* for the real economy, the BRRD provides for a list of liabilities which must not be bailed-in, in particular covered deposits and secured liabilities (BRRD Article 44.2) (European Parliament 2016: 1). Article 45 of the Directive also provides that all financial institutions should meet a *minimum requirement for own funds and eligible liabilities* ('MREL'), as determined by the resolution authority. MREL constitutes an 'anchor point for the new resolution framework, as it determines the credibility of the bail-in regime' (ibid.), in other words, a mandatory loss-absorbing buffer composed of equity and debt which banks have attempted to comply with by issuing new securities in the form of senior debt (Bloomberg 2018). MREL requirements apply the regulatory system of the FSB to *all* financial institutions and are (in theory) to be phased in alongside the BRRD by 2019.

According to the Spanish bank Bilbao Vizcaya Argentaria (2016: 17), MREL is determined on a case-by-case basis, while TLAC is a 'common minimum standard'. Eligible instruments include equity, junior and senior debt, subordinated debt and other liabilities (ibid.: 19). As Table 6.2 shows, at the *apex* of the creditor hierarchy is Tier 1 capital, consisting of common stock which, according to FSB rules, should constitute 4.5 per cent of all banks' balance sheets by 2019. Second in line for repayment is 'Additional Tier 1', comprised of securities and convertible capital instruments designed to absorb losses if capital buffers recede below required levels, while in third place is Tier 2 capital, namely supplementary capital including undisclosed reserves and other hybrid financial instruments. In fourth place stands subordinated

TABLE 6.2 Hierarchy of liabilities in BRRD resolution scheme

Rank	Category
1	Tier 1 capital
2	Additional Tier 1 capital
3	Tier 2 capital
4	Subordinated debt
5	Commercial paper
6	Corporate deposits
7	Retail deposits

debt and Tier 3 capital, and below this in fifth place lie senior debt, covered bonds, mortgage bond, securities, structured notes, promissory notes and various categories of commercial paper including deposits by credit institutions, central banks and public administration. Finally, at level six and seven, respectively, are corporate deposits and retail deposits which are most vulnerable in an emergency bail-in situation. The report opines optimistically that while not all the jurisdictions require exactly the same scheme, a 'certain minimum harmonization is necessary', and that the 'need for coordination in the EU and especially in the Eurozone is much higher'. Indeed, convergence of TLAC and MREL is seen as 'crucial' for the EU where a 'minimum level of harmonization is necessary' (ibid.). However, the authors conclude, 'the real test of the bail-in regime is *practical application*' (ibid.; emphasis added). This point is crucial for the present discussion, for behind the technical jargon of 'eligible instruments', 'orderly resolution', 'loss absorption capacity', etc. lies a more explosive question of fiduciary trust, legitimacy and accountability.

In what follows, we examine the 'legitimacy' of new bail-in rules first, looking at its inception in the eurozone crisis, and, more particularly, the banking crisis in Cyprus in 2013. We will then address the question of 'effectiveness' and the potential for the rules to overcome the need for socializing losses in a systemic crisis. We will see that financial socialism is not only legally (and morally) questionable but that it is wildly optimistic to believe that encouraging regulators to turn unsecured liabilities into 'bail-inable' debt will incentivize creditors to monitor risk more closely and reaffirm the fabled principle of 'market' discipline. Although some commentators believe the BRRD resolution framework renders future outright bailouts almost impossible (Hadjiemmanuil 2017), examined realistically it is clear that limitations exist on the workability of the new rules in all but 'idiosyncratic' cases of bank failure.

Authority necessitates law

To make sense of the new regulatory framework as a political-economic strategy for preserving elite corporate wealth, it is important to distinguish theoretically the *legal* status of the BRRD as a codified legal framework for the orderly resolution of banks based on EU 'rules', and the *political* origins of 'bail-in' as a constitutive precedent resulting from the ECB's emergency response to the insolvency of euro-zone banks during the eurozone crisis. As Derrida (1992) argued, the meaning of a constitutional order emanates not from a rule or any other measure of legal valid-ity, but from a foundational moment or constitutive agency *not subject to* normative regulation: no posited system of rules can 'will' itself into being; neither can it bind sovereign power. Rather, rules augment or validate prior constitutive acts, creating a secure framework for the exercise of authority. The prior foundational moment of new rules is necessarily violent and destabilizing, until rules are *formally enacted* as law or informally observed as custom. Debate on this issue has simmered since Agamben's celebrated discussion of the 'force of law', as a result of which a 'state of exception' is inscribed in a juridical context (1995: 32). Agamben's critique of Schmitt shifted the terms of the debate towards the normalization of the state of exception as the 'dominant paradigm of government', providing a theoretical refer-ence point to scrutinize governmental practices in modern democracies (cf. Cotula 2017). A similar constitutive/regulative dynamic informs the legal codification of the BRRD following the decision by the EU to impose financial martial law to resolve a banking crisis in southern Europe by forcing depositors to assume liability for the resolution of distressed banks – thereby placating indignant taxpayers in northern Europe. The subsequent enactment of the BRRD is merely a legal encod-ing of a prior constitutive act ('precedent') which has its origins in the decision by Eurogroup finance ministers to relinquish responsibility for the integration of 'Club Med' economies into the eurozone – and, in the absence of eurozone solidarity, to pass this responsibility on to local depositors and foreign nationals living in Cyprus to enjoy its relaxed banking laws. Opinions on the events in Cyprus in 2013 vary depending on the nationality, location and political perspective of writers.

One perspective is offered by former head of the Central Bank of Cyprus, Athanasios Orphanides (2016), who defends the island's banks against the stupidity/malfeasance of its central bank and government. He observes that the island's GDP fell by 10 per cent from 2008 to 2012 under the socialists, who were fiscally imprudent and failed to follow basic rules of public finance. Warnings were ignored and the island was shut out of capital markets from 2011, which the government tried to cover up for political motives – until too late. For elec-toral reasons, it blamed the banks, which, Orphanides claims, had been trying to reinforce capital adequacy ratios to conform with Basel III – although proximity to Athens meant they were dangerously exposed to the Greek drama. Despite its ineptitude, however, the Cypriot government was determined to remain solvent and not to follow the path of Greece, Ireland and Portugal by seeking aid from the EU/IMF/ECB 'Troika', whose demands for stricter capital adequacy conditions exacerbated the crisis. Rather than go to the IMF – which would have imposed strict SAP conditions on loans – Cyprus negotiated a large loan from Russia:

> The [Russian] loan antagonized the island's European partners, and could not solve the government's sustainability problem, just postpone its

resolution until a later date. [...] The amount of the loan was calculated so that the government could meet its fiscal needs until the next presidential elections, in February 2013. With the loan, the government could avoid undertaking the meaningful fiscal adjustments necessary to restore market access. The delay in corrective action made the problem worse. Once again, short-term political calculations dominated. (Orphanides 2016: 188)

The ECB would not allow Cyprus to issue further government debt unless it had an investment-grade rating – which was impossible because Cyprus, unlike Ireland or Portugal, was acting outside the framework of the Troika. One solution was to offer fiscal concessions, but the president rejected these as politically unacceptable. As a result, the credit rating of Cyprus was downgraded to junk. This led the government to accuse the banks of 'casino practices' to divert attention from their own failure to manage the economy and seek aid earlier. It claimed that the financial weakness of the banks was the reason it had to seek help, not its own incompetence and bad-faith manoeuvring. The recapitalization needs of the banks were then exaggerated by PIMCO (a US investment management firm) under contract from the government, which made 'irregular' measures more likely. Orphanides concludes that although this condemned the banking system to collapse, it could be justified as a response to 'casino banking'. As such, the 'campaign against the banks in the context of the February 2013 election led to the haircut [bail-in] of deposits in Cyprus' (ibid.: 200).

A different perspective is offered by critics of the eurozone crisis which revealed severe financial imbalances in the eurozone banking system and underlying political conflict between core capitalist economies in the EU and the less developed southern periphery. Financialization had facilitated a gross distortion of the Cypriot banking system itself, which before the crisis was bloated with total assets of $143 billion – eight times the value of the island's GDP:

> Cyprus offered savings rates which could not be matched. [...] The island became a financial nexus without a financial district: a hub for flows of capital without the trappings of distinction that dominated the cityscapes of London, Frankfurt, New York and Zurich. Many of those depositors happened to be Russians; Cyprus, as much as London, was a playground for ex-Soviet business tycoons because of low dividend taxes and the use of business-friendly English law. [...] Moody's, the credit ratings agency, estimated in 2013 that Russian banks had $12 billion and private individuals another $19 billion on deposit with banks in Cyprus. (Theodore & Theodore 2015: 40)

The authors contend that the Cyprus crash was really just a new phase in the Greek debt crisis and that the actions of the Troika were motivated largely by containment. 'It is strikingly clear', they observe, 'that the Troika and the ECB *failed to deal in a timely manner* with the fall-out from the haircut on Greek sovereign bonds [in 2012]. Cyprus was sacrificed on the altar of Greece' (Theodore &

Theodore 2015: 61). In fact, the banking crisis on the island was used by the EU, ECB and IMF to 'road-test' financial martial law:

> Road-testing this technique on Cyprus has an obvious logic to it. The economy of the island was too small for anything more than a ripple effect for this new modus operandi, at least in direct financial terms: minimising the systemic consequences which the entire approach was crafted to avoid. The country's plutocratic ties outside the eurozone made the policy much easier to sell to the European media, if not to the people of Cyprus themselves. The bail-in served the purpose of avoiding the use of taxpayers' money to bail *out* the very banks that had contributed to the problem in the first place: the central, and enormously unpopular, characteristic of bank rescue plans since the collapse of Lehman Brothers in 2008. (Theodore & Theodore 2015: 71)

When Cypriot depositors took legal action against the central bank after an extended bank holiday (arguing that the bail-in was disproportionately negative for them as individual savers), the central bank referred the matter to the Supreme Court which ruled that they had no 'formal legal grounds' (*locus standi*) for their protest; in the absence of a government-led bailout of the banks, the court declared the issue a 'private' rather than public matter, and depositors were directed to the civil courts. As a result, an impression was created that the bail-in had deliberately targeted uninsured deposits (both Cypriot and non-Cypriot) in order to contain and localize the crisis and reduce the immediate risk of contagion for German and French banks by ensuring a continued flow of funds from their poorer 'Club Med' equivalents.

Chorafas (2013a) takes this argument a stage further, locating the eurozone crisis in the broader structural crisis of neoliberal globalization, which has limited the capacity of governments to regulate and stabilize their own financial systems. Although the banking union survived the crisis by immunizing core EU economies from contagion from the 'Club Med' periphery, the 2013 bail-in ultimately had a devastating impact on the integrity and unity of the EU project:

> The way Cyprus has been treated by its eurozone partners shows that far from the currency bloc acting as a partnership of equals, it is a disjointed group of countries where the national interests of the big nations stand higher than the interests of the whole. (Passarides cited in Chorafas 2013a: 10)

Chorafas concludes that we have entered a new era of '*banksterism, state gangsterism, and too-big-to-fail* policies' (ibid.: 13). He warns furthermore that policies of this type are always introduced 'softly', by 'little Caesars without even asking parliaments to give an opinion. Then, before we know it, we wake up as slaves of a new economic fascism [...]' (ibid.).

The dramatic events in Cyprus illustrate the structural violence of financial socialism, namely the coercive appropriation of depositors' assets without compensation to limit contagion in core EU economies. This foundational act provides a powerful precedent for the future use of financial martial law, and the controversial nature of new bail-in rules is acknowledged in official circles – in principle, at least:

> [B]ail-in remains among the most contested elements of new resolution frameworks and the debate on the scope and reasonability of its application continues, both in the Union and internationally. The concerns are at least partially rooted in the intrusive nature of bail-in. In resolution, authorities determine when which creditor must bear which amount of a bank's losses. They do so based on the principles and objective elements set out in the law, but often with a large interpretative latitude and margin of discretion. As case law and established practices have yet to develop, the resulting challenges are manifold – some clearly legal, some of a more political nature. (Grünewald 2017: 288)

It is important here to note that the BRRD framework supersedes and is distinct from the traditional notion of insolvency resolution due to the introduction of an additional criterion for pre-insolvency intervention, namely 'failing or likely to fail' (FOLTF). Determining whether a bank should be categorized as 'FOLTF' is a technical issue for supervisory authorities, the intention of which is 'to enable the authorities to intervene early enough, i.e. before actual insolvency. The more likely insolvency becomes, the more of a bank's value may be destroyed irrecoverably, but the less intrusive is an ensuing bail-in regarding shareholders' and creditors' right to property' (ibid.). As such, FOLTF attempts to extrapolate a bank's future insolvency 'beyond reasonable doubt', even though any decision to intervene is likely to be based on a subjective valuation of its assets and liabilities. The subjectivity of this determination is further extended by its 'dependency on macroeconomic assumptions and, over time, changing market conditions' (ibid.: 291).

Grünewald concedes that the combination of these complex stipulations indicates that the technocratic yet subjective nature of bail-in interventions, which also allow for the preferential treatment of some creditors over others, 'render bail-in a practice that interferes with the fundamental right to property as protected by Article 17(1) CFR and Article 1 of the Protocol to the ECHR' (ibid.: 293). Nonetheless, it is argued, the process can in theory avoid this legal minefield if three conditions are met, namely: (i) the legal basis of intervention is 'accessible, precise and foreseeable in its application'; (ii) intervention is in the 'public interest' as defined by the ECHR, which allows states considerable latitude excluding only a deprivation of possessions that is 'manifestly without reasonable foundation'; and (iii) proportionality can be achieved between the public interest and the rights of property owners using a means test to ensure that a 'least onerous measure' is implemented (ibid.: 294). Inevitably, however, there will be difficulties in determining the calibration of bail-in operations in the light of these proportionality conditions, and the legal basis of the rules remains untested, complex, controversial and opaque.

The BRRD framework requires that up to 8 per cent of a financial institution's assets may be bailed ahead of public insolvency resolution, yet as the Cyprus precedent attests, this figure is possibly irrelevant. Once the Memorandum of Understanding between the bank of Cyprus and EU had been finalized in 2013, 47.5 per cent of its uninsured deposits had been converted into stock to stabilize the banks, with the stipulation that 'uninsured depositors would be refunded through a buy-back of shares, should Bank of Cyprus turn out to be overcapitalised relative to the Core Tier 1 (CET1) target of 9 per cent under stress' (ibid.: 295). In a subsequent legal case contesting the legitimacy of the bail-in, the court ruled that given the priority of

> ensuring the stability of the banking system in the euro area, and having regard to the imminent risk of financial losses to which depositors with the two banks concerned would have been exposed if the latter had failed, such measures do not constitute a disproportionate and intolerable interference impairing of the [...] appellants' right to property. (Case C-8/15 P, Ledra Advertising v Commission and ECB, ECLI:EU:C2016:701, para. 74., cited in Grünewald 2017: 296)

In other appeals against the EU, similar judgements have been passed legitimizing *ex post facto* the precedent of emergency intervention in Cyprus in 2013, with judges at the General Court of the EU upholding rulings by the European Court of Justice by rejecting litigants' requests for compensation in accordance with the ECHR's right to property, the principle of legitimate expectations and the principle of equal treatment. The Court reiterated the legality of converting uninsured Bank of Cyprus deposits into shares and the 'temporary' freeze of other uninsured deposits which did not, in its opinion, 'constitute a disproportionate and intolerable interference which infringes the right to property' (General Court of the European Union 2018: 1–2).

Artemou focuses on legitimate expectations of risk among depositors in the case of bail-ins. He argues that while it is self-evident that creditors and depositors must accept an element of risk when lending money to banks, the validity of deposit protection (and the accountability which flows from this) may only be adequate for what he terms 'small crises', in other words, the failure of a specific bank (Artemou 2016: 213). Following Article 17 of the ECHR, he defines bank deposits as 'existing property', that is, 'rights with an "asset value creating an established legal position under the legal system, enabling the holder to exercise those rights autonomously and for his benefit"' (ECHR, cited in Artemou 2016: 217). Bank deposits are, he adds, assets with value 'through the currency they represent, and have an established legal position under the legal and monetary system. The holder may do as they wish with their currency such as deposit, withdraw, or invest' (ibid.). The Cyprus bail-in 'was not a situation where deposit holders effectively waived their right to property [...] waiving one's right to property requires an explicit and voluntary consent in full awareness of the circumstances' (ibid.).

In reality, of course, depositors were deprived of their property by the issuance of capital controls and the imposition of an extended 'bank holiday' during the course of the intervention, after which depositors were restricted to limited withdrawals of physical currency from cash dispensers:

> Even if the option to withdraw money from the banks were feasible, depositors had no control over the agreement. [...] Although the Cypriot parliament agreed to the terms of the bailout [sic], *no vote occurred among depositors which would constitute explicit and voluntary consent and thus a waiver of the right to property under Article 17* [...]. (ibid.: 218; emphasis added)

This coercive intervention has undermined confidence in the EU banking system, for while 'only uninsured deposits were materially affected by these obligations, bank consumers may not feel safe knowing that there is a risk that any portion of their deposits may be lost during an economic crisis' (ibid.: 228). To ameliorate this, argues Artemou, the EU Commission and ECB should rule out future emergency coercive appropriation of bank deposits 'unless all other reasonable options have been frustrated, thus leaving a higher standard in the regulation of bank deposits for the general interest according to Article 17' (ibid.).

In practice, however, the feasibility of the BRRD framework is challenged by a range of other factors, including fears of vanishing confidence, investor flight, contagion risk beyond the regional cluster, and the extreme reluctance of national central banks, technically subordinate to the ECB, to abide by the stipulations of the Directive while their domestic banks collapse. Hadjiemmanuil reminds us that

> beyond their potentially ruinous fiscal consequences, bailouts create expectations regarding future state responses to financial troubles. [...T]he subsidization of bank stakeholders' risk-taking by means of the externalization and absorption by the taxpaying public of the costs of insolvency exerts a very powerful effect on *ex ante* incentives, entrenching moral hazard. (Hadjiemmanuil 2017: 2)

Since the depths of the eurozone crisis in 2011, however, the EU and ECB have continued to authorize national support measures by member states to ensure the stability of their respective banking systems – and hence the stability of the banking union. Hadjiemmanuil argues that the EU's priority is not to eliminate burden-sharing but to rule out 'open-ended interventions which may generate undue fiscal risk and distortions of competition' (ibid.: 5), and governments should seek remuneration to the state for the costs of refinancing. Yet he also recognizes the potential legal and political wisdom of a regulatory regime which rules out public support to compensate accumulated losses: 'Resolution, as distinct from liquidation, is supposed to be justified on grounds of systemic stability. In contrast, in conditions of economic distress and system-wide banking weakness bail-in as the preferred and essentially mandatory resolution tool can aggravate the situation' (ibid.: 12).

In other words, if stability is more important than market competition or moral hazard then is it rational to penalize governments for using discretionary interventions to compensate for accumulated losses, non-performing loans and general unprofitability of banks – an economic sector which relies on central banks to act as lenders of last resort? It should be remembered here that, while imposing stringent rules on bank capitalization to comply with new FSB rules, the ECB has continued to do 'whatever it takes' to defend EU financial institutions and has issued more than €2.5 trillion in its QE programme to soften the impact of the eurozone recession (Jones 2018). While the ECB claims its banks are better capitalized and more resilient than before the crisis, as the FT reported in September 2018, lenders can still obtain

> ultra-cheap cash from the central bank [ECB], which is committed to providing liquidity in potentially unlimited quantities at an interest rate of zero. The ECB expects to keep interest rates at record lows 'through [to] the summer of 2019'. (ibid.: 2)

Avgouleas and Goodhart assess the plausibility of the bail-in tool in a critical analysis of the BBRD framework. While accepting the implicit technical advantages of bail-in as an alternative to bailout, in contrast to Hadjiemmanuil, they contend that the aspiration to force creditors and depositors to accept liability will not eradicate the need for emergency liquidity injections in systemic crises and may simply transfer the burden from one set of payers (taxpayers) to another (savers). In the midst of serious banking crises, four variables must be taken into account, including: timing, market confidence, required levels of restructuring, and accurate loss estimation (Avgouleas & Goodhart 2015: 14). The key unknown is the potential behaviour of transnational investors once a bail-in process is initiated in a specific financial jurisdiction – that is, once it becomes clear those same investors may be forced to accept liability for losses in other financial institutions the next day, or the day after. In addition to fears of creditor flight, it is difficult to maintain investor confidence given that bank failures generally occur 'when macroeconomic conditions have worsened, and asset values are falling' (ibid.: 16). It is also difficult to restore trust among depositors once bail-in tools have been used and courts are flooded with compensation claims. Mobile creditors (unlike *immobile* taxpayers) are unlikely to remain within a jurisdiction for the duration of a bank recapitalization: 'Consequently', the authors argue,

> triggering the bail-in process is likely to generate a capital flight and sharp rise in funding costs whenever the need for large-scale recapitalizations becomes

apparent. Creditors, who sense in advance the possibility of a bail-in, or creditors or institutions that are similar in terms of nationality or business modes
will have a strong incentive to withdraw deposits, sell debt, or hedge their
positions through the short selling of equity or the purchase of credit protection at an even higher premium, disrupting the relevant markets. [...] market
propensity to resort to herding during shocks means that it is not realistic
to believe that generalized adoption of bail-in mechanism would not trigger
contagious consequences that would have a destabilizing effect. (ibid.: 22–23)

These issues become yet more complex in cross-border resolutions involving
G-SIFIs where the proportion of foreign creditors is higher than domestic banks
accountable to one supervisory authority.

This indicates the importance of the distinction between 'single point of entry'
(SPE) and 'multiple points of entry' (MPE) regimes alluded to at the beginning
of the chapter. SPE regimes entail a group-level approach, involving cooperation between jurisdictions, while MPE regimes leave local monetary authorities
responsible for the welfare of financial entities within their territories. The categories SPE/MPE are really ideal types: 'actual regimes are likely to fall somewhere in between, but the distinction is nonetheless important. In particular,
most regulators recognise that the best approach depends on the nature of the
bank' (Philippon & Salord 2017: 5). Yet the choice of resolution regime is not just
a technical question for experts; it reflects a broader tension between monetary
nationalism and monetary *internationalism* in IPE which has become a pressing
issue for monetary elites as they seek to determine rules to limit financial contagion risk in future crises and defend the accumulated wealth of the investor class.

As noted earlier in this study, the mode of resolution of contradictions in preceding crises creates the necessary structural conditions for the unfolding form
of future contradictions – which are displaced to a higher level of abstraction. If
Cyprus were a test-case/precedent for the efficacy of bail-in, then the attempt
to routinize the BRRD framework in Italy – and the coercive tactics used by
the EU to force Italy's populist government to comply with the rules of the EU
Fiscal Compact – highlight fundamental limitations of bail-in as an alternative
approach to investor socialism. Although the crisis in the Italian banking sector long predates the election of Italy's Lega-Five Star coalition in May 2018, it
highlights contradictions in the EU banking union which in turn reveal contradictions in the monetary and fiscal structure of the eurozone.

Before concluding this section, therefore, it is worth considering the resistance in EU economies – in particular Italy – towards the use of bail-in tools to
resolve the longstanding problem of unprofitable EU banks. Wihlborg suggests
that there are two issues to be determined when considering the efficacy of bail-
in tools for promoting market discipline:

First, effective market discipline requires that there are a sufficient number
and size of creditors subject to credible bail-ins. If not, the marginal cost of

funding for a financial institution will not reflect its default risk. Second, it must be possible to apply the bail-in rules without serious systemic consequences. Authorities are not likely to allow bail-ins if they are not convinced that they can be applied with a minimum of systemic consequences. Therefore, the credibility of the bail-in rules and their systemic effects are intertwined. (Wihlborg 2017: 7)

The first issue is a technical one which need not concern us here; the second issue is, however, a structural one, which has definite consequences for the decision by local supervisory authorities (national central banks) to attempt pre-insolvency intervention by forcing creditors and depositors to accept initial liabilities. Weighing the risk of contagion and systemic instability, Wihlborg argues that 'limitations on bail-ins and eligible liabilities imply that authorities must have additional instruments to address contagion risk and its consequences for system-wide liquidity' (ibid.: 9). As a result, he affirms that 'central banks' traditional lender of last resort role as supplier of liquidity remains an important part of the financial system even if effective resolution procedures are in place' (ibid.). Papanikolaou (2018) also finds that, confronted by the collapse of large complex banks, governments will continue to resort to bailout measures – despite the downside risk of inefficiency and low future profitability. A similar scepticism characterizes the view of central banks in many eurozone states, where resistance to bail-in is acute, leading to tension between the EU and member states over the appropriate response to instability in the banking system.

An early indication of the problems of bail-in before the term had entered the official lexicon of Euro-speak was the collapse of Amagerbanken in 2011, a relatively small lender in Denmark. The collapse threatened to lock all but the largest Danish financial institutions out of the funding markets, leading to financial panic among investors. This localized financial event, which attracted little of the media attention devoted to Cyprus in 2013, has since led Danish regulators to conclude that *all* banks are 'essentially too big to fail' (Bloomberg 2018: 1):

> Jesper Berg, Director General of the Financial Supervisory Authority in Copenhagen, said in an interview: 'If you look at the rest of Europe, it has not exactly been a walk in the park imposing losses on investors in Tier 2'. The observation is among a list of weaknesses Berg says risk undermining Europe's efforts to prevent the next financial crisis. […] loss-absorbing buffers intended to prevent taxpayer rescues could fail because of the way they are designed. (ibid.)

Specifically, the issue concerns the demand of MREL that banks maintain a first line of defence of loss-absorbing senior/non-preferred debt based on specific maturities. Such maturities should be much longer, argues Berg, to eliminate refinancing risk in a crisis, thus reducing the risk of market contagion and systemic failure. At the same time, the demand for early creditor resolution and market discipline is contradicted by the continuing moral hazard of deposit protection insurance.

Problems in the Italian banking sector have gained much more attention due to the size of the country's debt, its stagnant economy and the polarization of its political system. A report by the *Economist Intelligence Unit* summarizes the regulatory problems faced by supervisory authorities in Italy, which largely refrained from extending state support to its banks in the 2008–2009 crisis due to the fiscal weakness of the state. Since then, the report argues,

> the Italian authorities and Italian banks have been slow to tackle the structural weaknesses in the banking system: high operating costs, low profitability, fragmentation and gaps in the supervision of the sector. In addition, the sector's balance sheet deteriorated sharply as a result of a protracted recession, leaving banks ill-prepared for the implementation of the new EU banking rules [BRRD], which require, with few exceptions, that the burden of rescuing ailing banks should be shouldered by bank creditors before taxpayers make any contribution. (EIU 2017: 1)

Predictably, confronted by the prospect of two large bank failures in 2017 (Veneto Banca and Banca Popolare di Vicenza), the Italian authorities chose to ignore BRRD rules and liquidate the financial institutions using national insolvency rules with state support of €5.2 billion (plus a further €12 in guarantees), selling the banks' assets to a larger competitor, Banca Intesa Sanpaolo for €1. Although this plan was conducted with the approval of the EU, the motive for its inception was the constraints imposed by new EU banking rules. 'As in the case of other failed or failing banks in Italy', the report concludes, a bail-in would have ruined 'small savers and pensioners who hold (or were mis-sold) bank bonds. [...] about €200 billion of €600 billion in total Italian bank bonds are held by retail investors' (ibid.: 2).

How was it possible for the Italian government to resort to bailout measures in the case of these two banks, while remaining within the rules of the BRRD? One writer suggests that hidden flexibility in the rules actually allows national supervisory authorities greater discretionary powers than at first appear. Both of the banks had been declared 'FOLTF' (see above) by the ECB because neither had been able to raise adequate capital to cover non-performing loans (Maxwell 2017). While their importance to the financial system was not critical, outright failure would have been politically and economically damaging for the government in the vital northeast industrial region (Lombardy-Venetia). Yet the return to taxpayer-funded resolution (renamed 'precautionary recapitalization') seems to imply 'public coffers are still fair game for aiding failing banks', which raises the question whether the BRRD can indeed function as intended (ibid.: 4). The decision seems to reflect a degree of expediency in the interpretation of the rules: would the EU have 'allowed public injection of funds if these two banks were based in a country other than Italy – where a populist anti-euro party would be a force to be reckoned with in a general election before mid-2018 [?]' (ibid.).

The subsequent election of the Lega-Five Star coalition did indeed complicate relations between Italy and Brussels, although the most combustible issue was not the BBRD but the Fiscal Compact which Italy could violate by exceeding EU deficit rules. Yet the EU continues to threaten legal consequences and punitive fines for eleven EU economies which have failed to integrate BRRD rules into their national law, including Bulgaria, the Czech Republic, Poland, Sweden, Lithuania, Malta, Romania, Luxembourg, the Netherlands, France and Italy – the last two of which have deep structural problems in their interlinked banking systems. Although Austria, normally subservient to Germany, technically removed all public support for investor deposit insurance in July 2018, it too retreated from this position in September 2018 by reintroducing a hybrid national deposit insurance scheme to be funded at 0.4 per cent from the national budget. As a key backer of the BRRD, Germany aims to impose limits on 'how much government debt a bank can take onto its books. It also wants to require banks to set aside capital against these government bonds' (Berschens & Hildebrand 2018: 2). In marked contrast, Italy 'opposes this requirement because the highly indebted country fears it will significantly increase its borrowing costs. There seems to be little chance these issues can be resolved ahead of the December summit of EU government heads' (ibid.).

In December 2018, Italy appeared to be heading for an explosive showdown with the EU Commission and ECB which would undermine the stability of the eurozone more seriously than the stand-off with Greece in 2015. As Evans-Pritchard notes, Italians are less intimidated by the EU now than they were in 2011, when the government of Silvio Berlusconi was toppled by a crisis in the bond markets engineered by the Eurogroup. Italy, he argues,

> is right that the Stability Pact and the Fiscal Compact are an absurdity with no foundation in economic science, and have a contractionary bias that leaves high-debt legacy states in a deflationary cul-de-sac. The rules are an unworkable attempt by lawyers to overcome the original sin of binding incompatible economies together in a single currency half a century too soon and then allowing a massive North-South chasm in real exchange rates to build up for fifteen years. (Evans-Pritchard 2018b: 2)

For Italians, the threat of financial destruction is less powerful than it was for Greece, yet the Eurogroup has the power to close down a country's access to refinancing markets with dire potential consequences for its banking system. This is a powerful incentive for compliance, and the stakes for Italy are immense: 'Italy's sovereign debt is €2.3 trillion. The exposure of French banks alone amounts to 11pc of France's GDP. The Bank of Italy "owes" a further €492 billion via the ECB's Target2 payment system which converts into Lira under *Lex Monetae* in a euro break-up' (ibid.). This is no idle threat, for Italy could in theory redenominate its debts in a new currency (as Greece could also have done in 2015). As a legal principle, *lex monetae*, vests a sovereign issuing a currency with full powers of control over the nominal value of that currency, which could force creditors to accept major losses. Unfortunately for Italy, however, this may be inadequate, for 'the prevailing contract currency [of Italy's debt] is issued by the European Central Bank, and would continue to exist even after the lira's return as legal tender' (Gelpern 2017: 1). Redenomination could only work if 'supported by legislation in Italy, throughout the euro area, and in major financial jurisdictions around the world, recognizing that euro-denominated contracts could now be paid in lira' (ibid.: 2).

Given the bitter dispute which erupted between the UK and EU over Brexit, however, it initially appeared that the likelihood of the EU agreeing to a compromise with Italy was close to zero. In December 2018, however, with investors fleeing Italian bond markets, Rome agreed to moderate its planned budget deficit for 2019 by a margin acceptable to the EU. Senior powerful figures in the Eurogroup had originally hoped to use the dispute to rein in Italy's public spending further but appeared to back down at the risk of inducing a more serious political crisis in Italy (Brundsen & Kahn 2018). For the EU, the prospect of a sovereign debt crisis in Italy stokes fears of a renewed crisis across the eurozone which would threaten EU banks and expose dangerous fragilities in the BRRD. As a BIS report from September 2018 notes, eurozone banks' equity values have

> vastly underperformed those of their peers from other advanced economies. An aggregate index tracking euro area banks' stock price performance dropped almost 20% from mid-May through mid-September [...]. In contrast, US banks traded sideways and other advanced economies' banks experienced much more moderate losses. The divergence between bank equity price performance in the euro area and the United States started in May, when political uncertainty in Italy increased. (BIS 2018c: 12)

The ill-concealed bitterness of the Italian sovereign debt dispute indicates the power of the Eurogroup which exists outside the formal legal structures of the EU but which occupies a central position in financial decision-making and crisis management (Varoufakis 2015). It also indicates the willingness of the EU to use punitive legal tactics to silence popular opposition to the treaties in member-states and consolidate the power of the supranational institutions over member-states.

Monetary internationalism

What therefore are the implications of bail-in for the theory of financial socialism, and how can we resolve the disconnect between monetary *nationalism* and monetary *internationalism* implicit in attempts by elites to impose binding rules on economies to regulate their monetary and fiscal policy, and, more specifically, the conduct of financial resolution within their jurisdictions? In this final section we sketch some of the issues in international monetary political economy as we approach 2020, by which date it is expected G20 economies will have adapted to demands for greater monetary internationalism and incorporated transnational rules on macroprudential regulation, capital adequacy and insolvency resolution into their own national law in the interests of stabilizing global capital. The aim is to assess the scope for change in the global monetary system beyond regulation, and to indicate a possible direction for global liquidity provision and reserve currency allocation against the background of an evolving geoeconomic order. The central issue is the capacity of the US dollar to provide a basis for global liquidity. Despite the dramatic economic rise of Asia, the dollar remains a hegemonic reserve currency, yet one which renders rival economies dependent on the willingness of the Federal Reserve to pursue a pro-cyclical growth regime (Vermeiren 2014: 13).

To understand the changing reality of international monetary relations of power, it is necessary to consider how the economic growth of China and the consolidation of the eurozone have allowed more economies to challenge the asymmetries of a US-centric international monetary system. Although the US dollar remains pre-eminent, the global economy is increasingly diffuse, leaderless and multipolar. At the centre of this problematic is a tension between the US as financial hegemon – providing the dollar as a 'global public good', which at the same time affords the Federal Reserve and the US Treasury enormous economic power:

> Especially in the monetary realm, the US still assumes a hegemonic role because of the persistent dominance of the dollar as in the world economy. The dollar remains the dominant exchange rate anchor and reserve currency in East Asia, which suggests that the accumulation of dollar reserves by East Asian states can at least as much be seen to reflect their subordination to persistent US monetary hegemony as the alleged dependency of the US upon East Asian capital. Such contrasting interpretations of US-East Asian monetary relations suggest that mercantilist realist accounts lack an accurate understanding of the nature of power in the global monetary system. (Vermeiren 2014: 8)

The price for accepting the US dollar in global trade and finance is the vulnerability of rival economies to the capriciousness of US monetary policy, the orientation of which oscillates between US-centric and global priorities. Given that no other economy can (yet) substitute itself or its currency for the preponderance of the US in international relations or predominance of the dollar in world trade, alternatives to the present unstable model of global liquidity provision suggest a future progression towards a more genuine form of monetary internationalism, placing in question the primary of the US dollar in global trade and finance and the (unintended) role of the US consumer economy as a 'global surplus-recycling system' (Varoufakis 2011).

One leading luminary of elite opinion argues that pressures towards deglobalization in the world-system have reached such fever pitch that it is legitimate to consider developing the IMF's existing mechanisms of liquidity provision as an alternative to the present model. 'Creating an international currency that would be managed by the IMF', he argues, it might be possible 'to underpin and enhance the international monetary system with a non-national official reserve asset' (El-Arian 2017: 1). El-Arian argues that hostility to globalization – 'caused in part by poor global policy coordination in the context of too many years of low and insufficiently inclusive growth' (ibid.), could be addressed by reconsidering the 'ecosystem of SDR use, with the composite currency – which last year [2016] added the Chinese renminbi to the British pound, euro, Japanese yen and US dollar – potentially benefiting from a virtuous cycle' (ibid.). The composite structure of the SDR is reviewed every five years to make sure that it reflects the 'relative importance of currencies in the world's trading and financial systems' (IMF 2018b: 1). Currency amounts are fixed for the duration of five-year SDR valuation periods, yet the respective weight of each currency fluctuates as exchange rates fluctuate. Most importantly, the 'value of the SDR is determined daily based on market exchange rates' (ibid.), allowing the composite currency to reflect real price movements in foreign exchange markets.

In addition to its three existing roles (reserve asset, unit of exchange and numeraire [reference point for global trade]), El-Arian argues that the SDR 'could ensure greater official liquidity, expand the range of new assets used around the world in public and private transactions, and boost its use as a unit of account' (2017: 1). He rules out a 'big-bang' global monetary event (comparable to the creation of the euro) in favour of its *gradual legitimation* through cooperation between the IMF, World Bank, G20 and other relevant non-governmental organizations, leading to the creation of 'public-private partnerships to enhance issuance, the development of market infrastructure, and liquidity provision'. In an ideal world, he suggests,

> the SDR would have evolved into more of a reserve currency during the era of accelerated trade and financial globalization. In the world as it is today, the international monetary system faces two options: fragmentation, with all the risks and opportunity costs that this implies, or an incremental approach to bolstering the global economy's resilience and potential growth, based on bottom-up partnerships that facilitate systemic progress. (ibid.: 2)

In other words, a market-oriented 'M-SDR' facility could evolve as more than simply an official unit of account between sovereign governments overseen by the IMF into a template for the future development of a global exchange-traded currency.

A bolder perspective is offered by Middelkoop (2016), a noted specialist on the gold standard and international currencies. In a celebrated study of the role of gold in monetary systems (2015), he suggested that as China assumes a more powerful role in global finance, the pressure to develop the SDR facility will grow, beginning with efforts to expand its convertibility and address the lack of liquidity that have limited its appeal vis-à-vis the US dollar. Traditionally, there have been inadequate SDRs in circulation for it to play a central role in monetary finance (Middelkoop 2016). To overcome the liquidity issue, and the reluctance of US elites to retire the dollar from its pre-eminent position in global trade and finance, a logical course of action would be to create a 'substitution fund' to enable countries like Japan and China with large US dollar positions to exchange all or part of their holdings into SDRs at a 1:1 ratio. An SDR substitution fund could

> kick-start the SDR as a truly world reserve currency (WRC). If only half of the almost 20 trillion outstanding U.S. treasuries would be exchanged through this Substitution Fund, almost 10 trillion of SDRs would be created instantly. The SDR would become one of the most liquid financial instruments almost immediately. A number of (academic) publications about this topic have been published recently. (ibid.: 4)

Following Wijnholds (2009), Middelkoop highlights two fundamental changes to transform the SDR into a de facto WRC: (a) inclusion of additional currencies from emerging economies in the composite basket; (b) an increase in its commodity content – in other words, acknowledging a future role for gold in the international monetary system (2016: 5). This reflects a deeper concern among elite economists, who believe that formally re-including gold in the international monetary system could '"provide a counterweight to the impact of the depreciation/appreciation of the US dollar", and could "reduce vulnerability to the USD exchange rate"' (Catherine Schenk, in ibid.: 6), and could also address a disproportionality created by the size of China's economy and the diminutive position of the renminbi as a globally traded currency.

This view is shared in principle by Rickards, who maintains that the creation of the SDR system in 1969 was a compromise solution to declining confidence in the US dollar: 'The goal was to create a reserve asset that was neither dollar, nor gold, but a hybrid. The SDR simultaneously alleviated the dollar glut and the gold shortage. The SDR was a paper claim on the IMF's combined resources linked to a fixed gold quantity' (Rickards 2016: 68). He also believes that a commodity-backed SDR can resolve Triffin's dilemma which forces the provider of a global reserve currency to run persistent and debilitating deficits 'to supply the world with sufficient reserves for normal trade' (ibid.: 69). The question is how the SDR facility can be extended and integrated into the international monetary system without disrupting the prevailing idea of national currencies (and the US dollar in particular) as the primary units of national account and means of payment. Unlike El-Arian, who adopts a cautious systemic approach based on the gradual promotion of the SDR model to advance the cause of global multilateral trade and finance in a new era of anti-globalization, Rickards calls openly for the remonetization of gold, which Middelkoop (2015) also champions vociferously in his work on monetary reset.

For Rickards, the point is not to rehabilitate the gold standard to facilitate or extend trade liberalization, but to create a denationalized global unit of account/ exchange by sleight of hand when the next economic downturn occurs, leading to instability in emerging markets, declining equity prices, rising energy costs and overzealous inflation targeting. A future crisis would present global economic elites with an opportunity to intensify capital controls ('international financial martial law') to *freeze* the global financial system in order to sidestep a repeat of the liquidity crisis which threatened global capitalism in 2008. At the same time, increasing the commodity component of the SDR would address the imbalance in the global financial system caused by China's financial limitations, that is, its lack of a 'deep liquid bond market, with hedging instruments, repo financing, settlement and clearing facilities, and a good rule of law' (ibid.: 70). It would enable China to compensate for its diminutive global reserve currency status (the renminbi constitutes only 1 per cent of allocated global foreign exchange reserves) and join the elite club of gold-hoarding nations who use control over bullion as a tool for financial leverage in global trade and a guarantee of economic security.

Although gold is officially disparaged by international financial institutions like the IMF, most national governments – with the exception of the UK – continue to hoard it. In a bid to catch up with traditionally gold-rich economies like the US, Germany, France and Italy, the largest acquisitions of gold since 2008 have been made by Russia and China, both of whom view the metal as a guarantee that their economies will survive a monetary reset caused by de-dollarization or a transition to the SDR system. The capacity of the SDR model to displace the dollar as an international currency unit depends not only on its use by governments but by financial institutions and private investors. Gradually, predicts Rickards, a

> private market for SDRs will develop. Large corporations like GE, IBM, and Volkswagen will issues SDR-denominated bonds. Large banks like Goldman Sachs will make markets in this SDR bonds and write derivatives contracts in SDRs for hedging. [...] Imperceptibly, the dollar will become just another local currency. Important transactions will be counted in SDRs. (ibid.: 71)

This implies that the world's major central banks – which together hold roughly $12 trillion in foreign exchange reserves (Richter 2018), will in the near future be willing to 'de-dollarize' and embrace monetary internationalism. It also implies that wealth held in US dollars and other fiat currencies will be vulnerable to major devaluation, pauperizing millions of ordinary depositors (particular in the US) who are unaware of the risks entailed in entrusting wealth in the form of cash deposits in the banking system. For ordinary depositors, it is difficult to conceptualize the idea that gold is the *only* financial asset with no counterparty liability; or that, despite the existence of insider manipulation of gold markets through price-fixing in the Comex market, physical bullion is less vulnerable to inflation and financial repression than fiat money. As we saw in Chapter 4, the scale of 'commodity money' in derivatives markets dwarfs the combined value of debt, equities, commodities and currencies in the global economy and makes it possible for powerful financial institutions to profit from high-volume trading in these assets through financial instruments which extract notional value from the future.

But is this monetary internationalism in its *true* sense, or merely the globalization of central bank power through the institutionalization of global financial governance – in other words, 'global financial socialism'? Hayek (1971) famously argued that 'full blown' monetary internationalism would require a 'globally homogeneous monetary system': an end to the plethora of state currencies, controlled by national central banks and confined within territorial jurisdictions (White 1996: 2). In an authentic global monetary system, he believed, 'ordinary money (including deposits as well as currency) crosses national borders freely to settle international payments; money can flow among regions without hindrance, regardless of whether the regions are part of the same nation-state' (ibid.). From an Austrian perspective, considerations of market efficiency imply that international flows of money should be determined solely or primarily by private financial and commercial transactions rather than *state* policies. Yet Hayek in fact recognized the need for an international central bank:

> So long as an effective international monetary authority remains a utopian dream, any mechanical principle (such as the gold standard) which at least secures some conformity of monetary changes in the national area to what would happen under a truly international monetary system is far preferable to numerous independent and independently regulated national currencies. If it does not provide a really rational regulation of the quantity of money, it at any rate tends to make it behave on roughly foreseeable lines, which is of the greatest importance. (ibid.: 3)

This reflects a pragmatic dimension of transnational neoliberalism, namely the requirement – in a globally integrated economy – for a common monetary standard and global authority to accelerate the integration of financial markets and regulate imbalances between economies. It is this logic which reinforces the belief among both elite insiders and critical political economists that global capitalism is unviable in the absence of effective transnational co-governance of the international monetary system.

In reality, of course, co-governance mechanisms already exist for managing international monetary relations reflecting the institutional rationality of the global financial system. At the BIS offices in Basel, the Global Economy Meeting led by the Chairman of the FSB (presently Mark Carney) meets regularly to advise policymakers on the Committee on Global Financial System and other advisory bodies which formulate policy recommendations for central bankers. In addition, as Lebor (2013) notes, the 18 members of the elite Economic and Consultative Committee meet bimonthly to analyse and prepare proposals for

Global Economy Meetings. Using the least accessible language possible, economists at BIS concede that central bank activism (accommodative monetary policies analysed in Chapter 5) may ultimately be economically counterproductive:

> A central tenet of monetary economics is that money is, in the jargon [of BIS analysis], neutral and even super-neutral – which is to say that increasing the amount of money in the economy does not create more output and employment in the long run, and that increasing the growth rate of money simply translates into a higher steady-state rate of inflation. (BIS 2016: 6)

Yet, the authors concede, central bank activism is 'the only game in town' (ibid.) and has become indispensable for capitalist central planning in advanced economies whose central bankers meet in Basel to plan future strategies. Their official and unofficial meetings are conducted *in camera,* and – as within the 'deep establishment' of the European Union (Varoufakis 2015) – networks of power connecting managers at the FSB, BIS and IMF are opaque to outsiders.

Although the SDR system still remains a shadow currency – yet to be fully developed or implemented – it is clear that any political decision to extend its profile/use in the international monetary system will inevitably be taken by a very narrow circle of high-ranking financial technocrats who already constitute a de facto 'global monetary policy committee' functioning quietly in Washington, London, Frankfurt and Basel beyond the scrutiny of democratically elected parliaments. If implemented, the SDR model would lead to a global monetary system far more complex and ambitious than the gold standard of the nineteenth century, the collapse of which contributed to the economic slump of the interwar period and the rise of fascism. When Hayek was writing in the late 1930s, economic elites were still grappling with the legacy of the gold standard, which had regulated currency exchange while confirming Britain's hegemony in the international imperial order. The end of this imperial order resulted in trade protectionism and nationalism, which liberal economists blame for the Depression. It also ushered in a period of hegemonic transition in international relations as the US assumed the mantle of world leadership bequeathed by Britain after 1945. In the present epoch of US retrenchment, a new experiment in monetary internationalism would require not only a major constitutive event such as financial collapse, but a *positive* consensus among global monetary and political elites in favour of monetary reset, confirming a transition in the international balance of power. Although the US is belatedly attempting to slow China's emergence as a rival global power, a shift towards monetary internationalism would confirm a significant movement in the centre of global economic gravity from the Euro-Atlantic sphere to Eurasia, hastening the erosion of US financial preponderance and its supersession by a supra-sovereign global monetary system beyond the direct control of a single hegemon.

Notes

1 According to BIS, not only does the US remain the primary currency of reserve in global banking, but in the course of 2018 became 'even more dominant as the prime foreign currency for international borrowing. Dollar credit to the non-bank sector outside the US rose from 9.5% of global GDP at end-2007 to 14% in Q1 2018' (BIS 2018c: 18).

2 For a complete breakdown of all categories of bank capital, see Gleeson (2012: 81).

3 The opposite is in fact the case. As we saw in Chapter 5, a growing practice of business in the present period is corporate share buybacks where cash-rich firms purchase back their own stock rather than issue new stock to raise money for investment.

7
CONCLUSION

Any discussion of monetary political economy in the present crisis inevitably raises more questions than can be resolved within the framework of a single monograph. The range of variables is simply too vast to predict with any certainty the impact of central bank policies for the advanced economies over the next decade. As we approach 2020, however, three preliminary conclusions can be made from our analysis with some degree of conviction. First, political and monetary elites have learned important lessons from the 2008 financial crisis, most importantly that systemic risk in the banking system exceeds the capacity of regulators to manage turbulence. Hence the frantic efforts of transnational regulatory authorities to strengthen macroprudential regulation, loss absorbance capacity and insolvency resolution procedures to compensate for the continued growth of G-SIFIs which *despite everything* remain 'too-big-to-fail'. But while Keynesian faith in the capacity of international financial institutions to rein in the compulsive logic of self-expansion without purpose that characterizes capital remains unbounded, as one perceptive critic observed as early as December 2008, the notion that regulation can resolve the inner contradictions of capital is misguided:

> The fantasy of avoiding a repetition of the financial crunch with new legal measures has regained force. But these commotions are inherent to capitalism and there is no way to stop their re-emergence. The system itself periodically generates pressures to increase the value of capital and it creates antibodies to sterilize [macroprudential] regulations in force. This phenomena [sic], for instance, can be verified with the debut of neoliberalism itself and will return anew when capitalism needs to restore the rate of profit. (Katz 2008: 1)

Second, there are indications that the malinvestment of trillions of dollars in global equity, bond and futures markets has created unsustainable speculative bubbles of fictitious capital which are once again running dangerously ahead of growth in the nonfinancial sector, and which are exceptionally vulnerable to any shift away from accommodative monetary policy in advanced economies – particularly the US and the UK. Central banks bear direct responsibility for this decade-long strategy, and have stood back from 'normalizing' monetary policy (allowing interest rates to rise) in order to defend bond markets, shore up leveraged debt, and forestall another collapse in investor confidence. At the first sign of geoeconomic turbulence, central banks have 'blinked', most recently in late 2018 as monetary elites abandoned monetary tightening amid anxieties over a renewed global slowdown (Fleming & Smith 2019; cf. Wigglesworth 2019). Third, and finally, it is clear that, whatever other reforms may have been introduced to improve regulation, an 'international monetary system underpinned by private liquidity provision in US dollars no longer seems as inevitable as it did only ten years ago' (Wilkie 2012: 225). As we saw in Chapter 6, the 2008 crisis revealed the limits of the power of the Federal Reserve to provide global liquidity, leading to the supersession of the G7 by the G20 while affording China an historic opportunity to take its place at the highest table of global governance as the renminbi joined the IMF's prestigious SDR basket of currencies. Any future transition to a supra-sovereign multireserve currency system – even within the framework of a Western-dominated IMF – would signal the de facto approaching decline of US dollar hegemony and with it the capacity of the US to dominate international political economy.

In 2018, instability returned to the international financial system as global equity markets shed more than $13 trillion of market capitalization, which Martenson (2018b) estimates as a 15 per cent year-on-year decline. Whether a precipitous crash or controlled decline will occur before 2020 is unclear, but evidence suggests that the coordinated 'recovery' in advanced economies propagated by corporate media is an illusion facilitated by central bank activism: capitalist central planning has delayed monetary collapse by defending 'too-big-to-fail' financial institutions and inflating new price bubbles to forestall a catastrophic deleveraging of asset values in financial markets, rather than limit the misallocation of resources by a corporate elite whose oligopolistic power results in the 'creative obstruction' of progressive socioeconomic change (Wasserberg 2013). As suggested in Chapter 1, this can be interpreted as a 'katechontic deferral', the function of which is to delay an alteration in capitalist relations of power through continued multiplication of debt as a precondition for an uninterrupted self-expansion of capital value. The aim of this can only be understood as an attempt to prevent a catastrophic deleveraging of capital value sufficient to bankrupt G7 economies, undermining the established financial and geopolitical influence of the West while limiting the power of the investor class to appropriate the surplus product of the global economy.

The theoretical framework employed in the present study derives from a materialist critique of capitalism based on Marx's analysis of the value form in commodity-determined society. The Marxian 'law' of the falling rate of profit remains a controversial theory of capitalist decline which did not appear in a unified systematic form in Marx's works (as Heinrich [2013] notes, it was Engels who pieced together the disparate parts of Marx's analysis in the third volume of *Capital*). Yet Marx's emphasis on the rising organic composition of capital provides a powerful insight into the inner contradictions of the form of value in commodity-determined society. It satisfies the requirements of logical empiricism to the extent that capital, in its drive for self-expansion, strives compulsively to achieve higher levels of productivity by reducing its dependence on labour power as a principal source of surplus value. Marx realized that it is precisely because variable capital (labour power) is the *only* factor in the production process which assumes the 'form of value whilst it is not produced within the capitalist sphere of production that it potentially creates value-added' (Reuten & Williams 1987: 69). Conversely, the value of constant capital (technical means of production) derives not 'from the ideal value of the output of the production process in which they actually figure as means of production, but from the process of production in which *they* were actually produced' (ibid.). Despite the rising proportion of value generated outside the sphere of production, the ratio of productive to unproductive labour in advanced economies has continued to widen until labour power as a commodity is now reduced to a fraction of its historic scale. To combat the declining rate of profit, production has been systematically moved offshore to special production zones in low-wage Asian economies, allowing global corporations to escape temporarily the internal and external barriers to (profitable) accumulation in the US, the EU and Japan.

Yet the declining profitability and deindustrialization of advanced capitalist economies has indeed been partially compensated for by the growing importance of financial services, equities and commodity markets in Europe, North America and Northeast Asia, disguising the decadence of metropolitan capital which is dependent on price speculation, asset bubbles and rising debt. As a specific feature of accumulation in advanced monetary economies, financialization derives value from alternative sources: it creates fictitious capital through a multiplication of complex financial instruments to leverage capital value by multiplying claims to particular assets (CDOs, futures), the growth of which provides seemingly infinite scope for an expansion of interest-bearing capital in the markets. This global commodity money provides a means of *commensuration* – enabling financial corporations to synthesize global trade between multiple complex asset classes. As a disembodied bearer of value supported by state-issued fiat currency, commodity money constitutes a specific articulation of monetary abstraction in advanced capitalism which assumes additional relevance in financialized economies that depend disproportionally on an appropriation of *future* value to sustain *present* accumulation. Yet the escalating instability and near-collapse of financial market money during the 2008 crisis demonstrates the perilous nature of financialization as a basis for profitable accumulation through the derivation of abstract wealth from leveraged assets: fictitious capital – as 'form without content' – expands seemingly inexplicably, enabling money to augment itself rather than realize value through exchange in the (temporary) form of an commodity. Through financialization, self-augmenting money (M–M') substitutes itself for the traditional sequence *money* → *commodity* → *augmented money* (M–C–M'). In contrast to simple commodity exchange, where money functions as a universal equivalent mediating between market actors, derivative assets that generate fictitious capital deconstruct money into its constituent attributes, giving value a specific materiality – 'not in terms of what it symbolically represents, but in terms of what it, itself, is and does' (Bryan & Rafferty 2010: 107).

The crisis of the capitalist monetary economies derives not from financialization *as such*, therefore, nor from disproportional growth of overextended financial service relative to the 'real' economy of goods and services, but from falling profit rates across the advanced economies due to a displacement of living labour power from commodity production, which has in turn severed the link between productivity growth and real wage growth. The cause of the present crisis, exacerbated by the general insolvency of the global banking system, is not 'neoliberalism' as a global accumulation regime. It is, rather, the periodic hyperproductivity of capitalist economies in which the valorization of capital depends on a paradoxical displacement of human labour power as the real substance of commodity value. Intensifying competition accelerates advances in productivity by forcing firms to continually invest in new techniques of production in a race to remain profitable, which in turn leads to overproduction and falling prices as an abundance of capital is invested which cannot be adequately valorized. As noted in Chapter 3, this is presently leading corporate firms in major developed economies to jettison human labour power at alarming rates, in preference for investment in new forms of AI and automation, leading international organizations to warn governments that impatience to integrate new production technologies is causing 'creative destruction' in the labour market as the number of workers required to perform skilled labour functions dwindles (Cocco 2019).

But is this argument correct? Is postliberal capitalism degenerating into a decadent mode of production, confronting internal barriers to the self-expansion of capital and external barriers to the useful employment of human labour? The answer to both questions is affirmative: as has been shown throughout the present study, the actions of global monetary and political elites since 2009 have concentrated overwhelmingly on two coordinated strategic policies, namely *accommodation* and *risk mitigation*. Accommodation has resulted in a fatal decision to disguise the unprofitability and moribund nature of advanced economies through central bank activism, leading to a massive expansion in the monetary base and the socialization of private losses to taxpayers. This strategy has thus far prevented a Japanese-style deflationary recession, and has maintained G7 economies in 'limp mode', intensifying moral hazard with government support for G-SIFIs in the process. And this in turn has undermined the public finances of major economies, leading to rising sovereign debt among OECD nations. Risk mitigation, on the other hand, has resulted in the implementation of new macroprudential rules designed to limit the destabilizing contagion effect of bank failure for the global financial system, ring-fencing a network of 'too-big-to-fail' international financial institutions whose survival is deemed critical to the survival of the transnational investor class itself. To complement this, new rules have been enacted in major economies of the EU and North America to bail-in depositors' and investors' assets in a bid to limit the requirement for public insolvency support by placing the burden instead on ordinary citizens to ensure the interests of major bank creditors are not harmed in future banking crises. As illustrated in Chapter 6, these rules – which may not be adequate to rule out a return to 'too-big-to-fail' – have been implemented by stealth and without democratic oversight, suggesting significant levels of anxiety among monetary and political elites towards the legitimacy deficit of global governance and populist dissatisfaction with corporate globalization.

Against Marxian theory, it might of course be argued that a return to profitable accumulation is viable using a minority of the current labour force to operate and service the constant capital invested to produce commodities or services in an economy led by the exaggerated derivative values of investment in finance and real estate. Globalization has allowed a large number of routine labour functions to be 'offshored', and new forms of 'immaterial labour' to emerge which enable capital to generate value through 'intangible' assets. Automation and AI could obviate the need for skilled workers and render socially necessary labour less critical: if robots can make cars and washing machines, and AI can be used to provide legal advice, interview candidates and assess the creditworthiness of mortgage applicants at a fraction of the cost of medium-skilled white-collar workers, then the generation of relative surplus value through socially necessary labour may be less necessary to sustain growth over time, while the creation of new jobs in the 'knowledge' economy may be adequate to contain disorder in advanced economies as traditional mechanisms of social integration and solidarity disintegrate. It may therefore be more humane and pragmatic to introduce a universal basic income (or universal credit) for economically redundant workers to consume a modest range of essential commodities and quietly reproduce the material conditions of their own existence than to fund expensive education systems which create a surplus of overeducated generalists with inflated or unrealistic career expectations. Although high levels of personal debt and bankruptcy represent increasingly serious concerns (Barrett 2019), credit expansion could in theory supplement declining real incomes as redundant skilled workers are directed towards residual deskilled employment opportunities.

While this counterargument sounds plausible, however, it is flawed in two main respects. On the one hand, although commodity production in capitalist society is not predetermined by the 'content of labour and the products that derive from it' (Amorim 2014: 95), capital can only achieve self-expansion over time by satisfying 'human wants for mass produced use values, the efficient standardized production of which is made possible by available industrial technologies' (Westra 2010: 94).

It is through the creation of commodities with *socially universal use-value* and *profitable exchange value* in the market that capital has expanded most successfully in the last century. Benefiting from abundant cheap carbon-based energy, capitalism flourished in the long reconstruction boom which followed the Second World War centred on the production of automobiles – a high-value commodity which embodied the aspirational individualism of Fordism, as well as other consumer durables which create a powerful yet inflated prosperity effect among nationally integrated aristocracies of labour. The fact that automobile industries can no longer function (without government support) as a basis for the self-expansion of capital is clearly apparent, however. This is not simply because of rising energy costs or new environmental concerns, but because – as a consequence of financialization – the *real* source of current profitability in the production and sale of private vehicles derives from automobile finance as workers with declining real incomes take out expensive loans to pay for vehicles they will never own – exacerbating an already serious personal debt crisis.

Yet declining purchasing power/demand is in and of itself an inadequate explanation, since the rationalization of the automobile industry and the rising organic composition of capital in 'state-of-the-art' robotically enhanced factories have reduced competition to a struggle for market share between a handful of global vehicle manufacturers headquartered in the G7 economies. These giant corporations are supported by government subsidies, trivial aesthetic product enhancements (commodity fetishism) and exaggerated claims to fuel efficiency. The real point is, however, that in view of the structural constraints on long-term profitability in the global car industry, few equivalent commodities exist with a similar capacity to satisfy requirements for social universality and long-term, built-in obsolescence provided by the marketing and consumption of desirable vehicles. In affluent areas of Western cities, property speculation still stimulates demand for home improvement among propertied classes, while glamorous marketing of ultra-sleek digital communication devices continues to support the market capitalization of technology firms. Yet property speculation is dependent on stable employment and rising incomes among intermediate strata, and even the latest generation of iPhones will succumb to the same logic of overinvestment, overproduction and declining profitability which characterizes the product life cycle of *all* commodities as general rates of productivity rise, relative surplus value declines and profit rates fall – irrespective of their historical genesis, functional utility or creative potential. In addition, as suggested in Chapter 3, the much-vaunted transition to cognitive capitalism founded on immaterial labour is highly problematic: its significance is based on the faulty assumption that changes in the materiality of production instantiated by the end of Fordism somehow reduce the objective requirement for average socially necessary labour time to valorize capital invested in 'intangible' commodities. It is equally implausible to believe that such changes will bring in their wake progressive changes in social and political organization in knowledge-based economies, enabling workers to gain more control over the labour process.

Here we can identify the exhaustion of capitalist value as a 'necessary dimension of labour and of the useful objects produced by it in the bourgeois mode of production. It is a *social* dimension and a social universal' (Reuten & Williams 1987: 60). Ultimately, the particular 'products of labour necessarily have to take on a social-universal form which is the value form, for without them being validated as such they are socially non-existent' (ibid.: 60–61). It is not financialization which *explains* the present crisis, but a crisis of valorization in the sequence of money, production and profit that underpins commodity production. Herein lies an explanation for the failure of central banks to engineer recovery through debt-purchases, government bailouts and accommodative monetary policy. This highlights the futility of reformist arguments in favour of reconstituting the Keynesian national welfare-state as a political framework for 'democratic' capitalism. Wishful thinking or nostalgia for the post-war Fordist compromise reappears with predictable regularity in leftist critiques of neoliberal globalization as if the expansion and development of capitalism beyond core industrialized economies had not taken place, and as if the specific material-economic conditions necessary for the 'long boom' in the post-1945 period could simply be replicated without reversing the deindustrialization of core economies like the UK and the US.

A return to inefficient import substitution might be possible under the banner of economic nationalism, in defiance of comparative advantage theory; and proletarianized consumers might (with suitable levels of coercion) be persuaded to adjust their economic expectations and purchase domestically produced commodities with lower marginal utility, ushering in a new era of deglobalization and ascetic localism. Yet this would in practice hasten the collapse of capitalist commodity society, for the logic of production without reason in capitalism has little to do with political rationality or functional utility since capital is a mode of value-augmentation in which useful and useless items are produced *in excess* until such point that objective-societal advances in productivity entail that their production and sale can no longer realize a profit within specific spatial contexts. As Schmidt notes, to understand the mode of functioning of capital we must acknowledge the 'primacy of the logical over the historical' in Marxian theory: 'Marx's major work', he notes, 'does not (as one might first expect) begin with the developmental history of capitalist relationships but rather with the immediately given, everyday fact that the wealth of capitalist societies appears as an "immense collection of commodities"' (Schmidt 1981: 33). Marx derived his empirical insight by positing capital in an abstract-theoretical rather than concrete-historical form: by 'adhering strictly to the logic of capital [...] Marx comes closer to the historical content of empirical history than he would have had he been content with chronologically following developments immediately at hand' (ibid.: 34). To survey capitalist commodity society in the first instance abstractly as a fully formed 'immense collection of commodities' enables us to subsequently form a deeper understanding of the concrete-historical, economic and political-legal forms of capitalist societies as they derive from the commodity as it assumes particular social-universal forms.

On the other hand, it is clear that hyperconsumerism and the proletarianization of the subject which logically attend capitalism in its decadent phase cannot be reversed or dismantled by means of traditional forms of political action. Capital determines the material-social conditions for its own self-augmentation; and capital generates legal and political norms which enable elite accumulation to function legitimately in the absence of effective criticism. As we have seen in the course of the present study, the accumulation of capital without value in the global financial system is paralleled by a cultivation of belief in consumerism to sustain an illusion of progress and rising prosperity among subjects with disposable income or access to credit. For Stiegler, belief in this mode of production and consumption – which is contingent on continual access to new commodities and belief in the myths of 'industrial populism' which support modern monetary economies – is threatened by the growth of a new 'spiritual misery' linked to the 'destruction of the *kingdom of ends* in which, as Kant taught, reason consists' (Stiegler 2006: 4). Which is to say, not only is the capacity for substantive reason diminished by the uncontrolled manipulation and exploitation of consumer desire, but popular performance of the narratives of financialized capital are undermined as growing numbers of subjects of capital, overburdened by personal debt and excluded from the material advantages of commodity capitalism, confront the abject nature of their social condition and question the common-sense 'financial literacy' which permeates the cultural imaginary of modern monetary economies.

As surplus value is drained from the productive base of advanced capitalism, financial socialism is leading to an alteration in the legal structure of property rights in capitalist monetary economies, which will not only erode the wealth of intermediate strata, but limit the capacity of subjects without significant monetary assets to engage in meaningful action outside the framework of managed consumerism. Although opportunities for emancipatory action outside the realm of constituted power may develop, as Agamben (2014) argued, the conditions of possibility for a transformation of asymmetric power relations in postliberal capitalism can only be realized through the *cultivation of radical indifference to power itself*. This implies not simply a renunciation of materialism and power as ends in themselves, but presupposes, rather – through the negating force of inoperativity – the accelerated depletion of relative surplus value as the basis for the material reproduction of commodity-determined society. The question is whether such a process takes place voluntarily or involuntarily. That is to say, whether the *objective* tendency towards accumulation without value analysed in the present study – which is mitigated to a great extent by the economic and monetary policies of financial socialism – proceeds towards its own logical-historical end, or whether this process is exacerbated by 'destituent power', rendering law *inoperable* by negating the 'anarchy of power' that attempts to govern disorder in postliberal capitalism.

Parallel with the objective failure of capitalist production and implosion of financialization is a growing subjective loss of belief in capitalist *Geist* among disaffected proletarianized consumers divested of the necessary life skills to benefit materially from capital. Capitalism, according to Stiegler, is threatened not so much by labour protest but by *itself*:

> The destruction of spirit leads to the loss of all hope, but also to the loss of the very possibility of constituting horizons of expectation of a *we*. This is the result when capitalism – in order to penetrate every market and to exploit every possibility revealed by industrial innovation, at the same time continuously disrupting social structures, that is, those systems of collective individuation through which psychic individuals find their place – succeeds in destroying every barrier to the circulation of commodities. The circulation of commodities, then, comes to replace the circulation of the works of the spirit, and as such leads to the outright *liquidation of the superego* as a system of prohibitions, and to the liquidation of *sublimation as that socialization through which desire always constitutes itself* [...]. (ibid.: 5)

To sustain corporate profitability through hyperconsumerism capital depends on the negation of every last barrier to the circulation and exchange of commodities: maximal exploitation of 'available brain-time', facilitated by new forms of commodification and marketing which continually assess real-time data on human affects and consumer preferences – extending regimes of surveillance, disempowerment and deautonomization into the lifeworld of the subject. The consequences of this trend are explosive, creating 'dissociated milieus' in poor peripheral communities characterized by extreme forms of indifference and hostility. For Stiegler (2014: 42), this is creating its own destructive form of destituent power, leading a 'becoming-barbaric' of society confronted by loss of meaning and the ruination of affective capacities which neutralize the traditional fear of the established legal structures and social conventions which previously regulated industrial class societies.

It is this phenomenon which underlies, perhaps, the intense explosion of anger that overtook France in 2018–2019 in reaction to social inequality, leading President Emmanuel Macron to call in the armed forces to suppress protesters (*les gilets jaunes*) from the peripheral conurbations which encircle the bourgeois urban heartlands of the French Republic. And it is a similar phenomenon that caused the infamous looting in London in August 2011, in a frightening display of 'defective consumerism' where the ordinarily lethal rivalries that simmer between inner-city youth were temporarily suspended in an ironic articulation of collective solidarity against security forces. Following Bauman (2009), sociologists investigating these events highlight not just the antipathy and resentment that fuelled the rioting in response to the systemic and symbolic violence operating via the normal structures of exclusion in capitalist society, but the cynical nonchalance of participants bemused by the opportunities afforded by a sudden breakdown of order and the chance to acquire commodities without performing socially necessary labour. Like Stiegler, Bauman (2009) identifies a clear link between hyperconsumerism and 'adiaphorization' – the moral indifference of subjects conditioned to measure their social agency only by pragmatic or technical criteria, extinguishing alternative criteria of ethical responsibility and concern (Palmer 2013: 7). For Bauman, 'the "collateral victim of the leap to the consumerist rendition of freedom is the Other as object of ethical responsibility and moral concern"' (Bauman, cited in Palmer 2013: 6). For Stiegler (2006), on the other hand, this indicates an unspoken crisis of *cognitive and affective saturation* in hyperconsumerist societies – revealing the necessary social pathologies of capital which enable a continual valorization of new commodities regardless of economic dislocation and social exclusion as capital approaches irresolvable internal and external barriers to its own profitable self-expansion.

BIBLIOGRAPHY

Accenture (2016) *Liquidity Coverage Ratio: Implications and a Pragmatic Approach to Implementation*, www.accenture.com/t20150626t121140__w__/us-en/_acnmedia/accenture/conversion-assets/dotcom/documents/global/pdf/dualpub_9/accenture-liquidity-coverage-ratio.pdf.

Adalsteinsson, G. (2014) *The Liquidity Risk Management Guide: From Policy to Pitfalls*, Chichester: Wiley.

Admati, A. & Hellwig, M. (2013) *The Bankers' New Clothes*, Princeton: Princeton University Press.

Agamben, G. (1995) *Homo Sacer: Sovereign Power and Bare Life*. English trans., Stanford: Stanford University Press.

Agamben, G. (2007) *Profanations*, New York: Zone Books.

Agamben, G. (2011) *The Kingdom and the Glory: For a Theological Genealogy of Economy and Government*. English trans., Stanford, CA: Stanford University Press.

Agamben, G. (2014) 'For a theory of destituent power', Transcript of Athens lecture, 16 November 2013, http://criticallegalthinking.com/05-02-2014.

Ahumada, P. (2012) 'The mercantile form of value and its place in Marx's theory of the commodity', *Cambridge Journal of Economics*, 36, 4: 843–867.

Ailon, G. (2013) 'Financial risk-taking as a sociological gamble: Notes on the development of a new perspective', *Sociology*, 48, 3: 606–621.

Allen, R. E. (2016) *Financial Crises and Recession in the Global Economy*. Fourth edition, Cheltenham: Edward Elgar.

Althusser, L. (1969) 'Ideology and ideological state apparatuses', in L. Althusser (ed.) *Lenin and Philosophy and Other Essays*. English trans., New York: Monthly Review Press.

Althusser, L. (2005 [1969]) *For Marx*. English trans., London: Verso.

Althusser, L. et al. (2015 [1965]) *Reading Capital: The Complete Edition*. English trans., London: Verso.

Altvater, E. (1975) 'Wertgesetz und Monopolmacht', in *Staat und Monopole (I). Zur Theorie des Monopols*, Berlin: Argument.

Amato, M. & Fantacci, L. (2012) *The End of Finance*. English trans., Cambridge: Polity.

Amato, M. & Fantacci, L. (2014) *Saving the Market from Capitalism: Ideas for an Alternative Finance*, Cambridge: Polity.

Amorim, H. (2014) 'Theories of immaterial labour: A critical reflection based on Marx', *Work Organisation, Labour and Globalization*, 8, 1: 88–103.

Appelbaum, R. (1978) 'Marx's theory of the falling rate of profit: Towards a dialectical analysis of structural social change', *American Sociological Review*, 43, 1: 67–80.

Arendt, H. (1958) *The Human Condition*, Chicago: University of Chicago Press.

Arestis, P. (2011) 'Recent banking and financial crises: Minsky and the financial liberalizationists', in R. Belliofiore & P. Ferri (eds.) *Financial Keynesianism and Market Instability. The Economic Legacy of Hyman Minsky Vol. I*, Cheltenham: Edward Elgar.

Arestis, P. & Karakitsos, E. (2013) *Financial Stability and the Aftermath of the 'Great Recession'*, Basingstoke: Palgrave Macmillan.

Arias, M. A. & Wen, Y. (2014) 'The liquidity trap: An alternative explanation for today's low inflation', www.stlouisfed.org/publications/regional-economist/april-2014.

Artemou, P. (2016) 'Rights of European Union depositors under Article 17 of the Charter of Fundamental Rights after the Cyprus bailout', *Pace International Law Review*, 28, 1/5: 205–232.

Arthur, C. (2002) *The New Dialectic and Marx's Capital*, Leiden: Brill.

Augar, P. (2018) *The Bank that Lived a Little: Barclays in the Age of the Very Free Market*, London: Allen Lane.

Avgouleas, E. & Goodhart, C. (2015) 'Critical reflections on bank bail-ins', *Journal of Financial Regulation*, 1, 1: 3–29.

Ayres, R. U. (2014) *The Bubble Economy: Is Sustainable Growth Possible?* Cambridge, MA: MIT Press.

Baker, A., Epstein, G. & Montecino, J. (2018) *The UK's Finance Curse: Costs and Processes*, University of Sheffield Political Economy Research Institute, http://speri.dept.shef.ac.uk.

Bakir, E. & Campbell, A. (2010) 'Neoliberalism, the rate of profit and the rate of accumulation', *Science and Society*, 74, 3: 323–342.

Barlett, D. L. & Steele, J. D. (2007) 'Washington's $8 billion shadow', www.vanityfair.com/news/2007/03.

Barrett, C. (2019) 'Inside the UK's debt crisis', www.ft.com/content/26-04-2019.

Bataille, G. (1979) 'The psychological structure of fascism', *New German Critique*, 16: 64–88.

Bateman, B. W. (2010) 'Keynes returns to America', in B. W. Bateman, T. Hirai & M. C. Marcuzzo (eds.) *The Return of Keynes*, Cambridge, MA: Belknap Press.

Bauman, Z. (2009) *Does Ethics Have a Chance in a World of Consumers?* Cambridge, MA: Harvard University Press.

Baumol, W. J. & Benhabib, J. (1989) 'Chaos: Significance, mechanism and economic applications', *Journal of Economic Perspectives*, 3, 1: 77–105.

BBVA [Banco Bilbao Vizcaya Argentaria] (2016) *New Requirements for Loss-Absorbing Capacity: TLAC and MREL*, www.bbvaresearch.com/wp-content/uploads/2016/03.

Beggs, M. (2017) 'The state as a creature of money', *New Political Economy*, 22, 5: 463–477.

Bell, P. & Cleaver, H. (2002) 'Marx's theory of crisis as a theory of class struggle', *The Commoner*, 5: 1–61.

Bello, W. (2013) *Capitalism's Last Stand? Deglobalization and the Age of Austerity*, London: Zed Books.

Bellofiore, R. (2014) 'The great recession and the contradictions of contemporary capitalism', in R. Bellofiore & G. Vertova (eds.) *The Great Recession and the Contradictions of Contemporary Capitalism*, Cheltenham: Edward Elgar.

Benjamin, W. (2004 [1921]) 'Capitalism as religion', in M. Bullock & M. Jennings (eds.), *Walter Benjamin Selected Writings, Vol. 1: 1913–1926*, Cambridge: Harvard University Press.

Berghoff, H., Scranton, P. & Spiekermann, U. (2012) (eds.) *The Rise of Marketing and Market Research*, Basingstoke: Palgrave Macmillan.

Berlinksi, C. (2018) 'In Helsinki, Trump and Putin are pulling Europe apart', www.haaretz.com/us-news/16-07-2018.

Bernal, J. D. (2010 [1939]) *The Social Function of Science*, London: Faber & Faber.

Bernanke, B. S. (2010) 'Implications of the financial crisis for economics', Speech to the Center for Economic Policy Studies and Bendheim Center for Finance, Princeton, 24 October 2010, www.bis.org/review/r100929a.pdf.

Bernanke, B. S., Gertler, M. & Gilchrist, S. (1996) 'The financial accelerator and the flight to quality', *Review of Economics and Statistics*, 78: 1–15.

Bernanke, B. S., Gertler, M. & Gilchrist, S. (1999) 'The financial accelerator in a quantitative business cycle framework', in J. B. Taylor & M. Woodford (eds.) *Handbook of Macroeconomics vol. 1c*, pp. 1341–1393. Amsterdam: Elsevier.

Berschens, R. & Hildbrand, J. (2018) 'Austria's compromise on European deposit insurance irritates Berlin', https://global.handelsblatt.com/finance/13-09-2018.

Bhaskar, R. A. (1975) A Realist Theory of Science, London: Verso.

Bhaskar, R. (2015) *The Possibility of Naturalism: A Philosophical Critique of the Contemporary Human Sciences*. Fourth edition, London: Routledge.

Bibow, J. (2009) *Keynes on Monetary Policy, Finance and Uncertainty: Liquidity Preference Theory and the Global Financial Crisis*, London: Routledge.

BIS [Bank for International Settlements] (2010) *Basel III: A Global Regulatory Framework for More Resilient Banks and Banking System*, Basel: Basel Committee on Banking Supervision.

BIS [Bank for International Settlement] (2013) *Basel III: The Liquidity Coverage Ratio and Liquidity Risk Monitoring Tool*, www.bis.org/publ/bcbs238.pdf.

BIS [Bank for International Settlement] (2016) *Financial Systems and the Real Economy*. BNM-BIS Conference October 2016, Malaysia; BIS Papers No 91, www.bis.org/publ/bppdf/bispap91.pdf.

BIS [Bank for International Settlements] (2018a) *Structural Changes in Banking after the Crisis*, CGFS Papers No. 60, January 2018, www.bis.org/publ/cgfs60.pdf.

BIS [Bank for International Settlements] (2018b) *Annual Economic Report June 2018*, www.bis.org/publ/arpdf/ar2018e.pdf.

BIS [Bank for International Settlements] (2018c) 'International banking and financial market development', *BIS Quarterly Review*, September 2018, www.bis.org/publ/qtrpdf/r_qt1809.pdf.

Birch, K. & Tickell, A. (2010) 'Making neoliberal order in the United States', in K. Birch & V. Mikhnenko (eds.) *Rise and Fall of Neoliberalism: Collapse of an Economic Order*, London: Zed Books.

Bloomberg (2018) 'An ugly bank bail-in shows why EU may have to rethink its rules', www.gulf-times.com/story/580517/04-02-2018.

Blundell-Wignall, A., Atkinson, P. & Roulet, C. (2014) 'Complexity, interconnectedness: Business models and the Basel system', in C. Goodhardt, D. Gabor, J. Vestergaard & I. Ertürk (eds.) *Central Banking at a Crossroads: Europe and Beyond*, London: Anthem Press.

Boettke, P. J. & Luther, W. J. (2010) 'The ordinary economics of an extraordinary crisis', in S. Kates (ed.) *Macroeconomic Theory and its Failings: Alternative Perspectives on the World Financial Crisis*, Cheltenham: Edward Elgar.

Boccuzzi, G. & De Lisa, R. (2017) 'Does bail-in definitely rule out bailout?' *Journal of Financial Management, Markets and Institutions*, 5, 1: 93–110.

Borak, D. (2019) 'Fed indicates it will slow down rate hikes in 2019', https://edition.cnn.com/09-01-2019.

Bossu, S. & Henrotte, P. (2002) *Finance and Derivatives: Theory and Practice*. English trans., Chichester: Wiley.

Boyle, B. & McDonough, T. (2010) 'Critical realism, Marxism and the critique of neoclassical economics', *Capital and Class*, 35, 1: 3–22.

Braudel, F. (1982) *Civilization and Capitalism, Vol II: 15th–18th Century*. New York: Harper and Row.

Brenner, R. (1998) 'Uneven development and the long downturn', *New Left Review*, 229: 1–265.

Brenner, R. (2002) *The Boom and the Bubble*, London: Verso.

Brenner, R. (2006) *The Economics of Global Turbulence: The Advanced Capitalist Economies from Long Boom to Long Downturn 1945–2005*, London: Verso.

Brenner, R. (2009) 'The economy in a world of trouble [interview with Seong-jin Jeong]', www.internationalviewpoint.org.

Brodbeck, S. (2019) 'Nearly 500 ATMs close a month as Britain's rush to a cashless society accelerates', www.telegraph.co.uk/personal-banking/12-02-2019.

Brooks, R. (2018) *Bean Counters: The Triumph of the Accountants and How They Broke Capitalism*, London: Atlantic.

Brown, E. (2013) 'The Detroit bail-in template: Fleecing pensioners to save the banks', https://dandelionsalad.wordpress.com/2013/08/05.

Brundsen, J. & Kahn, M. (2018) 'EU and Italy strike budget agreement to avoid fines', www.ft.com/content/19-12-2018.

Brunkhorst, H. (2011) 'The return of crisis', in P. F. Kjaer et al. (eds.) *The Financial Crisis in Constitutional Perspective: The Dark Side of Functional Differentiation*, Oxford: Hart.

Bryan, D. & Rafferty, M. (2003) 'Financial derivatives and value theory: Towards a theory of capitalist money', University of Western Sydney, School of Economics and Finance Working Paper 2003/07.

Bryan, D. & Rafferty, M. (2006a) *Capitalism with Derivatives: A Political Economy of Financial Derivatives, Capitalism and Class*, Basingstoke: Palgrave Macmillan.

Bryan, D. & Rafferty, M. (2006b) 'Money in capitalism and capitalist money', *Historical Materialism*, 14, 1: 75–95.

Bryan, D. & Rafferty, M. (2010) 'Time and place: Foundations of commodity money', in M. Amato & L. Fantacci (eds.) *Money and Calculation: Economic and Sociological Perspectives*, Basingstoke: Palgrave Macmillan.

Bryan, D. & Rafferty, M. (2014) 'Financial derivatives a social policy beyond crisis', *Sociology*, 48, 5: 887–903.

Buchheit, P. (2016) 'The collapse of the middle class job', www.commondreams.org/views/2016/05/09.

Buck, P. D. (2008) 'Keeping the collaborators on board as the ship sinks: Toward a theory of fascism and the US "middle class"', *Rethinking Marxism: A Journal of Economics, Culture and Society*, 20, 1: 68–90.

Buick, A. (2017) 'MMT: New theory, old illusion' [from the Feb 2017 issue of Socialist Standard], "https://socialiststandardmyspace.blogspot.com/search?q=crankism" https://socialiststandardmyspace.blogspot.com.

Buiter, W. (2008) *Central Banks and Financial Crises*, LSE Financial Markets Group Research Centre, Discussion Paper No. 619.

Buiter, W. (2009) 'What's left of central bank independence?' http://blogs.ft.com/maverecon/2009/05.

Bullough, O. (2018) *Moneyland: Why Thieves and Crooks Now Rule the World and How to Take It Back*, London: Profile Books.

Burghardt, T. (2013) 'Echelon today: The evolution of an NSA black program', www.globalresearch.ca/14-11-2013.

Bussolo, N., Karver, J. & López-Calva, L. (2018) 'Is there a middle class in Europe?' www.brookings.edu/blog/future-development/2018/03/22/is-there-a-middle-class-crisis-in-europe/22-03-2018.

Buzan, B. (2011) 'A world order without superpowers: decentred globalism', *International Relations*, 25, 1: 3–25.

Cahill, D. (2014) *The End of Laissez-Faire? On the Durability of Embedded Neoliberalism*, Cheltenham: Edward Elgar.

Callinicos, A. (2017) 'The neoliberal order begins to crack', *International Socialism*, 154: 1–19.

Carlin, W. & Soskice, D. (2006) *Macroeconomics: Imperfections, Institutions and Policies*, Oxford: Oxford University Press.

Carlson, J. (2017) 'The globalism threat: Socialism's new world order', https://themarketswork.com/2017/02/24.

Carroll, W. K. (2010) *The Making of a Transnational Capitalist Class: Corporate Power in the 21st Century*, London: Zed.

Carson, K. (2014) 'Economic calculation under capitalist central planning', in G. L. Nell (ed.) *Austrian Theory and Economic Organization: Reaching Beyond Free Market Boundaries*, Basingstoke: Palgrave Macmillan.

Chassang, S. & Padró i Miquel, G. (2010) 'Savings and predation', *Journal of the European Economic Association*, 8, 2/3: 645–665.

Chiaramonte, L., Casu, B. & Bottiglia, R. (2013) 'The impact of new structural liquidity rules on the profitability of EU banks', in J. Falzon (ed.) *Bank Performance, Risk and Securitization*, Basingstoke: Palgrave Macmillan.

Chorafas, D. N. (2013a) *Breaking Up the Euro: The End of a Common Currency*, Basingstoke: Palgrave Macmillan.

Chorafas, D. N. (2013b) *The Changing Role of Central Banks*, Basingstoke: Palgrave Macmillan.

Christiano, L. J. (2017) 'The Great Recession: A macroeconomic earthquake', *Federal Reserve Bank of Minneapolis Economic Policy Paper 17-1*, February 2017.

Chu, B. (2018) 'Seeds for new financial crisis "being planted" warns economist Douglas Diamond', *Independent*, 23 April.

Clark, B. (2016) *Political Economy: A Comparative Approach*. Third edition, Santa Barbara: Praeger.

Clark, W. R. (2005) *Petrodollar Warfare: Oil, Iraq and the Future of the Dollar*, New York: New Society.

Clarke, S. (1994) *Marx's Theory of Crisis*, Basingstoke: St Martins.

Clarke, S. (1999) 'Capitalist competition and the tendency to overproduction: Comments on Bob Brenner's "Uneven development and the long downturn",' Centre for Comparative Labour Studies, University of Warwick, https://homepages.warwick.ac.uk/~syrbe/pubs/Brenner.pdf.

Clarke, S. (2001) 'State, class struggle, and the reproduction of capital', https://homepages.warwick.ac.uk/~syrbe/pubs/kapstate.pdf.

Cleaver, H. (1992) 'Theses on secular crisis in capitalism', https://libcom.org/library.

Cocco, F. (2019) 'Rich nations urged to prepare workers for age of automation', www.ft.com/content/25-04-2019.

Cockshott, P. (2013) 'Is the theory of the falling profit rate valid?' *World Review of Political Economy*, 4, 3: 323–340.

Cohen, G. A. (2000 [1978]) *Karl Marx's Theory of History: A Defence*. Expanded edition, Oxford: Oxford University Press.

Coleman, L. (2015) *The Lunacy of Modern Finance Theory and Regulation*, London: Routledge.

Collins, R. (2013) 'The end of middle-class work: No more escapes', in I. Wallerstein et al. (eds.) *Does Capitalism Have a Future?* Oxford: Oxford University Press.

Connell, C. M. (2013) *Reforming the World Monetary System: Fritz Machlup and the Bellagio Group*, London: Pickering & Chatto.

Cooper, G. (2008) *The Origins of Financial Crises: Central Banks, Credit Bubbles and the Efficient Market Fallacy*, Petersfield: Harriman House.

Cooper, C. (2014) 'Accounting for the fictitious: A Marxist contribution to understanding accounting's roles in the financial crisis', https://strathprints.strath.ac.uk/51490/1.

Cord, R. (2013) *Reinterpreting the Keynesian Revolution*, London: Routledge.

Costanza, R. (2010) 'Towards a new sustainable economy', in S. Kates (ed.) *Macroeconomic Theory and Its Failings: Alternative Perspectives on the Global Financial Crisis*, Cheltenham: Edward Elgar.

Cotula, L. (2017) 'The state of exception and the law of the global economy: A conceptual and empirico-legal inquiry', *Transnational Legal Theory*, 8, 4: 424–454.

Cox, J. (2018) 'Companies buying back their own shares is the only thing keeping the stock market afloat right now', www.cnbc.com/02-07-2018.

Crotty, J. 2005. 'The neoliberal paradox: The impact of destructive product market competition and "Modern" financial markets on nonfinancial corporation performance in the neoliberal era," in G. Epstein (ed.) *Financialization and the World Economy*, Cheltenham: Edward Elgar.

Crotty, J. (2009) 'Profound structural flaws in the US financial system that helped cause the financial crisis', *Economic and Political Weekly*, 44, 13: 131–135.

Crouch, C. (2013) *Making Capitalism Fit for Society*, Cambridge: Polity.

Cynamon, B. Z., Fazzari, S. & Setterfield, M. (eds.) (2013) *After the Great Recession*, Cambridge: Cambridge University Press.

Cypher, J. M. (2007) 'From military Keynesianism to global-neoliberal militarism', *Monthly Review*, 59, 2: 37–55.

Cypher, J. M. (2015) 'The origins and evolution of military Keynesianism in the United States', *Journal of Post-Keynesian Economics*, 38, 3: 449–476.

Das, S. (2018) 'Volatility trading is a problem: It increases risk, harms the real economy and distorts the financial system', www.bloomberg.com/opinion/articles/2018-06-04.

Dailami, M. & Masson, P. (2009) *The New Multipolar International Monetary System*, World Bank Development Economics and Development Prospects Group, Policy Research Paper 5147.

De Grauwe, P. (2013) 'Central bank communication when agents experience cognitive limitations', in P. L. Siklos & J.-E. Sturm (eds.) *Central Bank Communication, Decision Making and Governance*, Cambridge, MA: MIT Press.

De Graw, D. (2010) 'The financial coup d'état: consolidation of America's economic elite', www.globalresearch.ca/17742.

Dean, J. (2009) *Democracy and other Neoliberal Fantasies: Communicative Capitalism and Left Politics*, Durham, NC: Duke University Press.

Debord, G. (1994) *Society of the Spectacle*. English trans., London: Rebel Press.

Decker, S. (2018) 'From degrowth to deglobalization', www.degrowth.info/en/23-01-2018.

Decker, S. & Sablowksi, T. (2017) *Die G20 und die Krise des globalen Kapitalismus: Studien 4/2017*, Berlin: Rosa-Luxemburg-Stiftung.

Dejuán, Ó., Febrero, E. & J. Uxó (eds.) (2013) *Post-Keynesian Views of the Crisis and its Remedies*, London: Routledge.

Dejuán, O. (2013) 'The debt trap', in O. Dejuán, E. Febrero & J. Uxó (eds.) *Post-Keynesian Views of the Crisis and Its Remedies*, London: Routledge.

Deleuze, G. (1994) *Difference and Repetition*. English trans., New York: Colombia University Press.

Denys, A. (2014) 'Methodological individualism and society: Hayek's evolving view', in G. L. Nell (ed.) *Austrian Economic Perspectives on Individualism and Society: Moving Beyond Methodological Individualism*, Basingstoke: Palgrave Macmillan.

Derrida, J. (1992) 'The force of law: The "mystical foundations of authority"', in D. Cornell et al. (eds.) *Deconstruction and the Possibility of Justice*, London: Routledge.

Derrida, J. (1994) *Spectres of Marx*. English trans., London: Routledge.

Desjardins, J. (2017) 'Animation: The collapse of the middle class in 20 major US cities', www.visualcapitalist.com/18-04-2017.

Desjardins, J. (2018) 'The 8 major forces shaping the future of the global economy', www.visualcapitalist.com/04-10-2018.

Deutsche Bank (2018) *Information on Bank Resolution Procedures and Creditor Participations (bail-ins) and on Article 41 of the Delegated Regulation (EU) 2017/565*, June 2018, www.deutsche-bank.de/pfb/data/docs/ser-bankenabwicklung-und-glaeubigerbeteiligung-engl.pdf.

Dewatripont, M. et al. (2010) *Balancing the Banks: Global Lessons from the Financial Crisis*, Princeton: Princeton University Press.

Dodd, N. (2014) *The Social Life of Money*, Princeton, NJ: Princeton University Press.

Dodd, R. (2012) 'Derivatives markets: Sources of instability in vulnerability in US financial markets', in G. A. Epstein (ed.) *Financialization and the World Economy*, Cheltenham: Edward Elgar.

Doff, N. (2018) 'Russia dumps Treasuries for gold', www.bloomberg.com/news/articles/2018-06-20.

Dolack, P. (2017) 'The bait and switch of public-private partnerships', www.counterpunch.org/2017/02/24.

Donnan, S. & Fleming, S. (2016) 'America's Middle Class meltdown', www.ft.com/content/09-12-2015.

Dorn, J. A. (2018) 'Money in an uncertain world: The case for rules', www.cato.org/winter 2018.

Duménil, G. & Lévy, D. (2001) 'Periodizing capitalism: Technology, institutions, relations of production', in R. Albritton et al. (eds.) *Phases of Capitalist Development*, Basingstoke: Palgrave Macmillan.

Duménil, G. & Lévy, D. (2012) 'Costs and benefits of neoliberalism: A class analysis', in G. A. Epstein (ed.) *Financialization and the World Economy*, Cheltenham: Edward Elgar.

Duménil, G. & Lévy, D. (2014) 'The crisis of the early 21st century: Marxian perspectives', in R. Bellofiore & G. Vertova (eds.) *The Great Recession and the Contradictions of Contemporary Capitalism*, Cheltenham: Edward Elgar.

Durand, C. (2017) *Fictitious Capital: How Finance Is Appropriating Our Future*. English trans., London: Verso.

Eatwell, R. (2004) 'Introduction', in R. Eatwell & C. Mudde (eds.) *Western Democracies and the New Extreme Right Challenge*, London: Routledge.

ECB [European Central Bank] (2007) *Risk Measurement and Systemic Risk* [Fourth Joint Central Bank Research Conference November 2005 in Cooperation with the Committee on the Global Financial System], www.ecb.europa.eu/pub/pdf.

Economist (2018) 'The next recession', *Economist*, 13 October.

Ehret, M. (2012) 'Financial socialism: The role of financial economics in economic disorganization', *Journal of Business Research*, 67, 1: 2686–2692.

Eisenberg, G. (1999) '"Wer nicht arbeitet, soll auch nicht essen": Zur Sub- und inneren Kolonialgeschichte der Arbeitsgesellschaft', in R. Kurz, E. Lohoff & N. Trenkle (eds.) *Feierabend! Elf Attacken gegen die Arbeit*, Hamburg: Konkret Literatur Verlag.

EIU (2017) 'Fixing Italy's banks: avoiding bail-ins', http://country.eiu.com/06-07-2017.

El-Erian, M. A. (2012) 'Evolution, impact, and limitations of unusual central bank policy activism', *Federal Reserve Bank of St. Louis Review*, 94, 4: 243–264.

El-Arian, M. A. (2017) 'Could the IMF's "world currency" help encourage global unity?' www.theguardian.com/business/24-04-2017.

El-Erian, M. A. (2018) 'Emerging markets face further pressure before the all-clear: Forced sales and repeated pockets of illiquidity complicate matters for investors', www.ft.com/03-09-2018.

Elliott, L. (2018) 'An economic recovery based around high debt is really no recovery: Ten years after the Lehman collapse the necessary reforms to a flawed model have not taken place', www.theguardian.com/business/2018/sep/16.

Elster, J. (1985) *Making Sense of Marx*, Cambridge: Cambridge University Press.

Engdahl, W. (2018) 'Washington's silent weapon for not-so-quiet wars', https://journal-neo.org/20-08-2018.

Escobar, P. (2018) 'How Iran will respond to Trump', www.counterpunch.org/25-05- 2018.

European Parliament (2016) 'Loss absorbing capacity in the Banking Union: TLAC implementation and MREL review', www.europarl.europa.eu/RegData/etudes.

Evans-Pritchard, A. (2016) 'IMF admits disastrous love affair with the euro and apologises for the immolation of Greece', www.telegraph.co.uk/business/2016/07/28.

Evans-Pritchard, A. (2018a) 'Turkey is the first big victim of Fed tightening, but it won't be the last', www.telegraph.co.uk/business/2018/08/15.

Evans-Pritchard, A. (2018b) 'The EU's unstoppable showdown with Italy risks a market crash and a euro break-up', www.telegraph.co.uk/24-10-2018.

Faia, E. & Schnabel, I. (2015) 'The road from micro- to macroprudential regulation', in E. Faia et al (eds.) *Financial Regulation: A Transatlantic Perspective*, Cambridge: Cambridge University Press.

Fantacci, L. (2013) 'Reforming money to exit the crisis: Examples of non-capitalist monetary systems in practice', in J. Pixley & G. C. Harcourt (eds.) *Financial Crises and the Nature of Capitalist Money*, Basingstoke: Palgrave Macmillan.

FDIC [Federal Deposit Insurance Corporation] & Bank of England (2012) 'Resolving globally active systemically important financial institutions', www.fdic.gov/about/srac/10-12-2012.

Federal Reserve Bank (2019) www.federalreserve.gov/monetarypolicy.

Feld, L., Köhler, E. A. & Nientiedt, D. (2015) 'Ordoliberalism, pragmatism and the Eurozone crisis: How the German tradition shaped economic policy in Europe', CESifo Working Paper, No. 5368.

Feldner, H. & Vighi, F. (2015) *Critical Theory and the Crisis of Contemporary Capitalism*, New York: Bloomsbury.

Feldstein, M. (2008) 'Defence spending would be great stimulus', *Wall Street Journal*, 24 December, www.wsj.com/articles/SB123008280526532053.

Fine, B. (2004) 'Addressing the critical and the real in critical realism', in P. Lewis (ed.) *Transforming Economics*, London: Routledge.

Fine, B. (2010) 'Looking at the crisis through Marx – Or is it the other way around?' in S. Kates (ed.) *Macroeconomic Theory and Its Failings: Alternative Perspectives on the Global Financial Crisis*, Cheltenham: Edward Elgar.

Fleming, S. & Fox, B. (2018) 'Economists warn on dominance of US corporate giants: The rising grip of a small group of large companies comes under scrutiny', www.ft.com/content/15-08-2018.

Fleming, S. & Smith, J. (2019) 'Global economy: Why central bankers blinked', www.ft.com/content/08-02-2019.

Flitter, E. & Rappaport, A. (2018) 'Big banks to get a break on risky trading', www.nytimes.com/2018/05/30/business/volcker-rule-banks-federal-reserve.html.

Florio, M. (2011/2012) 'The real roots of the great recession: Unsustainable income distribution', *International Journal of Political Economy*, 40, 4: 5–30.

Foster, J. B. & Magdoff, H. (2009) *The Great Financial Crisis: Causes and Consequences*, New York: Monthly Review Press.

Foy, H. (2018) 'Russian sanctions: Why "isolation is impossible". Rhetoric has not matched reality as Moscow sells arms and build alliances', www.ft.com/content/12-11-2018.

Fratianni, M. & Pattison, J. C. (2015) 'Basel III in reality', *Journal of Economic Integration*, 30, 1: 1–28.

Friedman, J. & Kraus, W. (2011) *Engineering the Financial Crisis: Systemic Risk and the Failure of Regulation*, Philadelphia: University of Pennsylvania Press.

Friedman, M. (1993) *Why Government Is the Problem*, Stanford, CA: Hoover Institution Press.

FSB [Financial Stability Board] (2009) *Improving Financial Regulation: Report of the Financial Stability Board to G20 Leaders 25-09-2009*, www.fsb.org/wp-content/uploads/r_090925b.pdf.

FSB [Financial Stability Board] (2013) *Progress and Next Steps Towards Ending 'Too-Big-to-Fail'*, www.fsb.org/wp-content/uploads/r_130902.pdf.

FSB [Financial Stability Board] (2015) *Principles on Loss-Absorbing and Recapitalization Capacity of G-SIBs in Resolution*, www.fsb.org/wp-content/uploads/TLAC-Principles-and-Term-Sheet-for-publication-final.pdf.

FSB [Financial Stability Board] (2017) *2017 list of global systemically important banks (G-SIBs)*, www.fsb.org/wp-content/uploads/P211117-1.pdf.

Fuchs, C. (2014) *Digital Labour and Karl Marx*, London: Routledge.

Gai, P. (2013) *Systemic Risk: The Dynamics of Modern Financial Systems*, Oxford: Oxford University Press.

Gamble, A. (1988) *The Free Economy and the Strong State*, Basingstoke: Palgrave Macmillan.

Gamble, A. (2006) 'Two faces of neoliberalism', in R. Robinson (ed.) *The Neoliberal Revolution: Forging the Market State*, Basingstoke: Palgrave Macmillan.

GAO (2012) *Dodd-Frank Act: Agencies Efforts to Analyze and Coordinate Their Rules*, Washington, DC: US Government Accountability Office.

Gelpern, A. (2017) 'Bad Latin: *lex monetae, pari passu*, and other Italy exit irritants', www.piie.com/commentary/op-eds/06-06-2017.

General Court of the European Union (2018) Press Release No 108/18 Luxembourg, 13 July 2018: *Judgments in Cases T-680/13 K. Chrysostomides & Co. and Others v Council and Others and T-786/14 Bourdouvali and Others v Council and Others*. Luxemburg: CVRIA.

Genschel, P. & Seelkopf, L. (2015) 'The competition state: The modern state in a global economy', in S. Leibfried et al. (eds.) *The Oxford Handbook of Transformations of the State*, Oxford: Oxford University Press.

Girouard, J. E. (2018) 'Corporate Buybacks, The illusion of profit and the looming disaster for your portfolio', www.forbes.com/sites/investor/11-05-2018.

Gleeson, S. (2012) *International Regulation of Banking: Capital and Risk Requirements*. Second edition, Oxford: Oxford University Press.

Goodfriend, M. & King, R. G. (1997) 'The new neoclassical synthesis and the role of monetary policy', *NBER Macroeconomic Annual 1997*, vol. 12. Cambridge, MA: MIT Press.

Goodhart, C. (2014) 'Bank resolution in comparative perspective: What lessons for Europe?' in C. Goodhardt, D. Gabor, J. Vestergaard & I. Ertürk (eds.) *Central Banking at a Crossroads: Europe and Beyond*, London: Anthem Press.

Goodspeed, T. B. (2012) *Rethinking the Keynesian Revolution: Keynes, Hayek and the Wicksell Connection*, Oxford: Oxford University Press.

Gordon, D. M. (1975) 'Recession is capitalism as normal', *New York Times*, www.nytimes.com/1975/04/27/archives.

Grant, J. (2007) 'The Fed's subprime solution', www.nytimes.com/26-08-2007.

Grant, J. (2015) 'Monetary activism is a virus that infects politics', www.ft.com/content/05-01-2015.

Greenstein, T. (2018) The Feds $16 trillion bailouts under reported', www.forbes.com/sites/traceygreenstein/2011/09/20.

Griffin, R. (2007) *Modernism and Fascism: The Sense of a Beginning Under Mussolini and Hitler*, Basingstoke: Palgrave Macmillan.

Groff, R. (2004) *Critical Realism, Post-Positivism and the Possibility of Knowledge*, London: Routledge.

Grossmann, H. (2005 [1929]) *Law of Accumulation and Breakdown.* Abridged English trans. from *Das Akkumulations- und Zusammenbruchsgesetz des kapitalistischen Systems*, Leipzig: Hirschfeld, www.marxists.org/archive/grossman/1929/breakdown/ch02.htm.

Grünewald, S. (2017) 'Legal challenges of bail-in', in *European Central Bank, Eurosystem. ECB Legal Conference 2017. Shaping a New Legal Order for Europe: A Tale of Crises and Opportunities.* September 2017, Frankfurt am Main: ECB.

Habermas, J. (1987) *Knowledge and Human Interests.* English trans., Cambridge: Polity.

Hadjiemmanuil, C. (2017) *Limits on State-Funded Bailouts in the EU Bank Resolution Regime*, European Banking Institute Working Paper Series 2017/2.

Haiven, M. (2010) 'Finance as capital's imagination? Reimagining value and culture in an age of fictitious capital and crisis', *Social Text*, 29, 3: 93–124.

Haiven, M. (2015) *Cultures of Financialization: Fictitious Capital in Popular Culture and Everyday Life*, Basingstoke: Palgrave Macmillan.

Hall, D. (2014) *Why Public-Private Partnerships Don't Work: The Many Advantages of the Public Alternative*, www.world-psi.org/sites.

Hall, R. E. (2010) 'Why does the economy fall to pieces after a financial crisis?' *Journal of Economic Perspectives*, 24, 4: 3–20.

Hamacher, W. (2002) 'Benjamin's sketch "Capitalism as Religion"', *Diacritics*, 32, 3/4: 81–106.

Hardouvelis, G. A. (2016) 'Overcoming the crisis in Cyprus', in A. Michaelides & A. Orphanides (eds.) *The Cyprus Bail-In: Policy Lessons from the Cyprus Economic Crisis*, London: Imperial College Press.

Hardt, M. and Negri, A. (2000) *Empire*, Cambridge, MA: Harvard University Press.

Harris, D. (1983) 'Accumulation of capital and the rate of profit in Marxian theory', *Cambridge Journal of Economics*, 7, 3/4: 311–330.

Harrison, M. (2014) 'Capitalism at war', in L. Neal & J. G. Williamson (eds.) *The Cambridge History of Capitalism*, Cambridge: Cambridge University Press.

Hart, N. (2010) 'Macroeconomic theory and the global economic recession', *International Journal of Business Research*, 10, 2: 205.

Hartlage, A. W. (2012) 'The Basel III liquidity coverage ratio and financial stability', *Michigan Law Review*, 111, 3: 453–483.

Harvey, D. (1989) *The Conditions of Postmodernity: An Enquiry into the Origins of Cultural Change*, Oxford: Blackwell.

Harvey, D. (2003) *The New Imperialism*, Oxford: Oxford University Press.

Harvey, D. (2005) *A Brief History of Neoliberalism*, Oxford: Oxford University Press.

Harvey, D. (2010) *The Enigma of Capital and the Crises of Capitalism*, London: Profile.

Haug, W. F. (1980) 'Annäherung an die faschistische Modalität des Ideologischen', in M. Behrens et al. (eds.) *Faschismus und Ideologie* [Argument-Sonderband Bd. 60], Berlin: Argument-Verlag.

Haug, W. F. (1983 [1971]) *Critique of Commodity Aesthetics*. English trans., Cambridge: Polity.

Haug, W. F. (2006) 'Commodity aesthetics revisited: Exchange relations as the source of antagonistic aestheticization', *Radical Philosophy*, 135: 18–24.

Haug, W. F. (2012) *Hightech-Kapitalismus in der großen Krise*, Berlin: Argument Verlag.

Hayek, F. (1971 [1937]) *Monetary Nationalism and International Stability*, New York: Augustus Klly.

Hayek, F. (1976) *The Denationalization of Money: An Analysis of the Theory and Practice of Concurrent Currencies*, London: Institute of Economic Affairs.

Hayek, F. (1980 [1939]) 'The economic conditions of interstate federalism', in F. Hayek (ed.) *Individualism and Economic Order*, Chicago: Chicago University Press.

Hedges, C. (2018) 'The coming collapse', www.truthdig.com/articles/20-05-2018.

Hein, E. (2008) *Money, Distribution Conflict and Capital Accumulation: Contributions to Monetary Analysis*, Basingstoke: Palgrave Macmillan.

Hein, E. (2012) *The Macroeconomics of Finance-Dominated Capitalism and Its Crisis*, Cheltenham: Edward Elgar.

Hein, E. (2013) 'Finance-dominated capitalism, redistribution and the financial and economic crisis: A European perspective', in O. Dejuán, E. Febrero & J. Uxó (eds.) *Post-Keynesian Views of the Crisis and Its Remedies*, London: Routledge.

Heinrich, M. (1991) *Die Wissenschaft vom Wert. Die Marxsche Kritik der politischen Ökonomie zwischen wissenschaftlicher Revolution und klassischer Tradition*, Hamburg: Westfälisches Dampfboot.

Heinrich, M. (2013) 'Crisis theory, the law of the tendency of the profit rate to fall, and Marx's studies in the 1870s', https://monthlyreview.org/01-04-2013.

Henry, J. F. (1990) *The Making of Neoclassical Economics*, London: Unwin Hyman.

Henry, L. (2009) 'One huge "Minsky moment": Lessons from the financial crisis', *Social and Economic Studies*, 58, 2: 77–89.

Higgs, R. (1997) 'Regime uncertainty: Why the Great Depression lasted so long and why prosperity resumed after the war', *The Independent Review*, 1, 4: 561–590.

Hilferding, R. (1981 [1910]) *Finance Capital*. English trans., London: Routledge & Kegan Paul.

Hiro, D. (2012) *After Empire: The Birth of a Multipolar World*, New York: Perseus.

Hoda, A. (2016) *Bluff: The Game Central Banks Play and How It Leads to Crisis*, London: One World.

Holcombe, R. G. (2018) *Political Capitalism: How Political and Economic Power Is Made and Maintained*, Cambridge: Cambridge University Press.

Hoogerverst, H. (2018) 'Are we ready for the next crisis?', www.ifrs.org/news-and-events/2018/12.

Hossein-Zadeh, I. (2014) *Beyond Mainstream Explanations of the Financial Crisis: Parasitic Finance Capital*, Abingdon: Routledge.

Hudson, M. (2010) 'From Marx to Goldman Sachs: The fictions of fictitious capital', http://michael-hudson.com/2010/07.

Hudson, M. (2014) *The Bubble and Beyond: Fictitious Capital, Debt Deflation and Global Crisis*. Second edition, Dresden: ISLET.

Huerta de Soto, J. (2008) *The Austrian School: Market Order and Entrepreneurial Creativity*, Cheltenham: Edward Elgar.

Hummel, J. R. (2015) 'Reserve requirements Basel style: The Liquidity Coverage Ratio', www.alt-m.org/2015/07/31.

Ikenberry, G. J. (2018) 'The end of liberal international order?' *International Affairs*, 9, 1: 7–23.

IMF (2018a) *Considerations of the Role of the SDR*, IMF Policy Paper April 2018. Washington, DC: International Monetary Fund.

IMF (2018b) *Special Drawing Right Factsheet*, www.imf.org/19-04-2018.

IMF/BIS/FSB (2016) *Elements of Effective Macroprudential Policies: Lessons from International Experience*, www.imf.org/external/np/g20/pdf/2016/083116.pdf.

Ingham, G. (2004a) *The Nature of Money*, Cambridge: Polity.

Ingham, G. (2004b) 'The emergence of capitalist credit money', in L. Randall Wray (ed.) *Credit and State Theories of Money*, Cheltenham: Edward Elgar.

Inman, G. (2018) 'Household debt in UK "worse than at any time on record"', www.theguardian.com/money/26-07-2018.

Innes, B. (1914) 'The Credit Theory of Money', *Banking Law Journal*, January: 151–168. Republished as 'The credit theory of money' in L. R. Wray (ed.) Credit and State Theories of Money, Cheltenham: Edward Elgar, 2004.

Institute of Fiscal Studies (2018) 'The decline of homeownership among young adults' [IFS Briefing note BN224], www.ifs.org.uk/uploads.

Itoh, M & Lapavitsas, C. (1999) *Political Economy of Money and Finance*, Basingstoke: Macmillan Press.

James, H. (2017) 'Deglobalization as a global challenge', *Centre for International Governance Innovation Papers*, No.135. Ontario: Waterloo.

Jay, M. (1984) *The Adventures of a Concept from Lukács to Habermas*, Berkeley: University of California Press.

Jefferis, C. (2017) *The Dialectics of Liquidity Crisis: An Interpretation of the Financial Crisis of 2007–08*, Abingdon: Routledge.

Jehu (2017) 'How does fascist state fiat affect capitalist accumulation?' https://therealmovement.wordpress.com/2017/02/09/how-does-fascist-state-fiat-affect-capitalist-accumulation.

Jenkins, P. (2019) 'The private equity bubble is bound to burst. There are worrying signs that the sector is becoming a victim of its own success', www.ft.com/content/12-04-2019.

Jessop, B. (2000) 'The crisis of the national spatio-temporal fix and the tendential ecological dominance of globalising capitalism', *International Journal of Urban and Regional Research*, 24, 2: 323–360.

Jessop, B. (2001) 'What follows Fordism? On the periodization of capitalism and its regulation', in R. Albritton et al. (eds.) *Phases of Capitalist Development: Booms, Crises and Globalizations*, Basingstoke: Palgrave Macmillan.

Jessop, B. (2007) 'What follows neoliberalism? The deepening contradictions of US domination and the struggle for a new global order', in R. Albritton et al. (eds.) *Political Economy and Global Capitalism*, London: Anthem.

Jessop, B. (2013) 'Credit money, fiat money and currency pyramids: Reflections on the financial crisis and sovereign debt', in J. Pixley & G. C. Harcourt (eds.) *Financial Crises and the Nature of Capitalist Money*, Basingstoke: Palgrave Macmillan.

Jolly, J. (2017) 'Federal Reserve announces balance sheet unwinding starting in October as interest rates left unchanged', www.cityam.com/272422.

Jones, C. (2016) 'Why German wages need to rise and fast', www.ft.com/16-11-2016.

Jones, C. (2018) 'Is the ECB still ready to say goodbye to QE?', www.ft.com/13-09-2018.

Jones, D. M. (2014) *Understanding Central Banking: The New Era of Activism*, Armonk: M. E. Sharpe.

Kates, S. (2010) 'The crisis in economic theory: The dead end of Keynesian economics', in S. Kates (ed.) *Macroeconomic Theory and Its Failings: Alternative Perspectives on the Global Financial Crisis*, Cheltenham: Edward Elgar.

Katouzian, H. (1980) *Ideology and Method in Economics*, London: Macmillan.

Katz, C. (2008) 'The crisis of capitalism: Beyond regulation and greed', reprinted in English translation at: https://isreview.org/issue/65.

Kautsky, K. (1914) *The Class Struggle [Erfurt Program]*. English trans., London: Twentieth Century Press.

Kautsky, K. (1937) 'Die Krise des Kapitalismus und die Verkürzung', *Gewerkschaftliche Rundschau*, March 1937. Re-printed in *Neue Gesellschaft*, 31 (1984): 123–129. www.marxists.org/deutsch/archiv/kautsky/1937/03/arbeitszeit.htm.

Keen, S. (2011) *Debunking Economics: The Naked Emperor Dethroned?* Second revised edition, London: Zed Books.

Keita, L. D. (1997) 'Neoclassical economics and the last dogma of positivism: Is the normative-positive distinction justified?' *Metaphilosophy*, 28, 1/2: 81–101.

Keynes, J. M. (1936) *The General Theory of Employment, Interest and Money*, Basingstoke: Palgrave Macmillan.

Keynes, J. M. (2017 [1939]) *The General Theory of Employment, Interest and Money*, Ware: Wordsworth Editions.

Khan, M. (2015) 'EU takes members states to court over "bail-in" laws to protect taxpayers', www.telegraph.co.uk/finance/economics/22-10-2015.

Kimball, M. (2013) 'Breaking through the zero lower bound', https://warwick.ac.uk/fac/soc/economics/seminars.

Kindleberger, C. P. & Aliber, R. Z. (2005) *Manias, Panics and Crashes: A History of Financial Crises*, Basingstoke: Palgrave Macmillan.

Kliman, A. (2012) *The Failure of Capitalist Production: Underlying Causes of the Great Recession*, London: Pluto.

Knapp, G. F. (1973 [1924]). *The State Theory of Money*, Clifton, NY: Augustus Kelley.

Koepnick, L. P. (1999) *Walter Benjamin and the Aesthetics of Power*, Lincoln: University of Nebraska Press.

Kojève, A. (1969) *Introduction to the Reading of Hegel*, Ithaca: Cornell University Press.

Kołakowski, L. (1978) *Main Currents in Marxism*, 3 vols. English trans., Oxford: Oxford University Press.

Kondratieff, N. D. (1979 [1926]) 'The long waves in economic life', *Fernand Braudel Center Review*, 2, 4: 519–562.

Koo, R. C. (2015) *The Escape from Balance Sheet Recession and the QE Trap: A Hazardous Road for the World Economy*, Hoboken, NJ: Wiley.

Kotz, D. (2007) 'The erosion of non-capitalist institutions and the reproduction of capitalism', in R. Albritton et al. (eds.) *Political Economy and Global Capitalism*, London: Anthem.

Kotz, D. (2015) 'Roots of the current economic crisis: Capitalism, forms of capitalism, politics, and contingent events', https://thenextrecession.files.wordpress.com.

Kotz, D. M. (1994) 'Interpreting the social structure of accumulation theory', in D. M. Kotz et al. (eds.) *Social Structures of Accumulation*, Cambridge: Cambridge University Press.

Kozul-Wright, R. (2018) 'The global economy's fundamental weakness', www.project-syndicate.org/commentary/13-09-2018.

Krahl, H.-J. (1984) *Vom Ende der abstrakten Arbeit: die Aufhebung der sinnlosen Arbeit ist in der Transzendentalität des Kapitals angelegt und in der Verweltlichung der Philosophie begründet*, Frankfurt-am-Main: Materialis.

Krugman, P. (2009) 'How did economists get it so wrong?' *New York Times*, 6 September 2009.

Kuhn, T. (1970) *The Structure of Scientific Revolutions*. Second edition, Chicago: University of Chicago Press.

Kurz, R. (1986) 'The crisis of exchange value: Science as productive force, productive labor, and capitalist reproduction', English translation, reprinted in N. Larsen et al. (eds.) *Marxism and the Critique of Value*, Chicago: MCM' Publishing.

Kurz, R. (1994) 'The end of politics: Theses on the crisis of the regulatory system of the commodity form', https://libcom.org/library.

Kurz, R. (1995) 'The apotheosis of money: The structural limits of capital valorization, casino capitalism and the global financial crisis', https://libcom.org/library.

Kurz, R. (2010) 'On the current global economic crisis: Questions and answers', English translation, reprinted in N. Larsen et al. (eds.) *Marxism and the Critique of Value*, Chicago: MCM' Publishing.

Kurz, R. (2012) *No Revolution Anywhere*. English trans., London: Chronos.

Kurz, R. (2016) *The Substance of Capital: The Life and Death of Capitalism*. English trans., Lincoln: Chronos Publishing.

La Berge, L. C. (2014) 'The rules of abstraction: Methods and discourses of finance', *Radical History Review*, 118: 93–112.

Lanchester, J. (2018) 'After the fall', *London Review of Books*, 40, 13: 3–8.

Lapavitsas, C. (1991) 'The credit theory of money: A structural analysis', *Science and Society*, 55, 3: 291–322.

Lapavitsas, C. (1997) 'Two approaches to the concept of interest-bearing capital', *International Journal of Political Economy*, 27, 1: 63–79.

Lapavitsas, C. (2000) 'Money and the analysis of capitalism: The significance of commodity money', *Review of Radical Political Economics*, 32, 4: 631–656.

Lapavitsas, C. (2011) 'Theorizing financialization', *Work, Employment and Society*, 25, 4: 611–626.

Lapavitsas, C. (2013) *Profiting without Producing: How Finance Exploits Us All*, London: Verso.

Larsen, N. et al. (2014) 'Introduction', in N. Larsen et al. (eds.) Marxism and the Critique of Value, Chicago: MCM' Publishing.

Lash, S. & Urry, J. (1987) *The End of Organized Capitalism*, Madison: University of Wisconsin Press.

Lavoie, M. (2013) 'After the crisis: Perspectives for post-Keynesian economics', in F. S. Lee & M. Lavoie (eds.) *In Defense of Post-Keynesian and Heterodox Economics: Reponses to Their Critics*, London: Routledge.

Lawson, C. (1999) 'Realism, individualism and theory in the work of Carl Menger', in T. Lawson (ed.) *Critical Realism in Economics: Development and Debate*, London: Routledge.

Lawson, T. (2009) 'The current economic crisis: Its nature and the course of academic economics', *Cambridge Journal of Economics*, 33, 4: 759–777.

Lawson, T. et al. (eds.) (1998) *Critical Realism: Essential Readings*, London: Routledge.

Lazzarato, M. (1996) 'Immaterial labor', in M. Hardt & P. Virno (eds.) *Radical Thought in Italy*, Minneapolis, MN: University of Minnesota Press.

Lazzarato, M. (2009) 'Neoliberalism in action: Inequality, insecurity and the reconstitution of the social', *Theory, Culture and Society*, 26, 6: 109–133.

Lazzarato, M. (2012) *The Making of The Indebted Man*. English trans., New York: Semiotext(e).

Lazzarato, M. (2015) *Governing by Debt*. English trans., New York: Semiotext(e).

Lebor, A. (2013) *Tower of Basel: The Shadowy History of the Secret Bank That Runs the World*, New York: Public Affairs.

Lebowitz, M. A. (1976) 'Marx's falling rate of profit: A dialectical view', *Canadian Journal of Economics*, 9, 2: 232–254.

Levine, Y. (2018) 'Google Earth: How the tech giant is helping the state spy on us', www.theguardian.com/news/20-12-2018.

Leys, C. (2008) *Total Capitalism: Market Politics, Market State*, Monmouth: Merlin Press.

Li Puma, E. & Lee, B. (2004) *Financial Derivatives and the Globalization of Risk*, Durham, NC: Duke University Press.

Lin, Y.Y. & Dailami, M. (2011) 'Are we prepared for a multipolar world economy?' www. project-syndicate.org/commentary.

Lindblom, T. & Willesson, M. (2013) 'Basel III and banking efficiency', in J. Falzon (ed.) *Bank Performance, Risk and Securitization*, Basingstoke: Palgrave Macmillan.

Lohoff, E. (2003) 'The violent core of the commodity subject', English trans., reprinted in N. Larsen et al. (eds.) *Marxism and the Critique of Value*, Chicago: MCM' Publishing.

Lohoff, E. (2009) 'Off limits, out of control: Commodity society and resistance in the age of deregulation and denationalization', English trans., reprinted in N. Larsen et al. (eds.) *Marxism and the Critique of Value*, Chicago: MCM' Publishing.

Lohoff, E. (2014) 'Kapitalakkumulation ohne Wertakkumulation: Der Fetischcharakter der Kapitalmarktwaren und sein Geheimnis', *Krisis: Kritik der* Warengesellschaft, www.krisis. org/1/2014.

Lohoff, E. (2016) 'Die letzten Tages des Weltkapital: Kapitalakkumulation und Politik im Zeitalter des fiktiven Kapitals', *Krisis: Kritik der Warengesellschaft*, www.krisis. org/5/2016.

Lohoff, E. & Trenkle, N. (2012) 'Making every central bank a bad bank: Ernst Lohoff and Norbert Trenkle discuss the economic and financial crisis', *Krisis: Kritik der Warengesellschaft*, www.krisis.org].

Lohoff, E. & Trenkle, N. (2013) *Die große Entwertung: vom finanzkapitalistischen Krisenaufschub zur globalen Notstandsverwaltung*, Berlin: Unrast Verlag.

Lotz, C. (2014) *The Capitalist Schema: Time, Money, and the Culture of Abstraction*, New York: Lexington.

Lozano, B. (2014) *Of Synthetic Finance: Three Essays of Speculative Materialism*, London: Routledge.

Lukács, G. (1962) *The Destruction of Reason*. English trans., London: Merlin.

Lukács, G. (1975 [1923]) *History and Class Consciousness*. English trans., London: Merlin.

Luxemburg, R. (1972 [1913]) *Accumulation of Capital: An Anti-critique*. English trans., New York: Monthly Review Press.

Macfarlane, L. (2017) 'It's time to call the housing crisis what it really is: The largest transfer of wealth in living memory', www.opendemocracy.net /13-11-2017.

MacKinnon, N. (2017) 'A financial crisis in 2018? The danger signs are starting to emerge', www.cityam.com/277580/15-12-2017.

Mai, N. (2018) 'Global debt and the new neutral: The global economy remains highly lever- aged and sensitive to interest rate movements', www.pimco.co.uk/en-gb/insights/view- points/May 2018.

Manzarolle, V. & Kjøsen, A. M. (2016) 'Digital media and capital's logic of acceleration', in C. Fuchs & V. Mosco (eds.) *Marx in the Age of Digital Capitalism*, Leiden: Brill.

Marazzi, C. (2010) *The Violence of Financial Capital*. English trans., New York: Semiotext(e).

Martenson, C. (2018a) 'We are all lab rats in the largest-ever monetary experiment in his- tory', www.peakprosperity.com/blog/114291/18-08-2018.

Martenson, C. (2018b) 'Is the long-anticipated crash now upon us? Is this the market's break- ing point?' www.peakprosperity.com/blog/26-10-2018.

Martin, K. (2018) 'Riksbank holds rates but lifts inflation forecasts', www.ft.com/content/ aad8736c-7e93-11e8-8e67-1e1a0846c475/0-3-07-2018.

Marx, K. (1954 [1886]) *Capital: A Critique of Political Economy Volume I*. English trans., London: Lawrence & Wishart.

Marx, K. (1959 [1894]) *Capital: A Critique of Political Economy Volume III*. English trans., London: Lawrence & Wishart.

Marx, K. (1970 [1843]) *Critique of Hegel's 'Philosophy of Right'*. English trans., Cambridge: Cambridge University Press.

Marx, K. (1973 [1858]) *Grundrisse: Foundations of the Critique of Political Economy*. English trans., London: Pelican.

Marx, K. (1978 [1867]) 'The value form: Appendix to the first German edition of *Capital*, Vol.1'. English trans. published in *Capital and Class*, 4: 130–150. www.marxists.org/archive/marx/works/1867-c1/appendix.htm.

Matthews, C. (2016) 'The death of the middle class is worse than you think', http://fortune.com/2016/07/13.

Mattick, P. (2011) *Business as Usual: The Economic Crisis and the Failure of Capitalism*, English trans. London: Reaktion Books.

Mauldin, J. (2017) 'The pension storm is coming to Europe: It may be the end of Europe as we know it', www.forbes.com/sites/03-10-2017.

Maxwell, F. (2017) 'Italy tests ECB's new bank rules – again: The use of taxpayers' money to mop up the mess of two regional lenders courts controversy', www.politico.eu/26-06-2017.

McCrum, D. (2017) 'Mario Draghi's "whatever it takes" outcome in 3 charts: Where do we stand 5 years after the ECB head's famous pledge?' www.ft.com/content/25-07-2017.

McDuff, P. (2017) 'Even the IMF says austerity doesn't work. It's the zombie idea that will not die', www.theguardian.com/07-07-2017.

McKinsey Global Institute (2016) *Poorer Than Their Parents? Flat or Falling Incomes in Advanced Economies*, www.mckinsey.com.

McNally, D. (2003) 'Beyond the false infinity of capital', in R. Albritton & J. Simoulidis (eds.) *New Dialectics and Political Economy*, Basingstoke: Palgrave Macmillan.

Meaney, M. (2014) 'Capital breeds: Interest-bearing capital as purely abstract form', in F. Moseley & T. Smith (eds.) *Marx's Capital and Hegel's Logic: A Re-Examination*, Leiden: Brill.

Mejorado, A. & Roman, M. (2014) *Profitability and the Great Recession: The Role of Accumulation Trends in the Financial Crisis*, London: Routledge.

Middelkoop, W. (2015) *The Big Reset: War on Gold and the Financial Endgame*. Revised edition, Amsterdam: Amsterdam University Press.

Middelkoop, W. (2016) 'IMF's "Substitution Fund" to kick-start SDR as new global currency', *Commodity Discovery Fund SDR Special August 2016*, www.cdfund.com/wp-content/uploads.

Milios, J. & Sotiropoulos, D. (2009). *Rethinking Imperialism: A Study of Capitalist Rule*. Basingstoke: Palgrave Macmillan.

Miller, D. (2010) 'How neoliberalism got where it is: Elite planning, corporate lobbying and the release of the free market', in K. Birch & V. Mykhnenko (eds.) *The Rise and Fall of Neoliberalism: Collapse of an Economic Order?* London: Zed.

Milne, S. (2015) 'The Davos oligarchs are right to fear the world they've made', www.theguardian.com/22-01-2015.

Minerd, S. (2016) 'The global liquidity trap turns more treacherous: The adoption of negative interest rates will do little to stimulate growth', www.ft.com/06-04-2018.

Minsky, H. (1977) 'The financial instability hypothesis: An interpretation of Keynes and an alternative to "standard" theory', *Nebraska Journal of Economics and Business*, 16, 1: 5–16.

Minsky, H. (1982) *Can 'It' Happen Again? Essays on Instability and Finance*, Armonke, NY: Sharpe.

Minsky, H. (1986) *Stabilizing an Unstable Economy*, New York: McGraw Hill, 2008.

Mises, L. von (1980 [1912]) *The Theory of Money and Credit*. English trans., Indianapolis: Liberty Classics.

Möller, K. (2018) 'From constituent to destituent power beyond the state', *Transnational Legal Theory*, 9, 1: 32–55.

Morishima, M. (1973) *Marx's Economics: A Dual Theory of Value and Growth*, Cambridge: Cambridge University Press.

Moseley, F. (1988) 'The rate of surplus value, the organic composition and the general rate of profit in the US economy 1947–1967: A critique and update of Wolff's estimates', *American Economic Review*, 78, 1: 298–303.

Moseley, F. (1992) 'Unproductive labour and the rate of profit in the post-war US economy', in F. Moseley & E. Wolff (eds.) *International Perspectives on Profitability and Accumulation*, Fairfield, VT: Edward Elgar.

Moseley, F. & Smith, T. (eds.) (2014) *Marx's* Capital *and Hegel's* Logic: *A Re-examination*, London: Haymarket.

Murray, P. (1988) *Marx's Theory of Scientific Knowledge*, Atlantic Highlands, NJ: Humanities Press International, 1988.

Nefiodow, L. & Nefiodow, S. (2017) *The Sixth Kondratieff: A New Long Wave in the Global Economy*. Second edition, Charleston: CreateSpace Independent Publishing.

Neocleous, M. (2008) *Critique of Security*, Montreal: McGill-Queen's University Press.

Nitzan, J. & Bichler, S. (2009) *Capital as Power: A Study of Order and Creorder*, London: Routledge.

Nitzan, J. & Bichler, S. (2012) 'The asymptotes of power', *Real World Economics Review*, 60: 18–53. http://bnarchives.yorku.ca.

Norris, P. (2005) *Radical Right: Voters and Parties in the Electoral Market*, Cambridge: Cambridge University Press.

OECD (2018) *Putting Faces to the Jobs at Risk of Automation*, www.oecd.org/employment/future-of-work/Automation-policy-brief-2018.pdf.

Offe, C. (1976) *Disorganized Capitalism*. English trans., Cambridge: Polity.

Offe, C. (1985) *Disorganized Capitalism*. English trans., Cambridge: Polity.

Ohanian, L. E. (2010) 'The economic crisis from a neoclassical perspective', *Journal of Economic Perspectives*, 24, 4: 45–66.

Ollman, B. (2015) 'Marxism and the philosophy of internal relations: Or, how to replace the famous "paradox" with "contradictions" that can be studied and resolved', *Capital and Class*, 39, 1: 7–23.

Olson, D. A. & Wu, D. D. (2015) *Enterprise Risk Management in Finance*, Basingstoke: Palgrave Macmillan.

Onishi, H. (2011) 'The ongoing world crisis as already explained by *Capital* in 1867 and *Imperialism* in 1917', *World Review of Political Economy*, 2, 1: 26–34.

Orphanides, A. (2016) 'What happened in Cyprus? The economic consequences of the last communist government in Europe', in A. Michaelides & A. Orphanides (eds.) *The Cyprus Bail-In: Policy Lessons from the Cyprus Economic Crisis*, London: Imperial College Press.

Özel, H. (2000) 'The explanatory role of general equilibrium theory: An outline onto a general theory of neoclassical economics', https://dergipark.org.tr/download/article-file/322337.

Patnaik, P. (2016) 'Globalization and the impasse of capitalism', *Social Scientist*, 44, 11/12: 3–14.

Palley, T. I. (2013a) *Financialization: The Economics of Finance Capital Domination*, Basingstoke: Palgrave Macmillan.

Palley, T. I. (2013b) 'America's exhausted paradigm: Macroeconomic causes of the financial crisis and great recession', in B. Z. Cynamon, S. M. Fazarri & M. Setterfield (eds.) *After the Great Recession: The Struggle for Economic Recovery and Growth*, Cambridge: Cambridge University Press.

Palmer, J. (2013) 'Flawed Consuming: An analysis of the riots of August 2011 informed by the thought of Zygmunt Bauman' [Bauman Institute Think Pieces No. 1], http://baumaninstitute.leeds.ac.uk.

Papanikolaou, N. I. (2017) 'To be bailed out or to be left to fail? A dynamic competing risks analysis', *Journal of Financial Stability*, 34: 61–85.

Papanikolaou, N. (2018) 'To be bailed out or to be left to fail: A dynamic competing risks hazard analysis', *Journal of Financial Instability*, 34, C: 61–85.

Parenteau, R. (2005) 'The Late 1990s' US bubble: Financialization in the extreme', in G. Epstein (ed.) *Financialization and the World Economy*, Cheltenham: Edward Elgar.

Parenteau, R. (2012) 'The late 1990s US bubble: Financialization in the extreme', in G. A. Epstein (ed.) *Financialization and the World Economy*, Cheltenham: Edward Elgar.

Parvin, M. (1992) 'Is teaching neoclassical economics as the science of economics immoral?' *Journal of Economic Education*, 23, 1: 65–78.

Pento, M. (2018) 'When the yield curve inverts soon, the next recession will start', www.peakprosperity.com/michael-pento-when-the-yield-curve-inverts-soon-the-next-recession-will-start.

Perelman, M. (1996) *The End of Economics*, London: Routledge.

Pettifor, A. (2018) 'Why building more homes will not solve Britain's housing crisis', www.theguardian.com/27-01-2018.

Philippon, T. & Salord, A. (2017) *Bail-Ins and Bank Resolution in Europe: A Progress Report*, Geneva Reports on the Global Economy, Special Report 4. Geneva: International Centre for Monetary and Banking Studies.

Phillips, K. (2009) *Bad Money: Reckless Finance, Failed Politics and the Global Crisis of American Capitalism*, New York: Penguin.

Picciotto, S. (2011) *Regulating Global Corporate Capitalism*, Cambridge: Cambridge University Press.

Pilkington, P. (2011) 'Marginal utility as a mechanism for social control', "www.nakedcapitalism.com/2011/10." www.nakedcapitalism.com/2011/10.

Pilkington, M. (2014) *The Global Financial Crisis and the New Monetary Consensus*, London: Routledge.

Postone, M. (1993) *Time, Labour and Social Domination: A Reinterpretation of Marx's Critical Theory*, Cambridge: Cambridge University Press.

Postone, M. (2007) 'Theorizing the contemporary world: Robert Brenner, Giovanni Arrighi, David Harvey', in R. Albritton et al. (eds.) *Political Economy and Global Capitalism*, London: Anthem.

Prasch, R. E. (2010) 'Bankers gone wild: the crash of 2008', in S. Kates (ed.) *Macroeconomic Theory and Its Failings: Alternative Perspectives on the Global Financial Crisis*, Cheltenham: Edward Elgar.

Pressman, S. (2004) 'The two dogmas of neoclassical economics', *Science and Society*, 68, 4: 483–493.

Prins, N. (2018) *Collusion: How Central Bankers Rigged the World*, New York: Nation.

Prozorov, S. (2014) *Agamben and Politics: A Critical Introduction*, Edinburgh: Edinburgh University Press.

PWC. (2017) *Will Robots Steal our Jobs? An International Analysis of the Potential Long-Term Impact of Automation*, "www.pwc.fr/fr/assets/files/pdf/2018/02/impact-of-automation-on-jobs-international-analysis-final%20report-feb-2018.pdf" www.pwc.fr/fr/assets/files/pdf/2018/02.

Racy, G. (2016) 'Walter Benjamin's *Capitalism as Religion*: Is there any chance for freedom?' *Heathwood Journal of Critical Theory*, 1, 3: 84–96.

Rankin, K. (2010) 'Krugman on the malaise of modern macro: Critique without alternative', *Agenda: Journal of Policy Analysis and Reform*, 17, 1: 95–100.

Rechtschaffen, A. N. (2014) *Capital Markets, Derivatives and the Law: Evolution after the Crisis.* Second edition, Oxford: Oxford University Press.

Reinhart, C. M. & Rogoff, K. S. (2009) *This Time is Different: Eight Centuries of Financial Folly,* Princeton: Princeton University Press.

Rennison, J. (2019) 'CLOs: The specialist loan vehicles luring yield-hungry investors. Designers of CLOs say that structures are much safer than crisis-era cousin', www.ft.com/content/db97c650-1ec6-11e9-b126-46fc3ad87c65.

Rennison, J. (2019) 'CLOs: The specialist loan vehicles luring yield-hungry investors. Designers of CLOs say that structures are much safer than crisis-era cousin', www.ft.com/content/28-01-2019.

Rennison, J. & Smith, C. (2019) 'Debt machine: Are risks piling up in leveraged loans? Regulators fear looser lending standards for low-rated companies could precipitate the next downturn', www.ft.com/content/64c9665e-1814-11e9-9e64-d150b3105d21.

Reuten, G. (1991) 'Accumulation of capital and the foundation of the tendency of the rate of profit to fall', *Cambridge Journal of Economics*, 15, 1: 79–934.

Reuten, G. & Williams, M. (1987) *Value-Form and the State: The Tendencies of Accumulation and the Determination of Economic Policy in Capitalist Society*, London: Routledge.

Reuters (2017) 'Daily FX trade more like $3 trillion than 5', www.reuters.com/article/13-03-2017.

Reuters (2018) 'Tough to stop Nord Stream 2 now it's being built: EU's Oettinger', www.reuters.com/article/us-germany-russia-pipeline/28-12-2018.

Richter, W. (2018) 'The world is refusing to kill off the dollar as its reserve currency', www.businessinsider.com/02-01-2018.

Rickards, J. (2014) *Currency Wars*, London: Penguin/Random House.

Rickards, J. (2016) *The Road to Ruin*, London: Penguin/Random House.

Rickards, J. (2017) 'Four financial components to improved Russian relations: With the US preparing to confront China and go to war with North Korea, Russia is an indispensable ally for the US', https://dailyreckoning.com.

Roberts, M. (1997) *Analytical Marxism: A Critique*, London: Verso.

Robinson, W. I. (2004) 'From state hegemonies to transnational hegemony: A global capitalism approach', in T. E. Reifer (ed.) *Globalization, Hegemony and Power: Anti-systemic Movements and the Global System*, Boulder: Paradigm.

Robinson, W. I. (2007) 'Beyond the theory of imperialism: Global capitalism and the transnational state', *Societies Without Borders*, 2: 5–26.

Robinson, W. I. (2011) 'The global capital leviathan', *Radical Philosophy*, 165: 2–6.

Robinson, W. I. (2019) 'Global capitalist crisis and twenty-first century fascism: Beyond the Trump hype', *Science and Society*, 83, 2: 481–509.

Rochet, J.-C. (2008) *Why Are There So Many Banking Crises?* Princeton: Princeton University Press.

Roemer, J. (1982) *A General Theory of Exploitation and Class*, Cambridge, MA: Cambridge University Press.

Rogoff, K. S. (2016) *The Curse of Cash*, Princeton: Princeton University Press.

Rothbard, M. (1963) *What Has Government Done to Our Money?* Auburn, AL: Ludwig von Mises Institute.

Rotheim, R. J. (1998) 'New Keynesian macroeconomics and markets', in R. J. Rotheim (ed.) *New Keynesian Economics/Post-Keynesian Alternatives*, London: Routledge.

Rubin, I. I. (1973) *Essays on Marx's Theory of Value.* English trans., Montreal: Black Rose.

Rüddenklau, E. (1981) *Gesellschaftliche Arbeit oder Arbeit und Interaktion? Zum Stellenwert des Arbeitsbegriffes bei Habermas, Marx und Hegel*, Frankfurt-am-Main: Peter Lang.

Rüddenklau, H. (1982) *Gesellschaftliche Arbeit oder Arbeit und Interaktion? Zum Stellenwert des Arbeitsbegriffs bei Habermas, Marx und Hegel*, Frankfurt-am-Main: Lang.

Saleuddin, R. (2015) *Regulating Securitized Products: A Post-Crisis Guide*, Basingstoke: Palgrave Macmillan.

Sands, P. (2016) 'Making it harder for the bad guys: The case for eliminating high denomination notes', *Harvard Kennedy School Mossavar-Rahmani Center for Business and Government Associate Working Paper Series* 52, www.hks.harvard.edu/mrcbg.

Sardoni, C. (2015) 'Is a Marxist explanation of the current crisis possible?', *Review of Keynesian Economics*, 3, 2: 143–157.

Saul, J. R. (2009) *The Collapse of Globalism and the Reinvention of the World*. Second edition, London: Atlantic.

Savitsky, A. (2018) '"It's the economy, stupid": What really drives US sanctions against Russia', www.strategic-culture.org/news/29-09-2018.

Sawaya, R. R. & Garlipp, J. R. D. (2011) 'The crisis of a post-war logic of global accumulation', *World Review of Political Economy*, 2, 3: 441–460.

Sawyer, M. L. (2011) '"It" keeps almost happening: Post-Keynesian perspectives on the financial crisis and the great recession', *History of Economic Ideas*, 19, 2: 147–162.

Scheler, M. (1964) 'The Thomist ethic and the spirit of capitalism', English trans., reprinted in *Sociological Analysis*, 25, 1: 4–19.

Schlichter, D. S. (2014) *Paper Money Collapse: The Folly of Elastic Money*. Second edition, New York: Wiley.

Schmidt, A. (1981) *History and Structure: An Essay on Hegelian-Marxist and Structuralist Theories of History*. English trans., Cambridge, MA: MIT Press.

Schmied-Kowarzik, W. (1981) *Die Dialektik der gesellschaftlichen Praxis. Zur Genesis und Kernstruktur der Marxschen Theorie*, Freiburg: Alber.

Schneiderman, D. (2013) *Resisting Economic Globalization: Critical Theory and International Investment Law*, Basingstoke: Palgrave Macmillan.

Schoenmaker, D. (2013) *Governance of International Banking: The Financial Trilemma*, Oxford: Oxford University Press.

Schumpeter, J. A. (1942) *Capitalism, Socialism and Democracy*, New York: Harper & Row.

Scott, B. (2018) 'The cashless society is a con and big finance is behind it', www.theguardian.com/19-08-2018.

Scutt, D. (2016) 'Charts: Here's how much currency is traded everyday', www.businessinsider.com.au/02-07-2016.

Seccareccia, M. (2011) 'The financial crisis, structural transformations and the need for a new regulatory structure', *International Journal of Political Economy*, 40, 2: 3–4.

Seccareccia, M. (2011/2012) 'The role of public investment as principal macroeconomic tool to promote long-term growth: Keynes' legacy', *International Journal of Political Economy*, 40, 4: 62–82.

Shaxson, N. (2018) *The Finance Curse: How Global Finance Is Making Us All Poorer*, London: Bodley Head.

Siklos, P. L. (2017) *Central Banks into the Breach: From Triumph to Crisis and Beyond*. Oxford: Oxford University Press.

Simmel, G. (2004 [1907]) *The Philosophy of Money*. Third enlarged edition, ed. & trans. D. Frisby, London: Routledge.

Simpson, D. (2013) *The Rediscovery of Classical Economics: Adaptation, Complexity and Growth*, Cheltenham: Edward Elgar.

Singh, M. (2012) *Banking Crises, Liquidity and Credit Lines: A Macroeconomic Perspective*, London: Routledge.

Singh, M. (2017) 'Understanding the Federal Reserve balance sheet', www.investopedia. com/articles/economics/11-09-2017.

Singleton, J. (2011) *Central Banking in the Twentieth Century*, Cambridge: Cambridge University Press.

Smaga, P. (2014) 'The concept of systemic risk', *SRC Special Paper* 5, http://eprints.lse. ac.uk/61214/1/sp-5.pdf.

Smith, C. H. (2010) 'The stealth coup d'état: USA 2008–2010', www.businessinsider. com/28-08-2010.

Smith, R., Walter, I. & De Long, G. (2012) *Global Banking*. Third edition, Oxford: Oxford University Press.

Smith, T. (2003) 'Systematic and historical dialectics: Towards a Marxian theory of globalization', in R. Albritton & J. Simoulidis (eds.) *New Dialectics and Political Economy*, Basingstoke: Palgrave Macmillan.

Smith, T. (2014) 'Hegel, Marx and the comprehension of capitalism', in F. Moseley & T. Smith (eds.) *Marx's Capital and Hegel's Logic: A Re-Examination*, Leiden: Brill.

Sohn-Rethel, A. (1978) *Intellectual and Manual Labour: A Critique of Epistemology*. English trans., London: Macmillan.

Sotiropoulos, D. P., Milios, J. & Lapatsioras, S. (2013) *A Political Economy of Contemporary Capitalism and Its Crisis*, Abingdon: Routledge.

Spence, P. (2015) 'Negative interest rates could be necessary to protect UK economy, says Bank of England chief economist', www.telegraph.co.uk/finance/11874061/18-09-2015.

Springford, J. (2018) 'The German wage puzzle', www.cer.eu/insights/german-wage-puzzle.

Staniszkis, J. (1992) *The Ontology of Socialism*. English trans., Oxford: Clarendon Press.

Stiegler, B. (2004) *The Decadence of Industrial Democracies. Disbelief and Discredit Vol. 1*. English trans., Cambridge: Polity.

Stiegler, B. (2006) *Uncontrollable Societies of Disaffected Individuals. Disbelief and Discredit Vol. 2*. English trans., Cambridge: Polity.

Stiegler, B. (2011) *For a New Critique of Political Economy*. English trans., Stanford: Stanford University Press.

Stiegler, B. (2014) *The Re-enchantment of the World: The Value of Spirit Against Industrial Populism*. English trans., London: Bloomsbury.

Stiglitz, J. (2009) 'The current economic crisis and lessons for economic theory', *Eastern Economic Journal*, 35: 281–296.

Stockhammer, E. (2012) 'Financialization, income distribution and the crisis', *Investigación Económica*, LXXI, 279: 39–70.

Strauss, D. (2019) 'Central banks shift stance in face of "pervasive uncertainty": Policymakers take dovish tilt amid rapidly worsening outlook for global growth', www.ft.com/content/09-03-2019.

Streeck, W. (2014) *Buying Time: The Delayed Crisis of Democratic Capitalism*. English trans., London: Verso.

Stultz, R. M. (2004) 'Should we fear derivatives?', *Journal of Economic Perspectives*, 18, 3: 173–192.

Suarez-Villa, L. (2015) *Corporate Power, Oligopolies and the Crisis of the State*, Albany: SUNY Press.

Subacchi, P. & Pickford, S. (2011) 'Legitimacy vs. effectiveness for the G20: A dynamic approach to global economic governance', *Chatham House International Economics Briefing Paper*.

Sullivan & Worcester (2016) 'EU bail-in legislation', www.sandw.com/news-1449.

Sundblad, W. (2019) 'Industry 4.0: The journey toward perfect production', www.forbes. com/sites/willemsundbladeurope/16-07-2018.

Swedberg, R. (1992) 'Can capitalism survive? Schumpeter's answer and its relevance for new institutional economics', *Archives Européennes de Sociologie*, 33, 2: 350–380.

Szendy, P. (2012) 'Katechon', www.politicalconcepts.org.

Tabb, W. K. (2010) 'Marxism, crisis theory and the crisis of the early 21st century', *Science and Society*, 74, 3: 305–323.

Tabb, W. K. (2012) *The Restructuring of Capitalism in Our Time*, New York: Columbia University Press.

Theodore, J. & Theodore, J. (2015) *Cyprus and the Financial Crisis: The Controversial Bailout and What It Means for the Eurozone*, Basingstoke: Palgrave Macmillan.

Therborn, G. (1980) *The Power of Ideology and the Ideology of Power*, London: Verso.

Thompson, H. (1997) 'Ignorance and ideological hegemony: A critique of neoclassical economics', *The Journal of Interdisciplinary Economics*, 8: 291–305.

Thompson, P. (2005) 'Foundation and empire: A critique of Hardt & Negri', *Capital and Class*, 86: 39–64.

Tischleder, B. B. & Wasserman, S. (2015) 'Introduction: Thinking out of sync – a theory of obsolescence', in B. B. Tischleder & S. Wasserman (eds.) *Cultures of Obsolescence: History, Materiality and the Digital Age*, Basingstoke: Palgrave Macmillan.

Tognato, C. (2012) *Central Bank Independence: Cultural Codes and Symbolic Importance*, Basingstoke: Palgrave Macmillan.

Tooze, A. (2018) *Crashed: How a Decade of Financial Crises Changed the World*, London: Penguin.

Toporowski, J. (2014) 'Debt, class and asset inflation', in R. Bellofiore & G. Vertova (eds.) *The Great Recession and the Contradictions of Contemporary Capitalism*, Cheltenham: Edward Elgar.

Trenkle. N. (1998) 'Value and crisis: Basic questions', English trans., reprinted in N. Larsen et al. (eds.) *Marxism and the Critique of Value*, Chicago: MCM' Publishing, 2014.

Trenkle, N. (2006) 'Struggle without classes: Why there is no resurgence of the proletariat in the currently unfolding capitalist crisis', reprinted in N. Larsen et al. (eds.) *Marxism and the Critique of Value*, Chicago: MCM Publishing.

Udehn, L. (2001) *Methodological Individualism: Background, History and Meaning*, London: Routledge.

Ulrich, W. (2008) *Habenwollen: Wie funktioniert die Konsumkultur?* Berlin: Fischer.

Urry, J. (2014) *Offshoring*, Cambridge: Polity.

Variato, A. M. (2001) 'Hyman Minsky: What kind of a (post-) Keynesian?' in R. Belliofiore & P. Ferri (eds.) *Financial Keynesianism and Market Instability: The Economic Legacy of Hyman Minsky Vol. I*, Cheltenham: Edward Elgar.

Varoufakis, Y. (2011) *The Global Minotaur: America, Europe and the Future of the Global Economy*, London: Zed.

Varoufakis, Y. (2015) *Adults in the Room: My Battle with Europe's Deep Establishment*, London: Vintage.

Veblen, T. (1923) *Absentee Ownership and Business Enterprise in Recent Times: The Case of America*, New York: B. W. Huebsch.

Vercelli, A. (2001) 'Minsky, Keynes and the structural instability of a sophisticated monetary economy', in R. Bellofiore & P. Ferri (eds.) *Financial Fragility and Investment in the Capitalist Economy: The Economic Legacy of Hyman Minsky Vol. II*, Cheltenham: Edward Elgar.

Vermeiren, M. (2014) *Power and Imbalances in the Global Monetary System: A Comparative Capitalism Perspective*, Basingstoke: Palgrave Macmillan.

Vincent, M. (2018) 'Why Carillion has gone into liquidation rather than administration', www.ft.com/15-01-2018.

Walker, T. C. (2010) 'The Perils of paradigm mentalities: Revisiting Kuhn, Lakatos, and Popper', *Perspectives on Politics*, 8, 2: 433–451.

Wallerstein, I. (1974) *The Modern World-System*, New York: Academic Press.

Wallerstein, I. (1992) 'The collapse of liberalism', reprinted in I. Wallerstein (ed.), *After Liberalism*, New York: W. W. Norton, 1995.

Wallerstein, I. (2000) 'Globalization or the age of transition? A long-term view of the trajectory of the world-system', *International Sociology*, 15, 2: 251–267.

Wallerstein, I. (2009) 'Crisis of the capitalist system: Where do we go from here?' https://mronline.org/2009/11/12.

Wallerstein, I. (2011) 'The limits of capitalism are hit/bifurcation: New hierarchic order or more democracy', www.kontext-tv.de/broadcast/29062011.

Wallerstein, I. (2013) 'Structural crisis, or: Why capitalists may no longer find capitalism rewarding', in I. Wallerstein et al. (eds.) *Does Capitalism Have a Future?* Oxford: Oxford University Press.

Warner, J. (2018) 'From economic slowdown to political chaos, the global outlook gives us plenty to worry about', www.telegraph.co.uk/news/23-11-2018.

Wasserberg, A. (2013) *Capitalist Discipline: On the Orchestration of Corporate Games*, Basingstoke: Palgrave Macmillan.

Watkin, W. (2012) '*The Kingdom and the Glory*: The articulated inoperativity of power', *Res Publica: Revista de Filosofía Política*, 28: 235–264.

Watts, W. (2019) 'Here's how hard China's slowdown could hit global economic growth', www.marketwatch.com/30-01-2019.

Weber, M. (2002 [1905]) *The Protestant Ethic and the Spirit of Capitalism*. English trans. London: Penguin.

Weeks, D. (1989) *A Critique of Neoclassical Economics*, Basingstoke: Macmillan.

Wellmer, A. (1971) *Critical Theory of Society*, New York: Herder & Herder.

Wessel, R. (2018) 'Is lack of competition strangling the US economy?' *Harvard Business Review*, March–April 2018, https://hbr.org/2018/03.

Westra, R. (2010) *The Political Economy of Globalization*, London: Routledge.

White, L. H. (1996) 'Monetary nationalism reconsidered', www.independent.org/publications/policy_reports/detail.asp?id=9248.

White, W. (2018) 'Start preparing for the next financial crisis now', www.ft.com/content/18-02-2018.

Wigglesworth, R. (2018) 'Shorting volatility: Its role in the stocks sell-off', www.ft.com/02-02-2018.

Wigglesworth, R. et al. (2018) 'Global markets retreat as tech rout spreads: Big five "FAANG" stocks have now shed more than $1tn in value since recent highs', www.ft.com/21-11-2018.

Wigglesworth, R. (2019) 'Markets yield to fears of a global downturn', www.ft.com/content/16-08-2019.

Wihlborg. C. (2017) *Bail-ins: Issues of Credibility and Contagion*, European Money and Finance Reform Policy Note 10, www.suerf.org/policynotes.

Wijnholds, O. (2009) 'The dollar's last days', www.project-syndicate.org/commentary/09-05-2009.

Wildau, G. (2018) 'China to designate more financial groups as "too big to fail": Central bank cites international frameworks as model for national regulation', www.ft.com/content/27-11-2018.

Wile, A. (2011) 'Gaddafi planned gold dinar; now under attack', www.thedailybell.com/all-articles/editorials/05-05-2011.

Wilkie, C. M. D. (2012) *Special Drawing Rights (SDRs): The First International Money*, Oxford: Oxford University Press.

Williamson, J. (2004) 'The strange history of the Washington Consensus', *Journal of Post Keynesian Economics*, 27, 2: 195–206.

Wilson, C. (2018) 'SDRs: the "world money" plan', www.bullionvault.com/gold-news/18-05-2018.

Wolf, M. (2018) 'Martin Wolf on the next financial crisis', www.landandliberty.net/28-04-2018.

Wolff, R. P. (1981) 'A critique and reinterpretation of Marx's theory of value', *Philosophy and Public Affairs*, 10, 2: 89–120.

Wolin, S. (2010) *Democracy Incorporated: Managed Democracy and the Specter of Inverted Totalitarianism*, Princeton: Princeton University Press.

Woll, C. (2014) *The Power of Inaction: Bank Bailouts in Comparison*, Ithaca: Cornell University Press.

Woodley, D. E. (2013) 'Radical right discourse contra state-based authoritarian populism: Neoliberalism, identity and exclusion after the crisis', in R. Wodak & J. Richardson (eds.) *Analysing Fascist Discourse: European Fascism in Talk and Text*, London: Routledge.

Woodley, D. E. (2015) *Globalization and Capitalist Geopolitics: Sovereignty and State Power in a Multipolar World*, Abingdon: Routledge.

World Bank (2016) *Bank Resolution and Bail-in the EU: Selected Case Studies Pre- and Post-BRRD*, Washington, DC: World Bank Group.

World Bank (2018) 'What is a public-private partnership?' https://ppp.worldbank.org/public-private-partnership/overview/02-06-2018.

Wray, L. R. (1999) 'The development and reform of the modern international Monetary system', in J. Deprez & J. T. Harvey (eds.) *Foundations of International Economics: Post-Keynesian Perspectives*, London: Routledge.

Wray, L. R. (2014) 'From the state theory of money to modern money theory: An alternative to economic orthodoxy', Levy Economics Institute Working Paper No. 792, www.levyinstitute.org/pubs.

Wray, L. R. (2015) *Modern Money Theory: A Primer on Macroeconomics for Sovereign Monetary Systems*. Second edition, Basingstoke: Palgrave Macmillan.

Wright, E. O. (2015) *Understanding Class*, London: Verso.

Xavier, M. (2016) 'Subjectivity under consumerism: The totalization of the subject as a commodity', *Psicologia & Sociedade*, 28, 2: 207–216; English version available online at: www.scielo.br/pdf.

Zakaria, F. (2011) *Post-American World*. Second edition, London: Penguin.

Zeremba, A. (2015) *The Financialization of Commodity Markets: Investing during Times of Transition*, Basingstoke: Palgrave Macmillan.

Žižek, S. (1989) *The Sublime Object of Ideology*, London: Verso.

Zouboulakis, M. S. (2014) *The Varieties of Economic Rationality: From Adam Smith to Contemporary Behavioural and Evolutionary Economics*, London: Routledge.

INDEX

Note: Page numbers followed by n refers to notes.

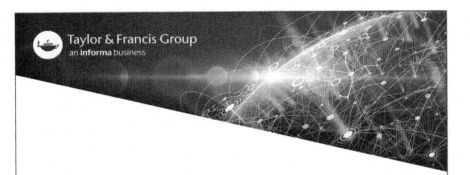